International Insolvency Procedures

International Insolvency Procedures

Second edition

Edited by Mike Wheeler and Roger Oldfield

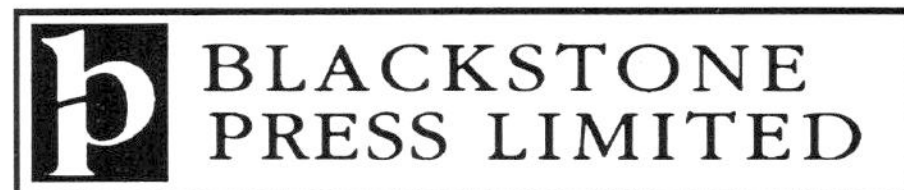

This edition published in Great Britain 1997 by Blackstone Press Limited,
9-15 Aldine Street, London W12 8AW.
Telephone 0181-740 2277

ISBN: 1 85431 624 9

British Library Cataloguing in Publication Data
A CIP catalogue record for this book is available from the British Library.

Typeset by Style Photosetting Ltd, Mayfield, East Sussex
Printed by Ashford Colour Press, Gosport, Hants

Contents

Caveat

The information provided in this book has been summarised to cover insolvency procedures in general. Insolvency legislation and practice is inherently complicated and much of it is subject to refinement and change through new primary legislation, other commercial legislation and, in certain countries, court decisions on specific legal issues.

Accordingly, for specific application of a country's insolvency procedures the local KPMG contact partner (shown under each country) should be consulted.

Preface

As we approach the second millenium, it is clear that almost all major companies now operate in an international market place. Accordingly, it is an inescapable fact that an economic downturn in any given country will have an impact on companies in many other countries. It is essential, therefore, that companies, lenders and advisers are able to obtain a basic understanding of insolvency procedures around the world. This new, second edition of *International Insolvency Procedures* is designed to give just such an overview.

It is almost nine years since the first edition of this book appeared. Since then, many national borders have changed. Many more countries have come into existence, resulting in much new legislation. Other countries have amended their rules and regulations governing business practice in general. We at KPMG are encouraged by the trend that is emerging in much of this new legislation. It is now apparent that more and more often legislators are recognising the need to introduce procedures for trying to save or rehabilitate ailing businesses, rather than merely providing a framework for their liquidation.

As legislation begins to take similar paths around the world, the global presence of KPMG, a professional services firm located in 150 countries, places us in a strong position to co-ordinate local and cross-border corporate and personal insolvency. Our international Corporate Recovery practice integrates the specialist skills of senior insolvency practitioners around the world with an unparalleled network of relevant industry expertise.

At KPMG, our commitment to quality of service is global. In keeping with this commitment, we are keen to support initiatives to promote an enhanced understanding of corporate recovery procedures around the world. Accordingly, KPMG is an active supporter of organisations such as INSOL, the world-wide federation of accountants and lawyers specialising in insolvency. Through coming together in this way to share views and experiences, insolvency practitioners from around the world have the opportunity to develop their knowledge, share ideas and ensure that the profession is able to adapt to the requirements of an increasingly international market.

In compiling this overview of international insolvency procedures, many many hours of labour have been offered with good grace by my colleagues all over the KPMG world. Without their efforts this book quite simply, could not have been produced. I would also like to acknowledge the efforts of and express particular thanks to Samantha Bewick and Andrew Wetherall in London who, with unfailing good humour, co-ordinated the production of this book in a remarkably short period of time.

Mike Wheeler
KPMG
London
March 1997

Anguilla

Legislation

Insolvency and receivership procedures are provided for in the recently revised Companies Ordinance 1994 and the Anguilla Registered Land Ordinance of 1974.

Insolvency procedures

Company insolvency and winding up (Companies Ordinance Part IV)

A company that has not issued any shares may be dissolved at any time by resolution of the directors. A company that has no property or liabilities may be dissolved by special resolution of the shareholders. Articles of dissolution are sent to the Registrar of Companies who issues a certificate of dissolution. The company ceases to exist on the date shown in the certificate.

With respect to a voluntary liquidation and dissolution of the company, a statement of intent to dissolve must also be sent to the Registrar who issues an intent to dissolve certificate. When this certificate has been issued the company must cease to carry on business except to the extent necessary for liquidation. The company must immediately send notice of its intent to dissolve to each known creditor of the company and must also publish its intent to dissolve at least 120 days prior to dissolution in the *Official Gazette* of Anguilla and in an appropriate newspaper. The company may then proceed to discharge its obligations and distribute its remaining property to shareholders according to their respective rights.

The Registrar or any interested person may, at any time during the liquidation of the company, apply to the court for an order for supervision of the liquidation by the court. Similarly, a revocation of the intent to dissolve might be sent to the Registrar. If there is no revocation the company must proceed by preparing articles of dissolution which must be sent to the Registrar for approval.

The court may order the liquidation and dissolution of a company or any of its affiliate companies upon the application of a shareholder, debenture holder, creditor, director or officer. The application must state the reasons why liquidation is appropriate and the reasons must be verified by affidavit. The court will allow four weeks for any person to show why the company should not be liquidated or dissolved. The court may order the directors and officers of the company to provide:

- financial statements of the company;
- the name and address of each shareholder;
- the name and address of each known creditor or claimant even with future or contingent claims and any person with whom the company has a contract.

The court may make any order as it thinks fit to liquidate the company and appoint a liquidator. Directors might be restrained by the court from exercising any of their powers or collecting or receiving any debt or property of the company or transferring any property unless permitted by the court.

Upon appointment, the liquidator must give notice of his appointment to the Registrar and to each claimant and creditor known to the liquidator. Notice must be placed in the Anguilla *Official Gazette* and once a week for two consecutive weeks in a newspaper distributed in Anguilla requiring:

- any person indebted to the company to render an account;
- any person possessing property of the company to deliver it to the liquidator;

- any person having a claim against the company to present particulars of the claim in writing to the liquidator not later than two months after the first publication of the notice.

The liquidator must:

- take control of the property of the company;
- maintain trust accounts for the company of moneys received and paid out by him;
- keep accounts of moneys of the company received and paid by him;
- maintain separate lists of shareholders, creditors and other persons having claims against the company;
- apply to the court for directions if the company is unable to discharge its obligations;
- deliver to the court and Registrar financial statements of the company at least once in every 12 months after his appointment or as often as the court might require.

A liquidator may:

- retain attorneys at law, accountants, engineers, appraisers or other professional advisers;
- bring, defend, or take part in any civil, criminal or administrative action in the name or on behalf of the company;
- carry on the business of the company as required for an orderly liquidation;
- sell by public auction or private sale any property of the company;
- borrow money on the security of the property of the company;
- settle or compromise any claims by and against the company;
- provide for the custody of the documents and records of the company after its dissolution.

A liquidator incurs no liability as liquidator if he relies in good faith upon:

- the financial statements of the company represented to him by an officer or auditor of the company;
- any report or opinion presented to him by a professional adviser.

The liquidator must pay the costs of liquidation out of the property of the company and must make adequate provision for all claims against the company. The liquidator must apply to the court for approval of final accounts and for permission to distribute moneys or remaining property to the shareholders. After the court approves the final accounts the court will issue an order instructing the registrar to issue the certificate of dissolution. Property due to creditors or claimants who cannot be found must be converted into money and paid into a consolidated fund.

Receivership (Registered Land Ordinance 1994)

If default is made in payment of the principal sum or any interest due under a charge, and remains unpaid for one month, the lender may serve on the borrower notice in writing to pay the money owing.

If the borrower does not comply, within three months of the date of service of notice, the lender may:

- appoint a receiver of the income of the charged property; or
- sell the charged property.

Section 73 of the Ordinance covers the appointment, remuneration, and duties of a receiver as follows:

- the appointment of a receiver must be in writing signed by the lender;

- a receiver may be removed at any time and a new receiver appointed by the lender;
- a receiver shall be deemed to be the agent of the lender for the purposes for which he is appointed; and the lender shall be solely responsible for the receiver's acts and defaults unless the charge otherwise provides;
- the receiver has power to demand and recover all the income of which he is appointed receiver;
- the receiver is entitled to retain out of any money received by him all costs, charges and expenses incurred by him as receiver, and, for his remuneration, a commission at such rate, not exceeding 5 per cent of the gross amount of all moneys received, as is specified in his appointment, or if no rate is so specified at the rate of 5 per cent of that gross amount, or such other rate as the charger and the chargee and other chargees, if any, agree or the court thinks fit to allow on application made by the receiver for that purpose.

A receiver must apply all money received by him in the following order of priority;

- in discharge of all rents, rates, taxes and outgoings whatever affecting the charged property;
- in settling all annual sums or other payments, and the interest on all principal sums, having priority to the charge;
- in payment of his commission, costs, charges and expenses and of the premiums on fire, life and other insurance, if any, properly payable under the charge instrument or under the Land Ordinance, and the cost of executing necessary or proper repairs directed in writing by the chargee;
- in payment of the interest accruing due in respect of any principal money due under the charge;
- in or towards the discharge of the debt secured by the charge, if so directed in writing by the chargee;
- and shall pay the residue, if any, of the money received by him to the person, who, but for the appointment of the receiver, would have been entitled to receive the income of which he is appointed receiver, or who is otherwise entitled to the charged property.

A discharge, whether of the whole or of a part of a charge, shall be made by an instrument in the prescribed form, and (if of the whole) the word 'Discharged' endorsed on the charge.

KPMG contact partner

Claudel V.V. Romney
Caribbean Commercial Centre
PO Box 136
The Valley
Anguilla

Telephone: +1 (809) 497 5500
Fax: +1 (809) 497 3755

Antigua

Legislation

Insolvency procedures are governed by the provisions of:

- the Companies Act, c. 358 (as amended) of the Laws of Antigua and Bermuda with respect to liquidation and receiverships;
- the Bankruptcy Act, c. 19 with respect to bankruptcies.

The legislation is based largely on the UK Companies Acts of the early 1900s.

Insolvency procedures

Bankruptcy of individuals

Bankruptcy procedures are conducted by order of the court which may make a 'receiving order' on a petition presented either by a creditor or the debtor. Bankruptcies are not common.

Liquidation of companies

Liquidation of companies may be commenced:

- by the court;
- by creditors (through the court);
- voluntarily, i.e., by members of a company;
- subject to the supervision of the court (on application by either creditors or members).

A liquidator, more often than not a practising public accountant, is appointed either by the court or named in the resolution to wind up by the members of the company. He must be an individual.

Upon appointment, a liquidator takes possession of all of the property of the company and is vested with power to sell such property or to carry on the business of the company so far as may be necessary for its beneficial winding up. He may appoint a special manager for that purpose.

When the property of the company is realised, the liquidator is to apply it in payment of:

- costs, charges etc., necessarily incurred, including the liquidator's remuneration;
- secured creditors (to the extent of their security);
- preferential creditors;
- unsecured creditors, pari passu;
- members according to their rights and interests in the company.

Receivership

A receiver, or receiver and manager, is usually appointed in accordance with provisions contained in a debenture or mortgage deed and acts as agent of the company. Only an individual may be appointed receiver.

A receiver is required to take possession of the assets secured either by a fixed or floating charge and, if the company is not being wound up, must pay the debts of the company which would be paid in priority to all other debts if the company were being wound up. The priority of payments out of a receivership is the same as that for a liquidation.

A receiver or receiver and manager may carry on the business of the company if such course will enhance, or prevent the deterioration of, the assets coming into his possession.

A receiver is usually indemnified by the secured creditor against any claims against him other than those caused by his negligence.

KPMG contact partner

Cleveland Seaforth
KPMG Peat Marwick
High & Market Streets
PO Box 3109
St John's
Antigua

Telephone: +1 268 462 8868
Fax: +1 268 462 8808

Argentina

Legislation

The Argentine Insolvency Law 1955 1 was extensively modified by Laws 22 917 in 1983 and 24 522 in 1995. The legislation deals both with commercial insolvencies and insolvencies of private persons not being in business. It also applies, albeit with some differences, to the liquidation of banks and insurance companies.

Insolvency procedures

Two so-called 'preventive' procedures exist in addition to liquidation and bankruptcy. Receivership is not used in Argentina.

Preventive out-of-court agreement

This type of arrangement consists essentially of an agreement between the debtor and all or part of his creditors in order to overcome financial and economic difficulties or a situation of insolvency. The agreement will only be validated if it is considered to be the only way to avoid bankruptcy. The agreement may be presented for approval before a judge after the publication of a summons in the *Official Gazette* and in a daily newspaper in order that anyone with a legitimate interest may challenge it. If the judge approves the agreement, it cannot later be challenged by the creditors involved in an eventual formal preventive composition proceeding or a bankruptcy proceeding.

Preventive composition proceeding (PCP)

This procedure may be started only after a formal petition by the debtor, who must comply with certain legal requirements. If these are met, the judge appoints a court scheme manager (*sindico*) to whom the creditors must present their petition before a fixed deadline.

Once the PCP is formally opened, a provisional creditors' committee is appointed by the judge, made up by the three largest creditors reported by the debtor, with an informative and a control function. Also, as from that date, the debtor cannot dispose of any assets — except goods sold in the ordinary course of business — maintaining, however, their administration. Other collateral effects are: interest charges do not accrue as from the date the PCP was filed by the debtor and execution procedures are frozen in order to protect the principle of *pars conditio creditorum* (equal protection of the creditors). From the date of filing and for 30 days, the debtor has the right to propose categorising creditors into three or more groups. The law foresees three basic categories: secured liabilities, unsecured liabilities and unsecured labour liabilities. To each of the groups of creditors, a proposal will have to be made, but these proposals may be different for each group (e.g. 40 per cent discount on financial creditors, 50 per cent discount on suppliers' credits, etc.). The categorisation of creditors is subject to approval by the judge, who may reject it if in his opinion it is unreasonable. When the judge approves the categorisation of creditors, a new creditors' committee should be appointed by him which must at least include the largest creditor. Within 30 days after approval of the categorisation of the creditors or within a longer period of time set by the judge, within a maximum of 60 days, the debtor may negotiate an agreement with the various categories of creditors. Five days before the deadline, an informative meeting is summoned by the judge. The debtor must submit the scheme of arrangement to the court in writing, with proof of its approval by the creditors. If the scheme of arrangement has been approved by the required majorities of the groups of creditors, the judge must approve the PCP, appointing the final creditors' committee.

A scheme of arrangement may propose a moratorium of payment, a reduction of debts, or both. Indeed it may offer various options to the creditors and can take any form considered acceptable by the creditors, except that it may not contain a clause by which compliance with its stipulations are made subject to the sole volition of the debtor. Also, the discount proposed may not exceed 60 per cent of the debts. Since the last change in the legislation, the judge may not reject a scheme that has been approved by the creditors.

A scheme of arrangement must be approved by a majority of the creditors holding at least two thirds of the debt.

In the case of joint stock companies, limited liability companies and the like, should the debtor be unable to achieve approval of a scheme of arrangement by the various categories of creditors, the judge will open a register, for five days, where interested parties may record their wish to buy the equity of the company in question. These interested parties may in turn attempt to negotiate a scheme of arrangement with the creditors, there being in this case no limitation to the discounts that can be agreed. Should these efforts prove successful, the entirety of the equity of the debtor may be acquired by the successful party, at a price which may not be lower than the equity value established by the judge.

Once the agreement with the various groups of creditors has been sanctioned by the judge, the rights of these creditors are definitively reduced to the agreed amount.

Liquidation

In case no agreement has been reached with the creditors and no interested party has registered as a potential buyer, the judge must declare the debtor bankrupt. This may also happen at the request of the debtor or at the request of a creditor. In this latter case, the debtor may petition to change the procedures into a PCP, whereby the procedure discussed above is set into motion.

Creditors

The principle of equality of division of assets among creditors of similar standing used to be basic to the Argentine insolvency law, but this has been changed by the recent amendment whereby different categories of creditors may receive different treatment.

Privileged (or secured) creditors

A privileged creditor is one who holds a mortgage, charge or lien on property of the debtor as a security for a debt. He has a right to recover partly or wholly from the disposition of the property in question with priority to an unsecured (or common) creditor. To a certain extent other creditors are also considered privileged on the basis of the nature of their rights (judicial costs, labour credits, etc.).

Common (or unsecured) creditors

The term ‘common creditor’ encompasses all creditors not qualified as privileged. These creditors are paid once the privileged creditors have been satisfied.

Treatment of foreign creditors

Current treatment gives a foreign creditor similar rights to a local creditor, provided the foreign creditor’s country of domicile reciprocates.

Other matters

Insolvency legislation in Argentina is rather complex and rarely helps the creditor. By recent legal changes, the speed by which the assets in question are returned to business activity seems to have been given priority over the rights of creditors and owners.

KPMG contact partner

Juan Carlos Pickenhayn
KPMG Finsterbusch Pickenhayn Sibille
Avenida L.N. Alem 1050, 5th floor
1001 Buenos Aires
Argentina

Telephone: +54 (1) 313-9633
Fax: +54 (1) 311-7117

Aruba

Legislation

Procedures for initiating and conducting the dissolution of a company (or coming to an arrangement with creditors) under the Commercial Code of Aruba (CCA) are laid down in the Act of 6 July 1990 and the Bankruptcy Decree of 1931.

Insolvency procedures

Procedures in general follow those of the Netherlands. A company may be wound up by the Attorney General (if the company is deemed to be acting against the public interest) or by the court having been petitioned by creditors or debenture holders. There is a 'protection from creditors' provision which is also instigated by the court having been petitioned either by creditors or debenture holders or by the company.

The court decides the effective date and appoints trustees. The trustees, usually a lawyer and an accountant, are empowered to demand and collect all outstanding debts and liabilities on shares. Notice of the arrangement must be placed in the *Official Gazette* and with the Commercial Register and must set forth the scheme of distribution showing the basis for the division of the company's assets.

Rights of creditors and priorities of payment are the same as under Dutch law. Thus the trustees or liquidator, court and other government liabilities rank ahead of secured creditors.

Liquidation, dissolution

A corporation may be dissolved pursuant to a general shareholders' resolution to that effect, on the expiration of its term (as provided for in the articles of the corporation) or on its insolvency after a declaration of bankruptcy (CCA, art. 141). In practice, the articles of most corporations provide for an unlimited period of existence so that liquidation of a corporation on expiry of its term is rare.

A general shareholders' resolution initiating dissolution must be published in the *Official Gazette* and filed in the Commercial Register of the Chamber of Commerce (CCA, art. 143). After dissolution, the corporation only continues to exist to the extent necessary for winding up its business (CCA, art. 144(1)). The general meeting which took the decision to dissolve may appoint one or more liquidators. If no liquidators are appointed, the managing directors act as such (CCA, art. 145(1)).

The liquidator has the duty of paying the claims of the corporation's creditors, including tax claims. Only after the creditors have been paid are the remaining assets available for distribution to shareholders (CCA, art. 146). Corporate assets may not actually be distributed to shareholders until two months after publication of a notice in the *Official Gazette* and a detailed plan of distribution has been prepared and filed with the Chamber of Commerce and at the offices of the corporation (CCA, art. 147(1)).

During this two-month period any interested party, whether creditor or shareholder, may oppose the distribution plan. After the final distribution has been made the liquidator must, within one month, prepare a final account of his administration. This written final account must be registered at a location designated by the liquidator (and in Aruba) and at the Chamber of Commerce for public inspection for a period of three months. Notice of registration of the final account must also be published in the *Official Gazette* (CCA, art. 151(1)).

If no legal proceedings are initiated against the liquidator within three months after the filing of the final account and publication in the Official Gazette, the account of the liquidator is considered approved and the dissolution of the corporation is automatically complete (CCA, art. 151(2)).

KPMG contact partner

Tico R. Croes
KPMG Accountants
Caya G.F. (Betico) Croes 85
PO Box 701
Oranjestad, Aruba

Telephone: +297 (8) 32098
Fax: +297 (8) 24378

Australia

Legislation

Practitioners involved in liquidations, receiverships and other corporate administrations work within the statutory framework of the Corporations Law. That Commonwealth legislation has, by agreement, been adopted by each of the States in Australia by legislation.

Practitioners involved with personal bankruptcies operate under the Bankruptcy Act 1966, which applies nationally.

Insolvency procedures

The following office holders may be appointed:

- liquidator — with the exception of members' voluntary liquidations, only liquidators registered with the Australian Securities Commission, being natural persons, can be appointed liquidators of corporations. Generally, only accountants in public practice with appropriate experience are registered as liquidators;
- receiver — only registered liquidators may be appointed to act as a receiver of the property or part of the property of a company;
- company administrator or administrator of deed of company arrangement — only registered liquidators may consent to act as company administrators;
- scheme manager — only registered liquidators can accept an appointment to act as scheme managers.

There are provisions that disqualify appointment to most of the above positions for auditors, officers and mortgagees etc. of the debtor corporation.

Receivership

A receiver and manager, or a receiver, appointed by a creditor holding security in the nature of an equitable mortgage, assumes control of the company's assets and realises them in order to satisfy the claims of the secured creditor. However, although the appointee is clearly acting for the secured creditor, the receiver and manager is the agent of the company and also has a common law responsibility to give due regard to the position of other creditors.

A receiver appointed by the court must act in accordance with the terms of the order under which he is appointed.

Commonly, a company grants a mortgage charging the whole of its assets and undertaking. The instrument creating the charge confers on the holder of the charge or his trustee a right to appoint a receiver and manager where a condition precedent, such as default in meeting a repayment obligation, occurs.

A secured creditor may elect not to exercise his rights to appoint a receiver and manager under the instrument and allow a liquidator to realise the assets which are subject to the charge. The secured creditor will still benefit from these realisations provided there is acceptance by the liquidator of the validity of the security.

The appointment of a receiver and manager can be implemented very quickly and with minimal dislocation to the company's business. He may be appointed in terms of a floating charge (most common appointment) a real property mortgage or other form of fixed or specific mortgage, or a court order.

The powers of the receiver and manger are usually contained within the security document or the instrument appointing him. The powers generally include full powers to carry on the business, to receive income and realise assets. The Corporations Law provides for the receiver to meet certain employee entitlements before satisfying the claims of the secured creditor.

Agent for mortgagee in possession

Following or upon a mortgagee entering into possession of assets (and, in some circumstances, an ongoing business) pursuant to powers contained in a mortgage or floating charge, the mortgagee may appoint an agent to do all things that the mortgagee is entitled to do in terms of the mortgage or charge. Like a receiver, an agent for the mortgagee, or the mortgagee itself if in possession, is required to meet certain employee entitlements before satisfying the claims of the mortgagee. Unlike a receivership, where the business of the mortgagor is carried on, the mortgagee will be vicariously liable for any losses incurred by the agent.

Liquidation

A company can be liquidated by order of the court, by the company voluntarily placing itself in liquidation or during the course of a voluntary administration. Whilst all are similar in operation and effect, there are significant differences in the method of appointing the liquidator. The court may order the winding up of a company where it is insolvent, among other reasons. Where the directors and shareholders of a company realise that the company is insolvent and cannot continue its operation, it is usual for the directors to convene a general meeting of the shareholders and creditors to place the company in voluntary liquidation. A company may also be wound up upon a resolution of creditors at the end of the moratorium period in a voluntary administration (see below) or during the period of a deed of company arrangement.

Scheme of arrangement

A scheme of arrangement is a court-approved arrangement between a company and its creditors, providing either for time to pay debts, or an arrangement whereby the company's creditors abandon the balance of their claims after receiving a specified distribution. This type of arrangement is usually entered into where the creditors are of the opinion that they are more likely to obtain a greater benefit from the company continuing its operations under the control of a scheme manager than if the company is wound up.

Voluntary administration and deed of company arrangement

Voluntary administrations and deeds of company arrangement are a relatively new insolvency procedure, resulting from amendments to the Corporations Law in June 1993. An administrator of a company may be appointed by a liquidator of the company, a secured creditor in a position to enforce its security, or, most commonly, by a resolution of the directors of the company.

Upon the appointment of the administrator of the company, a statutory moratorium restricts the rights of creditors to seek the winding up of the company or to enforce their usual rights. The moratorium continues for up to 28 days, but can be extended either by a resolution of creditors for another 60 days, or by the court. There are limited exceptions to the moratorium. The principal exception is that a secured creditor with a charge over substantially the whole of the assets of the company may still exercise its rights within the first two weeks of the moratorium.

The purpose of the moratorium period is to allow the administrator of the company to form a recommendation as to the future of the company. The recommendation may be to return control of the company to its directors, that the company be wound up, or that the company enter into a deed of company arrangement with its creditors. The terms of such a deed are very flexible with few legislative requirements and no need for court approval.

The administrator's recommendation is considered by a meeting of creditors at the conclusion of the moratorium. Should the creditors resolve that the company enter into a deed of company arrangement, a simple majority in value and number in favour of the resolution is sufficient to bind all unsecured creditors and secured creditors who voted in favour of the deed. The creditors may alternatively resolve that the company proceed into liquidation in which case the administrator automatically becomes the liquidator.

The voluntary administration and deed of company arrangement procedure has been readily adopted by the business community and has rapidly become the most common form of insolvency procedure in Australia.

Creditors

The principle of an equality of division of assets among creditors is fundamental to the whole statutory scheme but there are some exceptions to the general rule, all of which are statutory in origin:

- secured creditors — a secured creditor is one who holds a mortgage, charge or lien on property of the debtor as security for a debt, and is in a position whether at law or in equity to recoup partly or wholly from the assets of the debtor in priority to unsecured creditors. A secured creditor has many courses of action available and these include the appointment of a receiver, entering into possession as mortgagee, appointing a company administrator or doing nothing and allowing the company or administrator to realise the security;
- unsecured creditors — the term 'unsecured creditor' includes all creditors not being secured creditors. Unsecured creditors can, in accordance with the provisions of the Corporations Law, resolve to effect a scheme of arrangement or voluntary administration for a company, to wind the company up or to enter into a deed of company arrangement with the company. In certain circumstances they also have the power to nominate who they wish to be the liquidator of a corporation. They also generally have the power to appoint some of their number to creditors' committees.

Priority claims

The Corporations Law makes provision for the payment of certain unsecured creditors in priority to others. As a general guide in company liquidations and receiverships, priority is provided to the following:

- injury compensation payments;
- costs of liquidation, including petitioning creditors' costs;
- costs of any previous insolvency administrator;
- wages and salaries (not exceeding $2,000 in respect of directors and their relatives);
- amounts due to employees in respect of leave of absence (not exceeding $1,500 in respect of directors and their relatives).

Other matters

Insolvency administration and legislation in Australia are highly sophisticated and provide a workable framework for creditors to exercise their legal rights to ensure that a company, unable to pay its debts, is placed in an appropriate form of insolvency administration. Similarly, a debtor company is able to avail itself of the insolvency provisions to provide a framework for it to trade out of financial difficulties. Generally, all forms of insolvency administrations are administered by accountants in public practice.

KPMG contact partner

Lindsay Maxsted
KPMG
161 Collins Street
Melbourne VIC 3000
Australia

Telephone: +61 (3) 9288 5555
Fax: +61 (3) 9288 6666

Austria

Legislation

Insolvency laws were thoroughly reformed in 1982 and comprise:

- Bankruptcy Code (Konkursordnung);
- Settlement and Recomposition of Debts Act (Ausgleichsordnung).

Insolvency laws were introduced in order to speed up insolvency proceedings, to abolish privileged creditors, such as tax authorities and social security institutions, and to secure the continuation of enterprises for the purpose of improving the employment situation.

Generally, insolvency proceedings may be divided into moratorium, settlement or bankruptcy proceedings. In 1995 private bankruptcy proceedings were introduced for individuals, both for entrepreneurs and non-entrepreneurs.

Creditors

The principle of an equality in the distribution of the proceeds realised out of the sale of assets among creditors has been strengthened. Property rights of secured creditors, for example, on assets leased to the debtor, remain intact.

Priority claims

Priority claims are the cost of proceedings and the cost of carrying on the business. These include the cost of administration and maintenance of the debtor's assets, taxes, social security contributions, salaries, wages and fees of certain associations for the protection of creditors' interests.

Terminology

Insolvenzverfahren	insolvency proceedings
Vorverfahren	moratorium
Konkurs	bankruptcy
Ausgleich	settlement proceedings
Zahlungsunfähigkeit	insolvency (incapacity to meet liabilities on a regular basis)
Überschuldung	excess of liabilities over assets
Privatkonkurs	private bankruptcy
Zwangsausgleich	forced settlement
Abschöpfungsverfahren	garnishment
Geschäftsaufsicht	official management
Masseverwalter, Ausgleichsverwalter	receiver
Sachwalter	supervisor
Gläubigerschutzverband	association for the protection of creditors' interests

Court

All insolvency proceedings are conducted under the supervision of the bankruptcy court, which appoints a (temporary) receiver and a creditors' committee to administer the insolvency proceedings.

The law provides for the existence of associations for the protection of creditors' interests. The associations professionally represent creditors in insolvency proceedings and often play a decisive role in such proceedings.

Insolvency procedures

Moratorium

The purpose of a moratorium is to rehabilitate and reconstruct businesses that are only in temporary financial difficulties, but are basically healthy enough to stay in business. Only the insolvent debtor can file an application to the bankruptcy court for the opening of a moratorium. A temporary receiver is appointed by the court to supervise the proceedings, verify the feasibility of reorganisation, and check the risk of continuation of the enterprise. The debtor must submit a detailed proposal for the reorganisation of its business. The length of the moratorium may not exceed eight weeks. Usually, the temporary receiver inquires whether banking or financing institutions are willing to provide new funds to the debtor and give guarantees in favour of the existing creditors in case of failure of the reorganisation.

Any claims that come into existence after the opening of these temporary proceedings have priority over old claims in subsequent insolvency proceedings. Usually, the proceedings will be terminated and the debtor will be free to continue its business activities. If the debtor is not able to continue its business activities, the court will decide to open formal settlement proceedings upon application of the debtor or to open bankruptcy proceedings, if such application has not been filed.

The moratorium as currently provided by law is hardly used in practice. It is expected that the moratorium will be replaced by a law specifically dealing with the reconstruction of enterprises with effect from mid 1997.

Bankruptcy proceedings

The application for the opening of bankruptcy proceedings may be filed either by the debtor itself or by a creditor. Bankruptcy proceedings have to be opened by the bankruptcy court upon application if the insolvent debtor is incapable of meeting its financial obligations, which means that debts cannot be settled within due time. If the debtor is a legal entity, bankruptcy proceedings must also be opened if liabilities exceed assets. The debtor is under a statutory obligation to file an application within 60 days after becoming insolvent.

With the opening of the bankruptcy proceedings, the debtor is deprived of all rights to make any dispositions with respect to its property, and the administration of it is conferred exclusively on a receiver appointed by the court. Transactions concluded by the debtor after the opening of bankruptcy proceedings are void with respect to its creditors.

The court appoints a receiver (in most instances an attorney at law) and in addition a creditors' committee, if it deems this necessary in view of the size of the debtor's business. The receiver's first task is to establish the economic status of the debtor's business and whether it would be possible to carry it on. If there are no prospects of doing so, the receiver is obliged to sell all assets of the debtor and to distribute the proceeds to the creditors.

All claims against the debtor must be notified to the bankruptcy court within a period set by the court in its decision on the opening of the bankruptcy proceedings. A creditor who does not file a claim in bankruptcy proceedings will not participate in the distribution of the debtor's assets. Secured creditors, i.e., creditors in whose favour a mortgage, lien, encumbrance or any other security was constituted either by way of contract or by way of seizure in enforcement proceedings, have priority in the settlement of their claims with respect to the assets over which they hold security. Transactions undertaken and securities perfected within 60 days prior to the opening of bankruptcy proceedings are therefore, as a general rule, always voidable. Secured creditors are banned from exercising their rights for a maximum period of 90 days after the opening of bankruptcy proceedings, if the exercise of such rights would endanger the carrying on of the bankrupt's business by the receiver.

The bankruptcy proceedings terminate as soon as all assets of the debtor have been sold and the proceeds have been distributed to the creditors. The creditors are free for a further period of 30 years to attempt collection of the unsettled portion of their claims from the debtor, should the debtor come into the possession of any assets within such a period.

Settlement proceedings

Whereas bankruptcy proceedings ultimately lead to the sale and distribution of the debtor's assets with the debtor remaining liable for its residual debts, settlement proceedings are aimed at enabling the debtor to continue its activities and to be discharged from a part of its debts.

The application for the opening of settlement proceedings can only be filed by the debtor and must include a correct and complete description of the debtor's financial status and a proposal stating the percentage of its debts that the debtor is willing to settle.

The minimum statutory requirement for a settlement offer to be accepted by the court is payment by the debtor of at least 40 per cent of the creditors' claims within a period of two years from the day of the creditors' acceptance (of the debtor's settlement offer regarding the forced settlement).

The court-appointed receiver has a right of veto over any ordinary transaction of the debtor and must expressly agree to any transaction of the debtor beyond the ordinary course of business.

The court will also schedule a meeting of creditors and will give notice to all known creditors of the opening of settlement proceedings and request the creditors to file their claims with the court. Within 90 days of the opening of the settlement proceedings, the creditors must decide whether to accept the debtor's offer. A vote of acceptance by the creditors requires an absolute majority of all creditors present and a majority of three-quarters of the total sum of all claims of the creditors present. If a debtor's offer is accepted by the creditors, the court will issue an order confirming the agreement reached between the parties. The debtor must repay the portion of its debts specified in the order. Excess claims are foreclosed, if the debtor fulfils the terms of the offer.

If the debtor's offer is not accepted by the creditors, the court must decide whether bankruptcy proceedings should immediately be opened.

The approval of creditors can be made subject to the appointment by the court of a supervisor for the period granted to the debtor for the settlement of the approved portion of its debts.

Forced settlement

A bankrupt is given the possibility to turn the bankruptcy proceedings into a forced settlement. The debtor's settlement offer during bankruptcy must provide for the settlement of at least 20 per cent of the debtor's obligations within two years. If the debtor's proposal for forced settlement is approved by the creditors, bankruptcy proceedings are terminated pending the debtor's fulfilment of the terms of the agreement reached between the parties.

Private bankruptcy

In 1995 Austrian insolvency law introduced personal bankruptcy proceedings for individuals, specifically designed for non-entrepreneurs. The purpose is to oblige the insolvent individual to make a reasonable contribution, from future earnings, towards his creditors.

After the failure of an out-of-court settlement, an insolvent individual must file an application for bankruptcy proceedings to the bankruptcy court within 60 days from the beginning of his insolvency.

In case the debtor wants to prevent the liquidation of his property, he must apply for a forced settlement. The debtor's settlement offer in the course of bankruptcy proceedings must provide for the settlement of at least 20 per cent of the debtor's obligations within two years. Individual debtors who are not entrepreneurs may alternatively choose to provide for a settlement of at least 30 per cent within five years.

Any forced settlement relies on the creditors' acceptance of the debtor's offer (absolute majority of all creditors present and three-quarters majority of the total sum of all claims of the creditors present).

A debtor who cannot meet the requirements of a forced settlement may propose a payment plan to its creditors, which contains a payment schedule for up to seven years.

In the course of bankruptcy proceedings, the debtor may also request garnishment in order to discharge any residual debt. The debtor must cede the attachable part of his income to a court appointed trustee for a period of seven years. The bankruptcy court will terminate the garnishment process, if the creditors receive at least 50 per cent of their claims within three years of the proceedings or at least 10 per cent within seven years.

Official management

Only banks can be put under official management.

KPMG contact partner

Gottwald Kranebitter
KPMG Austria Alpen-Treuhand Gmbh
Kolingasse 19
A-1090 Vienna
Austria

Telephone: +43 (1) 313320
Fax: +43 (1) 313325

Azerbaijan

Legislation

Azeri insolvency legislation is relatively new and undergoing continuous development. Under the Soviet system, all enterprises were deemed to be branches of the State, and therefore no bankruptcy was possible. Liquidation through reorganisation was possible, but it was an administrative and logistical exercise.

Although insolvency legislation has been passed in Azerbaijan and there is some evidence that insolvency proceedings have been instituted, the process is neither common nor even the automatic result of an irredeemable financial position. This is due partly to lack of experience and partly to what seems to be a 'Soviet' belief that companies, once founded, cannot or should not die.

Current insolvency legislation is closely related to the legislation in Russia as both have evolved from the same system and Russian legislation is more readily accessible. Azeri insolvency legislation is based on the Law on Insolvency (Bankruptcy), which was passed in July 1994. Since then the legislation has been considerably modified and developed by Presidential Decrees and other enabling legislation.

Further development is certain and so these notes are merely indicative of the current situation.

Insolvency procedures

Types of insolvency procedure

- reorganisation — the business is placed in the hands of an external management, which may be charged with its rehabilitation;
- liquidation — this occurs (a) if a court has declared the enterprise insolvent, or (b) if the enterprise declares itself insolvent;
- amicable settlement — the enterprise comes to an agreement with its creditors involving the deferral of payment of debts, payment by instalment, or debt forgiveness.

Insolvency courts

Insolvency cases are examined by 'arbitration' courts. Cases may be brought when claims have been outstanding for three months from the due date for repayment and constitute 10 per cent of the charter capital of the enterprise.

Parties to an insolvency action

The legislation recognises various parties in an insolvency action, including:

- arbitration manager — the arbitration manager is authorised, *inter alia*, to carry on the business, hire and fire workers, dispose of assets, call meetings of the creditors, and draw up a plan for an external management and execute the plan;
- receiver — the receiver may dispose of assets, act in an arbitration court to contest the validity of contracts closed up to six months prior to the initiation of arbitration proceedings, collect debts and receivables, form a liquidation commission and call a creditors' meeting;
- creditors;
- representatives of the workforce;
- the debtor.

Petition

An insolvency action is initiated by a petition to the arbitration court from:

- the debtor, either the owner of the enterprise or its management — such a petition cannot be withdrawn;
- a creditor, after the lapse of three months from the due date for payment for goods or services.

The court may either refuse the petition if it is established that the creditor's claim can be met or the defendant is solvent, or it may recognise the defendant as insolvent, in which case liquidation proceedings will be instituted.

If a petition is received for the debtor enterprise to be reorganised, the court may decide to postpone the declaration of insolvency and instead institute rehabilitation procedures.

Reorganisation

Reorganisation of the enterprise may be considered if there is a real possibility that the solvency of the enterprise may be restored by selling off parts of the debtor organisation, reorganising it, or instituting some other economic measures. Three months is allotted to gain approval for a reorganisation plan.

The arbitration court must review the plan and decide whether it should continue or the debtor should be declared insolvent and liquidation proceedings be instituted.

Rehabilitation

If the enterprise can be restored to solvency as a result of financial aid by the owner or third parties, the arbitration court may institute rehabilitation proceedings. If an arbitration court rules in favour of rehabilitation, it must put the rehabilitation contract out to tender.

Within 12 months of the start of rehabilitation, the enterprise must have met at least 35 per cent of the combined creditor claims. Rehabilitation may not last for more than 18 months. Rehabilitation ceases when 18 months has elapsed or it is determined by the court that rehabilitation is ineffective, in which case liquidation proceedings must be instituted. Rehabilitation is deemed successful when all claims have been met and the insolvency action can be closed.

Liquidation proceedings

Once a debtor has been declared insolvent, liquidation proceedings are instigated. The arbitration court appoints a receiver and the creditors' committee determines the receiver's remuneration. The receiver has the duty, monitored by the creditors' committee, to obtain the highest price for the debtor's assets.

The liquidation proceedings must also involve representatives of the workforce and other interested parties.

The proceeds of the realisation of assets are distributed in the following order of priority:

- claims of individuals whom the debtor has injured or jeopardised;
- payment of the workforce;
- taxes and social security contributions etc.;
- creditor claims.

The first three of these classes are considered privileged creditors.

Voluntary liquidation

An enterprise may declare voluntary liquidation in the event of its managers determining that it can no longer meet its obligations or restore solvency. The receiver is appointed by the enterprise's creditors.

Amicable settlement

A settlement among the non-privileged creditors may be reached at any point in the insolvency proceedings; it may not infringe on the settlement of the privileged claims and must be endorsed by the court. Creditors must receive at least 35 per cent of their settlement within two weeks of the settlement date. The settlement may be rendered void if (a) the terms are not satisfied, (b) the financial position of the debtor deteriorates, (c) the debtor infringes the rights and interests of the creditors.

KPMG contact partner

Roger Munnings
KPMG
37 Ul. Novaya Basmannaya
3rd Floor
Moscow 107066
Russia

Telephone: +7 (502) 222 4030
Fax: +7 (502) 222 4024

Bahamas

Legislation

The laws of the Bahamas are based on English law and thus insolvency procedures are similar to those in England and Wales. Such laws include the Companies Act 1992, the International Business Companies Act 1989 and the Companies (Winding-up) Rules 1975.

Insolvency procedures

Receivership

Receivers are most commonly appointed by lenders under the terms of mortgage debentures where there has been a failure by the borrower to repay the debt to the lender when requested to so do.

The procedures regarding receiverships are similar to those set out in the section on England and Wales except that the term 'administrative receiver' is not used in the Bahamas and no meeting of creditors has to be called by the receiver. The procedures provide a speedy remedy and allow the company to continue to trade.

Voluntary winding up

Voluntary winding up means the winding up of a company by the shareholders without seeking the assistance of the court. The assets and liabilities of the company are placed under the control of a liquidator who winds up the affairs of the company.

A company may be wound up voluntarily:

- whenever the articles of association of the company provide for it to be dissolved, and the company in general meeting has passed a resolution requiring it to be wound up voluntarily;
- whenever the company has passed a special resolution requiring it to be wound up voluntarily;
- whenever members of the company have passed a resolution to the effect that it has been proved to their satisfaction that it cannot by reason of its liabilities continue its business, and that it is advisable to wind up.

A voluntary winding up is deemed to commence at the time of the passing of the resolution authorising the winding up. The effects of the commencement of winding up are that:

- the company shall cease to trade except as required for the beneficial winding up;
- the company's corporate powers and status continue until its affairs are wound up;
- upon the appointment of a liquidator all the powers of the directors cease.

There are certain procedural differences in the voluntary winding up of companies incorporated under the provisions of the Companies Act 1992 and the International Business Companies Act 1989.

As soon as the affairs of the company are fully wound up, the liquidator must prepare an account showing the manner in which the winding up has been conducted and the property of the company disposed of.

Winding up under supervision of the court

When a resolution has been passed by a company to wind up voluntarily, the court may make an order directing that the voluntary winding up should continue but subject to such supervision of the court as the court thinks fit. The company or any creditor of the company or any contributory may petition the court to order such supervision.

Compulsory winding up

A company may be wound up by the court whenever:

- the company has passed a resolution requiring the company to be wound up by the court;
- the company does not commence its business within a year from its incorporation, or suspends its business for a period of one year;
- the members are reduced in number to less than two;
- the company is unable to pay its debts;
- the court is of the opinion that it is just and equitable that the company should be wound up;
- the Central Bank petitions for the winding up of a bank whose licence has been suspended.

Companies incorporated under the International Business Companies Act 1989 may also be compulsorily wound up under the provisions of the Companies Act 1992.

Section 198 of the Companies Act 1992 defines when a company is deemed to be unable to pay its debts. The date of commencement of winding up by the court is the date of presentation of the petition for the winding up.

The court shall appoint one or more persons to be called official liquidator or liquidators and all proceedings in the winding up of the company by the official liquidators are subject to the court's directions. The powers and duties of official liquidators are contained in the Companies Act 1992, the International Business Companies Act 1989 and the Companies (Winding-up) Rules 1975.

Striking off

A company may be struck off under the provisions of the Companies Act 1992 where:

- it fails to submit any return, notice, document or prescribed fee to the Registrar as required by the Act;
- it is dissolved;
- it has amalgamated or merged with one or more companies;
- it refuses to comply with any request or direction given by the Registrar pursuant to the Act;
- its registration is revoked or cancelled in accordance with the Act;
- it has ceased to carry on business.

The striking off of any company under the Act shall not affect the liability of the company and any director, officer and member of the company, and such liability shall continue and may be enforced as if the company had not been struck off. Any property vested in or belonging to any company struck off under the Act thereupon vests in the Treasurer of the Bahamas.

Using this procedure, a company may be dissolved at minimum cost and there is no need for a liquidator.

KPMG contact partner

David Hamilton
KPMG Peat Marwick
1st Floor, International Building
West Mall
PO Box F-40025
Freeport
Grand Bahama

Telephone: +1 (242) 352 9384
Fax: +1 (242) 352 6862

Bahrain

Legislation

Bahrain insolvency law is included in:

- Company Law 1975;
- Commercial Law 1987;
- Bankruptcy and Composition Law 1987.

Who may be appointed

The following officers may be appointed:

- liquidator — this usually, but not essentially, is an experienced accountant in private practice;
- trustee — appointed by the court.

Insolvency procedures

Liquidation

Liquidation is the statutory process for winding up the affairs of a company. Liquidation may be:

- voluntary liquidation — this is normally initiated by the directors who call a meeting of the shareholders who, by majority, appoint a liquidator;
- compulsory liquidation — this is normally initiated when a creditor presents a winding-up petition to the court. The court then normally makes a winding-up order and appoints the liquidator.

As soon as the resolution or court order is received the liquidator prepares a balance sheet of the net assets of the company. After receiving the various claims from the creditors, the liquidator prepares a final report and submits it to the court for approval.

Bankruptcy

Bankruptcy applies to a trader or company whose financial business is disrupted and ceases to meet its commercial debts as they fall due. A petition of bankruptcy may be made to the court by the individual, one of his creditors or the public prosecutor.

The court appoints a judge to supervise the bankruptcy and a trustee to manage it. The trustee carries out an inventory of the bankrupt's asset and takes over the assets, books and papers of the bankrupt person. The trustee then prepares a balance sheet which is submitted to the court.

Other forms of insolvency administration are set out in the Bankruptcy and Composition Law 1987. These other forms are new and are designed to avoid bankruptcy and protect the creditors. They are the scheme of arrangement, composition, and union of creditors.

Scheme of arrangement

A scheme of arrangement is a court-approved arrangement between an individual or company and its creditors, mainly providing either for a moratorium of time to pay the debt or relief from part of the debt, or both. This type of arrangement is usually entered into where the creditors are of the opinion that, if the business activities continue as normal, they are more likely to recover their debt than if the company is wound up. This arrangement is more popular than a composition since the scheme is discussed and decided in court.

Composition

A composition is a compromise whereby the debtor agrees to pay a certain amount to each unsecured creditor whilst continuing the company's business. The composition may stipulate time limits to pay and may also discharge the debtor from part of the debt. If agreement from a majority of the creditors is reached the composition is submitted to the court for approval.

Union of creditors

A union of creditors may exist where the creditors believe that the only means of recovering their debt is by providing financial assistance to the debtor. A union of creditors is formed where the debtor fails to apply for a composition or the debtor applies for a composition but is rejected by the creditors or the debtor obtains a composition, which is later annulled or rescinded. The court must approve the union of creditors and agree the level of financial assistance required.

Creditors

Creditors are categorised as:

- secured creditors — someone who holds a fixed charge over the assets of the debtor;
- preferential creditors — someone who has priority in payment before unsecured creditors;
- unsecured creditors — all other creditors.

Preferential creditors normally include all government dues, social insurance and amounts due to employees. The courts have in certain recent cases awarded payment to employees before secured creditors.

KPMG contact partner

Hussain Kasim Abdul Rasool
KPMG Fakhro
Chamber of Commerce and Industry Building
PO Box 710
Manama
State of Bahrain

Telephone: +973 224807
Fax: +973 227443

Barbados

Legislation

Insolvency procedures are governed by the Companies Act of 1982. Insolvency matters dealt with relate to receivership, liquidation and bankruptcy.

Insolvency procedures

Receivership

The Companies Act is based largely upon Canadian legislation and also reflects the Barbadian common law legal system. Secured creditors often take fixed and floating charge debentures as security over the assets of the borrower. A typical debenture gives the secured creditor the right to appoint a receiver or receiver and manager. Receivers have an obligation to act honestly and in a commercially reasonable manner.

Corporate bodies are not allowed to act as receivers and so partners in a firm accept appointments in their individual names. The secured creditor provides the receiver with a full indemnity against claims other than those caused by gross negligence. Government and severance pay obligations to employees rank in priority to floating charge security.

Liquidation

A company may be placed in liquidation by the directors through a voluntary action or through a creditor applying to the Supreme Court for the winding up of the business. An individual is appointed liquidator as companies are not allowed to act as liquidators. Appropriate notices must be given in the local press of a liquidation procedure.

Bankruptcy

Bankruptcy procedures are conducted under the supervision of the court and are not widely used at present.

KPMG contact partner

David A. Millington
KPMG Peat Marwick
Hastings
Christ Church
Bridgetown
Barbados

Telephone: +1 (246) 427 5230
Fax: +1 (246) 427 7123

Belgium

Insolvency procedures

Insolvency procedures are:

- bankruptcy;
- arrangement under court supervision;
- suspension of payment.

The above procedures apply to traders only. Traders are defined as follows:

- natural persons who, as their normal trade or profession, carry out transactions defined by law as commercial, whether they carry out these transactions as their principal occupation or as a contributory occupation;
- legal persons whose objects are commercial transactions.

Bankruptcy

Any trader who stops paying his creditors and whose credit is exhausted is in a state of bankruptcy.

Cessation of payments — this means that arises when it is impossible for a trader to continue paying his debts. The debts taken into account are those which have fallen due and payable. The unpaid debts may be both unsecured and preferential. There is no cessation of payment when the debtor borrows to meet his obligations. Whether the debt is civil or commercial is also unimportant. A trader can be adjudicated bankrupt even if he only fails to pay one debt. The source of the debt is irrelevant. Cessation of payments is proved by an admission by the debtor, service of writs, distraints, protests, refusal of an amicable arrangement, filing of an application for an arrangement under court supervision, disappearance of the trader, closure of the business premises, or recourse to fraudulent preference. The commercial court is the final judge of the facts advanced to establish a cessation of payments.

Exhaustion of credit — this means that a trader's business associates have lost confidence in him. His suppliers suspend supplies, his sources of funds refuse any new financing etc. However, only commercial credit is involved and considered. The commercial court judges whether a trader has exhausted his credit.

Bankruptcy — is declared by judgment of the commercial court, in response to an admission by the bankrupt or to a petition from one or more creditors, or of the court's own motion.

Admission — within three days of ceasing payment, a bankrupt is obliged to make an admission of the fact to the registry of the commercial court of his domicile or be subject to penalties.

Petition from one or more creditors — the petitioning creditor must prove that the trader cannot continue to pay his debts and that his credit is exhausted. Such a petition has to be initiated by service of a writ: the debtor is served the writ and allowed to defend himself.

Declaration of bankruptcy by the commercial court of its own motion — this usually occurs when the debtor has not admitted that he has ceased payment and his creditors prove negligence, or when they seek to reap the benefit of individual actions. Also when the petition by a creditor proves to be defective, or at certain stages in arrangement proceedings, the commercial court may declare the trader bankrupt.

The Services for Trade Investigations (*depistagediensten, services de dépistage*) attempt to identify traders and trading companies which have serious financial problems, in order to discover potential bankruptcies as soon as possible. The Services for Trade Investigations have different ways of detecting whether companies are in financial difficulty. For instance, the Services are informed when a company is fined for not paying its debts on repeated occasions or when real property has been seized. When the Services undertake their investigations, they invite the company's directors and officers to comment on whether the company is bankrupt or not. Although the Services operate under the supervision of the commercial court they are not empowered to tell the company what to do. However, many companies that come before the Services for Trade Investigations take additional measures to avoid bankruptcy.

When the commercial court declares a trader bankrupt, the following procedures occur:

- the commercial court appoints a trustee (usually a lawyer) whose responsibility is to wind up the bankrupt's operation and sell all of the assets in order to satisfy creditors' claims. He also investigates creditors' claims and determines whether any actions by the bankrupt's management group or any third party contributed to the insolvency;
- the commercial court appoints a judge to supervise the handling of the winding up;
- the commercial court sets a date by which time creditors must file their claims.

Arrangement under court supervision

The debtor must submit his application for an arrangement to the commercial court. The arrangement application must indicate:

- why the debtor is making the request;
- a list of the debtor's assets;
- a list of creditors;
- the arrangement proposals.

The commercial court appoints a judge for the preliminary investigation of the request. If the commercial court decides that the proceedings may continue, a meeting of the creditors is arranged to discuss the arrangement details. A vote is held and the commercial court must confirm a positive decision.

If the arrangement is accepted, the judgment confirming the arrangement nominates one or more commissioners to supervise, with the appointed judge, the performance of the arrangement.

Suspension of payment

This procedure is rarely used. Basically, it allows the debtor to suspend payments temporarily because of extraordinary circumstances, even though he is not insolvent.

KPMG contact partner

Guy Pierson
KPMG Peat Marwick sc-cv
Neerveldstraat 101 rue Neerveld
1200 Brussels
Belgium

Telephone: +32 (2) 773 38 05
Fax: +32 (2) 772 33 05

Belize

Legislation

The Belize statutes relating to insolvency procedures are drawn from UK statutes of many years ago and have not been revised. Their origins and major features are noted below:

Companies Act, c. 206

The Companies Act is drawn from the UK Companies (Consolidation) Act 1908, with minor revisions. It was enacted on 23 April 1914. The revisions to insolvency legislation which were made by the UK Companies Act 1948 and Insolvency Act 1986 have not been incorporated into Belize law and there is very little reference to receivership within the Act. In the absence of statutory provisions covering receiverships, a receiver's powers and obligations are drawn from the debenture document itself and from case law. Additional legislation concerning the winding up of companies is included within the Companies (Winding-up) Rules 1909. These are a part of UK law which have been directly incorporated into the laws of Belize.

Law of Property Act, c. 154

This Act originated in 1954 and is primarily drawn from the UK Law of Property Act 1925. A subsequent Act, the Registered Land Act, was issued in 1977.

Aliens Landholding Act, c. 144

This Act, issued in 1973, is not drawn from UK legislation and was brought about to restrict the ability of 'aliens' to hold land in Belize. An alien is defined as any one other than a British subject born in Belize, a Belizean resident for over three years or a Belizean company controlled by Belize residents.

Sale of Goods Act, c. 214

This Act was passed in 1923 and while it does not embody the revisions brought about by subsequent UK legislation, it incorporates the main provisions that are required by a receiver.

Insolvency procedures

Winding up

The winding up of a company may be:

- by the court;
- voluntary;
- subject to the supervision of the court.

Winding up by court

A company may be wound up by the court if:

- the company has by special resolution resolved that the company be wound up by the court;
- default is made in filing the statutory report or in holding the statutory meeting;

- the company does not commence its business within a year from its incorporation, or suspends its business for a whole year;
- the number of members is reduced in the case of a private company, below two, or, in the case of any other company, below seven;
- the company is unable to pay its debts;
- the court is of the opinion that it is just and equitable that the company should be wound up.

An application to the court for winding up is by petition presented by the company, or any creditor or creditors, or any contributory or contributories, or by all or any of those parties, together or separately, and a winding-up order operates in favour of all the creditors and contributories of the company.

A winding up by the court is deemed to commence at the time of presentation of the petition for winding up.

When a winding-up order has been made, no action or proceeding shall be proceeded with or commenced against the company except by leave of the court and subject to such terms as the court may impose.

Where the court has made a winding-up order, the Official Receiver, as soon as practicable after receipt of the statement of the company's affairs is required to submit a preliminary report to the court. The report should comment on:

- the amount of capital issued, subscribed and paid up, and the estimated amount of assets and liabilities;
- if the company has failed, the causes of the failure;
- whether in his opinion further inquiry is desirable as to any matter relating to the promotion, formation or failure of the company, or the conduct of its business.

Voluntary winding up

A company may be wound up voluntarily:

- when the period (if any) fixed for the duration of the company by the articles expires, or the event (if any) occurs, on the occurrence of which the articles provide that the company is to be dissolved, and the company in general meeting has passed a resolution requiring the company to be wound up voluntarily;
- if the company resolves by special resolution that the company be wound up voluntarily;
- if the company resolves by extraordinary resolution to the effect that it cannot by reason of its liabilities continues its business, and that it is advisable to wind up.

A voluntary winding up is deemed to commence at the time of the passing of the resolution authorising the winding up.

From the commencement of its voluntary winding up a company ceases to carry on its business, except so far as is required for its beneficial winding up but its corporate state and corporate powers continue until it is dissolved.

The effects of a voluntary winding up are:

- the property of the company is applied in satisfaction of its liabilities *pari passu*, and the residue distributed among the members according to their rights and interests;
- the company in general meeting is required to appoint one or more liquidators for the purpose of winding up the affairs and distributing the assets of the company, and may fix the remuneration;
- on the appointment of a liquidator all the powers of the directors cease, except so far as the company in general meeting, or the liquidator sanctions the continuance thereof;

- the liquidator may, without the sanction of the court, exercise all powers given by the Act in a winding up by the court.

Winding up under supervision

When a resolution has been passed by a company to wind up voluntarily, the court may make an order for the voluntary winding up to continue subject to the supervision of the court, and on such terms and conditions as the court thinks just. In making or refusing a supervision order, the court has regard to the wishes of creditors and contributories and may appoint an additional liquidator or liquidators to act with the existing liquidator.

Removal of defunct companies from the register

A company may be struck off the register under the provisions of s. 218 of the Companies Act, c. 306, where:

- the Registrar General has reasonable cause to believe that the company is not carrying on business;
- the company is being wound up and the Registrar General has reasonable cause to believe that either no liquidator is acting or that the affairs of the company are fully wound up.

The striking off of any company under the Act does not affect any liability of a director, officer or member of the company and such liability continues and is enforceable as if the company had not been struck off. Property belonging to the company so struck off vests in the Accountant General of Belize.

KPMG contact partner

Stanley Ermeav Sr
35A Regent Street
PO Box 756
Belize City
Belize

Telephone: +501 (2) 76629
Fax: +501 (2) 76072

Bermuda

Legislation

The laws of Bermuda are based on English law and thus winding up procedures are similar to those in the United Kingdom. Such procedures are now laid down in the Bermuda Companies Act 1981 which became effective on 1 July 1983.

Insolvency procedures

There are four methods by which a company can be wound up:

- members' voluntary liquidation;
- striking off;
- creditors' voluntary liquidation;
- compulsory liquidation.

Whilst the first two methods do not deal with insolvent situations they are the most common ways of disposing of Bermudian companies and are, therefore, dealt with first. The normal reason for winding up is because the purpose for which the company was originally incorporated is no longer required.

Members' voluntary liquidation

In order to commence a members' voluntary liquidation a majority of the company's directors must make a declaration of solvency and a special general meeting (SGM) must be called to pass a resolution to wind up the company and to appoint a liquidator.

The declaration of solvency (an affidavit sworn by the directors which states that they have made a full inquiry into the affairs of the company and have formed the opinion that the company will be able to pay its debts within a period of 12 months) must include a statement of total assets and liabilities as at the most recent practicable date. It must be filed with the Registrar of Companies prior to the date of the SGM and the SGM must be held within five weeks of making the declaration.

Upon the appointment of a liquidator, the responsibility for the company's affairs rests entirely in his hands and no future executive action may be carried out without his approval.

Notice of the winding-up resolution, together with a notice from the liquidator pertaining to his appointment must be published in the *Official Gazette* within 21 days of holding the SGM. The Registrar of Companies must also be notified. The liquidator then proceeds to publish notice for the proof of debts, settles the liabilities and distributes the surplus assets, if any, to the members.

A final general meeting (FGM), which requires one month's notice in the *Official Gazette*, concludes the winding up. At this meeting the liquidator's report is received and resolutions dissolving the company, and determining the manner in which the books and records of the company are to be disposed of, are passed. The liquidator files the notice of the FGM with the Registrar of Companies who then records the fact, and the date of dissolution, in the appropriate register.

Striking off

Facilities do exist in Bermuda for a company to be struck off the register without going through the formal process of liquidation. This can arise in cases where a company has failed to pay its annual government fee, or where the company is not properly constituted due, for example, to the resignation of the Bermudian directors.

If such circumstances come to the notice of the Registrar of Companies, the Registrar will advertise in the *Official Gazette* to the effect that if the shortcoming is not rectified within six months the company will be struck off.

Companies are strongly advised not to allow this to happen without first taking proper advice. The reason is that it is most unlikely that the owners of a company struck off in this way would be permitted to incorporate another company in Bermuda in the future.

Creditors' voluntary liquidation

A company shall cause a meeting of its creditors to be summoned for the day, or the next day following the day, on which there is to be held the meeting at which the resolution for creditors' voluntary winding-up is to be proposed, and shall cause the notices of the meeting of creditors to be sent by post to the creditors simultaneously with the sending of the notices of the meeting of the company. The company must advertise notice of the meeting of creditors in an appointed newspaper on at least two occasions.

The directors of the company must:

- lay before the meeting of creditors a full statement of the position of the company's affairs together with a list of the creditors of the company and the estimated amount of their claims;
- appoint one of their number to preside at the meeting.

The creditors and the company at their respective meetings may nominate a person to be liquidator, and if the creditors and the company nominate different people, the person nominated by the creditors becomes the liquidator. The creditors may, if they think fit, appoint a committee of inspection consisting of not more than five people. The committee of inspection, or if there is no such committee, the creditors, may fix the remuneration to be paid to the liquidator or liquidators.

On the appointment of a liquidator all the powers of the officers of the company cease, except so far as the committee of inspection, or if there is no such committee, the creditors, sanction their continuance. If a vacancy occurs, by death, resignation or otherwise, in the office of a liquidator, other than a liquidator appointed by, or by the direction of, the court, the creditors may fill the vacancy. The powers of the liquidator in a creditors' voluntary liquidation cannot be exercised except with the sanction either of the court or of the committee of inspection.

As soon as the affairs of the company are fully wound up, the liquidator must make an account of the winding up showing how it has been conducted and the property of the company has been disposed of, and thereupon call a general meeting of the company and a meeting of the creditors for the purpose of laying the account before the meetings and giving any explanation of it.

Within one week of the meetings the liquidator must send to the registrar a copy of the account, and must make a return to him of the holding of the meetings and their dates. The registrar, on receiving the account and returns, registers them and after three months from their registration the company is deemed to be dissolved.

Compulsory liquidation

A company may be wound up by the court if:

- the company so resolves;
- the company defaults in holding statutory meetings;
- the company does not commence business within one year of incorporation;
- the number of members falls below three;
- the company is unable to pay its debts;

- the Minister's consent for registration was obtained as a result of misstatements in the application;
- the court considers that it is just and equitable that the company be wound up.

An application to the court for a winding up must be by petition and can be presented either by the company or any creditor or contributory.

KPMG contact partner

Malcolm M Butterfield
KPMG Peat Marwick
Vallis Building
PO Box HM 906
Hamilton
Bermuda

Telephone: + 1 (441) 295 5063
Fax: +1 (441) 295 9132

Bolivia

Legislation

Bankruptcy and preventive insolvency proceedings are governed by Title II, arts 1487 to 1692 of the Commercial Code.

Insolvency procedures

Voluntary Preventive

To file voluntary preventive insolvency proceedings, a company must present evidence of its inability to pay its debts. The proceedings must be filed within 10 days of any payment default provided, however, that the company has not:

- been declared bankrupt in the previous 10 years;
- applied for voluntary insolvency in the previous three years;
- been convicted for crimes against third-party properties or the national economy.

The judge advertises notices in newspapers so creditors can consider the agreement proposed by the company and designate a trustee.

All judicial collections, except for mortgage debts, are suspended as a result of the voluntary proceedings.

Notwithstanding that the judge has to comply with the terms it is difficult to specify the duration of such proceedings. However, if creditors are in agreement, the proceedings will probably last for less than a year.

Bankruptcy procedures

If there have not been preventive insolvency proceedings, any creditor may file bankruptcy proceedings based on one of the following grounds:

- default of one or more debts;
- the debtor's absence or the closing of his offices for more than five days without notice;
- the sale of goods much below the market price;
- transfer of property damaging creditors' rights;
- fraudulent acts or insufficient assets.

Once the bankruptcy proceedings have been filed the judge appoints a trustee, orders the debtor's detention and the delivery of any of the debtor's property and accounting records to the trustee and sets the date for creditors to file their claims and have their first meeting.

The trustee is depository of all the company's property and acts as administrator and liquidator of the company. The trustee is appointed from banks, lawyers or auditors. Creditors have the right to appoint up to five controllers.

As a result of the bankruptcy proceedings all overdue debts and unpaid debts cease to accrue interest except mortgage debts.

Creditors

Priority of payments among creditors is as follows:

- salaries and labour social compensation;
- judicial expenses, trustee and lawyers' fees;
- mortgages on real estate, mining concessions, industrial equipment and vehicles in accordance with the date the collateral was filed in the real estate office and commercial registry;
- collateral on movable property in accordance with the date of registration;
- debts in favour of the government or governmental entities in accordance with the date of registration — a private debt registered before a governmental debt has priority payment;
- creditors without a collateral, proportionally on the balance of the assets.

KPMG contact partner

Gonzalo Ruiz Ballivian
KPMG Peat Marwick
Calle Capitan Revelo No. 2131
La Paz
Bolivia

Telephone: +591 (2) 372106
Fax: +591 (2) 372952

Botswana

Legislation

- The Insolvency Act, c. 16:01, Proclamation No. 25 of 1929, as amended;
- Companies Act, c. 42:0 1, Proclamation No. 71 of 1959, as amended;
- Regulations in terms of the Companies Act, c. 42:0 1, for winding up and judicial management of companies (ss. 166–276).

Insolvency procedures

The available insolvency procedures are:

- compulsory winding up by the court of an individual or partnership or company;
- members' or creditors' voluntary winding up of a company;
- voluntary surrender of an estate by an individual;
- judicial management;
- scheme of arrangement or compromise.

Compulsory winding-up

An insolvent's estate or company may be wound up by the court if:

- judgment has been obtained for a debt and cannot be satisfied or paid;
- any attempt is made to dispose of assets thereby prejudicing creditors or preferring one creditor above another;
- any attempt is made to compromise debts with creditors;
- notice in writing is given to any creditor that his debt cannot be paid;
- an executor of a deceased estate which is found to be insolvent petitions the court;
- a judicial manager makes application to court;
- the debtor departs from his dwelling or otherwise absents himself with intent to delay the payment of his debts.

Voluntary winding up

The court may grant a voluntary winding-up order if an individual petitions the court. No court order is required if a company has by special resolution resolved that it be wound up either by its members or creditors.

Judicial management

The court may grant a judicial management order when so petitioned by a director, member or creditor. Judicial management is a temporary moratorium to enable a company to surmount its financial problems under the management of a person specifically appointed for this purpose who acts in the place of the board of directors.

Scheme of arrangement or compromise

A scheme of arrangement or compromise may be proposed between a company in liquidation and its creditors or its members. Should the scheme or compromise be approved by creditors and sanctioned by the court the winding-up order is set aside and the company is reinstated.

A private individual may also submit an offer of composition to his trustee for consideration by his creditors. However, any condition which makes the offer subject to the rehabilitation of the insolvent is of no effect.

Insolvency procedures can be instituted by:

- generally speaking, anyone who is a creditor and has been unable to obtain settlement by legal means;
- directors, members, shareholders and an individual on his own recognisance;
- a judicial manager;
- an executor of an insolvent deceased estate;
- an *ex parte* application.

The effect once the procedure has commenced is to:

- divest the company or individual of all assets which can then vest in the master of the High Court until a liquidator or trustee is appointed by him;
- stay civil proceedings;
- cease trading except in the case of judicial management or where it is necessary to preserve an asset or by direction of the court on application by a liquidator;
- generally curtail all activities except those of an individual who is entitled to earn an income but subject to certain restrictions and conditions;
- make void every disposition of property (including rights of action) made after commencement of the winding up unless the court declares otherwise;
- make void any attachment or execution order against the assets after the commencement of the winding up;
- make void, in the case of a company, every transfer of shares or alteration of the status of its members effected after the commencement of the winding up.

The control, functions and duties are exercised by:

- the master of the High Court initially;
- a liquidator in the case of a company and a trustee in the case of an individual or a partnership who must account to the master of the High Court;
- a judicial manager in the case of judicial management.

The duties of the liquidator or trustee are to:

- investigate and report on the affairs of the company or insolvent including contravention by directors, members or individuals;
- trace and realise all assets;
- lodge a liquidation and distribution or contribution account with the master of the High Court.

The duty of a judicial manager is to continue the business of the company and to report to creditors on the viability of continuing under judicial management or placing the company in liquidation.

Secured creditors are entitled to value their security and prove their claims. On realisation of the security the creditor receives payment of the amount realised less administration costs.

Any free residue resulting from assets realised, including any excess on secured assets realised, is awarded to preferential creditors such as the Receiver of Revenue, staff salaries and wages and audit fees within certain limits.

Thereafter:

- concurrent creditors are entitled to a pro rata share of whatever balance is available;
- foreign creditors enjoy the same considerations but payment in foreign currency is subject to government approval;
- shareholders are entitled to receive dividends only after all other creditors are settled in full;
- in the event of insufficient funds being available to cover liquidation costs, a contribution will be levied on the petitioning creditor and/or creditors who proved claims.

Being subject to the dictates and strict control of the master of the High Court, the present procedure ensures an equitable distribution of the proceeds of assets realised. The procedure may last for periods from nine months to two years.

At present it does not appear as though there is any intention to review the existing legislation.

KPMG contact partner

Tom Piper
KPMG Management Services (Pty) Ltd
1st Floor, Professional House
BBS Mall
Gaborone
Botswana

Telephone: +267 312 400
Fax: +267 375 281

Brazil

Legislation

A debtor is considered to be insolvent when his debts exceed the value of his assets. An insolvent debtor who is not engaged in trade is subject to declaration of insolvency procedure, as governed by the Civil Code. An insolvent debtor who is engaged in trade on a regular basis is subject to the process of bankruptcy, in accordance with the Bankruptcy Law (Decree Law No. 7661/45).

Insolvency procedures

Insolvency

A declaration of insolvency may be applied for by the debtor himself, by the administrator of his estate or by an ordinary creditor. The court appoints a receiver chosen from among the principal creditors and orders a notice to be issued inviting the creditors to file their claims within 20 days.

A general list of creditors is drawn up, and their claims are listed in the following order of priorities:

- employment-related claims;
- tax claims;
- personal claims enjoying special privilege;
- personal claims enjoying general privilege;
- ordinary claims.

Unpaid liabilities are deemed to have been discharged five years from the date of termination of the insolvency proceedings. The court order declaring the debtor's liabilities to have been discharged rehabilitates the debtor and restores his full legal capacity.

Bankruptcy

A debtor must petition for his bankruptcy when, without legal justification, he fails to pay a debt at maturity. If he does not do so, his successors, or any of his creditors, may petition for his bankruptcy.

As in the case of insolvency, a commercial debtor may, within the time limit for presenting a defence, avoid bankruptcy by depositing the amount claimed before discussing the merits of the claim. Also as in insolvency, the court appoints a receiver or trustee in bankruptcy (who has basically the same duties as the receiver in an insolvency) and sets a time limit of not more than 20 days for the creditors to file their claims. Once bankruptcy has been decreed, any actions and executions instituted against the debtor individually by the creditors are stayed.

A general schedule of creditors is drawn up and the claims are classified in the following order:

- employment-related claims;
- tax and fiscal claims;
- claims for expenses and debts incurred by the estate;
- secured claims;
- specially privileged claims on certain goods;

- claims with general privilege;
- ordinary claims.

Foreign creditors participate in the distribution of the assets of the debtor equally with Brazilian creditors but foreign currency claims are converted into Brazilian currency at the rate of exchange in effect on the date the bankruptcy was decreed or the *concordata* (see under 'Creditors' agreement' below) was ordered to be processed, and it is only at the value so established that the claim is considered.

Once the bankruptcy proceedings have been instituted, the debtor loses the right to administer and dispose of his assets. Bilateral contracts previously entered into by the bankrupt are not suspended and may be performed by the trustee in bankruptcy. The bankrupt may be required to undergo a judicial examination to establish facts and circumstances which may form the basis for criminal proceedings against him for a bankruptcy offence.

Creditors' agreement ('*concordata*')

Brazilian law allows a commercial debtor, who is temporarily unable to meet his obligations, to avoid bankruptcy by a '*concordata*'.

A preventive *concordata* is one applied for before the declaration of bankruptcy. The debtor must have carried on business regularly for more than two years without resorting to a *concordata*; he must possess assets the value of which exceeds one half of the amount of his unsecured liabilities; he must not be bankrupt, or, if he has been previously declared bankrupt, he must have discharged his liabilities; and he must not have any bill protested for failure to pay. In his petition, the debtor must offer his creditors payment of at least 50 per cent of their claims at sight, or 60 per cent, 75 per cent, 90 per cent or 100 per cent within 6, 12, 18 or 24 months respectively. In the latter two cases, at least two fifths must be paid in the first year.

The period for complying with the terms of the *concordata* begins on the date on which the petition is filed in court. During the preventive *concordata* proceedings, the debtor regains the right to administer his assets and may continue to run his business under the supervision of an inspector who, as in the case of the trustee in bankruptcy, is appointed by the court from among the principal creditors. The debtor may not, however, dispose of real property or give guarantees without authorisation of the court.

Should the debtor fail to comply with his obligations in the proceedings the *concordata* may at any time be transformed into a bankruptcy.

Creditors enjoy the same rights and the same priority in filing their claims in *concordata* proceedings as in a bankruptcy. Once the processing of the *concordata* is ordered, any actions or executions instituted against the debtor are stayed.

A bankrupt debtor may obtain the suspension of his bankruptcy by applying to the judge in the bankruptcy proceedings to grant him a suspensive *concordata* provided that he offers to his ordinary creditors payment of at least 35 per cent of their claims at sight, or 50 per cent within a maximum of two years; in the latter instance he must pay at least two fifths in the first year. The rules for preventive *concordata* also apply to suspensive *concordata* in so far as appropriate.

Other matters

Probably the most controversial issue which has affected insolvency and bankruptcy proceedings (including the *concordata* process) is the question of indexation of claims in view of the continued high rates of inflation.

The present situation is that indexation is applicable only in *concordatas* and then only as from the date that cash deposits are required to be made by the debtor on account of his declared liabilities.

Bankruptcy Bill

A Bill in the Brazilian Congress proposes substantial changes to bankruptcy law, including extending the two-year period for repayment of liabilities within the *concordata* to a three-year or five-year period, the latter in exceptional cases. The Bill also requires creditors to file proof of three additional unpaid liabilities, other than the filing creditor's own unpaid debt, in order to petition for bankruptcy.

KPMG contact partner

David Bunce
KPMG Peat Marwick
Rua Dr Renato Paes de Barros, 33
04530–904 São Paulo, SP
Brazil

Telephone: +55 (11) 3067 3000
Fax: +55 (11) 883 2916

Brunei Darussalam

Legislation

The insolvency procedures are regulated by the Companies Act 1956 which includes:

- receivership;
- winding up by the court;
- voluntary winding up;
- winding up subject to the supervision of the court.

Insolvency procedures

Receivership

The court, on the application of the debenture holders or other creditors of a company, may appoint a receiver, who could be the official receiver but in practice is more likely to be an outside person (usually a professional accountant). A receiver may also be appointed by the debenture holders if the debenture empowers them to do so.

The purpose of appointing a receiver is to protect the rights of the debenture holders, and if it is desired that the business of the company be continued, a manager must be appointed. This is to ensure the best possible realisation of the assets or sale as a going concern.

Winding up by the court

A company may be wound up by the court if:

- the company has by special resolution resolved that it be wound up by the court;
- default is made in delivering statutory reports to the registrar or in holding statutory meetings;
- the company does not commence its business within a year from its incorporation, or suspends its business for a whole year;
- the number of members is reduced, in the case of a private company, below two, or, in the case of any other company, below seven;
- the company is unable to pay its debts;
- the court is of opinion that it is just and equitable that the company should be wound up.

A petition to the court for the winding up may be made by the company, creditors, contributories or the official receiver. If granted, the official receiver becomes the provisional liquidator. The creditors and contributories may appoint a liquidator in the place of the official receiver failing which the official receiver becomes the liquidator.

The following acts made after the commencement of the winding up are, unless the court otherwise orders, void:

- any disposition of the property of the company;
- any transfer of shares;
- any attachment, sequestration, distress or execution put in force against the estate or effects of the company.

An order for the winding up of a company operates in favour of all creditors and contributories. The liquidator has power to do all acts necessary for winding up the affairs of the company and distributing its assets, subject to the control of the court. The committee of inspection (consisting of creditors and contributories) and the official receiver may also supervise the performance of the liquidator's duties.

A liquidator may resign or, on cause shown, be removed by the court. On completion of his duties, he applies to the court for his release as liquidator.

Voluntary winding up

A company may be wound up voluntarily:

- when the period, if any, for the duration of the company set by the articles expires, or the event, if any, occurs, on the occurrence of which the articles provide that the company is to be dissolved, and the company in general meeting has passed a resolution requiring the company to be wound up voluntarily;
- if the company resolves by special resolution that it be wound up voluntarily;
- if the company resolves by extraordinary resolution to the effect that it cannot by reason of its liabilities continue its business, and that it is advisable to wind up.

The winding up is deemed to commence at the time of passing of the resolution. The company ceases to carry on its business, except so far as may be required for the purpose of winding up the company.

If the directors make a statutory declaration to the effect that the company is solvent and will be able to settle its debts in full within 12 months, the winding up is then a 'members' voluntary winding up'. Otherwise it is a 'creditors' voluntary winding up'.

For a creditors' voluntary winding up, the creditors must be notified of the meeting to pass a resolution to wind up the company. A creditors' meeting is held on the same day or the next day. A committee of inspection, consisting of not more than five persons, may be appointed by the creditors.

In the event of the winding up continuing for more than one year, the liquidator summons a general meeting (and in the case of a creditors' voluntary winding up, a creditors' meeting also) at the end of the first year, and of each succeeding year. An account of his acts and dealings is laid before these meetings.

As soon as the company is fully wound up, the liquidator lays before a general meeting (and in the case of a creditors' voluntary winding up, a creditors' meeting also) an account of the winding up. The company is deemed to be dissolved on the expiration of three months from the registration of the accounts and the necessary returns with the Registrar of Companies.

Winding up subject to supervision of the court

When a company has passed a resolution for voluntary winding up, on petition, the court may make an order that the voluntary winding up be subject to the supervision of the court.

Creditors

The order of payment of debts is as follows:

- costs and expenses of the winding up;
- preferential debts including taxes, rates and wages (not exceeding Br$1,000) for services within five months before the winding up — the preferential debts rank equally among themselves;
- holders of debentures under a floating charge;
- unsecured creditors;
- contributories.

KPMG contact partners

Hj Shazali Hj Sulaiman
KPMG Peat Marwick
Room 31, Britannia House
38 Jalan Cator
Bandar Seri Begawan 2085
Brunei Darussalam

Telephone: +673 (2) 228382
Fax: +673 (2) 228389

Paul K.W. Ma
KPMG Peat Marwick
16 Raffles Quay #22-00
Hong Leong Building
Singapore 048581

Telephone: +65 3210603
Fax: +65 2250984

Bulgaria

Legislation

Bulgarian insolvency law consists of two areas: general regulations provided by the Commercial Code 1994 and special provisions of the Banking and Lending Act 1996 and the Insurance Act 1997 for insolvency of banks and insurance companies. Where no special provision is made by the Banking and Lending Act and the Insurance Act, the provisions of the Commercial Code apply.

Insolvency procedures

General rules

Insolvency proceedings are intended to provide equitable satisfaction of the creditors and to secure an opportunity for a recovery of the debtor's company. In these proceedings the interests of the creditors, the debtor and the debtor's employees shall be taken into consideration.

Insolvency

The insolvency procedure shall be initiated for sole traders, companies and banks which are unable to pay an executable and undisputed debt under a commercial transaction. The insolvency commences when the debtor has filed a petition at the court for instituting insolvency proceedings, upon discontinuance of payments or when the liabilities of a limited liability company or a joint-stock company exceed its assets. The declaration of insolvency of a bank shall be made by the Bulgarian National Bank (BNB).

A request for insolvency proceedings may be submitted within a year after the death of a sole trader or the closing down of a company.

No insolvency proceedings shall be initiated for State-owned companies exercising a State monopoly or established by a special Act.

Competent court

Under the Bulgarian legislation courts of insolvency are the district courts of the registration of the trader (the sole trader or the company) or the bank. The court's decisions for initiating the insolvency procedure as well as for declaring the insolvency shall be entered into the court's register and advertised in the *State Gazette*.

Instituting insolvency procedure

Insolvency procedures are instituted by a written petition submitted to the court by the debtor, by his heir, by a managing body of a company, by a creditor of his on a commercial transaction, by a partner who bears unlimited liability or by an authorised person who has been granted a power of attorney for that submission. Only the Bulgarian National Bank (BNB) can petition in relation to a bank.

The court's decision

When the court finds that the preconditions for an insolvency procedure have occurred it shall declare the debtor insolvent, institute insolvency proceedings and appoint a temporary trustee.

Trustee

The trustee may be either a natural person or a legal entity. The name and the address of the trustee shall be entered into the court's register and advertised in the *State Gazette*. The trustee must keep a full record of his activities relating to the management of the property of the debtor as well as submit reports to the court (respectively to the BNB in case the debtor is a bank) on a monthly basis or immediately on request.

The trustee shall represent the debtor, manage its current affairs, prepare an inventory, keep and maintain the books and business correspondence, identify and specify the debtor's property and creditors, request termination of the debtor's contracts, participate in legal proceedings in relation to the debtor's business, collect the debtor's receivables and deposit them in a particular bank account, terminate the debtor's participation in other companies, and realise the movable and immovable property and other ownership rights of the debtor.

Recovery plan

A plan for the recovery of a debtor's enterprise may be proposed by the debtor, the trustee, creditors holding at least one third of the secured receivables, creditors holding at least one third of the unsecured receivables, shareholders holding at least one third of the capital of a debtor company, an unlimited liability partner or 20 per cent of the total number of the debtor's employees. In an insolvency procedure of a bank no recovery plan can be proposed.

The recovery plan may provide for payments to be deferred or paid in instalments, debts may be remitted in full or in part, the enterprise may be reorganised, special terms and procedures for realising property may be provided as well as other activities and deals. The plan may also provide a sale of the whole enterprise or part of it. The recovery plan must be ratified by the court and, once adopted by the creditors, it is binding on the debtor and creditors.

The ratification of the recovery plan by the court terminates the insolvency procedure. Should the debtor not discharge his obligations under the plan the creditors whose receivables account for at least 15 per cent of the total amount of the receivables or the trustee may request restitution of the insolvency proceedings without having to prove the insolvency again.

The court declares the debtor to be insolvent in cases where either a recovery plan has not been proposed within the term stipulated by the law or the proposed plan has not been accepted or approved.

Creditors

Creditors' are paid in the following order:

- debts secured by a pledge or a mortgage — out of the value of the property which is the subject of the pledge or mortgage;
- debts with regard to maintenance, repair or improvement of a debtor's property carried out by the creditor as well as receivables with regard to damages inflicted by that property — out of the value of that property;
- insolvency costs — these are the fees due to the State for the insolvency procedure, the trustee's remuneration, payments due to the employees if the debtor's enterprise has not wound up its operation, the expenses of managing, assessing and distributing the debtor's property;
- receivables arising out of employment relations up to one year before the date of the court's decision for initiating the insolvency procedure;
- receivables arising out of a financial support owed by the debtor to the creditor under legal provision;
- receivables with regard to current social security contributions as well as to contributions which became due up to one year before the date of the court's decision for initiating the insolvency procedure;
- current public receivables of the State and of municipalities such as taxes, customs duties, fees etc. and such receivables which became due up to one year before the date of the court's decision for initiating the insolvency procedure;
- receivables arising out of a continuation of the debtor's activity after the date of the court's decision for initiating the insolvency procedure;

- interest (determined by the law or by an agreement) on unsecured receivables, due after the date of the decision for initiating the insolvency procedure;
- receivables arising out of a credit granted to the debtor by a partner;
- receivables arising out of a gratuitous deal;
- all other receivables.

KPMG contact partner

Richard Glasspool
KPMG Bulgaria 00D
13 Slavyanska Street
Sofia 1000
Bulgaria

Telephone: +359 (2) 980 5325
Fax: +359 (2) 980 0458

Cambodia

Legislation

There are currently no laws governing insolvency procedures in Cambodia. The Ministry of Commerce and the National Bank of Cambodia (the central bank) have confirmed to KPMG that provided a liquidation is performed using a common practice applicable to a given country, it will be acceptable in Cambodia. KPMG Phnom Penh has experience of applying the procedures prescribed by Malaysian legislation in Cambodia.

KPMG contact partner

Rany Chung
KPMG Peat Marwick
2nd Floor
435 Preah Sisowath Quay
PO Box 2352
Phnom Penh 3
Cambodia

Telephone: +855 (15) 918 478
Fax: +855 (23) 428279

Canada

Legislation

Canada is a federation of 10 provinces. The constitution divides legislative authority between the Federal Parliament and the provincial legislatures. The Federal Parliament has authority over bankruptcy and insolvency while the provincial legislatures have authority over securities laws, property and civil rights. The provinces have legislative responsibility for determining the rights and remedies of secured creditors.

With the exception of the province of Quebec, Canada is a common law jurisdiction like the United States and England. There is, therefore, an extensive body of jurisprudence arising from court decisions interpreting statute law. Quebec has recently enacted a new European-style civil code which codifies the general principles of law applicable in that province.

The three federal statutes which govern insolvency proceedings generally are:

- Bankruptcy and Insolvency Act ('BIA');
- Companies' Creditors Arrangement Act ('CCAA');
- Winding-up Act ('WUA').

Most of the provinces have enacted a Personal Property Security Act which establishes a regime for creating valid security interests, determining priorities amongst creditors and for the enforcement of security interests. This legislation is similar to the various Uniform Commercial Codes in effect in many jurisdictions in the United States.

The BIA is the principal statute dealing with the administration of insolvent and bankrupt corporations and individuals. It was originally enacted as the Bankruptcy Act in 1949. Major amendments were made to the Act in 1992, at which time it was renamed the Bankruptcy and Insolvency Act. Further amendments are expected to come into force in 1997.

Insolvency procedures

Bankruptcy

The administration of bankruptcy is carried out by trustees in bankruptcy, licensed and supervised by the federal government. When a debtor becomes bankrupt a licensed trustee is appointed and all of the bankrupt's assets are vested in the trustee. Claims of creditors, other than secured creditors, are stayed. The trustee has a duty to review the validity of all security over the bankrupt's assets and to apply to court to set aside security which is not valid. Subject to confirmation of the validity of its security and a very limited stay provision, a secured creditor is entitled to take possession and dispose of all collateral over which it holds security.

A bankruptcy may occur in one of several ways:

- by the debtor making a voluntary assignment into bankruptcy;
- by the court granting a receiving order declaring the debtor to be bankrupt on the petition of one or more creditors;
- by the failure of the unsecured creditors or the court to approve a restructuring proposal under Part III of the BIA;
- by the proposal being subsequently annulled by the court.

A board of inspectors is elected by the creditors which has input into the general conduct of the bankruptcy proceedings. The trustee requires consent of a majority of the inspectors to sell assets, carry on the business of the bankrupt, commence or continue legal proceedings or to compromise any claims made by or against the bankrupt estate.

The major classes of creditors in a bankruptcy are: secured creditors, preferred creditors and unsecured or ordinary creditors. Secured creditors hold security in various forms over the assets of the bankrupt. A secured creditor may be represented by an agent or a receiver for the purpose of realising assets subject to its security. Preferred creditors have priority over unsecured creditors. Preferred creditors' claims include the costs of administration, the fees of the trustee, employees' claims, municipal taxes and claims of a landlord. With the amendments to the 1992 Act, Crown claims are no longer preferred. With few exceptions, Crown claims are unsecured. The unsecured creditors are entitled to share pro rata in the realisation of the bankrupt's assets after payment of preferred creditors, subject to the claims of secured creditors.

The Canadian and provincial governments have been active in attempting to create security in the form of a statutory deemed trust or lien against assets in priority to traditional types of security to ensure preferential treatment of debts due to the federal and provincial governments. This has met with measured success. Many of these claims are not effective in a bankruptcy.

Interim receiver

An interim receiver may be appointed by the court under the BIA in three instances:

- on or after the filing of a bankruptcy petition;
- on the filing of a notice of intention to file a proposal or the filing of a proposal under Part III of the BIA;
- when an enforcement notice is about to be sent or has been sent by a secured creditor indicating its intention to enforce its security.

In the case of an interim receiver appointed upon a petition being issued or an enforcement notice being sent by a secured creditor, the creditor applying for the order must show that it is necessary for the protection of the estate assets and, in the case of an enforcement notice, of the interests of the creditor who sent the enforcement notice. In either case the appointment will be of short duration and the court order will specifically set out the powers of the interim receiver. In most cases, the interim receiver will be instructed to take possession of the assets, to control the receipts and disbursements of the debtor but not otherwise interfere with the day-to-day business. The interim receiver is the watchdog of the assets during the hiatus between the filing of the petition and its hearing or during the enforcement proceedings. The interim receiver must be very careful to comply strictly with the scope of the order and not overextend its mandate.

By contrast, the appointment of an interim receiver during the proposal process is of longer duration, often for the full term of the proposal. The powers granted to the interim receiver in this case may be broad or narrow depending upon the terms of the proposal. The main purpose of the appointment of an interim receiver under a proposal is to facilitate the carrying out of the proposal.

Enforcement of security

The 1992 amendments to the BIA contain provisions relating to the enforcement of security and the appointment of receivers. Where a secured creditor is enforcing its security on all or substantially all of the assets of an insolvent debtor, the secured creditor must give prior notice of its intention to enforce its security to the debtor and must wait until the expiry of 10 days after sending the notice before taking any steps to enforce its security. The debtor may consent to an earlier enforcement of the security after the notice has been given. The receiver must give notice of his appointment to all creditors, issue reports on a regular basis outlining the status of the receivership and prepare a final report and statement of receivership accounts when the appointment is terminated. These reports are available to creditors upon request.

A secured creditor holding security on the assets of a defaulting debtor may enforce its rights under its security by the appointment of a receiver. Typical security would be a fixed and floating charge debenture on all of the assets of a corporation, a general security agreement on equipment, inventory, receivables and intangibles or a mortgage on real property. A receiver may be appointed privately by an instrument in writing pursuant to the provisions of the security agreement or by court order.

Private appointment of a receiver

Provisions allowing for the private appointment of a receiver, together with the powers of the privately appointed receiver must be set out in the security instrument itself. In the typical security instrument, the powers granted to a receiver are broad and would normally include the power to carry on the business and to sell the debtor's assets by auction, tender or private sale. Secured creditors tend to favour private appointments because the costs and delays of the court process can be avoided and the secured creditor has greater control over the realisation process.

Before accepting a private appointment, the receiver should, on advice of counsel, determine that the security is valid and enforceable and that the notice provisions under the BIA have been complied with before the security is enforced by the appointment. Failure to ensure that this has been done may expose the receiver and the secured creditor to lengthy and costly litigation and damages.

Many lenders do not provide express indemnities to privately appointed receivers. The receiver looks to the assets under administration for his indemnity, although there is support for the view that there is an implied indemnity by virtue of the nature of the appointment.

Court appointment of a receiver

The jurisdiction for a court-appointment of a receiver is found in provincial legislation. An action is commenced by a secured creditor against the debtor and a receiver appointed in an interlocutory proceeding within the action. The typical court order stays proceedings against the debtor corporation and the receiver, provides the receiver with control over the assets of the debtor, authorises the receiver to carry on the debtor's business, to borrow money on the security of the assets and ultimately to sell the debtor's assets with the approval of the court. If necessary, the court order may authorise the receiver to commence and defend litigation in the debtor's name.

Whereas the duty of a privately appointed receiver is primarily to the secured creditor who appointed it, subject to a general duty to act in a commercially reasonable manner, the court-appointed receiver is an officer of the court and has the duty to protect the interests of all creditors of the debtor corporation. Because of the nature of its appointment, a court-appointed receiver may not be entitled to seek indemnities from those who sought the appointment. In practice, secured creditors do in some cases provide indemnities.

A court appointment may be necessary if the debtor is opposing the appointment of a receiver and will not let the receiver into possession. In some provincial jurisdictions, the courts will grant possession orders and affirm the appointment of a private receiver with the powers of a receiver as set out in the security documents, thereby avoiding a court appointment. There are other circumstances where a court appointment may be preferable, for example, in large complex matters where the assets and operations of the debtor are located in a number of jurisdictions. Where there are competing security interests, it is generally in the interest of all concerned to arrange for appropriate management and realisation of the assets pending an ultimate determination by restructuring the court of the rights of the various secured creditors. The order appointing the receiver usually contains a stay of proceedings against the receiver. This has the effect of staying landlords, utilities and others who might otherwise have the legal right to interfere with the receiver's management of the debtor's business. Any action of this nature against a court-appointed receiver requires leave of the court. Where a public company or other company subject to regulatory authority is insolvent, the regulatory authority may require a court order. Where a debtor's operations involve hazardous products or other environmental risks, the secured creditor and the receiver may seek the protection inherent in a court appointment.

A restructuring of a corporation's debt or a 'work-out' usually occurs in one of two ways. Either a restructuring is accomplished informally without court process between the debtor and its creditors or formally under a proposal under Part III of the BIA or a plan of arrangement under the CCAA.

Similarities between BIA and CCAA restructurings

A proposal under the BIA and a plan of arrangement under the CCAA are similar in that they are both written contracts between an insolvent debtor corporation and its creditors. The debtor corporation is simply making a written offer to settle the provable claims of various classes of its creditors. A CCAA plan of arrangement can be made with any particular class or classes of creditors whereas a proposal under the BIA must include an arrangement with the corporation's preferred creditors (which includes claims of the trustee, employee claims and landlord claims) and unsecured creditors. In both cases, various classes of secured creditors may be included.

There are certain other similarities between the operation of BIA and the CCAA. They are both federal statutes which provide for a stay of proceedings (although the CCAA stay is often broader in scope), classification of creditors, and a voting threshold for approval by creditors, and they both allow the debtor corporation to remain in possession of its assets during the restructuring process. In both cases, there is a two-stage approval process. The creditors in each class vote on the proposal or plan of arrangement. If approved by the creditors, the court will then be called upon to approve the proposal or plan of arrangement at a subsequent hearing.

A trustee must be named in a BIA proposal. The trustee has a general duty to monitor the debtor's business and financial affairs during the restructuring and to report on any material adverse changes. The trustee must also report on the reasonableness of the debtor's cash flow statement. While the CCAA does not require the appointment of a trustee, it is common for the court to appoint a monitor who is usually given the limited duty of reporting on factual matters based on the information supplied to it by the debtor corporation and in certain instances supervising the preparation and negotiation of a plan of arrangement.

Differences between BIA and CCAA restructurings

Despite the similarities between the BIA and the CCAA, there are presently significant differences which must be taken into account in determining which statute to proceed under. We expect many of these differences to be eliminated with the anticipated 1997 amendments to the CCAA. The benefits of proceeding under the CCAA are as follows:

- due to the generally liberal judicial approach given to the interpretation of the CCAA and the almost complete absence of statutory rules of procedure, proceedings under the CCAA offer significantly more flexibility to a debtor corporation than proceedings under the BIA;
- there is no statutory time limit for filing a plan under the CCAA while the BIA only allows for a maximum period of six months to file a definitive proposal;
- unlike the BIA, the court under the CCAA has the discretion to make third parties, who are not creditors of the debtor, subject to the stay of proceedings during the restructuring period;
- unlike the BIA, there are no mandatory payments that must be made as a condition of court approval; and
- under the BIA, if the unsecured creditors reject a proposal, or the court refuses to approve it, the debtor corporation is automatically declared to be bankrupt; the rejection of a plan of arrangement under the CCAA does not have this automatic effect.

The benefits of restructuring under the BIA are as follows:

- the stay of proceedings under the BIA is obtained by filing a notice of intention with an administrative officer while the CCAA stay must be obtained by seeking a court order;
- the CCAA only applies to corporations which qualify by having an issue of outstanding bonds and debentures under a trust deed; the BIA has no such restriction (the proposed amendments will do away with the trust deed qualification and replace it with a threshold amount of debt);
- the threshold for voter approval of a restructuring is lower under the BIA than under the CCAA; while both require a majority in number of votes cast, the BIA requires approval of only two thirds of the monetary value of a class while the CCAA requires approval of three quarters of the monetary value of a class (under the proposed amendments, both statutes will require a two-thirds majority);

- unlike the CCAA, the BIA contains specific guidelines for determining the classification of secured creditors;
- since the BIA contains a detailed code of procedure for restructurings, which is absent from the CCAA and a shorter time-frame, there are usually lower costs involved in a proposal under the BIA as fewer court applications are required; and
- the BIA binds the Crown (government claims) while the CCAA does not (the proposed amendments will do away with this distinction).

Liquidation

Certain corporations such as banks and insurance companies are specifically excluded from the scope of the BIA. Another federal statute, the WUA is used to liquidate the assets of these types of corporations when they become insolvent. Under the WUA, a corporation is wound up by a court order and a liquidator is appointed by the court. Upon the appointment of a liquidator, all the powers of the directors cease except with the sanction of the court or the liquidator. The conduct of the winding up is subject to the overall supervision of the court. The WUA provides a statutory framework for terminating the business, realising the assets of the corporation, determining the validity of creditors' claims, distributing proceeds of realisation among the creditors and shareholders in accordance with their respective priorities and ultimately dissolving the corporation.

Enforcement of Bank Act, s. 427, security

While chartered banks in Canada usually obtain debenture or general security agreements from their customers, they may also obtain security on accounts receivable and inventory pursuant to s. 427 of the Bank Act. This unique form of security is available only to Canadian chartered banks and can only be taken in certain specific circumstances. Section 427 security is most often taken from manufacturers to secure inventory which would include raw materials, work in process and finished goods. The security interest also extends to the accounts receivable arising from the sale of the inventory.

The provisions of the Bank Act must be strictly followed in order to create valid security on receivables and inventory. A notice of intention must be filed with the Bank of Canada prior to taking the security. Realisation is effected by the appointment of an agent pursuant to the security to realise on the receivables and inventory. The agent must follow the realisation provisions set out in the Act. With the recent amendments to the BIA, an agent appointed under Bank Act security would be a 'receiver' and must comply with all the requisite reporting requirements.

KPMG contact partner

Gary Colter
KPMG
Commerce Court West
PO Box 31
Commerce Court Postal Station
Toronto, Ontario
M5L IB2
Canada

Telephone: + 1 (416) 366 5764
Fax: +1 (416) 777-3364

Cayman Islands

Legislation

The provisions relating to the winding up of companies are found in Part V of the Cayman Islands Companies Law (1995 revision).

In addition, the English Insolvency Rules 1986 also apply.

Insolvency procedures

Receivership

Receivers are most commonly appointed under the terms of mortgage debentures where there has been a failure by the borrower to repay the debt to the lender when requested so to do.

The procedures regarding receivership are very similar to those set out in the section on England and Wales except that the term 'administrative receiver' is not used in the Cayman Islands and no meeting of creditors has to be called by the receiver.

Voluntary winding up

Voluntary winding up means the winding up of a company by the shareholders without seeking the assistance of the court. The assets and liabilities of the company are placed under the control of the liquidator who terminates the affairs of the company in cooperation with the creditors.

A company may be wound up voluntarily for the following reasons:

- when the period deemed by the articles of association to be the life of the company has expired;
- on the happening of any event upon the occurrence of which the articles provide that the company is to be dissolved;
- if the shareholders at any time pass a special resolution requiring the company to be wound up voluntarily.

A voluntary winding up is deemed to commence at the time of the passing of the resolution authorising it or, in the case of termination of any period or the happening of any event, at the date of the termination or happening, as appropriate.

Once the resolution authorising the winding up has been passed the company must cease to carry on its business except as necessary for the winding up. The liquidation is carried on by one or more liquidators appointed by the company in general meeting and upon such appointment the directors' powers cease except in so far as the company or liquidators sanction their continuance.

The resolution appointing the liquidator must be gazetted. Upon the completion of the winding up the liquidator must call a general meeting at which the liquidation accounts will be presented to the shareholders. The liquidator's account will show the manner in which the winding up has been conducted and the property of the company disposed of. A notice relating to this meeting must be published in the *Cayman Gazette* at lease one month before the meeting.

The liquidator will make a return of the meeting to the registrar of companies and three months after the registration of such return the company is deemed to be dissolved.

The order of payment of debts, liabilities and distributions is contained in the Companies Law and is broadly speaking as follows:

- the costs, charges and expenses properly incurred in the winding up of the company, including the remuneration of the liquidator;
- all rates, taxes or assessments or impositions imposed under provisions of any Cayman Islands law due and payable within 12 months next before the date of commencement of winding up;
- all wages or salaries of any clerk or servant due in respect of the four months before the relevant date with the sum not exceeding CI$100;
- all wages of any workman or labourer due during the two months before the relevant date not exceeding CI$50.

The situation has been complicated by the Labour Law (1996 revised) which states that in the case of the bankruptcy or winding-up of an employer, any liability for severance pay shall be paid in priority to all other debts, secured or unsecured. This apparent conflict between the two laws has not been resolved.

Winding up under supervision of the court

The court may make an order directing that a voluntary winding up should continue, but subject to such supervision of the court as the court may direct. Application for the supervision of the court in a voluntary winding up is generally made by petition to the court. Such petition may be presented by either the company or any creditor of the company or any contributory. The company is deemed to be in liquidation from the time of the presentation of the petition.

Compulsory winding up

In certain circumstances a company may be wound up by the court if:

- the company has passed a special resolution requiring it to be wound up by the court;
- the company does not commence its business within a year from it incorporation or suspends its business for a whole year;
- the company is unable to pay its debts;
- the court is of the opinion that it is just and equitable that the company should be wound up.

The court shall appoint one or more persons to be called the official liquidator or liquidators and all proceedings in the winding up of the company by the official liquidators are subject to the court's directions. The company is dissolved from the date of an order of the court to that effect and such order will be made when the liquidator appointed by the court reports that the liquidation is complete.

Striking off

Where the Registrar of Companies has reasonable cause to believe that a company is not carrying on business or is not in operation he may strike the company off the register and the company shall thereupon be dissolved.

However, a creditor or any member aggrieved by the striking off may apply to the court to have the company reinstated. A fee equal to the relevant incorporation fee for the company is payable upon reinstatement plus all unpaid annual fees.

If the company has assets at the time of striking off those assets vest in the Financial Secretary of the Cayman Islands.

Banks and trust companies

If the Governor of the Cayman Islands is of the opinion that a licensee appears likely to become unable to meet its obligations as they fall due; or is carrying on business in a manner detrimental to the public interest, the interest of its depositors or the beneficiaries of any trust; or has contravened the Banking Law; or has failed to comply with the conditions of its licence, then he may, amongst other courses of actions, appoint, at the expense of the licensee, a person to assume control of the licensee's affairs.

This person is generally called an administrator and has the powers of a person appointed as a receiver or manager of a business appointed under s. 18 of the Bankruptcy Law (Revised).

The administrator must report to the Governor within three months of his appointment at which time the Governor may decide to revoke his appointment, extend his appointment, allow the licensee to reorganise its affairs, or revoke the bank or trust licence.

In case of revocation of the licence, the Governor may apply to the Court that the bank or trust company be wound up by the court subject to the provisions of the Companies Law.

KPMG contact partner

Theo Bullmore
KPMG
The Genesis Building
PO Box 493 GT
Grand Cayman
Cayman Islands

Telephone: +1 (345) 949-4800
Fax: +1 (345) 949-7164

Channel Islands

Legislation

Each of the islands of Guernsey, Jersey and Alderney has its own laws and judiciary and legislative bodies. Corporate insolvency procedures vary accordingly.

Guernsey

Legislation

- Companies (Guernsey) Law 1994;
- Law of Property (Miscellaneous Provisions) (Guernsey) Law 1979;
- Preferred Debts (Guernsey) Law 1983.

Insolvency procedures

Voluntary liquidation

Voluntary liquidation commences whenever a company in general meeting passes a special resolution requiring the company to be wound up voluntarily and a nominated liquidator to be appointed. Alternatively, by special resolution, a company may delegate to its creditors, or a committee of them, the power to appoint a liquidator.

From the date of the liquidation, the company must cease to carry on its business except in so far as to ensure an orderly winding up.

A liquidator has complete control of the company and its affairs. His duty is to realise all the assets, ascertain all the liabilities and then distribute any proceeds to the various classes of creditors. Any surplus is distributed to shareholders in accordance with their rights.

Any arrangement entered into prior to liquidation between a company and its creditors is binding if approved by special resolution of the shareholders and by three quarters in number and value of the creditors.

Priority is given to creditors who hold a charge against realty (by virtue of a bond registered in the Royal Court) to the extent of the lesser of the bond or the net sale proceeds of the realty. Any shortfall against the value of the bond is dealt with as if the creditor was unsecured.

At the time of any distribution, certain creditors have priority over others, and over shareholders, as defined by legislation. In broad terms, the priorities are:

- secured creditors;
- preferential creditors;
- unsecured creditors;
- shareholders.

When the affairs of the company are fully wound up, the liquidator must call a general meeting of the company for the purpose of having his accounts laid before it. The company is deemed to be dissolved three months after Her Majesty's Greffier (registrar of companies) is notified that this meeting was held.

Compulsory liquidation

A company may be placed in compulsory liquidation by the Royal Court if the company itself, or any creditor owed more than £750, petitions the Royal Court and satisfies it that the company is unable to pay its debts or that it is just and equitable that the company be wound up.

A liquidator is appointed by the Royal Court and his powers and the procedures he follows are the same as in a voluntary liquidation, except that when the liquidator has realised all the assets and ascertained the liabilities, he petitions the Royal Court to appoint its Commissioner to verify the respective demands and preferences of creditors and to fix a day on which he will distribute the net assets.

Striking off

Every company incorporated in Guernsey is registered with Her Majesty's Greffier. When a company ceases to exist, it is struck off the register.

Failure to file an annual return setting out the current directors, shareholders and details of share capital renders a company liable to be struck off, due notice having been given. Often to avoid the costs of liquidation or otherwise, a company may allow itself to be struck off by not filing its annual return. At the date of striking off, any remaining assets are forfeit to the Crown.

En désastre

When no liquidator is appointed and before a company is struck off, a judgment creditor may apply to the Royal Court to place the company en desastre. The procedure is similar to that used in Jersey but is only adopted in the simplest of insolvencies or when no creditor will underwrite a liquidator's fees and costs.

Other matters

There are no provisions under Guernsey company law for the appointment of administrators or, receivers or managers but companies in financial difficulties occasionally continue to operate with the directors under the supervision of a committee of creditors.

KPMG contact partner

Jason Sherwill
KPMG
Orbis House
20 New Street
St Peter Port
Guernsey
Channel Islands
GY1 4AN

Telephone: +44 (1481) 721000
Fax: +44 (1481) 722373

Jersey

Legislation

The procedure for winding up companies is governed by the Companies (Jersey) Law 1991 ('the Law').

Insolvency procedures

Creditors' winding up

Although the Law refers to the insolvent liquidation procedure as a 'creditors' winding up' in fact there is no provision under the Law whereby the creditors of a company are able to petition for its winding up. A creditors' winding up may only be instituted by means of a special resolution of shareholders. A remedy for a creditor seeking to enforce a claim against an insolvent company is by means of an application for a declaration of désastre under the Bankruptcy Désastre (Jersey) Law 1990. On the conclusion of the désastre, the company is dissolved by the registration of a notice to that effect.

A company gives notice of winding up to its creditors and to its shareholders, convenes meetings of its creditors and of its shareholders, nominates a liquidator and advertises its intention to wind up.

The winding up commences from the passing of the special resolution of the shareholders, from which date the company must cease to carry on its business except as required for its beneficial winding up. Notice of the passing of the special resolution to wind up is advertised.

The directors submit a sworn statement of the affairs of the company to the creditors. The creditors have the option of accepting the person nominated by the company to act as liquidator or of appointing their own nominee as a liquidator. Within 14 days of his appointment, the liquidator must give notice thereof to all creditors and to the Registrar of Companies. On the appointment of a liquidator, the powers of the directors determine and are vested in the liquidator. The creditors or the Royal Court may at any time remove the liquidator.

The liquidator winds up the affairs of the company in accordance with the rules under the Bankruptcy Désastre (Jersey) Law 1990 governing provable debts, priorities and rights of creditors.

On a winding up, subject to the rights of secured creditors and to the general rules on preferential payments, a company's property is to be applied *pari passu* in satisfaction of its liabilities.

Once the affairs of the company are fully wound up, the liquidator presents an account of the winding up to meetings of the creditors and of the shareholders and files a return with the Registrar of Companies. Dissolution of the company becomes effective three months thereafter.

KPMG contact partner

Keith Jenkins
KPMG
PO Box 453
38/39 The Esplanade
St Helier
Jersey
Channel Islands
JE4 8WG

Telephone: +44 (1534) 888891
Fax: +44 (1534) 888892

Alderney

Legislation

The Companies (Alderney) Law 1994.

Insolvency procedures

The procedures are similar to those in Guernsey, except that any applications are made to the Alderney Court.

A company may be struck off in a similar manner to a Guernsey company.

KPMG contact partner

Jason Sherwill
KPMG
Orbis House
20 New Street
St Peter Port
Guernsey
Channel Islands
GY1 4AN

Telephone: +44 (1481) 721000
Fax: +44 (1481) 722373

China

Introduction

For cultural reasons, the concept of formal bankruptcy law is a relatively new one in China. There were sparse regional laws on business bankruptcy from about 1900 which were seldom practised. From 1949 to the early 1980s, business enterprises could not go bankrupt since, under a Communist regime, every enterprise was a State-owned Enterprise ('SoE'). Following the opening up of the economy of the People's Republic of China ('PRC') from the late 1970s and a gradual modification of the State-planned economy to a socialist market economy, and with the eventual formation of non-State-owned business enterprises, business failures have begun to occur as a result of competition and market operations. This has led to the introduction of a number of business laws including those relating to bankruptcy and liquidation.

Bankruptcy, used in the corporate sense, refers to the winding up of insolvent business enterprises. This process requires heavy involvement and supervision from the relevant court. Liquidation, on the other hand, refers to the winding up and dissolution of solvent business enterprises and no court involvement is required.

There is as yet no insolvency law to deal with receiverships or the bankruptcy of individuals.

Legislation

The first national bankruptcy legislation was targeted for SoEs. It was promulgated in 1986 and was put into effect as 'trial implementation' in 1988. Provisions for bankruptcy and/or liquidation are now contained in the following national laws (effective dates in brackets):

- Bankruptcy Law for State-owned Enterprises (November 1988);
- Chapter 19 of the Code of Civil Procedures (April 1991);
- Chapter 8 of the Companies Law (July 1994).

Provincial or regional bankruptcy and liquidation laws, rules and regulations, initially to deal with mainly foreign-related business operations, have also been enacted. The major ones include:

Shenzhen

- Bankruptcy of Foreign-Related Companies (July 1987);
- Bankruptcy of Enterprises (March 1994);
- Liquidation and Dissolution of Enterprises (October 1995).

Shanghai

- Liquidation Procedures for Foreign Investment Enterprises (October 1991).

Beijing

- Liquidation Measures for Foreign Investment Enterprises (June 1992);
- Dissolution of Foreign Investment Enterprises (July 1995).

Guangdong Province

- Bankruptcy of Companies (August 1993).

Although the underlying procedures and mechanisms under the various national and regional laws are not completely dissimilar, there are marked differences in how the laws are to be implemented locally. Further, it is pertinent to know of the exact legal status of the entity in question as different sets of law apply to different types of business enterprises even within the same region.

Insolvency procedures

Bankruptcy procedures

The following general procedures are drawn from the 1986 Bankruptcy legislation for SoEs and Chapter 19 of the Code of Civil Procedures. They apply in practice to both State-owned and non-State-owned enterprises in areas like filing of a bankruptcy application, notice to creditors, public announcement of bankruptcy applications, composition of bankruptcy committees and creditors' meetings.

Application for bankruptcy

An application may be made to the relevant court by a creditor with evidence in respect of the inability of the debtor to repay the debt and stating details of any security held.

Within seven days of receiving the application the court must decide on whether to admit the case for hearing or otherwise. If the case is admitted for hearing the debtor must be notified within 10 days. Within 10 days of receiving notification from the court the debtor has to submit to the court a list of its debts and claims.

Within 10 days of receipt of the list of debts and claims the court will notify the known creditors and make a public announcement of the bankruptcy application and send notice of a creditors' meeting to all known creditors, requiring that claims be reported to the court at the same time.

Creditors who receive notification from the court must report their claims, whether secured or not, to the court within one month. All other creditors are required to submit their claim within three months from the public announcement. If a creditor fails to report to the court within the time limit, his claim may be regarded as abandoned.

A debtor may also apply itself for bankruptcy. Explanations are required as to the circumstances and reasons for the losses incurred. A statement of account with a list of its debts and claims is also required. In the case of a SoE, approval from its direct 'supervising' body is needed.

The court does not then decide immediately on whether to bankrupt the enterprise or otherwise. Attempts are made to try to reorganise the business.

The court is required to call the first creditors' meeting, within 15 days after the expiration of the period allowed for reporting claims, to report on and consider the financial circumstances of the debtor.

Reorganisation proposal

Within three months of the court's acceptance of the bankruptcy application, a proposal for reorganisation may be made by the debtor, the creditors, or, in the case of an SoE, the supervising body of the debtor.

The bankruptcy proceedings will be suspended by the court if the proposal is agreed upon at a creditors' meeting and by the employees of the debtor.

Reorganising plans usually involve the rehabilitation of the business, a period of moratorium and debt restructuring. The period of reorganisation is two years or less.

Supervision of the reorganisation plan is by a committee of the creditors and the employees. In the case of an SoE, the supervision is by the original supervising body. Report of progress is made to creditors regularly.

The reorganisation plan may be suspended by the court if the debtor has carried out activities contrary to the interest of the creditors, or where the debtor's financial position continues to deteriorate during the reorganisation period.

The court will terminate the bankruptcy proceedings upon the successful completion of the plan.

The position of a creditor

A creditor may exercise his rights generally through the creditors' meeting. A secured creditor may participate in a creditors' meeting without the right to vote unless the security is surrendered.

The function of the creditors' meeting is to:

- appoint a chairman of the creditors' meeting;
- investigate the nature and adjudicate the amount of claims received;
- approve any reorganisation plan; and
- approve any plans to deal with and distribute the assets in the bankruptcy proceedings.

Resolutions at a creditors' meeting are adopted by a majority in both number and by value of the creditors present and voting at the meeting. Two-thirds majority by value is required to approve any reorganisation plan. All resolutions passed are binding on all creditors.

Either the court, the chairman of the creditors' meeting, the bankruptcy committee (in the course of formal bankruptcy) or creditors representing at least 25 per cent of the total claims may propose to hold a creditors' meeting.

Bankruptcy proceedings

The court may declare a business enterprise bankrupt under the following circumstances:

- where there are substantial business losses and matured debts may not be settled;
- where no reorganisation plan is approved;
- where any approved reorganisation plan may not proceed;
- where any approved reorganisation plan fails.

Within 15 days of declaring the debtor bankrupt, the court should establish a bankruptcy committee to take over the business and assets of the debtor. The bankruptcy committee handles the winding up of the affairs of the debtor and reports to the court.

Members of the bankruptcy committee are appointed by the court from amongst the relevant 'supervisory body' (where SoEs are involved), the local government financial agencies, other relevant government departments and creditors. The bankruptcy committee may engage professionals such as lawyers and accountants to assist with their work.

The bankruptcy committee may apply to the court to declare invalid the transactions which took place within six months prior to the application for bankruptcy, such as transfer of properties at undervalue or preference of selected creditors.

All bankruptcy expenses are discharged from assets available in the bankruptcy proceedings before making payments in the following order of priority:

- employees' wages and labour insurance dues;
- taxes due;

- claims in the bankruptcy proceedings generally.

A plan to make any payment in the bankruptcy proceedings by the bankruptcy committee must be approved by a meeting of the creditors and then sanctioned by the court.

If funds are not sufficient to cover bankruptcy expenses, the court may terminate the bankruptcy proceedings. If assets are not sufficient to cover payment of any class of the claims in full, payment within that class is made on a pro rata basis.

The court may terminate the bankruptcy proceedings after payment of all funds as approved.

In bankruptcy cases involving SoEs, the relevant government departments will investigate the causes for the business failure of the SoE concerned. The officers responsible for its management, including those from its 'supervising body', may be subject to administrative admonishment. Criminal prosecution may also result where appropriate.

Liquidation procedures

The following liquidation and dissolution procedures are extracted from Chapter 8 of the Companies Law and only apply to two types of legal entities in the PRC, namely: limited liability companies ('LLC') and companies limited by shares ('CLS'). Procedures for bankruptcy of LLCs and CLS's follow closely those set out in the 1986 bankruptcy legislation for SoEs and Chapter 19 of the Code of Civil Procedures.

A company may be liquidated and dissolved when:

- the term of operation specified in the company's articles of association expires;
- the circumstances for dissolution as specified in the company's articles of association arise; or
- the shareholders resolve at a meeting to liquidate and dissolve the company.

A liquidation committee should be formed within 15 days of commencing the liquidation process. In the case of LLCs the liquidation committee is composed of its shareholders or their representatives and in the case of CLSs the composition is decided upon by the shareholders at a general meeting. If no liquidation committee is formed within the time limit, creditors may request the court to designate a relevant person to form a liquidation committee.

The liquidation committee is responsible for winding up the affairs of the enterprise; they may engage relevant professionals to assist with their work.

The liquidation committee must notify all known creditors within 10 days from their appointment and, within 60 days, make at least three announcements in newspapers of the liquidation. Creditors must within 30 days of receiving notice or within 90 days from the date of first announcement declare and register with the liquidation committee their claims together with supporting documentation.

The liquidation committee must register all claims, prepare a set of liquidation accounts and formulate a liquidation plan for confirmation by the shareholders.

Should the liquidation committee discover that a company being liquidated is unable to pay its debts in full, it should apply to the court for a declaration of bankruptcy and turn over the liquidation to the court.

When the liquidation is completed, the liquidation committee should prepare a liquidation report and submit it for confirmation by the shareholders. The report is also required by the relevant Business and Industry Registration Office for cancellation of the company's registration.

If members of a liquidation committee should cause the company or its creditors to suffer any loss in the liquidation process, they are liable to make the necessary compensation.

KPMG contact partner

Alan C.W. Tang
KPMG Peat Marwick
8th Floor, Prince's Building
GPO Box 50
Hong Kong

Telephone: +852 2522 6022
Fax: +852 2845 2588

Colombia

Insolvency procedures

Law 222, 1995, changed the procedures of insolvency established in the Commercial Code (Decree 410 of 1971). This law set two kinds of insolvency procedures:

- the preventive scheme named '*Concordato*', which is an agreement for the recovery of the debtor's business;
- compulsory liquidation of the debtor's business assets.

The Superintendency of Corporations is the legal entity with jurisdiction to carry out insolvency procedures in relation to corporations. The civil court judge will deal with the insolvency of individuals.

Insolvency is defined as:

- default in paying two or more commercial liabilities during a period of up to 180 days;
- inability to pay debts as they fall due;
- serious risk that any of the two previous situations may occur.

Preventive scheme

The *concordato* is aimed to assist and preserve the company as an economic unit and employer of labour. This procedure could be requested by the debtor or his creditors. The Superintendency also has the right to order the procedure at any time.

The Superintency will agree claims. The debtor and creditors will agree the ranking of creditors and the basis of payment according to law. The Superintendency will approve these arrangements.

Compulsory liquidation

Compulsory liquidation could be requested by the debtor or ordered on its own by the Superintendency of Corporations.

Compulsory liquidation may occur:

- by a decision of the Superintendency of Corporations or as a consequence of the request for a *concordato*;
- where a *concordato* has failed;
- when the debtor has deserted his business.

The compulsory liquidation procedure has the following effects:

- the removal of the managers of the debtor entity;
- all contracts or obligations subject to time or contract term are determined;
- the dissolution of the corporation;
- stock will be valued;
- the commencement of execution procedures against the debtor.

A liquidator will be named by the Superintendency who will agree creditors' claims in order to determine the amount to be paid to them.

Once the stock is valued it will be sold through an official entity.

The compulsory liquidation ends with the payment by the liquidator of the liabilities.

KPMG contact partner

Rosa Elvira Velandia
KPMG Peat Marwick
Apartado Aéreo 9122
Santafe de Bogotá, DC

Telephone: +57 (1) 6166100
Fax: +57 (1) 6103245

Cook Islands

A small number of insolvencies of tax-haven companies are carried out under the Cook Islands International Companies Act. Other insolvencies are conducted under legislation adopting the provisions of the New Zealand Companies Act 1955 as amended up to 1970. Reference should, therefore, be made to the section in this book dealing with New Zealand.

KPMG contact partner

Mike Carr
KPMG
Parekura House
Rarotonga
Cook Islands

Telephone: +682 20486
Fax: +682 21486

Costa Rica

Legislation

Insolvency proceedings apply to all non-merchants and are governed by Book III, Title VII of the Civil Code. Bankruptcy proceedings apply only to merchants and are governed by arts 851–967 of the Mercantile Code. Judicial intervention, prior to any insolvency proceedings, is governed by Chapters I and II of Title V of the Civil Procedural Code.

Insolvency procedures

Administration and reorganisation with judicial intervention

These proceedings are available for a company or individual merchant in a dire financial condition if the closure of the enterprise or insolvency of the individual would have socially damaging consequences. It is required, however, that there are no ongoing insolvency or bankruptcy proceedings.

The petition must be made by the company, one of its creditors or, in the case of companies making public offerings of securities, by the National Securities Commission. The petition made by the company must include a description of the reasons for its difficult financial condition and must be accompanied by all relevant financial information. Additionally, it must include a reorganisation plan, devised by an independent consultant of recognised capacity and integrity describing all the necessary steps and measures for the company's recovery.

On the basis of this documentation and whatever other evidence is deemed relevant, the court must determine whether the company is fit for recovery. If not, the court may initiate insolvency or bankruptcy proceedings. If the petition is accepted, the court must order the establishment of an administration through a regime of judicial intervention regime and appoint an *interventor* (administrator). In cases of significant complexity a committee may be formed with independent consultants, representatives of the company's creditors and workers to advise the *interventor*.

The administration through judicial intervention regime entails the suspension of all claims against the company and of all distribution of earnings. Dividends may be accumulated and paid at the end of the intervention, if successful. Additionally, if necessary according to the recovery plan, the suspension of all payments on principal for all due debts may be ordered. Also, the regime entails the reduction of all interest payments to a standard rate, capitalising all unpaid interest.

While the recovery plan is being discussed by the company's creditors, corporate officials and the proposer, the company can only perform the actions necessary to assure its normal operation. Once the plan has been approved by the creditors and the court, it will be executed for a period of three years. The administration through judicial intervention regime ceases at the termination of this three-year period or when the company is able to show that its financial problems have been overcome. If the company has not recovered, the court would initiate insolvency or bankruptcy proceedings.

Insolvency

A debtor or one of its creditors can make a petition for a declaration of insolvency. A creditor must be able to show that he is a creditor and that the debt is unrecoverable.

Once the insolvency has been declared, the debtor is unable to administer or dispose of his assets. However, this does not apply to those acquired by the debtor's own efforts during the proceedings. Upon declaration, all existing obligations are deemed due and cease to yield interest unless protected by a lien on a specific asset.

All creditors must submit their claims for qualification and admittance to the proceedings or '*concurso*'. No creditor may initiate or continue a separate judicial proceeding for payment of his credit. Secured creditors may realise their security but are not admitted in the '*concurso*'.

In the same declaration of insolvency, the court appoints a receiver to administer the insolvent's assets. The receiver is deemed to be the legal representative for the proceedings. The receiver may annul certain contracts, including gratuitous dispositions of assets to the debtor's spouse, ascendants, descendants, siblings and other relatives, made within two years of the declaration of insolvency.

The following transactions are also void if executed after the declaration of insolvency:

- gratuitous or onerous contracts entered into by the debtor;
- any attempt to secure or prefer liabilities previously contracted;
- payment of debts if not fallen due;
- payment of debts already due but not made in money or commercial credit instruments.

Anyone who has assisted the debtor in defrauding creditors (concealment of assets or liabilities, false liabilities, dealings with the debtor rather than the receiver, etc.) may have to reimburse assets and pay damages.

After the court has decided on the validity of any claims, the insolvent assets are liquidated and distributed among the creditors. At any time, the insolvent may submit to his creditors a proposal for the payment of his debts. This proposal is effective if accepted in a meeting of creditors and approved by the court. Insolvency proceedings are terminated by the approval of an agreement between creditors and the insolvent or the distribution of all of the insolvent's assets.

In the case of insolvency or bankruptcy proceedings in other jurisdictions, all assets of the insolvent existing in Costa Rica may be seized and liquidated but may only be distributed among creditors residing in Costa Rica.

Bankruptcy

The following are grounds for bankruptcy:

- a request by the debtor;
- non-payment of a debt;
- disappearance of the debtor;
- unjustified closing of the debtor's business.

When the debtor files for his or its own bankruptcy the application must be accompanied by a sworn statement of assets and liabilities, lists of debtors and creditors, reasons for cessation of payments and the date on which payments ceased as well as all the books, accounts and current and past correspondence.

In order to apply for a declaration of bankruptcy of a debtor, a creditor must be able to show that he is a creditor, that the debt is unrecoverable and that the debtor is a merchant. A secured creditor may only petition for bankruptcy if he can show that the encumbered property has been or will be insufficient to satisfy his debt and after the debtor is given the opportunity to pay the debt.

Within 24 hours of receiving the petition, the court must issue the declaration of bankruptcy which must include:

- a prohibition to the bankrupt to make any payment or conveyance of property;
- an order to the appropriate authorities to refrain from registering any documents relating to the transfer of the debtor's right or the establishment of an encumbrance;

- a notification to banks, credit institutions, general deposit warehouses and customs houses to withhold delivery to the debtor, his agent or representative of any documents, commercial goods, merchandise or other article or document of economic value;
- notification to the post office, telegraph service, radio and cable service to deliver to the receiver all correspondence, parcels and deliveries addressed to the bankrupt;
- notification to immigration authorities and offices, post officials and any others concerned, to refuse issuance of a passport to the bankrupt and to refrain from facilitating his departure from the country in any other way;
- notification to the prosecutor's office to start an investigation of any felonies that may have been committed.

If a merchant or company having one or more branches or agencies in Costa Rica becomes bankrupt in a foreign country, the branches or agencies are put in liquidation if this is requested by the foreign authority in charge of the principal bankrupt independently of the main office, being considered as a separate legal entity for such purposes. In this bankruptcy, payment will be made first to creditors domiciled in Costa Rica at the time of the declaration of bankruptcy or at the time the debts were contracted. Once these debts have been paid in full, any remaining moneys will be remitted to the main office.

A receiver and an alternate must be appointed by the court in the declaration of bankruptcy. Both appointees must be practising lawyers although the judge may appoint as receiver a banking institution or a corporation if deemed appropriate. The receiver must ensure that all of the bankrupt's assets are secured and inventoried, collect all debts owed to the bankrupt, continue, in the name of the bankrupt, all judicial proceedings that are relevant to the bankruptcy and liquidate all of the bankrupt's assets for a suitable price, with the authorisation of the creditors and a court approval and distribute all moneys among the creditors.

At any time, the bankrupt may submit to his creditors a proposal for the payment of his debts. This proposal is effective if accepted in a meeting of creditors and approved by the court. Bankruptcy proceedings are terminated by the approval of an agreement between creditors and the bankrupt or the distribution of all of the bankrupt's assets.

KPMG contact partner

Federico Golcher
KPMG Peat Marwick
Am Cham Plaza, 2nd Floor
7th Avenue, Sabana Norte
San José
Costa Rica

Telephone: +506 220-1366
Fax: +506 220 0408

Cyprus

Legislation

Procedures relating to liquidation in Cyprus are governed by the winding-up provisions of the Cyprus Companies Law, c. 113.

Insolvency procedures

Court liquidation

Court liquidations in cases of insolvency are normally instigated by a creditor or a group of creditors who hold a valid debt exceeding C£500 and which is not discharged by the company within three weeks of formal notice for its payment being served, or when the execution of a judgment issued by the court is returned unsatisfied.

On the presentation of a petition for winding up, and before any winding-up order is made by the court, the company or any creditor has the power to stay or restrain any proceedings or actions against the company. On hearing the petition the court may issue a winding-up order, in which case the winding up of the company is deemed to have commenced with the presentation of the petition. The court appoints a liquidator (usually the official receiver and registrar) who takes immediate possession of all assets of the company. All rights and powers of the directors cease on the appointment of the liquidator.

The rights and duties of the liquidator are conferred by the Law and are subject to the direction of the courts. In broad terms, the liquidator may take any action, dispose as best as he can of any assets of the company and make any payments to creditors having regard to the relative ranking of their claims. Any surplus assets are distributed to the shareholders. The liquidator is free to carry on business so far as this is necessary for the beneficial winding up of the company. On completion of the liquidation to the satisfaction of the court, the liquidator makes an application to the court for the dissolution of the company.

Voluntary liquidation

There are two types of voluntary winding up, a members' voluntary winding up and a creditors' voluntary winding up. In all voluntary liquidations, procedures are instigated by the company itself by adopting an extraordinary resolution to the effect that the company be wound up. Notice of the resolution must be advertised in the *Official Gazette* within 14 days of its adoption but proceedings are deemed to commence at the time of the passing of the resolution.

A members' voluntary winding up takes place when the directors make a statutory declaration to the effect that in their opinion the company will be able to satisfy all its creditors within a period not exceeding 12 months. A liquidator is appointed by the shareholders in general meeting for the purposes of distributing the assets and he has wide powers to deal in the assets of the company. The liquidator must call general meetings of the members at the end of each year and lay before them a full report and accounts on the conduct of the winding up. As soon as the affairs of the company are fully wound up, a final meeting of the members is held and a final return is made to the registrar of companies. The company is deemed to be dissolved three months after the filing of the final return.

A creditors' voluntary winding up occurs when the directors are unable to make a statutory declaration of solvency or at any time when the liquidator in a members' voluntary winding up forms the opinion that the company will be unable to pay all its debts.

A meeting of creditors is called (both by direct notice and by advertisement in the *Official Gazette*) where the directors present the financial position of the company. The creditors may nominate a liquidator and elect a committee of inspection to supervise the liquidation. Proceedings continue in a similar way as in a compulsory winding up and the liquidator may, at any time, seek the direction of the court in the discharge of his duties.

There is no time limit for the completion of a winding up.

Receiverships

Any debenture holder may, on default of repayment by the company, appoint a receiver and manager for the purpose of disposing of the assets used as security. The powers of the receiver are contained in the debenture instrument, but he may apply to the court for directions in relation to any particular matter arising in connection with the performance of his functions.

On appointment, the receiver takes possession of all assets of the company and the rights of the directors are suspended. In carrying out his duties, the receiver's primary responsibility is to the debenture holders but he must also consider the interests of the company itself and the interests of other creditors. The responsibilities of receivers are very onerous and it is normal practice to obtain indemnities from principals.

On the completion of the assignment (i.e., the satisfaction of the debenture holder) the receiver may hand the company back to the directors or, if there are not sufficient assets remaining, may petition the court for a winding-up order in which case the company will be compulsorily wound up.

Where a creditor has applied to the court for a winding-up order, debenture holders may, if they so wish, appoint a receiver and manager to safeguard their interests.

Creditors

The law stipulates the relative ranking of debts as follows:

- preferential creditors, which include certain rates and taxes and wages and salaries up to a specified amount;
- creditors secured by a specific charge on assets;
- creditors secured by a floating charge on assets;
- all other creditors rank equally, irrespective of whether they are foreign or local creditors.

If there are insufficient funds to satisfy all creditors, the liquidator will require the shareholders to pay all or part of any unpaid calls on their share capital.

KPMG contact partner

Andreas Christofides
KPMG Peat Marwick
10 Mnasiadou Street
Nicosia
Cyprus

Telephone: +357 (2) 448700
Fax: +357 (2) 363842

Denmark

Legislation

The Danish insolvency legislation is laid down in the Act on Bankruptcy and comprises:

- suspension of payments;
- bankruptcy;
- compulsory composition;
- rescheduling of debt.

Insolvency procedures

All administrations of estates pursuant to the Act on Bankruptcy are carried out under the supervision of bankruptcy courts. Reconstructions are to a certain extent carried out without the involvement of the Act or the bankruptcy court. This may, for instance, take place by means of a voluntary composition with a major creditor.

Rescheduling of debt is a compulsory composition for private persons who do not carry on commercial business and it will not be commented on further.

Suspension of payments

It is the debtor who notifies the bankruptcy court of the suspension of payments. The suspension of payments is in force for a minimum of three months. It is not possible in the suspension of payments period to make payments to unsecured creditors. A supervisor, usually a lawyer, is appointed and approves all decisions.

The creditors are notified of the suspension of payments and are called to an exploratory meeting at which they are entitled to speak. The bankruptcy court may decide that creditors with special guarantees cannot apply for settlement in the assets in the suspension of the payments period.

The bankruptcy court may decide that the suspension of payments is to cease to operate if:

- the suspension of payments serves no reasonable purpose;
- the debtor fails to collaborate;
- the circumstances indicate that adequate endeavours to obtain a collective arrangement with the creditors are not being made.

The ordinary discontinuation grounds on which the suspension of payments ceases are:

- if the debtor revokes his notification;
- on the commencement of negotiations for a compulsory composition;
- on the commencement of debt rescheduling proceedings;
- on the pronouncement of an adjudication order;
- on expiry of the three-month period from the date of notice.

Bankruptcy

The debtor, as well as his creditors, can file a petition in bankruptcy with the bankruptcy court. Proceedings on the petition can be postponed if the debtor tries to make a composition with the creditors. The debtor then enters into suspension of payments. A petition for bankruptcy against a person in suspension of payments is usually postponed. Where negotiations for a compulsory composition have commenced, proceedings in respect of bankruptcy are stayed upon the debtor's application to such effect.

The petition for bankruptcy can be allowed when the debtor is insolvent. By this it is understood that he is unable to pay his obligations in the order in which they fall due and that this is not due to temporary reasons.

In connection with the submission of a bankruptcy notice a trustee is appointed. After this the debtor no longer has disposal of his assets. The trustee will realise all the bankrupt's assets in the best possible way and distribute the proceeds to the creditors. The trustee will usually be a lawyer. The creditors are notified of the bankruptcy and must prove their claims, made up as at the bankruptcy date. The trustee may employ requisite professional assistance for the account of the estate.

Guarantees and unusual transactions — up to three months before notification of suspension of payments or the bankruptcy date — can be set aside. Creditors with valid security can realise their security. The other creditors obtain settlement in the following order:

- costs in connection with the administration of the estate;
- costs in connection with preliminary attempts at a reconstruction;
- claims for wages and holiday allowances;
- unsecured creditors;
- unsecured creditors' claims for interest after the bankruptcy date.

The bankruptcy proceedings are terminated when all assets have been realised and the proceeds have been distributed, when all notified creditors have been paid in full, or when a compulsory composition is established.

Bankruptcy proceedings in small estates usually take at least one year, large estates usually take longer.

Compulsory composition

The debtor has to take the initiative himself to try to obtain compulsory composition. He approaches a suitably qualified professional (usually a State-authorised public accountant) to act as trustee of the composition. They prepare material required by law. The material is forwarded to all known creditors, usually by a lawyer. He obtains promises for a proposal from at least 40 per cent of the creditors, in number as well as value. After this the bankruptcy court can be approached with an application for the negotiations to be opened in respect of compulsory composition on the basis of the forwarded material. The composition may involve:

- a percentage reduction of the debt;
- a postponement of the payment of the debt;
- realisation of all assets and distribution among the creditors;
- combinations of the above.

The debt can, at the most, be written down to 25 per cent.

Adoption of the composition requires at least 60 per cent, in some cases more, to vote for the composition. The composition only concerns the unsecured creditors. If the composition is adopted, the agreed write-down is also binding on any previously unknown creditors.

A compulsory composition is usually prepared in a suspension of payments period. Consequently, the debtor has disposal of his assets, but is subject to supervision. Payments to creditors take place in the same order as bankruptcy.

KPMG contact partners

Henry Heiberg, Poul Erik Olsen
KPMG
Borups Alle 177
PO Box 250
DK-2000 Frederiksberg
Denmark

Telephone: +45 (38) 18 3000
Fax: +45 (38) 18 3045

Egypt

Legislation

The following laws regulate insolvency in Egypt:

- Civil Law, arts 249–264 on insolvency;
- Commercial Law, arts 195–419 on bankruptcy;
- Law 56 of 1945, which is a supplementary Law to the Commercial Law, on deeds of arrangement.

Insolvency procedures

Egyptian law provides three methods or procedures to be taken against insolvent debtors.

- adjudication of insolvency — this method is confined to persons who are not traders. The adjudication of insolvency is issued by virtue of a ruling of the relevant court of first instance;
- adjudication of bankruptcy — this method is confined to traders who default in settling their commercial debts. The adjudication of bankruptcy is issued by virtue of a ruling of the relevant court of first instance;
- deed of arrangement in avoidance of bankruptcy — under the deed of arrangement, the insolvent trader petitions the relevant court to treat him according to this method instead of in bankruptcy. The court accepts the trader's petition if he proves to have acted in good faith and provided that some other favourable conditions exist, but such arrangement cannot be concluded unless it is approved by the required majority of his creditors.

Adjudication of bankruptcy is the most prevalent method of dealing with insolvent debtors and this method is outlined below.

Adjudication of bankruptcy

Commencement

If a trader defaults in settling his commercial debts he is considered to be in a state of bankruptcy. Bankruptcy proceedings commence by the presentation of a petition to the court of first instance in whose district the place of business of the debtor is located.

A petition may be made by the debtor or by one of his creditors or by the public prosecutor. The court is also entitled to adjudicate the debtor in its own capacity, while considering the debtor's petition for a deed of arrangement.

Effect of the procedure

After presentation of the petition to adjudicate the debtor, the presiding judge designates an early date for a court hearing and summons the debtor to attend. The presiding judge may, in cases that require expeditious action, freeze the debtor's funds, or take any other preventive action he sees fit. If the court's judgment declares the debtor bankrupt, it will appoint a bankruptcy officer from among the court's judges, and a provisional agent (trustee) to represent the creditors. It may also order the freezing of the bankrupt's funds, and, if need be, imprisonment or preventive custody of the bankrupt. The judge also designates two newspapers in which the bankruptcy adjudication will be published.

The effect of the bankruptcy adjudication is to restrain the bankrupt from managing his affairs, prohibit him from initiating any litigation in connection with his funds, and to form a creditors' syndicate. In addition, creditors' term debts fall due.

Control of the procedure

The bankruptcy adjudication appoints one of the court's judges as 'bankruptcy officer' to supervise and control the bankruptcy proceedings. The bankruptcy officer should, first of all, secure the bankrupt's funds, books and documents, and invite all the creditors to an urgent meeting to verify their debts. He will also authorise the trustee (creditors' agent) to sell the bankrupt's movable property, merchandise and place of business and will ensure that all the proceeds of sale are deposited regularly in the court's treasury. The officer must submit reports to the court on important matters as required by law.

The bankruptcy adjudication also appoints a provisional trustee or agent to represent the creditors. Thereafter, the provisional trustee's appointment is confirmed or he is replaced by another person by a court order after perusal of a report submitted by the bankruptcy officer, who should consult with the creditors before giving his report. More than one trustee may be appointed but not more than three. The trustee may be selected from among the creditors or may be an outsider but, in either case, he should not be related, by blood or marriage, to the sixth degree removed from the bankrupt.

The trustee places the bankrupt's assets under preventive custody, administers his affairs, collects debts due to him, represents him before the law courts, participates in the verification of the debts due to him, liquidates his assets and distributes the proceeds among the creditors. He is required to exercise the care of a reasonable man in carrying out his duties.

Creditors

Ordinary and preferential creditors

The effects of bankruptcy adjudication on ordinary and preferential creditors are as follows:

- formation of a creditors' group or syndicate;
- no individual creditor may institute legal proceedings against the bankrupt, but proceedings may be made in the name of the creditors' syndicate;
- cessation of interest accruing on their debts (but interest accrues on debts due to the bankrupt);
- their term debts fall due.

Secured creditors

The effects of bankruptcy adjudication on secured creditors are as follows:

- such creditors are not entitled to participate in the creditors' syndicate, unless the realised value of the security is insufficient to pay the total amount of the relevant debt, in which case the secured creditor joins the syndicate for the unpaid part of his debt. Secured creditors are not restrained from litigating and are entitled to pursue their cases and to execute judgments against the bankrupt's assets securing their debts. The only difference is that the proceedings are brought against the trustee and not against the bankrupt;
- they are not subjected to suspension of interest accruing on their debts, but such interest will be collected from the proceeds of the assets securing their debts if such proceeds are sufficient enough to cover their debts and the interest thereon;
- their term debts fall due.

Foreign creditors

Foreign creditors are treated in the same manner as Egyptian creditors, whether they are ordinary, preferential or secured creditors.

Shareholders

The bankruptcy of a joint-stock company does not result in bankruptcy of its shareholders since they are not liable for losses except to the extent of their shares in the company and they are not considered as traders. The general meeting of shareholders will appoint a manager or managers for the company to represent them before the bankruptcy officer or the trustee, to take the preventive actions which the trustee fails to implement, to institute proceedings against him if his interest conflicts with that of the bankrupt company, and to negotiate an amicable arrangement with the creditors. If the company is wound up, the liquidator assumes the position of the company's manager referred to above.

The stock exchange commission will delete from its listings, by a two-thirds majority of its members, the shares of a company that has been declared bankrupt, and consequently the shareholders of such a company cannot deal in the shares.

Priorities of payment

- secured creditors are paid first out of the realised amount of their security;
- preferential creditors are paid in accordance with their rank of preference as defined by law;
- remaining funds are used to pay the ordinary creditors. If funds are insufficient to pay them all, they are paid on a pro rata basis whether they be Egyptian or foreign creditors;
- if any funds remain after paying all the creditors, the surplus goes to the debtor. In the case of a company, the surplus will be distributed among the shareholders.

KPMG contact partner

Halim Samy
KPMG Hazem Hassan
72 Mohi Eldin Abul Ezz Street
Mohandiseen
Cairo
Egypt

Telephone: +20 (2) 336 90 94
Fax: +20 (2) 34 97 224

El Salvador

Legislation

Insolvency is dealt with under the Commercial Code of El Salvador.

Insolvency procedures

Bankruptcy

The decree of bankruptcy is pronounced by a competent judge of a commercial court against a merchant who has ceased to pay his obligations constituting a condition of insolvency. This situation is assumed in the following cases:

- failure to pay net and matured obligations;
- having insufficient assets for seizure;
- absence of the merchant during 15 days or more without leaving anyone in charge of the business who can legally fulfil its obligations;
- voluntary closing of the premises during 15 days or more when there are obligations to be met;
- assignment of assets to detriment of creditors;
- resorting to disastrous, fraudulent or fictitious means in order not to fulfil obligations;
- personal request of bankruptcy;
- request for suspension of payments when an agreement with creditors has not been reached;
- failure to fulfil obligations agreed to under a suspension of payments.

The action to declare bankruptcy on behalf of all creditors may be carried out by the Attorney-General's office, by the bankrupt and by any of the creditors under the provisions of the Civil Proceedings Code. The effects of bankruptcy are retroactive to the date of discontinuance of payments.

Judgments declaring bankruptcy abroad take effect in El Salvador, but creditors domiciled in El Salvador have priority over creditors domiciled abroad.

Should one or several debtors of a joint obligation declare bankruptcy, the creditor is entitled to claim from the assets of each debtor the full amount of his loan until it is fully paid.

Any merchant, before being declared bankrupt, may ask to be declared in a status of suspension of payments and have his creditors called to execute a general agreement in order to prevent bankruptcy. During this time the debtor retains the administration of the assets and may continue operations under legal surveillance.

Bankruptcy is annulled by the following:

- payment;
- lack of assets;
- non-concurrence of creditors;
- unanimous agreement of concurring creditors;
- by agreement between creditors and bankrupt.

Once bankruptcy is annulled, if the bankrupt has not been convicted by the judge of a criminal court as responsible for a failure due to bad management or fraud, he may request his rehabilitation from a judge of the Mercantile Court.

KPMG contact partner

Hector Figueroa
KPMG Peat Marwick
Avenida Olimpica 3324
San Salvador
El Salvador

Telephone: +503 224 1351
Fax: +503 298 3354

Estonia

Legislation

The Law on Bankruptcy came into force on 1 September 1992. Liquidation procedures of a company are included in the Commercial Code which came into force on 1 September 1995.

In the Law on Bankruptcy similar rules apply to both natural and legal persons.

Insolvency procedures

Liquidation procedures according to the Commercial Code

A public limited company can be dissolved by a resolution of the general meeting, by a court order or on other bases prescribed by law or the articles of association.

A dissolution resolution can be adopted if at least two thirds of those voting at the general meeting are in favour and if the management board and the supervisory board are also in favour. The overview of economic activities approved by the general meeting indicates the term during which the company is unable to satisfy the claims of creditors. Compulsory dissolution may take place if the general meeting does not adopt a dissolution resolution if it had to according to the law or the articles of association or if the general meeting has not been held during the last two financial years. Before an order for compulsory dissolution of the company is issued, the court may specify a deadline for elimination of the circumstances which are the basis for compulsory dissolution. Upon dissolution a company is liquidated.

Generally the liquidators of a company are the members of the management board. A court appoints the liquidators in a compulsory dissolution or an appointment may be requested by stockholders.

The liquidators have the rights and obligations of the management board and supervisory board provided these are not in conflict with the object of the liquidation. The liquidators terminate the activities of the company, collect debts, sell assets and satisfy the claims of creditors. If the assets of a company are insufficient for satisfaction of all claims of creditors, the liquidators submit a bankruptcy petition.

Bankruptcy procedures according to the Law on Bankruptcy

According to the Law on Bankruptcy, bankruptcy proceedings are effected as court and out-of-court proceedings.

In case of insolvency of a bank, other credit institution or insurance company, the Law on Bankruptcy can be applied only in combination with special provisions of other Laws.

Grounds for bankruptcy petition

A bankruptcy petition may be submitted by a debtor or a creditor. If the debtor is a legal person the declaration of its bankruptcy may be pursued by the owner, administration, board of directors, liquidation commission. A bankruptcy petition can be submitted by a creditor on the following grounds:

- the debtor has intentionally caused its insolvency by an act punishable under the Criminal Code;
- the debtor destroys, hides or squanders its property, or performs other acts resulting in his insolvency;
- a distraint has been unsuccessful within the past three months due to the lack of assets, or in the course of the distraint the debtor's assets seem to be insufficient to pay all the debts;

- the debtor has not paid a debt within 10 days after the due date and the creditor has announced its intention to submit a bankruptcy petition, whereafter the debtor has failed to pay the debt within a period of 10 days;
- the debtor informs the creditor, a law court or the public about its inability or lack of intention to pay its debts.

A secured creditor cannot petition. The court examines a bankruptcy petition submitted by a debtor immediately, or, if there is a valid reason for an extension, within 20 days. A bankruptcy petition of a creditor should be examined within 20 days or, if there is a valid reason for an extension, within a period of two months.

Having examined the bankruptcy petition, the court decides whether to declare the debtor bankrupt, to reject the petition, or to close bankruptcy proceedings by its decree. The petition is rejected if the debtor's economic situation enables it to satisfy the claims. The court closes bankruptcy proceedings without declaring the debtor bankrupt if, after the submission of the petition the debtors' debts are paid, or the court accepts security for the claims, or if the debtor's assets are insufficient to defray the expenses of the bankruptcy proceedings. The debtor is declared bankrupt if the court has established his insolvency. The decision is published in a newspaper and in the supplement to the *State Gazette*.

Rights and obligations of the trustee

As of the date of declaration of bankruptcy, the right to administer the debtor's assets is transferred to the trustee who acts under the supervision of the court and creditors. The trustee defends the rights and interests of all creditors, likewise of the debtor, and guarantees a rapid completion of the bankruptcy proceedings. The trustee administers the bankrupt's estate, from which he pays the creditors' claims. If the debtor is a legal person, the trustee arranges the continuation of its activities (including reorganisation, restructuring), or its liquidation. The activities of the trustee are supervised by the bankruptcy committee which ensures that the trustee acts lawfully.

Within a period of two months from the date of publishing the bankruptcy notice in the newspaper, creditors are obliged to notify the trustee of their claims against the debtor. Within the same time all persons are obliged to inform the trustee of the debtor's property in their possession. The first meeting of the creditors is held not earlier than 15 days and not later than one month after the declaration of bankruptcy.

After the declaration of bankruptcy the trustee has to prepare a plan for the continuation of the activities (reorganisation or structuring) or liquidation of a company. The first meeting of the creditors has to decide whether to accept this plan.

The trustee is not allowed to begin the liquidation of a company before the decision of the creditors. Reorganisation and restructuring may start immediately after the declaration of bankruptcy, if there are enough assets of the debtor left after the satisfaction of all claims to continue the activities.

Compromise proposal

In the course of the bankruptcy proceedings the debtor can make a compromise proposal, seeking the agreement of non-priority creditors to reduce the amounts and extend the terms of maturity of debts. In the compromise proposal the debtor provides a plan for the continuation of economic activities or the reorganisation of the company. If the proposal involves paying less than half of the amount of the claims with no priority then at least three quarters of the creditors present must vote in favour of the proposal.

After the presentation of the compromise proposal the court may declare bankruptcy only if there are valid reasons to presume that the compromise resolution will not be adopted. The decision on confirmation of a compromise resolution is taken by the court within a period of two weeks after the decision of the meeting of creditors has been submitted to the court. On the basis of the court decision on confirmation of a compromise resolution the debtor regains the right to administer property, the sale of the assets ceases, control of the estate is returned to the debtor and the division of property does not take place.

The duration of validity of the compromise resolution is determined by the meeting of creditors upon the debtor's proposal. The trustee supervises implementation of the compromise resolution. The court may abate the compromise resolution at the request of the trustee or a creditor if the debtor is guilty of fraud or fails to fulfil the obligations arising from the compromise, or if, at the expiration of not less than half of the agreed period of validity of the compromise resolution, the debtor appears to be unable to fulfil the provisions of compromise. In case of abatement of the compromise resolution the bankruptcy proceedings are recommenced.

Division of assets in bankrupt's estate

After establishing claims the trustee prepares a proposal of division, but before the division of assets, any claims for exclusion and segregation of assets from the bankrupt's estate are satisfied and the expenses connected with the bankruptcy proceedings are covered whereafter the claims of the creditors are satisfied.

Claims of the creditors are satisfied in the following order:

- secured claims;
- wages and incomes regarded as wages (pension, fees etc.), alimony, compensation for personal or other damage to health, as well as compensation for the loss of maintenance;
- taxes and social security payments;
- all other accepted claims.

The subsequent claims are satisfied after the full satisfaction of preceding claims. If the assets are not sufficient to satisfy all claims of one priority such claims are satisfied in proportion to the amount of each claim.

In conclusion

As insolvency legislation in Estonia has only recently been introduced it is likely to be improved and adjusted according to the demands and needs of a developing economy and changes in other legislative acts.

KPMG contact partner

Kadri Arula
KPMG
Ahtri 10A
Tallinn EE 0001
Estonia

Telephone: +372 (62) 68 700
Fax: +372 (62) 68 777

Fiji

Legislation

Fiji company laws are based on the UK Companies Act 1948. Receivership and winding up of companies are governed by the Companies Act 1983 and Companies (Winding Up) Rules 1983.

Insolvency procedures

Receivership

On application, the Supreme Court of Fiji may appoint a receiver who could be the official receiver but, generally, receivers are appointed by a security holder, e.g., a bank. The receiver must notify the company of his appointment, and the directors are required to prepare a statement of affairs for him which he forwards with his comments to the Registrar of Companies. Every six months thereafter the receiver is required to forward an abstract of his receipts and payments.

The legal provisions of the Companies Act are limited, although the receiver can apply to the court for directions in performance of his functions. The terms and conditions established by the appointor govern his action although he is personally liable and so an indemnity is usually sought. There is no requirement to inform creditors of the company of his actions.

Liquidation

The regulations governing the winding up of a company are far more complex and involved. There are basically three types of liquidation:

- by the court;
- members;
- creditors' voluntary.

Court winding up

Court winding up commences when an order is made after a petition has been presented by either the company, or creditors, or contributories or the official receiver. All transactions involving the company then become void. The official receiver is normally appointed liquidator, although an outside party, such as a chartered accountant, may be appointed. A statement of affairs prepared by a director and the secretary is submitted to the liquidator. Whilst the court can limit the liquidator's power, he has general ability to dispose of the property of the company. A committee of inspection may be appointed to oversee and advise the liquidator.

Members' voluntary winding up

Voluntary winding up is instituted after the company passes a special resolution to wind up. If a declaration of solvency is made by the directors it becomes a members' voluntary winding up, otherwise it is called a creditors' voluntary winding up. If the court so orders, a voluntary winding up can continue, but under supervision of the court.

Creditors' voluntary winding up

In a creditors' voluntary winding up, a meeting of creditors must be held where the directors present a full statement of the position of the company, and creditors elect a liquidator and, should they think fit, a committee of inspection.

On appointment of a liquidator the directors' powers cease. An annual meeting must be held where the liquidator accounts to creditors for his actions.

Creditors

In every winding up, there is a priority to pay certain classes of creditors such as government taxes and wages, although most claims are substantially limited in value and time. Landlords also have the right to claim distress for rent, whereby they can effectively gain a first priority over assets on property to repay outstanding rental payments.

KPMG contact partner

Brian Murphy
KPMG
ANZ House
25 Victoria Parade
Suva
Fiji

Telephone: +679 301 155
Fax: +679 301 312

Finland

Legislation

The statutory framework is regulated by the following:

- Bankruptcy Act (1868:31);
- Priority Act (1992:1578);
- *Action Paulienne* in Bankruptcy (1991:758);
- Corporate Reorganisation Act (1993:47);
- Act on the Regional Competence of District Courts in Matters Concerning Corporate Reorganisation (1993:1032);
- Companies Act (1978:734).

Insolvency procedures

Determining the right forum

The choice of insolvency forum can be complicated, as only 17 of the 71 Finnish district courts have jurisdiction in corporate reorganisation cases.

The reorganisation forum is determined according to the Act on the Regional Competence of District Courts in Matters Concerning Corporate Reorganisation. The correct forum in both reorganisation and bankruptcy is determined according to the factual location of the company's administration, i.e., not necessarily according to the registered office of the company. As all district courts handle bankruptcies problems may arise because a petition for reorganisation and a petition for bankruptcy may be pending simultaneously in different courts.

Corporate Reorganisation Act

Petitioning for reorganisation does not automatically stay other actions, but this may be temporarily effected through a request presented with the petition. A bankruptcy petition is postponed until a court order on the reorganisation process has been given. Also the liability to apply for liquidation as stated in the Finnish Companies Act is subordinated to reorganisation proceedings. Major creditors are heard on the question of the probability of successful avoidance of permanent insolvency, unless at least two major creditors with receivables amounting to at least 20 per cent of all the debtor's liabilities have already given their consent.

A court order on starting the reorganisation proceedings after the preliminary hearing has an automatic stay effect with several exclusions, for example, salaries and interest on secured loans are to be paid during the proceedings as they fall due. The court order on starting the proceedings also stops interest accruing on overdue payments. A receiver is appointed by the court to supervise the interests of the creditors. The receiver should generally present the reorganisation programme to the court and creditors within four months of the court order. He is also to confirm the debtor's liabilities and assets, to supervise the actions of the debtor, to see that the previous activities of the debtor are audited in appropriate depth, to act on behalf of the debtor in any court proceedings and especially petition for the remedy of any transaction subject to the Finnish *action paulienne* (for reversal of transactions defrauding creditors).

Liquidation

The general meeting of a corporation is the primary body for deciding on a corporation's liquidation. In cases enumerated in the Finnish Companies Act, the corporation may be placed in liquidation also by court order. A creditor may petition for the debtor's liquidation if the debtor does not have a registered board of directors or a managing director when required by law. When making a decision on a corporation's liquidation one or more liquidators are appointed to manage the corporate affairs during the process. The liquidators request the court to summon publicly the creditors of the corporation, they convert corporate assets into cash and they pay the debts of the corporation. If the liabilities exceed the assets, the liquidator should apply for the bankruptcy of the corporation in liquidation.

Merger

A corporation may also be dissolved through a merger with another corporation. A merger may also be realised so that two or more companies join together to form a new corporation.

Receivers in bankruptcy and reorganisation

A receiver is appointed by the court handling the insolvency case. In a reorganisation a receiver is called examiner. A receiver must have the special knowledge and experience required by that appointment. He is to enjoy the creditors' confidence and in every other respect to be suitable for the assignment. The court usually appoints an attorney at law as official receiver. The interim receiver in bankruptcy is usually proposed by the debtor and habitually appointed unless the creditors are alerted to propose another person for the assignment. In reorganisation the receiver is usually proposed by a creditor.

Later in the process the interim receiver is in general appointed receiver. The receiver has a status close to that of a court officer. He or she usually receives the demands concerning the liabilities of the insolvent company.

Creditors' committee in reorganisation

A creditors' committee performs a supervisory function and may consult with the examiner. The committee consists of at least three members each representing a group of creditors in similar position. For example unsecured creditors may propose a member as their representative. A creditors' committee is appointed only if deemed necessary due to a large number of creditors.

Liquidator

A liquidator pursuant to the Companies Act, is appointed by the general meeting of the shareholders or by the court. A member of the board of directors or the managing director of the corporation may be appointed liquidator.

Creditors

Priority is provided in bankruptcy and reconstruction for liens, real estate property mortgages and to 50 per cent of the realisation value of the property that is covered by a floating charge. Set-off is in general accepted with limitations stated in the Reorganisation Act. Bank guarantees and other forms of personal securities given in commercial trade by professional guarantors are valid in insolvency, whereas a personal security given by a non-professional guarantor is subject to the limitations set forth in the Reconstruction Act.

Several amendments to the Companies Act are under way. The Bankruptcy Act has recently been brought more up-to-date as regards content and formulation.

KPMG contact partner

Nils Blumme
KPMG Wideri Oy Ab
Mannerheimintie 20B
FIN-00100 Helsinki
Finland

Telephone: +358 (9) 69 39 31
Fax: +358 (9) 69 39 399

France

Legislation

Insolvency procedures in respect of debtors who are unable to meet their liabilities as they fall due from available assets, have been modified by legislation enacted on 10 June 1994 and confirmed by decree dated 21 October 1994.

This legislation provides for a unified procedure which covers legal entities (non-commercial or commercial corporations) and individuals (traders or craftsmen), which have ceased their payments (i.e., deemed insolvent). A simplified procedure is applicable for small companies (i.e., turnover under FF20 million and less than 50 employees).

Insolvency procedures

Prevention of difficulties

For companies experiencing financial difficulties, the legislation has defined a warning procedure ('procedure d'alerte') which may be initiated by:

- the statutory auditor;
- the President of the Commercial Court;
- the works council representing the interests of employees;
- the shareholders.

The President of the Commercial Court may require an inquiry and nominate a 'mandataire ad hoc', to assist the management in their negotiations or nominate a judicial administrator to manage the company.

This procedure is aimed at reaching an agreement with the creditors. The agreement has to be authorised by the President of the Court. If no solution can be found, the company goes through the insolvency procedure.

Inability to pay debts

When a company is unable to pay its creditors from its available funds or borrowings, the situation has to be declared to the Commercial Court, usually by management, within 15 days of being deemed insolvent.

The insolvency procedure may be also initiated by either:

- the judicial administrator if any;
- one or several creditors;
- the court itself;
- the State Attorney (Procureur de la République).

Preliminary judgment

On the basis of a preliminary inquiry the court will usually decide either to liquidate or to place the company in receivership.

To carry out the receivership procedure the court appoints:

- a magistrate (called '*juge-commissaire*') to supervise the procedure;
- a judicial administrator (professional) (his appointment is optional in the simplified procedure) to help the defaulting company;
- a creditors' representative (professional) to look after the creditors' interests and to control the debts from the application made by the creditors;
- a liquidator (professional) if liquidation is decided.

The court fixes the 'observation period' at the end of which a final decision has to be made. This period is limited to six months but may be reviewed once.

The preliminary judgment stops all legal action by creditors and freezes any action in progress.

The employees have preferred status which guarantees payment of salaries due for the 60-day period before the preliminary judgment.

During the 'observation period' the judicial administrator prepares a report to the court covering two possible solutions:

- recovery plan;
- transfer plan.

Recovery plan

In this case the business can continue but it has to pay its debts to the creditors under delays imposed by the court (the average delay is seven years), and debts may be reduced.

There is no distinction between secured and unsecured creditors. All creditors are subject to consolidated terms of payment. The national guarantee fund of salaries is not subject to these terms for the sums paid in advance which correspond to two months of salaries ('super-secured debts').

In order to be efficient the recovery plan implies that the future profitability of the company will take into consideration the staggered future reimbursement of the debts.

Such a plan should present:

- the industrial and commercial assumptions and plan supporting the forecasts;
- an employment plan;
- a schedule of payment of the debts;
- the guarantees offered.

Transfer plan

A transfer plan allows for all or part of the assets of the business to be sold, under condition of the continuation and the function of the business and total or partial continuous employment. The employment consideration is very important. All the agreements concluded between the company and third parties (operating or capital leases etc.) can be transferred with the assets.

The court will choose the more reliable solution proposed and will nominate an administrator (official receiver) to implement the agreed plan.

Legal liquidation

Liquidation may be decided at any time by the court if no solution can be found. A liquidator (professional) is designated.

Directors' and shareholders' responsibilities

As soon as difficulties appear, it is necessary to be extremely cautious to avoid any action or decision which could engage the financial responsibility of either the directors or shareholders and be deemed as acts of mismanagement.

Creditors' rights and obligations

Within eight days of the preliminary judgment, the creditors are informed of the procedure. They have two months in which to present a claim for their liabilities (four months for creditors who are domiciled outside France).

For existing contracts, the administrator may require their execution, provided the company is able to pay.

Debts incurred after the preliminary judgment have to be paid on a timely basis if the business continues.

KPMG contact partner

Didier de Menonville
KPMG Audit
47 rue de Villiers
92200 Neuilly-sur-Seine
France

Telephone: +33 (1) 46 39 44 44
Fax: +33 (1) 47 58 71 38

Francophone Africa

Insolvency procedures in certain parts of Africa are still developing and in other parts political uncertainty exists. For further information or assistance on insolvency matters in the following countries, please contact KPMG Paris:

Algeria
Benin
Burkina Faso
Cameroun
Central African Republic
Chad
Congo
Equatorial Guinea
Gabon
Guinea
Mali
Mauritania
Niger
Senegal
Togo

KPMG contact partners

Jean Delsol, Jean-Marc Declety, Loic Steunou
KPMG Paris
47, rue de Villiers
92200 Neuilly-sur-Seine

J. Delsol
Telephone: +33 (1) 46 39 42 04
Fax: +33 (1) 47 58 71 38

J. Declety
Telephone: +33 (1) 46 39 43 04
Fax: +33 (1) 47 58 71 38

L. Steunou
Telephone: +33 (1) 46 39 40 00
Fax: +33 (1) 47 59 00 78

Germany

Legislation

Insolvency procedures are primarily governed by the Bankruptcy Act (Konkursordnung) and the Judicial Composition Proceedings Act (Vergleichsordnung). The Real Property Compulsory Administration Act (Zwangsversteigerungsgesetz) and the Creditors' Contest Act (Anfechtungsgesetz) are also relevant.

Besides the above-mentioned Acts, numerous insolvency provisions are contained in other laws, for example: the Stock Corporation Act (Aktiengesetz), the Limited Liability Companies Act (Gesetz betreffend die Gesellschaften mit beschränkter Haftung), the Employment Promotion Act (Arbeitsförderungsgesetz) and the Firm Pension Act (Gesetz zur Verbesserung der betrieblichen Altersversorgung). In addition, German law contains a series of special bankruptcy-related criminal acts that are mostly contained in the Criminal Code (Strafgesetzbuch).

Insolvency procedures

Bankruptcy proceedings

Individuals, partnerships and corporations may be declared bankrupt or may be obliged to declare bankruptcy. Exceptions are civil law associations, limited partnerships and government bodies.

The two reasons for opening bankruptcy proceedings are:

- insolvency — permanent incapability of meeting financial commitments due to lack of liquid funds (cessation of payment); or
- over-indebtedness — assets of a corporation are no longer sufficient to cover the debts. Over-indebtedness of individuals and general partnerships does not cause bankruptcy proceedings.

A bankrupt entity must file a petition for bankruptcy without delay but no later than three weeks from the time that the ground for bankruptcy comes into being. This petition is to be submitted to the court together with a list of its creditors and debtors and a summary of its assets. A creditor may also apply to have bankruptcy proceedings initiated against an entity that has ceased to honour its liabilities.

Upon application, a receiver is appointed by the court. Typically, attorneys are engaged but also accountants and tax advisers qualify. The receiver recommends opening bankruptcy proceedings provided sufficient funds are available to cover the administration and the legal expenses. Due to the fact that security interests created outside of the insolvency law have led to an ever-increasing lack of assets being left for the proceeding, currently approximately 80 per cent of all petitions are rejected. As a result, the present insolvency proceedings will be replaced by a new Insolvency Law which will come into force on 1 January 1999; details are presented below.

The insolvent must supply any pertinent information to the receiver and must hand over all the assets belonging to the bankruptcy estate. The management of the entity will be prohibited from concluding any legally binding contracts and loses the authority to dispose of any assets. Sole responsibility lies with the receiver.

Based on economic considerations the receiver must either close down the business, selling assets individually, or continue it for a certain period. The temporary continuation of the business is the exception and can only be done if it improves the situation of the creditors. The receiver is personally liable to the creditors for damages caused by such continuance compared to an immediate close-down.

Under the statutory definition all executable property of the bankrupt belonging to him at the time of adjudication of bankruptcy is to be included in the bankruptcy estate. Creditors may, however, have different rights according to their legal status versus the bankrupt person or entity:

- rights of separation (*Aussonderung*) — before the compulsory sale of the assets takes place, any owners of an asset not belonging to the insolvent person's property may claim return of the asset, because the title of ownership did not pass before payment of purchase price (retention of title rights);
- lien claims against certain assets (*Absonderungsrechte*) — lien rights against certain assets arise with respect to assets against which one or more creditors have a right of prior satisfaction. The lien right, first of all, covers the immovable property subject to an execution. Lien rights in movables are created by: equitable lien, security assignment, extended and prolonged reservation of title, conventional liens and the statutory liens of landlords and lessors as well as the trader's right of retention;
- privileged creditors and bankruptcy creditors (*Massegläubiger, Konkursgläubiger*) — there are two types of unsecured creditors. Certain creditors for costs, expenses and business debts incurred during the liquidation period have a preferred position for payment. Among these creditors, called '*Massegläubiger*', there are statutory priorities. All other unsecured creditors, called '*Konkursgläubiger*', share equally in the remaining proceeds from the disposal of assets in proportion to their claims. However, even among such creditors statutory priorities for payment exist (i.e., taxation, social security, employees).

No time for the conclusion of the bankruptcy proceedings is established. The process normally takes a number of years.

Composition proceedings

Bankruptcy may be avoided by a composition proceeding if the debtor applies for it. The court initiates bankruptcy proceedings only if the composition proceedings fail.

The application of the debtor will be accepted if the proposal offers the pro rata cash payment of at least 35 per cent of the debts, or at least 40 per cent if the debtor demands a payment schedule of one year. A trustee is then appointed by the court. The insolvent must prepare a proposal indicating how he anticipates repaying his creditors. The debtor retains the power of management and disposition over his property, hence the trustee only guides the debtor in his management and disposition duties.

New Insolvency Act 1999

The purpose of equal satisfaction of all creditors through liquidation of assets of the debtor has for some time not been met by the present statutory insolvency proceedings, since assets of the debtor are used up through numerous preferential claims outside the actual insolvency proceedings. As a result, a reform of the present law has been carried out and a new Insolvency Act (Insolvenzordnung) will come into force on 1 January 1999. Important changes are as follows:

- instead of the existing two-track bankruptcy and composition proceedings a uniform insolvency procedure has been created. Within the framework of the uniform proceedings a comprehensive reorganisation proceeding inspired by Chapter 11 of the US Bankruptcy Reform Act has been introduced;
- under the present bankruptcy proceedings the bankruptcy usually results in the sale and liquidation of the debtor's assets. The new Act offers a way for reorganising businesses and, in cases of failure, for liquidation;
- the two substantive grounds for opening insolvency proceedings, i.e., the inability to meet debts and over-indebtedness, remain principally unchanged. In addition, according to the new Act a debtor will be allowed to file an application to open insolvency proceedings when the inability to pay his debts is imminent. In such a case the debtor is legally not obliged but only entitled to file a petition in order to place himself under the shelter of the Insolvency Act at the earliest practicable date;

- security interests in movable property without possession are included in the liquidation proceedings and only the insolvency administrator is allowed to realise them. Nevertheless, the proceeds will substantially go to the creditor who is beneficiary of the security interest, i.e., after deduction of a procedure fee;
- the bankruptcy priority rights of tax authorities, social security authorities, as well as preferred claims of employees for outstanding compensation to them, have been abolished.

KPMG contact partner

Hans-Joachim Früh
KPMG Deutsche Treuhand-Gesellschaft AG
Am Bonneshof 35
D-40474 Düsseldorf
Germany

Telephone: +49 (211) 475-7000
Fax: +49 (211) 475-6000

Ghana

Liquidation procedures

Introduction

The purpose of this chapter is to deal with the procedures to be followed to make provision for the official liquidation of companies and other bodies corporate and other matters connected therewith.

The official winding up of a company may be commenced by:

- a special resolution of the company;
- a petition addressed to the Registrar of Companies;
- a petition to the court;
- a conversion from a private liquidation.

Procedure on resolution

A special resolution for the official winding up of a company must state that the company is to be wound up by way of an official winding up and a copy of the resolution, after it has been passed, sent to the Registrar for publication in the *Gazette*.

Petition to the Registrar

A creditor or member or contributory of a company may present a petition to the Registrar for the official winding up of the company.

A copy of the petition must be served on the company by the petitioner on or before the day on which it is presented.

The Registrar shall place a copy of the winding-up order in the file of the company concerned and shall publish the order in the *Gazette*.

Petition to the court

A petition for the official winding up of a company may be presented to the court by:

- the Registrar;
- a creditor of the company;
- a member or contributory of the company; or
- the Attorney-General.

On the hearing of a winding-up petition the court may dismiss or adjourn the hearing conditionally or unconditionally or make an interim order, or any other order that it thinks fit, but the court shall not refuse to make a winding-up order on the ground only that the assets of the company have been mortgaged to an amount equal to, or in excess of, those assets or that the company has no assets.

On the making of a winding-up order, a copy of the order shall forthwith be forwarded by the registrar of the court to the Registrar of Companies who shall make a minute thereof in his books relating to the company and publish it in the *Gazette*.

The court may appoint the Registrar to exercise all or any of the powers of a liquidator.

Conversion to official winding up

The liquidator under a private liquidation may give notice stating that the company is unable to pay its debts in full within the period stated in the declaration of solvency. This will enable the Registrar to make a winding-up order converting the private liquidation into an official winding up.

The liquidator's notice must be accompanied by a statement in the prescribed form of the company's assets and liabilities.

Stay of proceedings

On the commencement of winding up all civil proceedings against the company are stayed and any transfer of shares of the company is void.

Liquidator

The Registrar shall be the liquidator in any official winding up.

An official winding up commences on the passing of a resolution for the winding up of the company or on the making of a winding-up order.

All the functions of the directors of the company shall vest in the liquidator.

The company ceases to carry on business on the commencement of winding up, except so far as may be required for its beneficial winding up.

The liquidator shall take into his custody or under his control all the property and things in action to which the company is or appears to be entitled.

A statement of affairs of the company in a form approved by the liquidator and verified by an affidavit shall be made out within 14 days.

As soon as possible after the making of a winding-up order the liquidator must prepare a list of contributories with power to rectify the register of members in all cases where rectification is required and must cause the assets of the company to be collected and applied in the discharge of its liabilities.

In preparing the list of contributories, the liquidator must distinguish between persons who are contributories in their own right and persons who are contributories as representatives or liable for the debts of others.

When all the creditors of the company are paid in full, any money due to a contributory from the company may be allowed to the contributory by way of set-off against any subsequent call.

During the winding up any creditor of the company may lodge with the liquidator a statement, known as a proof of debt.

The liquidator must examine every proof of debt lodged with him and if, after considering any representations made by the company or any other creditor, it appears to him that any item is improperly included or any value incorrectly stated or that the proof is otherwise incorrect, he shall give notice of the objection to the creditor who may lodge an amended proof within the period specified in the notice or such period as the liquidator may allow.

Where the liquidator is satisfied with a proof of debt he shall give notice to the creditor that he admits the proof of debt subject to verification.

Where a creditor fails to lodge an amended proof of debt or a further amended proof of debt, as the case may be, within the period specified, and the liquidator is still of opinion that the previous proof of debt is incorrect he shall give notice to the creditor that he rejects the proof of debt.

The liquidator may by notice in the *Gazette* fix a time within which creditors are to prove their debts or claims or be excluded from the benefits of any distribution made before those debts are proved.

First meeting of creditors

The liquidator must call a first meeting of creditors not later than six weeks after the publication of the winding-up order.

The meeting shall be closed not later than eight weeks after the publication of the winding-up order.

Liquidator's duties

The liquidator may at any time after the making of a winding-up order summon before the court any officer of the company or person known or suspected of having in his possession any property of the company or supposed to be indebted to the company, or any person whom the liquidator deems capable of giving information concerning the promotion, formation, trade, dealings, affairs or property of the company.

The liquidator should ensure that any property of the company in his custody is made available by him for the purposes of the official winding up.

The liquidator should ensure repayment of preferred creditors of money, transfer of property or surrender of rights, the benefit of which has accrued to the creditor by reason of his being preferred.

The liquidator shall open an account to be known as the company's official account in which shall be credited:

- all moneys received by him in respect of the company;
- payments made to him in respect of the company for the purpose of increasing the assets available for dividend;
- repayments in respect of excess dividends made.

The liquidator should secure the payment to him or other discharge of all debts and other obligations the right to which has passed to him.

He may, by notice in the Gazette, direct that all property or any part of the property whatsoever belonging to the company or held by trustees on behalf of the company shall vest in him by his official name.

He shall realise as soon as practicable all assets not held as cash.

The liquidator must take such steps as are practicable to verify the correctness of every admitted proof.

The liquidator must amend an admitted proof if the value of the debt or security included in it has changed.

The liquidator shall, in relation to each debt which ranks for dividend, ascertain into which class the whole or any part falls.

The liquidator has the duty:

- to report to the creditors at intervals of not greater than six months on the progress of the liquidation;
- to consult the creditors on matters arising in the proceedings which substantially affect their interest;

- to give effect, so far as may be practicable, to any views expressed by the creditors in relation to the realisation and distribution of assets.

In the event of an official winding up continuing for more than one year, the liquidator must summon a general meeting of the company and a meeting of the creditors within three months of the end of the first year and each subsequent year.

Within one year from the commencement of the winding up, the liquidator may, if he is of the opinion that property will not be of benefit to the creditors, disclaim it by notice in the *Gazette*.

The liquidator is entitled to withdraw from the property of the company sums sufficient to satisfy fees of the prescribed amount charged in respect of the costs of the liquidation.

The liquidator must from time to time, and as early as possible, declare and distribute dividends to creditors.

The property of a company must, on its official winding up, be applied in satisfaction of its liabilities *pari passu* and any surplus must be distributed among the members according to their rights and interests in the company.

Disposal of unclaimed assets

Where, after provision has been made for all payments and transfers of property, any balance remains in the company's official account the Court may direct that it shall be transferred to the fees account and may give directions for the disposal of any property not converted into money.

Termination of proceedings

The liquidator shall, when he has completed the winding up of a company and his final accounts have been drawn up and have been passed by the Auditor-General, apply to the court for an order terminating the liquidation proceedings.

The liquidator shall give notice of his application to the court and to every creditor with an admitted proof together with a summary of the final accounts.

Dissolution of company

When the Registrar is satisfied that the official winding up of a company is complete, he shall strike the name of the company off the register and notify the same in the *Gazette* and the company shall, thereupon, be deemed to be dissolved as at the date of the publication of the notification in the *Gazette*.

Disposal of books and papers of company

The liquidator must preserve the books and papers of the company and of the liquidator for a period of five years from the dissolution of the company and thereafter may destroy such books and papers unless the Registrar otherwise directs, in which event the liquidator shall not destroy them until the Registrar consents in writing.

KPMG contact partner

Herbert A. Morrison
KPMG Peat Marwick Okoh & Co.
PO Box 242
2nd Floor, Mobil House
Liberia Road
Accra
Ghana

Telephone: +233 (21) 66 4881
Fax: +233 (21) 66 7909

Gibraltar

Legislation

The legislation which governs insolvency procedures is:

- Companies Ordinance 1930;
- Companies (Winding-Up) Rules;
- Bankruptcy Ordinance.

Insolvency procedures

Liquidation

The Companies Ordinance provides for three modes of liquidation:

- by the court;
- voluntary — either members' or creditors';
- subject to the supervision of the court.

Liquidation by the court

A company may be wound up by the court if:

- the company has by special resolution resolved that it be wound up by the court;
- default is made in delivering the statutory report to the Registrar or in holding the statutory meeting;
- the company does not commence its business within a year from its incorporation, or suspends its business for a whole year;
- the number of members is reduced, in the case of a private company, below one, or, in the case of any other company, below seven;
- if the company is unable to pay its debts;
- the court is of the opinion that it is just and equitable that the company should be wound up.

An application to the court for the winding up of a company must be made by petition presented, subject to varying circumstances, by either the company, or by any creditor or creditors, or by a contributory or contributories. In the case of a licensed bank an application can be made by the Commissioner of Banking on the grounds that the bank in unable to repay its depositors or that its assets are less than its liabilities.

The winding up of a company by the court is deemed to have commenced at the time of the presentation of the petition for the winding up.

On the issue of a winding-up order by the court, the court will usually appoint a liquidator who will normally be an accountant. In special circumstances a provisional liquidator may be appointed at the time that the petition for winding up is filed. If no liquidator is appointed by the court on the issue of a winding-up order then the Official Receiver will be the liquidator.

Voluntary liquidation

A company may be wound up voluntarily:

- when the period fixed for the duration of the company by the articles expires;
- if the company resolves by special resolution that the company be wound up voluntarily;
- if the company resolves by extraordinary resolution that it cannot by reason of its liabilities continue its business, and that it is advisable to wind up.

The voluntary winding up of a company is deemed to commence on the passing of the resolution to wind up by the company. At the meeting at which the resolution is passed a liquidator is also appointed.

When a company which is to be wound up voluntarily is solvent the winding up is referred to as a members' voluntary winding up. In such cases the directors of the company are required to file with the Registrar of Companies a statutory declaration of solvency declaring that the company will be able to pay all its debts within 12 months of the passing of the resolution to wind up the company.

If a company which is to be wound up voluntarily is insolvent then the winding up is referred to as a creditors' voluntary winding up. In any such case the company must cause a meeting of the creditors of the company to be summoned for the day, or the day next following the day, on which there is to be held the meeting at which the resolution for voluntary winding up is to be proposed. A full statement of the position of the company's affairs together with a list of creditors of the company and the amounts owed must be laid before the meeting of creditors. The creditors at their meeting may appoint a liquidator in place of the one previously appointed by the company.

Liquidation subject to the supervision of the court

When a company has passed a resolution for voluntary winding up, the court may make an order, following the presentation of a petition, that the voluntary winding up shall continue but subject to such supervision of the court as the court thinks fit.

Receivership

A receiver is usually appointed by the holder of a debenture constituting a security document. The person appointed receiver, normally an accountant, takes control of the assets of the company which are charged in favour of the creditor, and realises them to satisfy the claim of the creditor.

It is usual for the appointment of a receiver to be followed by the compulsory liquidation of the company.

Striking off

If the Registrar of Companies has reasonable cause to believe that a company is not carrying on business or in operation, he may, after making certain inquiries of the company, strike the company off the register.

The directors of a company which has ceased to trade and has no assets or liabilities may request the Registrar to strike the company off the register.

Creditors

The legislation provides for the order in which distributions by a liquidator are required to be made. This is as follows:

- creditors secured by a fixed charge;
- expenses of the liquidation;

- the liquidator's fees;
- preferential creditors;
- creditors secured by a floating charge;
- unsecured creditors;
- contributories (members).

KPMG contact partner

Emilio J. Gomez
KPMG
PO Box 191
Suite C, 3rd Floor
Regal House
Queensway
Gibraltar

Telephone: +350 74015
Fax: +350 74016

Greece

Insolvency procedures

Greek law provides two basic insolvency procedures:

- bankruptcy in the case of complete and permanent inability to pay debts;
- placement under compulsory administration in the case of partial inability to pay debts when due.

Bankruptcy

Bankruptcy is available only to businesses, which includes sole traders, partnerships, corporations and all other companies or entities which engage in commercial operations.

Bankruptcy proceedings commence either by a declaration to the court by the insolvent business or by a petition to the court by creditors. It can also be declared by the court of its own motion, at least in theory, although rarely in practice.

Once a business owner has been declared bankrupt by court decision, it is deprived of the management and administration of its entire estate. Assets acquired after the declaration of bankruptcy are exempted from the bankruptcy proceedings. A receiver, a lawyer, is appointed by the court after consultation with the general meeting of the creditors, in order to manage and administer the estate for the purpose of its being liquidated and distributed to the creditors in proportion to the size of their claims. A special judge is appointed by the court with whom the receiver must consult in all matters pertaining to the bankruptcy. All claims against the bankrupt become due as from the date of the decision pronouncing the bankruptcy and all interest ceases accruing except for claims secured by a mortgage or a lien.

The court fixes the date of the ceasing of payments which may be up to two years prior to the declaration of bankruptcy. From this date on, and within 10 days prior to it, all gratuitous transfers of assets are null and void. Payments of matured debts as well as any other transaction for value of the bankrupt which took place within this period may be rescinded if the payees or those who contracted with the bankrupt acted with knowledge of the stoppage of payments.

Creditors may announce their claims to the receiver and cannot sue or take enforcement measures against the bankrupt person. All creditors are treated equally, but secured creditors, i.e., those holding a mortgage or lien on the debtor's property, retain their preferential rights. Expenses of the administration of the liquidation are paid in first priority, and salaries, taxes, social security, legal fees and certain other claims also enjoy priority of payment, followed by ordinary creditors who share equally.

The assembly of creditors finally decides whether a compromise may be reached with the insolvent business, whereby bankruptcy proceedings end, otherwise a union of creditors is formed and the property is liquidated for subsequent distribution to creditors. If the bankruptcy proceedings cannot continue because of lack of assets, the court may, at the suggestion of the specially appointed judge, after consultation with the receiver, pronounce them terminated. In such case the creditors resume their rights against the person and the estate of the bankrupt.

A new bankruptcy code is presently under preparation to modernise the existing provisions and to bring them in line with the harmonisation endeavours within the European Union.

Compulsory and provisional administration of enterprises

A business may be subjected to compulsory administration for the purpose of satisfying pecuniary claims against it. The administrator is appointed by the court upon a petition brought by a creditor, a third person or even the debtor himself. The compulsory administration ends in case of foreclosure against the assets of the business or in case the business is declared bankrupt.

Special provisions apply when the business is operated under the legal forms of corporation or partnership. (In the following discussion, the term 'corporation' refers also to partnerships and 'shareholders' includes partners.) Corporations which stop payments, instead of being declared bankrupt, may be subjected by the court, at the petition of creditors representing the majority of the claims, either to the management and the administration of the creditors or to a special liquidation as described below.

Such a corporation is first placed under provisional administration upon the consent of a special committee which is appointed by the Governor of the Bank of Greece. The court will appoint the person proposed by creditors representing the majority of the claims as administrator, and in case of disagreement, the person proposed by the above committee. As from the day following the date of filing the petition of the creditors with the above committee for its approval, foreclosure against the corporation's assets is prohibited and any bankruptcy proceedings are suspended.

The general meeting of the shareholders must decide whether to approve the continuation of the management and administration of the corporation by the creditors. In case of disagreement, the President of the Court of Appeal will irrevocably decide on the matter.

If the decision is against the continuation, the matter is referred to the special committee of the Bank of Greece, which may either allow the corporation to return to its normal status or decide that it be placed under a special liquidation by a court decision.

If it is decided that the corporation will continue to operate under the management and administration of the creditors, all the functions of the general meeting of the shareholders are transferred to the assembly of the creditors and all management functions are transferred to a management committee appointed by the assembly of the creditors. The creditors are granted registered titles with a nominal value equal to the amount of their claim. These titles confer the right to annual dividends of 6 per cent of the nominal value and priority in the capital of the corporation in case of dissolution. Net profits are used to redeem the creditor's registered titles. If all such titles are redeemed, the control of the corporation reverts to the shareholders. The assembly of creditors may authorise the dissolution or special liquidation of the corporation, for which the approval of the special committee of the Bank of Greece is required. Such approval is not granted if fewer than five years or more than 12 years have elapsed following the placement of the corporation under the administration of the creditors.

The corporation is placed under special liquidation if it was so decided originally by the court when the corporation was placed under provisional administration or if it is so decided later by the court. In such instances the administrator functions as liquidator and he may sell the assets of the corporation at auction, which is governed by strict rules, not allowing for deferment of proceedings and aimed at an expeditious completion of the liquidation.

A special government agency has been established for the purpose of undertaking the administration and reorganisation of enterprises encountering severe financial problems.

KPMG contact person

Constantine Papacostopoulos
KPMG Peat Marwick Kyriacou
Stratigou Tombra 3
153 42 Aghia Paraskevi
Athens
Greece

Telephone: +30 (1) 6062 100
Fax: +30 (1) 6062 111

Hong Kong

Legislation

The legislation concerning corporate insolvency is contained largely in the Companies Ordinance and the Companies (Winding-up) Rules. Certain aspects of the Bankruptcy Ordinance (and the related Bankruptcy Rules) are also applicable in liquidation of insolvent companies.

Insolvency procedures

Corporate insolvency proceedings available include:

- contractual arrangements;
- schemes of arrangement;
- creditors' voluntary liquidation;
- compulsory liquidation;
- court liquidation under a regulating order;
- receivership.

In addition to the above insolvency procedures, solvent or defunct companies may be disposed of by way of:

- members' voluntary liquidation;
- striking off.

There are presently no specific licensing or registration requirements for insolvency practitioners; however, in nearly all cases, they are certified public accountants registered under the Professional Accountants Ordinance.

Contractual arrangement

Contractual arrangements are by mutual agreement between the debtor company and its creditors. There is no need to involve the court. The terms of the arrangement are set by the parties involved.

These terms require 100 per cent agreement by the relevant class or classes of creditors concerned; the company and the creditors thus becoming contractually bound by the terms of the arrangement. Once approved, creditors will have close control over the implementation of the arrangement. They would normally form a steering committee with an insolvency practitioner as supervisor or trustee to monitor progress.

Scheme of arrangement

These are essentially the same as the contractual arrangements except that they require agreement by at least 75 per cent in value and 50 per cent in number of the creditors voting at the relevant meetings and must be sanctioned by the court.

Although agreement by 100 per cent of the creditors voting is not required, once approved by the court, the terms are binding on all creditors.

Creditors' voluntary liquidation

Somewhat contrary to what the name suggests, creditors have no role in initiating creditors' voluntary liquidation. The directors of a company, realising that there may be no real prospects of the company meeting demands of creditors, call an extraordinary general meeting (EGM) when members may resolve, by a special resolution, to wind up the company.

A meeting of creditors held after the EGM (on the same day as or the day following the EGM) would then confirm the appointment of a liquidator (if any) as proposed by the members or make their own appointment. They may also form a committee of inspection of not more than five persons (including any nominated by members at the EGM) to assist the liquidator with the liquidation administration.

Creditors would have considerable influence over the handling of the administration by the liquidator as certain powers of the liquidator are only exercised with sanction from the creditors at a meeting, the committee of inspection or the court.

As an alternative to the above, the majority of the directors of a company, may resolve at a meeting called for that purpose to have the company wound up and that one of them should make the requisite statutory declaration and file the same with the Companies Registry under s. 228A of the Companies Ordinance. Thus a company may be put into liquidation without any resolution from members or creditors. Members and creditors meet subsequently to decide mainly on the choice of the liquidator. A provisional liquidator is usually appointed by the directors to safeguard the assets of the company during the interim period. This method of commencing a liquidation is unique to Hong Kong.

Compulsory liquidation

Compulsory liquidation is set in motion by the presentation of a winding-up petition. Although the company itself may, after passing a special resolution to that effect, apply by way of petition to the court to wind up, most compulsory or court liquidations are initiated by unsatisfied judgment creditors or creditors who have served a 'statutory demand' on the company but have not received payment within 21 days.

Relevant government officials may also file the petition if authorised to do so by law, e.g., the Financial Secretary under the Banking Ordinance or the Companies Ordinance or the Securities and Futures Commission under the Securities and Futures Ordinance.

A provisional liquidator (usually the official receiver) may be appointed by the court to protect the assets of the company after the filing but before the hearing of the petition. A special manager may also be appointed by the court upon the application of the provisional liquidator, to assist with management of the affairs of the company.

When the winding-up order is made, the official receiver, if not yet the provisional liquidator, automatically becomes the provisional liquidator. The official receiver then arranges for the first meetings of the contributors and creditors of the company (to be held normally within three months of the granting of the winding-up order unless a court order is granted for the liquidation, with estimated assets of less than HK$200,000, to be dealt with under the summary procedures). At these meetings, contributors and creditors may appoint a liquidator to replace the official receiver and appoint a committee of inspection, as in the case of a creditors' voluntary liquidation. Contributories refer to persons who may be liable to contribute to the assets of an insolvent liquidation. Though somewhat misleading, contributories include shareholders who have paid up in full for their shares in limited companies.

It is possible for creditors in a compulsory liquidation to resolve at a meeting to apply to the court to convert the liquidation into a creditors' voluntary liquidation. Application has to be made within three months from the first meeting of the creditors.

Formal proofs of debts are required to be filed with the liquidator before claims may be adjudicated.

Although the official receiver may not be acting as liquidator of a company under compulsory liquidation, he still maintains his supervisory role in the administration. Upon filing of the liquidation receipts and payments accounts (every six months), he may request that the liquidator's accounts be audited by his office. Funds received by the liquidator (subject to an amount agreed to be retained) must be remitted to and disbursed from the Companies Liquidation Account under the control of the Official Receiver's Office.

Court liquidation under a regulating order

Under specific circumstances, e.g., due to the large number of creditors or contributors, adherence to full procedures of a compulsory liquidation may not be appropriate. The court may order that a liquidation be conducted under a regulatory order.

The main divergence from normal compulsory liquidation procedures is that no meeting of contributories or creditors need be held to appoint a liquidator or a committee of inspection. These appointments are made directly by the court.

Receivership

A receiver is a person, normally an insolvency practitioner, appointed to take possession of specific property to safeguard it, to receive income from it or to dispose of it. Where the receiver takes control of the general conduct of a business (including assets), he is called a receiver and manager. A receiver does not wind up or liquidate the company.

Receivers are usually appointed under debentures or charge documents granted in favour of a bank, as security for lending or general banking facilities, after the customer fails to repay the loans as demanded by the bank. The debenture may incorporate charges on specific property (fixed charge) or the general business undertaking of a company (floating charge) under the Companies Ordinance. The security thus afforded to the debenture holder may be a fixed charge, a floating charge or a combination of both.

A receiver may be appointed by the court, for example, to safeguard property which is the subject of a dispute or pursuant to a charging order in debt recovery actions. A receiver may also be appointed under the provisions of a statute, e.g., the Drug Trafficking (Recovery of Proceeds) Ordinance.

The receiver's primary duty is to the debenture holder who appointed him and his task is to realise sufficient assets to pay off the debt due to his appointee. Where the appointment is under a floating charge, or a charge originally created as such, the receiver would need first to settle the claims of the preferential creditors, who take precedence over the floating charge debenture holder.

Whilst the receiver is not appointed by the general body of creditors and he does not have any statutory responsibility to call meetings of creditors or to account to them for his administration, a receiver should nonetheless have regard to the possible interest of the unsecured creditors in disposing of the assets under the charge. As a matter of professional courtesy and particularly where the receiver is attempting over a prolonged period of time to dispose of the business as a going concern, he may wish to retain the goodwill and cooperation of the general body of creditors by issuing to them periodic reports of the progress of the receivership.

If there are surplus funds after payment to the debenture holder, these should be returned to the company or passed to any liquidator appointed. The receiver would not be paying any dividends to unsecured creditors in any case.

General insolvency issues

Priority of claims

In insolvency proceedings generally, the assets available will be distributed amongst the various types of claims in the following order:

- costs and expenses of the insolvency proceeding, including the remuneration of the insolvency practitioner;
- creditors secured by a fixed charge;
- preferential creditors — e.g., certain debts due to employees or the government;

- creditors secured by a floating charge;
- unsecured creditors in general.

Where there are insufficient funds to pay any class of the claims in full, payment will be made pro rata. Where there are surplus funds after payment of all the above claims, interest accruing during the period of the insolvency proceedings (where appropriate) will be paid before any funds are returned to the shareholders.

Statement of affairs

In all kinds of insolvency proceedings, the financial position of a company would have to be summarised and presented as a statement of affairs within a period normally not more than between 28 days from commencement of the relevant proceedings, except in the case of members' voluntary liquidation where the statement has to be incorporated in the declaration of solvency. In a compulsory liquidation and a receivership, the statement in statutory prescribed form sets out the assets and liabilities of the company as at the date of the winding-up order or receivership, as well as the estimated realisable values of those assets. A list of creditors with their estimated claims is usually included. Statements of affairs used for voluntary liquidation or voluntary arrangements do not have any particular set format but practitioners tend to follow the format as prescribed with due modifications as appropriate.

Recovery of assets

Liquidators of companies are empowered to undertake investigations and, where offences involving fraud or deception are proved, may seek redress personally against the directors and officers concerned, who may be required to repay or restore the property to the company or make such other pecuniary compensation or contribution to the assets of the company as the court considers appropriate. In more severe cases, criminal prosecution may follow and, where convicted, the relevant director or officer may be imprisoned. Malpractice includes:

- fraudulent trading, where the business is carried on with intent to defraud creditors or for any other fraudulent purpose;
- misfeasance where directors have breached their fiduciary duties to the company or have misapplied or retained property of the company for their personal benefit;
- fraudulent preference or transactions at an undervalue: the liquidator may challenge transactions at an undervalue, or creditors who have been preferred against any other creditors by the company within six months of commencement of the liquidation;
- disposition after commencement of compulsory liquidation: these dispositions or payments are void against the liquidator and the recipients of these funds or assets have to return the funds or assets to the liquidator;
- destruction or falsification of books and records: directors and officers may be charged for the intentional destruction or falsification of books and records of a company within 12 months of the commencement of liquidation (no time limit for falsification) or thereafter.

Auditors, liquidators and receivers of a company may be regarded as officers for these purposes.

Dissolution of companies

In voluntary liquidation, the liquidator calls final meetings of contributories and/or creditors to obtain his release. The company is deemed to be dissolved three months after filing by the liquidator of the final accounts and return of the final meetings with the Registrar of Companies.

In compulsory liquidation, the liquidator files the final accounts with the court and he may then obtain from the court his release as liquidator. The official receiver then files the relevant certificate with the Registrar of Companies and the company is deemed to be dissolved two years after this certificate has been registered. Upon application for release, the liquidator may apply at the same time for the dissolution of the company in which case the company dissolves as and when the court orders.

Disposition of solvent defunct companies

Members' voluntary liquidations

In a members' voluntary liquidation, a company which no longer wishes to exist, or which has achieved the purpose for which it was set up, realises all its assets, discharges all its liabilities and distributes the surplus funds among the shareholders. Members' voluntary liquidations are also common in group restructuring situations.

To commence the liquidation procedures, the majority of the directors of the company are required to make a declaration of solvency not more than five weeks before the company is put into liquidation, stating, *inter alia*, that creditors of the company are to be paid in full within 12 months of the commencement of liquidation. A statement of affairs of the company at the latest practicable date (not defined in statute) is attached to the declaration.

Liquidation starts when members of the company then pass a special resolution to wind up the company voluntarily at an extraordinary general meeting convened for that purpose. No meeting of creditors is required. The liquidation process itself may take more than 12 months, but creditors must be paid in full within 12 months of commencement of liquidation.

If, in the course of the liquidation, it should be found that assets are insufficient to meet the liabilities of the company within 12 months, the liquidator is under a duty to call a meeting of the creditors as soon as possible and to take steps to convert to a creditors' voluntary liquidation.

Striking off

Every company incorporated in Hong Kong is registered with the Registrar of Companies. When a company ceases to exist, e.g., dissolved following formal liquidation procedures, it is struck off the register.

Where companies have become dormant for a prolonged period of time and have defaulted on various statutory duties regarding the filing of returns etc., the Registrar of Companies may take steps to strike off the company from the register. Alternatively, the directors of a dormant company may apply to the Registrar of Companies to strike off the company. The directors will be expected to provide reasons for the application, state the activities and financial position of the company and explain why formal liquidation procedures have not been adopted.

Where appropriate, the Registrar will advertise his intention to strike off companies in the *Government Gazette* and, if no objection is received before the set deadline, he will strike off the company, which will cease to exist.

Restoration of companies

There are express provisions in the Companies Ordinance for companies which have been dissolved or struck off to be restored to the register, for specific purposes and under circumstances specified. These invariably require that an application be made to the court by the interested party and the restoration will be by way of a court order.

KPMG contact partner

Nick Etches
KPMG Peat Marwick
8th Floor, Prince's Building
10 Chater Road
Hong Kong

Telephone: +852 2522 60 22
Fax: +852 2845 25 88

Hungary

Legislation

Insolvency legislation is set out in Law IL of 1991 on Bankruptcy Procedures, Liquidation Procedures and Final Settlement. This Law, which has been in effect from 1 January 1992, covers all business organisations. There is no legislation relating to the bankruptcy of individuals.

Insolvency procedures

Types of insolvency

Bankruptcy

This is similar to the Chapter 11 provisions in the USA. It is a process through which a business organisation facing financial difficulties may gain a 90-day moratorium in which to reach agreement with its creditors on the settlement of its debts.

The head of a business organisation is required to declare bankruptcy if the organisation is unable to meet its debts within 90 days of their falling due. The head must notify all financial institutions where the organisation's bank accounts are kept. The Court of Registration publishes its decision to accept the declaration of bankruptcy within 15 days of being notified. Bankruptcy may not be declared within three years of the publication of a previous bankruptcy.

During the 90 days following the publication of the bankruptcy proceedings, the organisation is entitled to a moratorium on the settlement of monetary claims against it. This moratorium does not include wages, salaries and similar amounts due to employees. The moratorium may be extended by a further 30 days upon the request of both the organisation and its creditors.

Upon the request of the creditors the court will appoint a bankruptcy trustee to represent the interests of the creditors. The creditors bear the trustee's costs. The bankruptcy trustee will be one of a panel of 'eligible liquidators' designated by Government decree.

The organisation is to prepare a plan detailing its proposals to restore its solvency and to settle its debts. Within 60 days of the start of bankruptcy proceedings the organisation is set a date for a settlement meeting with its creditors. Notification of the meeting should be accompanied by a copy of the plan and published in two national newspapers at least eight days prior to the meeting.

The creditors may form an elected board to represent their interests. The organisation and the bankruptcy trustee should be notified within eight days of the composition and the negotiating powers of such a board.

The settlement proposal must be approved by all creditors present at the settlement meeting. The organisation must prepare minutes of the settlement meeting including the names of those creditors invited to the meeting and those who attended. A settlement document is to be prepared detailing the terms of the settlement accepted by the creditors.

The organisation must notify the court within three days of the settlement meeting, filing the settlement document and the settlement minutes. If the settlement meets the statutory requirements of the Law, the court declares the termination of proceedings within 15 days. An appeal against this may be raised within eight days. Following this the court will publish the final decree declaring the termination of all proceedings.

Should no settlement be reached, liquidation procedures will commence.

Liquidation

The liquidation process begins:

- as a result of a bankruptcy where no settlement is reached;
- at the request of the business organisation, creditors, or the liquidator of a final settlement process (i.e., a process by which a business organisation ceases to exist without a legal successor);
- at the request of the Court of Registration.

The court examines the validity of the request for liquidation and, in the case of a liquidation requested by a creditor, will examine the insolvency of the organisation and may grant a delay of 30 days to enable the debt to be settled.

The court issues a decree declaring the insolvency of the organisation and publishes details in the *Gazette of Firms.* A liquidator is appointed and creditors have 30 days from the date of publication in which to file their claims. Claims made after 30 days, but within a year, will be met only if there are sufficient funds following the settlement of all other claims. The court informs the appropriate authorities of the liquidation.

The panel of eligible liquidators is designated by Government decree.

Within 30 days the head of the organisation is to prepare an inventory of assets, financial statements on the basis of standard valuation principles and a tax return. These documents are to be submitted to the liquidator. The head must also consider potential environmental liabilities and inform the employees of the liquidation.

During the liquidation process the organisation and creditors may reach agreement regarding settlement of debts. The consent of half the creditors in each class covering two thirds of the total claims is required. The court is to approve the settlement.

It is the responsibility of the liquidator to examine the validity of all claims, to review contracts entered into by the organisation during the 12 months prior to liquidation and to realise the organisation's assets.

Once the liquidation process has been completed the liquidator is to prepare a closing balance sheet, a receipts and costs account, a final tax return, a final report and a proposal for the distribution of assets. These documents are to be filed with the court and the tax authorities. This must take place within two years of the start of liquidation procedures.

Within 30 days of the receipt of the documents the court will arrange a hearing. The liquidator, creditors and the representatives of the organisation are to attend and reach agreement on the proposal for distribution.

The order of distribution is:

- the costs of liquidation (these include payments to employees, severance pay, expenses, costs associated with the sale of assets and the liquidator's fee);
- claims secured by mortgage provided that the security was pledged at least six months prior to the start of the liquidation process;
- certain statutory payments to employees and former employees;
- other claims of private persons deriving from non-economic activities;
- social security and taxation obligations;
- other debts;
- interim interest and late payment penalties.

The court orders the conclusion of the liquidation and the dissolution of the organisation. Should any assets remain following the satisfaction of all creditors' claims, these are to be distributed to the owners in proportion to their ownership stake.

If the assets are insufficient to cover the costs of liquidation or if the required documentation cannot be prepared due to a lack of accounting records, the court may, at the request of the liquidator, decree a simplified liquidation. In this case the assets are to be sold and the organisation dissolved within 90 days.

Final accounting (voluntary liquidation)

Final accounting takes place where an economic organisation ceases to exist without a legal successor, other than in the case of a liquidation. The head of the organisation must inform the court within eight days of the decision to dissolve the organisation. A liquidator is appointed. The liquidator may be an owner or employee of the organisation.

The court publishes details of the commencement of final accounting procedures in the *Gazette*. The liquidator is required to notify the relevant authorities (about 10). Creditors have 30 days in which to file their claims.

The head of the organisation is required to prepare financial statements and tax returns within 30 days. The liquidator settles all liabilities and realises all assets of the organisation. If the liquidator realises that the assets are insufficient to cover the liabilities he is obliged to promptly file an application for liquidation proceedings to begin.

Following the settlement of all liabilities and the realisation of assets, at latest within a year of the publication date, the liquidator is to prepare financial statements. Following the distribution of any profits, the liquidator prepares a final balance sheet, a closing tax return, a final report and a proposal for the distribution of the assets. These documents are to be submitted to the court which orders the striking off of the economic organisation from the Trade Register.

Due to the need for multiple advertising and the extent of the notification procedures, voluntary liquidation may take up to a year to be effective, during which time certain reporting obligations remain.

KPMG contact partner

Mark Bownas
KPMG
Vaci ut 99
1139 Budapest
Hungary

Telephone: +36 (1) 270 7100
Fax: +36 (1) 270 7101

Iceland

Legislation

The Bankruptcy Act was enacted in 1991 (Nr. 21) and contains provisions in respect of two types of insolvency procedures: postponement of payments and bankruptcy. Legislation enacted in 1924 contains the framework for a composition with creditors in an insolvency situation.

Insolvency procedures

Suspension of payments

A debtor (an individual or a company) having serious financial difficulties and wishing to restructure his finances may apply for a court order permitting a suspension of payments. A suspension of payments can be permitted initially for a maximum period of three months and an extension may be granted for not more than a further two months. The debtor is required to have the assistance of a lawyer or a State-authorised public accountant. During the suspension of payments the debtor must neither pay any due amounts nor undertake any substantial obligations. During this period it is not possible to complete any legal action against the estate of the debtor for the purpose of securing an amount due and creditors can neither bring about a forced sale of an asset belonging to the debtor nor start bankruptcy procedures.

Bankruptcy

The filing of a petition in bankruptcy of an individual or a company may be made either by the debtor or by a creditor who has unsuccessfully brought legal action against the debtor for the payment of a debt. The adjudication of bankruptcy is made by a bankruptcy court. After such a decree the debtor loses possession of his property, and legal actions directed against that property cannot be completed. The administration of the bankrupt estate is taken over by a liquidator appointed by the district court. The liquidator issues a proclamation requiring creditors to record their claims within normally two months.

The Bankruptcy Act contains provisions to ensure an equitable distribution of the bankrupt's net assets among the creditors. Various arrangements made by the debtor can be revoked if they were initiated within a certain period prior to the commencement of bankruptcy procedures. Certain acts performed by the creditors prior to bankruptcy to secure their claims automatically become revoked. The maximum period in respect of the invalidity or revocability of various acts or arrangements is two years. An asset in the possession of the bankrupt, but not owned by him, shall be handed over to the owner.

Claims against a bankrupt estate are paid in the following order:

- claims under contracts made by the liquidator and expenses in respect of the handling of the bankrupt estate;
- claims secured by a mortgage and other secured claims are paid out of the proceeds from the respective properties, subject to the claims set out above;
- wages and salaries, liability claims for breach of a work contract, dues to pension funds and similar funds, liability claims for accidental death or disability of employees, pension payments and expenses in relation to an attempted accord between the creditors prior to bankruptcy procedures — many of the claims in this category are protected by a statutory State guarantee;
- unsecured claims not specified elsewhere;
- claims for interest accruing after the issue of a bankruptcy decree;

- fines;
- donations and gifts.

Composition with creditors

A debtor may apply for a court order to establish a composition with his creditors either before bankruptcy procedures have started or after a bankruptcy has been decreed. A composition with creditors means that a certain proportion of unsecured creditors agree to accept a certain percentage of the amounts due as a full and final payment. If the court confirms such an arrangement it becomes binding upon all creditors that had the right to vote on the arrangement.

KPMG contact partner

Helgi V. Jonsson
KPMG Legal Services
Vegmúli 3
108 Reykjavik
Iceland

Telephone: +354 (1) 533 5555
Fax: +354 (1) 533 5550

India

Legislation

Indian insolvency law is divided into two distinct parts:

- law relating to corporate insolvencies which encompasses winding up and schemes of compromise, arrangements and amalgamation;
- law relating to individuals which is contained in the Presidency-Towns Insolvency Act (1909) and the Provincial Insolvency Act 1920.

The relevant legislative authority for liquidation and receivership fall within a statutory framework primarily composed of:

- the Companies Act 1956;
- the Companies (Court) Rules 1959;
- the Companies (Official Liquidators Account) Rules 1965;
- the Companies Liquidation Account Rules 1965.

Insolvency procedures

Compulsory liquidation

There are specific grounds for compulsory winding up by the court:

- the company passes a special resolution to that effect;
- membership is reduced below seven in a public company or below two in a private company;
- the statutory meeting is not held or the statutory report is not filed;
- the company does not commence business within one year or suspends business for one year;
- the company is unable to pay its debts;
- the court regards it as just and equitable that the company should be wound up.

The following may petition for the winding up:

- the company;
- any creditor;
- any contributory;
- the Registrar of Companies;
- any person authorised by the central government upon a report of an inspector;
- the official liquidator in the course of voluntary winding up or one subject to the court supervision in the interest of creditors or contributories.

Only an official liquidator appointed by the central government becomes, by virtue of his office, the liquidator of the company. In district courts, the official receiver for insolvency purposes attached to such court shall be the official liquidator; if there is no official receiver in the district court, any person may be appointed by the central government.

Voluntary liquidation

In a voluntary winding up, if the company is solvent and the directors are prepared to make a declaration of solvency, the winding up is a members' voluntary winding up. If, however, the company is not in a position to pay its debts in full or the directors are not prepared to make a declaration of solvency, then it is a creditors' voluntary winding up, i.e., the creditors will have the greater say in the winding up of the company.

In a members' voluntary winding up the company's general meeting must appoint one or more liquidators for winding up the affairs of the company. In a creditors' voluntary winding up the creditors and the company may nominate a person to be liquidator. If the creditors and the company nominate different persons, the person nominated by the creditors shall be the liquidator. However, on application to the court, the court may appoint any person as the liquidator.

Upon a liquidator's appointment:

- the powers of the board and all of the company's officers cease, unless the liquidator otherwise directs;
- usually, the liquidator sells the undertaking and all the property of the company for cash or against shares in another company, for distribution to the creditors and members.

Receivership

A debenture holder may appoint a receiver if such power is given to him by the debenture. The court may, however, appoint another receiver. On the appointment of a receiver by the debenture holder, the assets become specifically charged in favour of the debenture holder and the power of the company to deal with the charged assets in the ordinary course of business ceases. If the debenture holders have a charge on the whole of the undertaking of the company, the court usually appoints the receiver to be receiver and manager and thereupon the board of directors for all practical purposes becomes *functus officio*. The power of the receiver and manager is usually contained in the security documents, which normally provide for full powers to carry on business, receive income and to dispose of assets.

Scheme of compromise or arrangement

A company is empowered to compromise and settle disputes with its creditors. Where such compromise or arrangement is proposed between the company and its creditors, the scheme can be approved by the court and can be carried out under the supervision of the court. The advantage of taking a scheme to the court is that the court may stay suits and proceedings filed against the company.

Creditors

The principle of equality of division of assets among creditors is fundamental to the whole statutory scheme.

A secured creditor is one who holds a mortgage, charge or lien on the property of the debtor as a security for a debt, and who is in a position to recover partly or wholly from the assets of the debtor in priority to unsecured creditors. In a winding up a secured creditor has the following alternatives:

- he may ignore the liquidation altogether and rely on his security for the payment of all that may be due to him;
- he may value or realise his security and prove only for the balance;
- give up his security altogether and prove for the whole amount as an unsecured creditor.

An unsecured creditor is any person to whom the company owes a sum of money and who does not hold any security from the company. Unsecured creditors rank *pari passu* and if the assets are not sufficient their claims abate rateably. A secured or an unsecured creditor may apply to the court for a winding up by the court.

Preferential claims

Before distributions can be made to unsecured creditors, due regard must be given to 'preferential payments'. They are: rates and taxes having become due and payable to the central or State government or to a local authority within 12 months before commencement of winding up; all wages and salaries of employees not exceeding Rs1,000 for each employee and workman; compensation payable under Workmen's Compensation Act 1923; sums due to an employee from a provident fund, pension, gratuity or any other fund maintained by the company; expenses of investigation ordered by the central government into the affairs of a company; all accrued holiday remuneration; amounts due in respect of contributions payable during 12 months before winding up by the company as the employer of any person under the Employees' State Insurance Act 1948. These preferential payments rank *pari passu* and if the assets are not sufficient to pay all the preferential payments, they shall abate rateably. While preferential payments have priority over unsecured creditors, the costs of liquidation have priority over preferential payments.

Other matters

Liquidation is a laborious and lengthy process which could extend to several years.

Insolvency legislation in India provides a practical framework for creditors to exercise their legal rights to ensure that a company, unable to pay its debts, is placed in an appropriate form of insolvency administration. A debtor company is also able to avail itself of the liquidation proceedings or compromise proceedings to enable it to trade out of financial difficulties. Insolvency administration in India is generally not performed by accountants in public practice.

Under legislation in the country to help losing units, known variously as sick units or relief undertakings, the government from time to time places companies in this category with the consequence that pending litigation or claims are held in abeyance during the period that such status is given. It is not unusual for this status to continue over long periods and effectively for debts previously incurred virtually to be lost without a possibility of recovery in the foreseeable future. In such cases, insolvency proceedings have no meaning.

KPMG contact partner

Naresh Malhotra
KPMG
5th Floor, Shariff Chambers
14 Cunningham Road
Bangalore 560 052
India

Telephone: +91 (80) 220 46 00
Fax: +91 (80) 220 43 00

Indonesia

Legislation

The Commercial Law was first introduced regarding the insolvency law and subsequently Company Act No. 1/1995 was introduced in 1995.

The Commercial Law covers personal and institutional affairs while Company Act No. 1/1995 applies to limited corporation affairs only.

Insolvency procedures

The insolvency procedures, according to Company Act No. 1/1995 Chapter IX, can be instituted by an acclamation (decision without formal voting) or when 75 per cent or more of the shareholders agree to liquidate the company, or where the articles of association provide for a limited period of operation and extension is not required, or if there is an order from the court arising from a request by:

- State Attorney for the sake of public interest;
- one or more shareholder(s) who represent at least 10 per cent of the authorised shares;
- creditors because of unpaid liabilities;
- any concerned party where the articles of association have not been complied with.

The process for the liquidation of the company starts when the company is wound up where the company ceases its legal activities, makes an announcement in the local newspapers and sends registered letters to all of its creditors.

A liquidator is appointed by a shareholders' meeting or by the court but if a liquidator is not appointed, the board of directors acts as liquidator. The court may also appoint a new liquidator under the request of one or more shareholder(s), or by a request of the State Attorney. Shareholders' meetings are held to inform shareholders of the liquidation status. The liquidator is required to request cancellation of the company's registration licence and put a notice in the *State Gazette* of the Republic of Indonesia.

All creditors' claims have to be made within 120 days from the date of the newspaper announcement.

The Commercial Law defines that anyone who is unable to pay off liabilities can, by court order, institute bankruptcy proceedings. When a petition either by a person or institution is approved by court, the bankruptcy can be started.

The court also appoints a supervisory judge and a liquidating body called '*balai harta peninggalan*' to oversee the liquidation and distribution of assets.

Creditors may establish a committee, consisting of one to three creditors for the purpose of providing advice to the liquidating body during the liquidation process.

Creditors exercise their right to vote at creditors' meetings according to outstanding liabilities. For every Rp100 outstanding the creditor is entitled to one vote. The creditors' meeting is chaired by the supervisory judge and a decision is made when the majority agree to it.

Creditors

Creditors holding security will continue to have right to that security and may exercise its right over the assets without the liquidator. Creditors who have preferential or special treatment are given seniority status on the repayment distributions.

It is advisable that creditors, who do not get preferential or special treatment, promptly submit their claims immediately after the announcement because, in practice, the rule is first come first paid.

KPMG contact person

Kanaka Puradiredja
Hanadi Sudjendro & Rekan
Wisma Dharmala Sakti
10th Floor
JI Jenderal Sudirman 32
Jakarta 10220
Indonesia

Telephone: +62 (21) 570 6111
Fax: +62 (21) 570 3003

Ireland

Legislation

In the Republic of Ireland there are basically two types of insolvency:

- corporate insolvency, which relates to companies;
- personal insolvency or bankruptcy, which relates to individuals or partnerships.

A corporate insolvency may take the form of an examination, a receivership or a liquidation. The legislation governing examinations, receiverships and liquidations is contained in the Companies Acts 1963 to 1990 and in various Acts relating to employee entitlements. The law relating to personal insolvencies is contained in the Bankruptcy Act 1988.

Examiners, receivers and liquidators

There are no special qualifications prescribed by law for examiners, receivers or liquidators but, normally, an accountant in practice is appointed as an examiner, receiver or liquidator. However, certain persons are excluded from taking appointments as examiners, receivers or liquidators and these include the auditor and any officer of the debtor company.

Insolvency procedures

Examinations

The concept of examination was introduced into company law in the Republic of Ireland by the Companies (Amendment) Act 1990. The purpose of the legislation is to provide a mechanism for the rescue and return to health of ailing but potentially viable companies.

An examiner may be appointed to a company by an order of the court, following an application on petition to it for such an appointment.

A petition may be presented by:

- the company;
- the directors of the company;
- a creditor, including contingent creditors;
- members of the company holding not less than 10 per cent of the voting paid-up share capital.

In presenting a petition, it will be necessary to show that:

- the company is, or is likely to be, unable to pay its debts;
- no order has been made for the winding up of the company.

When the court makes an order appointing an examiner to a company, the company comes under the protection of the court from the time of the presentation of the petition. The period of examination is 90 days unless this is extended by the court. Whilst the company is under the protection of the court:

- no proceedings may be commenced or resolution passed for the winding up of the company;
- no receiver shall be appointed;
- no attachment, sequestration, distress or execution shall be put into force, except with the consent of the examiner;
- no repossession of goods under hire-purchase agreements, retention of title arrangements or lease arrangements may be made except with the consent of the examiner.

The role of the examiner is that of enquiry into and examination of the affairs of the company. The day-to-day management of the company remains with the board of directors.

The examiner must report to the court within 21 days of his appointment or such further time as the court will allow and must furnish to the court the results of his examination of the affairs of the company. Where the examiner expresses an opinion that:

- the whole or part of the undertaking is not capable of surviving as a going concern;
- a compromise or scheme of arrangement will not facilitate the company's survival;
- the continuance of the company's undertaking will not facilitate the company's survival;
- the continuance of the company's undertaking in whole or in part would not be more advantageous to the members or its creditors than a winding up;
- there is evidence of irregularities.

a court hearing will be held to consider the report and the court may make such order as it sees fit, including the termination of the protection of the court and the discharge of the examiner.

Where the examiner expresses a favourable opinion, namely, that the company is capable of survival as a going concern in whole or in part and that the formulation of proposals for a compromise or scheme of arrangement would facilitate the company's survival, there is no court hearing.

The examiner proceeds to formulate proposals for a scheme of arrangement and convenes meetings of members and creditors to consider and seek approval of the proposals. The examiner is obliged to report to the court within 42 days of his appointment and to furnish it with a report setting out details of the proposals and outcome of the meetings of the members and creditors.

The examiner's report is considered by the court which may decide to reject or confirm the proposals. When the proposals are confirmed the court must set a date for the implementation of the proposals. This date must not be later than 21 days after the date of confirmation by the court. The protection of the court to the company ceases on the implementation of the scheme of arrangement and the examiner's appointment is terminated on the same day.

Receivership

A receivership is a process by which a creditor who holds a charge on the assets of a company appoints an individual to take control of the assets and realise them to satisfy his claim. The right to appoint a receiver is normally contained in the security document, usually a debenture.

There are basically two types of charge: a fixed charge, which relates to such assets as land and buildings, and a floating charge, which covers all the assets of the company. The normal procedure is that lenders requiring security obtain both fixed and floating charges over the assets of the company to which they advance money. The function of a receiver is to deal with the claims of the secured and preferential creditors and, furthermore, he has a duty of care to the unsecured creditors.

Once a receiver is appointed, the powers of directors and executives are effectively terminated. The receiver is normally the agent of the company but he reports on his activities to the secured lender. He is obliged to file a six-monthly summary of his cash receipts and payments at the Companies Registration Office.

The proceeds of the realisations achieved by a receiver are distributed in the following order:

- creditors secured by way of a fixed charge, out of the proceeds of their security after costs of realisation;
- receiver's costs, including the receiver's remuneration;
- preferential creditors;
- creditors secured by way of a floating charge.

In the event that a receiver has surplus funds, having discharged the claims of the secured and preferential creditors, such funds are paid to the directors of the company or to a liquidator, if one has been appointed.

When the receiver has completed his assignment he is discharged by the secured lender who appointed him and he files a notice of ceasing to act in the Companies Registration Office.

Liquidations

There are two types of liquidation for insolvent companies: creditors' voluntary liquidation and court liquidation.

Creditors' voluntary liquidation

A creditors' voluntary liquidation arises where the company decides it is unable to pay its debts and continue in business. The members place the company in liquidation and nominate a liquidator to administer the liquidation. On the same day, the creditors meet and review the statement of affairs of the debtor company and they either confirm the appointment of the liquidator nominated by the members or they appoint a replacement of their own choice. Once appointed, the liquidator takes control of all the assets of the company and realises them for the benefit of all the creditors. There is a provision in the legislation that the conduct of the administration of a creditors' voluntary liquidation is supervised by a committee comprising representatives of the members and creditors, but this procedure is not always used.

During the course of the liquidation, a liquidator is obliged to hold annual meetings of members and creditors and he must file his cash account in the Companies Registration Office each year. When the affairs of the company are fully wound up, the liquidator holds final meetings of members and creditors and reports to them on the proceedings.

Court liquidation

A court liquidation may be commenced by either the members or a creditor lodging a petition with the High Court to have the company wound up.

Once the liquidator is appointed, he takes control of the assets of the company and realises them for the benefit of all the creditors of the company. A court liquidation is supervised by the Examiner of the High Court. When the affairs of a company are wound up, the liquidator is discharged by the court.

Function of a liquidator

The function of a liquidator is the same in either a creditors' voluntary liquidation or a court liquidation — it is to realise the assets of the company and to distribute the proceeds to the creditors in the order of priority. Distributions by a liquidator are in the following order:

- creditors secured by way of a fixed charge, out of the proceeds of their security after costs of realisation;
- expenses of liquidation;

- remuneration of the liquidator;
- super-preferential creditors;
- preferential creditors;
- creditors secured by way of a floating charge;
- unsecured creditors;
- members.

Members' voluntary liquidation

A members' voluntary liquidation applies only to solvent companies. The liquidator is appointed by the members and he realises the assets and distributes the proceeds in the same order as in a creditors' voluntary liquidation or in a court liquidation. When the affairs of the company are fully wound up, the liquidator holds a meeting of the members and reports to them on his activities.

Members' voluntary liquidations are commonly used to wind up the affairs of family companies and the subsidiaries of multinational corporations.

Creditors

Creditors are divided into three main categories; secured, preferential and unsecured.

Secured creditors

A secured creditor is one who holds some form of security, usually a fixed and/or floating charge on the assets of a company. In an insolvency, a secured creditor who holds a fixed charge would usually have the following options:

- appoint a receiver;
- allow a liquidator to dispose of the assets, the subject of his charge, on his behalf;
- take possession of the assets and dispose of them;
- value and take possession of the assets and claim for any unsecured balance.

A secured creditor who holds a floating charge can appoint a receiver.

Preferential creditors

A preferential creditor is one who has a preference over ordinary creditors. The preference is conferred by law and preferential creditors consist of local rates, debts due to the State in respect of taxes and other amounts due to the State for payments made by the State to the employees, subject to certain limits, in respect of their preferential claims. The preferential claims of employees include arrears of wages, holiday pay, minimum notice and redundancy.

In liquidations only, there is a special class of preferential creditor called a super-preferential creditor. A super-preferential creditor relates to amounts due to the State in respect of social welfare deductions made from the wages of employees and which have not been paid to the State.

Unsecured creditors

An unsecured creditor is one who does not hold any security and is not entitled to any preference. Such creditors are usually the suppliers of goods and services.

KPMG contact partner

Ray Jackson
KPMG,
1 Stokes Place
St Stephen's Green,
Dublin 2
Ireland

Telephone: +353 (1) 7081000
Fax: +353 (1) 7081122

Isle of Man

Legislation

The legislation is based on, and broadly speaking equivalent to, that in force in the United Kingdom prior to 1948. The principal state governing corporate insolvency is the Companies Consolidation Act 1931, especially parts III, V and VI.

Personal insolvency is governed by the Bankruptcy Code 1892, the Bankruptcy Procedure Act 1892, the Bankruptcy Code Amendment Act 1903, and the Bankruptcy Act 1987.

Relevant to both corporate and personal insolvency procedures on the Isle of Man are the Preferential Payments Acts 1908 and 1973, the Recovery of Rent Act 1954, and the Employment Act 1991.

Insolvency procedures

The principal corporate insolvency procedures on the Isle of Man are receivership, creditors' voluntary liquidation and compulsory liquidation.

Receivership

Banks and other lenders normally require a corporate borrower to give security over its assets in the form of a debenture giving the lender power to appoint a receiver, or receiver and manager, if certain events occur, for example, the failure of the borrower to repay the lender on demand.

A receiver, who is usually a chartered accountant, takes control of the assets specified in the debenture. In many cases the borrower has pledged all its assets and the receiver controls the whole of the company's business with a power to manage the business given in the terms of the debenture. The receiver will act as agent of the company.

With the object of maximising recovery for the debenture holder, a receiver must decide whether to carry on trading with a view to selling as a going concern or to close the business down and sell the assets separately.

A receiver must pay for any goods or services purchased by the company in the course of receivership but is not responsible for pre-receivership debts, except that preferential creditors must be paid out of the proceeds of sale of floating charge assets in priority to the debenture holder. Preferential creditors include, in order of priority:

- debts due to the Crown (e.g., taxation);
- rates payable within the previous 12 months (e.g., water and local authority rates);
- arrears of wages limited to a maximum of £2,000 and accrued holiday pay;
- national insurance contributions;
- rent arising within the previous 12 months.

Once the assets pledged by the borrower (or sufficient of those assets to satisfy the debenture holder and the preferential creditors) have been realised and the proceeds distributed as appropriate, the receiver will file a notice of ceasing to act. Control over any remaining assets will pass to the directors, or to the liquidator, if one has been appointed.

Creditors' voluntary liquidation

Creditors' voluntary liquidation is most frequently initiated by directors who have formed the view that the company cannot by reason of its liabilities continue its business and that it is advisable to wind up. The directors call a meeting of shareholders to place the company into liquidation and a meeting of creditors, which is chaired by one of the directors.

Both the shareholders' meeting and the creditors' meeting may nominate a liquidator, and if there is a conflict, the creditors' choice prevails. The meetings may also appoint a committee of inspection to act with the liquidator.

The liquidator is responsible for collecting in and converting into cash the company's assets. He will only allow the company to trade under exceptional circumstances. A creditor who has security over an asset of the company may realise that security in order to satisfy the debt due to him but must account to the liquidator for any surplus.

The liquidator has a duty to ascertain the company's liabilities, and to consider creditors' claims, admitting or rejecting these as appropriate. He then distributes the proceeds of the company's assets in the prescribed order of priority as set out below:

- creditors secured by a fixed charge (to the extent of the value of the assets charged);
- preferential creditors;
- creditors secured by a floating charge (to the extent of the value of the assets charged);
- other creditors with admitted claims;
- shareholders.

Compulsory liquidation

A creditor who is unable to obtain payment from a company is entitled to petition the court for the winding up of that company on the grounds that it is unable to pay its debts. The court may order that the company be wound up and in this case will normally appoint the petitioner's nominee, who would normally be a chartered accountant, as provisional liquidator and deemed official receiver ('the provisional liquidator').

The provisional liquidator secures the company's assets and calls upon the directors to submit a detailed statement of the company's affairs. He also calls meetings of the company's creditors and members.

The meetings decide whether an application should be made to the court to confirm the provisional liquidator as liquidator or to appoint another person as liquidator. A committee of inspection may also be appointed if the meetings so wish.

A compulsory liquidation is a liquidation by the court and both a provisional liquidator and a liquidator in a compulsory liquidation are accountable to the court for their actions. If there is no committee of inspection, they must seek sanction from the court before taking certain steps.

Otherwise, the procedures followed by a liquidator in a compulsory liquidation are similar to those followed in a creditors' voluntary liquidation.

KPMG contact partner

Peter Francis Pell-Hiley
KPMG
Heritage Court
41 Athol Street
Douglas
Isle of Man IM99 1HN

Telephone: +44 (1624) 681 000
Fax: +44 (1624) 681 098

Israel

Legislation

Procedures relating to liquidation in Israel are governed by the Companies Ordinance (New Version) 1983, and the Companies Regulations (Liquidation) 1987.

Insolvency procedures

Israel has two main methods of handling companies facing difficulties. The first method — in which the final aim is to terminate the business activity of the company, realise all its assets and erase its status as a business entity — is liquidation. The second method is nomination of a receiver for the company to try to rehabilitate the company by reorganisation of its business activity and its assets, arrange for repayment of its liabilities and, in the end, transfer management of the company to its owners.

In spite of the above differentiation between liquidation/nomination of a liquidator and receivership/nomination of a receiver, nomination of a liquidator may result in the company's rehabilitation while nomination of a receiver may be a preliminary stage in the winding up of the company and its erasure. Liquidation pertains to a registered company, foreign company or, at the request of the government's legal counsel/attorney-general, a company in the process of registration.

Below are the types of liquidation which may be implemented in Israel:

- liquidation by a court of law;
- voluntary liquidation by the shareholders of a company;
- voluntary liquidation by the shareholders of a company under court supervision.

The last two types of voluntary liquidation are based on existing regulations in the Companies Ordinance or can be undertaken by special resolution because of company debts.

Liquidation by a court of law

A company, its creditors (including contingent and future creditors) or a partner may lodge a request for liquidation of a company with a court of law.

Causes of liquidation

Causes of liquidation include:

- a special resolution of a company, being an inactive company;
- the number of shareholders becomes less than the minimum required;
- insolvency of the company;
- any other cause which a court of law may deem just and right to declare liquidation of a company.

Insolvency is defined as an overdue period of three weeks for debt repayment, non-compliance with a court order, or a judgment or presentation of evidence to the court that the company is unable to repay its debts.

Liquidation procedures

The first step in the liquidation procedure is presentation of a request for liquidation to a court of law and its publication in the official government gazette, *Reshumot*. A written objection to the liquidation may be lodged.

A court order to liquidate a company is effective retrospectively from the date of presentation of the request. Certain actions taken after presentation of the request are nullified (e.g., transfer of shares, change of status of shareholders, termination of contracts, etc.).

During the interval between the date of presentation of a request for liquidation and the date of the related court order, the court is authorised to delay certain procedures and to nominate a temporary liquidator, if so requested.

The liquidator must be an attorney at law or a certified public accountant.

Powers of a liquidator

A liquidator has the following powers (some subject to court order): to accumulate all property and assets of the company including those held by others (debtors, trustees etc.), to interrogate persons suspected of holding assets of the company or, in certain cases to present personal claims against managers and directors (in the event of disclosure of fraudulent acts etc.).

Implications of liquidation

A court order for liquidation of a company terminates the rights of its shareholders to supervise its activities. With the commencement of liquidation procedures, legal proceedings against the company cease, with several exceptions.

Creditors

The order of distribution of the resources of a company is determined by law as follows:

- liens in respect of taxation on specific real estate;
- rights of holders of liens;
- rights of creditors;
- secured creditors who have registered specific liens on assets;
- rights of set-off;
- payment of liquidation expenses;
- debts with preference under the law (e.g., employees' salaries);
- rights of creditors with floating liens;
- non-secured debts to creditors;
- payment of par value of shares to their holders;
- distribution of the balance of the assets among the shareholders (in the case of voluntary liquidation).

KPMG contact partner

Roni Sivan
KPMG Braude Bavly
27–29 Hamered Street
Tel Aviv 68125
Israel

Telephone: +972 (3) 5140808
Fax: +972 (3) 5101918

Italy

Legislation

The statutory framework of Italian bankruptcy and liquidation law is primarily contained in:

- Articles 2272–2283, 2309–2312, 2448–2457 Civil Code, for liquidation of partnerships and companies;
- Article 2221 Civil Code, for insolvency in a commercial activity;
- Bankruptcy Act 1942 (R.D.L. 16 March 1942, n. 267) for bankruptcy and other arrangement procedures;
- Insolvent Large Corporation Act (L. 3 April 1979, n. 95) for extraordinary controlled management of large corporations in insolvency.

Insolvency procedures

Italian law provides for bankruptcy procedures for both incorporated and unincorporated associations and does not regulate the dissolution of a company, whether bankrupt or not, with only one procedure such as winding up but provides for bankruptcy procedures on the one hand and liquidation procedures on the other.

Liquidation

In a general sense, the term 'liquidation' (*liquidazione*) refers to a winding-up procedure that does not necessarily imply an insolvency situation; liquidation can also be decided voluntarily by a partnership or company.

No particular requirements are provided for liquidation of individual firms.

Stock corporations and limited liability companies can be dissolved and consequently liquidated due to one of the following causes:

- completion of the time fixed in the by-laws;
- achievement of the purpose for which it was established or cases where it is no longer possible to achieve this purpose;
- that the shareholders' meeting can no longer work or remains inactive;
- the capital is reduced below the legal minimum and the shareholders' meeting does not provide for an increase;
- a resolution of the shareholders' extraordinary meeting;
- any other reason fixed in the by-laws;
- a judgment of the court ordering the sale of the assets (for some categories of enterprises: Civil Code Articles 2448, 2620);
- bankruptcy, compulsory administrative liquidation, extraordinary administration.

In order to put a company into voluntary liquidation a resolution to that effect must be passed at an extraordinary shareholders' meeting. This meeting must appoint one or more liquidators who act in place of the directors and whose main function is to dispose of the company's assets, pay off its creditors and prepare the final liquidation balance sheet and a report specifying the amount, if any, of the proceeds of the liquidation available for distribution to each shareholder.

During the liquidation the shareholders' meeting retains the powers of approving the balance sheet, appointing the statutory auditors and modifying the articles of incorporation. The board of statutory auditors still functions during the liquidation.

The company's board of statutory auditors is required to examine the final liquidation balance sheet and issue a report which, together with the balance sheet and liquidators' report, must be deposited with the court for a period of three months. During this period shareholders have the opportunity, if they wish, to raise objections to the liquidation balance sheet. If no objections are raised, however, the final liquidation balance sheet is deemed to have been approved and accordingly the liquidator may distribute the proceeds, if any, of the liquidation to the shareholders. Immediately subsequent to this, the company is struck off the register of business enterprises and the books are deposited with the court which retains them for a period of 10 years.

Bankruptcy

All entrepreneurs who engage in a commercial occupation, except for public bodies and small entrepreneurs, shall be subject to the provisions on bankruptcy (art. 1(1) of Royal Decree No. 267 1942 known as the Bankruptcy Act).

The entrepreneur who is insolvent shall be declared bankrupt (art. 5(1) of Royal Decree No. 267). Bankruptcy (*fallimento*) is declared on petition by the debtor or one or more creditors; on application by the public prosecutor; by the court of its own motion.

The court appoints a bankruptcy judge to supervise the bankruptcy procedure and a trustee (usually an accountant or a lawyer) to handle the details of the procedure. The trader loses his right to manage his business or sell his assets.

The trustee must dispose of all of the trader's assets, verify all creditors' claims and distribute available funds to the creditors as shown on the schedule approved by the court.

The head of the bankrupted undertaking is registered in the official register of bankrupts and his name may only be removed from the list when:

- all creditors have been paid in full;
- a composition has been arrived at and approved by the creditors;
- five years have elapsed since being declared bankrupt.

The ranking of creditors relating to the above mentioned procedures is regulated by art. 111 of the Bankruptcy Act and arts 2777 to 2783 of the Civil Code. The ranking is similar for all these procedures and can be summarised as follows:

- credits due for costs of management of the procedure and for the continuation of the enterprise, if authorised;
- credits secured by a pledge or mortgage, credits having a general privilege such as claims for salaries, social contributions, taxes;
- unsecured credits.

The procedure ends when:

- all assets have been shared between creditors;
- a bankruptcy agreement has been met;
- no creditor has proposed claims;

- all creditors have been paid in full;
- assets are insufficient to satisfy creditors' claims.

The duration of the procedure depends on the assets involved.

Preventive arrangement

Preventive arrangement (*concordato preventivo*) aims to avoid putting entrepreneurs into bankruptcy. However, certain conditions regarding the trader and conditions of facts are required for this procedure to be granted:

- the business has been registered in the register of enterprises for at least two years or from the starting of the business if its duration has been shorter (this condition is actually only enforced regarding companies);
- proper books of account have been kept;
- the debtor has not been the subject of bankruptcy or preventive arrangement within the preceding five years;
- the debtor has not been convicted of bankruptcy or any other insolvency offences (arts 216 ff, Bankruptcy Act);
- the debtor must either provide a tangible guarantee amounting to 100 per cent of secured and 40 per cent or more of unsecured claims within six months of ratification of the arrangement or assign all his assets (valued at at least 100 per cent of secured and 40 per cent of unsecured claims) to his creditors upon application.

Only the entrepreneur can initiate this procedure. On application he must account for the events which led to his insolvency and give reasons for requesting an arrangement. He must also file his books of account, an analysis and a forecast of his business and a list of the creditors.

The proposal of arrangement is investigated by the judicial commissioner (usually an accountant) appointed by the court. He must verify all items submitted by the entrepreneur upon application, and notify creditors as to the details of the meeting to discuss the proposed arrangement, the entrepreneur's financial position and reasons for insolvency.

After the arrangement has been approved by the majority of unsecured creditors, representing two thirds of creditors, the court must confirm the arrangement by a judgment, and the judicial commissioner supervises the carrying out of the details specified therein. If the arrangement is not approved, the court decrees immediately the adjudication in bankruptcy.

The ranking of the creditors is the same as provided for bankruptcy. The procedure usually has a shorter duration than bankruptcy.

Supervised administration

The system of supervised administration (*amministrazione controllata*) involves a suspension of payments for a maximum of two years, which a company may request if it is not yet actually insolvent but is experiencing temporary difficulties in meeting its commitments.

The company must submit to the court a scheme of reorganisation, and a majority of the unsecured creditors representing a majority of the claims must vote in favour of this arrangement. If the arrangement is rejected, the company may propose a preventive arrangement: otherwise it is declared bankrupt.

During the procedure the enterprise is managed by the debtor under control of a judicial commissioner appointed by the court. Every two months the commissioner must file an account concerning the management of the assets with a judge delegate.

If the enterprise is able to settle its debts before the expiration of the two-year period, the debtor can demand the termination of the procedure.

Compulsory administrative liquidation

Compulsory administrative liquidation (*liquidazione coatta amministrativa*) applies only to public undertakings, indemnity insurance and life assurance companies, banks, cooperative societies, mandatory consortia and certain joint-stock companies with State participation as majority shareholder or creditor.

Proceedings for compulsory administrative liquidation can be carried out only by the responsible controlling authority.

An application is made to the relevant authorities by the company or one or more of its creditors. The court discusses the case with the government department responsible for the entity and begins liquidation proceedings. A liquidator (public official) is appointed by the court. His duties are to verify creditors' claims and investigate whether a composition is feasible or not. If it is, the liquidator and the company prepare a proposal for the creditors to vote on. If a composition is not feasible, the trader's assets are disposed of and the funds are distributed amongst the creditors.

Extraordinary administration

This procedure (*amministrazione straordinaria*), established by Law 95 3 April 1979 called '*Legge Prodi*', is restricted to large enterprises or to large industrial groups subject to the following conditions:

- the debts are equal to five times the paid-up capital and at the same time exceed 53 billion lire (updated to 1986, subject to annual revaluation), incurred with banks and social security institutions;
- the company is unable to pay its debts or the salaries to company personnel who have not been paid for at least three months;
- the number of employees amounts to 300 for a period of at least one year.

In extraordinary administration the company is deprived of managing powers which are entrusted to (one to three) judicial commissioners for a maximum of four years (or five in the case of affiliated companies). It begins with a decree of insolvency by the court followed by a decision of industry and treasury ministers.

The procedure creates a duty to make every effort to recoup the productive ability of the enterprise. This procedure also extends to controlling and controlled companies and to corporations under the same management, and applies to the companies which have loaned more than one third of their assets to the company subject to the procedure. The procedure extends to these companies whether or not they meet the conditions listed above.

A rescue project is normally drawn up and specific procedural fiscal advantages are provided for the selling of factories or plants belonging to the companies subject to the procedures, in order to continue their operations.

KPMG contact partner

Stefano Tanzi
KPMG Consulting SpA
Via Vittor Pisani 25
20124 Milano
Italy

Telephone: +39 (2) 67631
Fax: +39 (2) 6763 2445

Ivory Coast

Legislation

In the Ivory Coast the main enactment governing winding-up procedures is embodied in the Bankruptcy and Winding Up Act of 4 March 1889, the Code of Mercantile Law (dispositions 437 to 583), Act of 4 April 1890 and Decree-Law of 8 August 1935.

These regulations define the legal requirements and effects regarding the winding-up procedures.

Insolvency procedures

Legal requirements and effects for both bankruptcy and winding-up procedures are broadly similar as the latter is considered as a mitigated bankruptcy.

Therefore, if in the opinion of the commercial courts, any fraud or contravention has been committed by a debtor who is requesting a winding-up procedure, the judge could adjudge him bankrupt.

For that reason, the commercial courts easily grant the winding-up procedure to debtors.

Legal requirements for a winding-up procedure

The legal requirements for a winding-up procedure are as follows:

- the debtor must be a businessman or a business company;
- the debtor must be in a position of default regarding his payments and a creditor must submit convincing evidence of this position;
- the debtor must file and submit a petition, to the court within 15 days following his default. He must also provide his latest balance sheet, an evaluation of all his assets and debts, the latest profit and loss account and a list naming all his creditors;
- a winding-up judgment, which is considered as a declaration of a new legal status, appoints a liquidator and judge as an official receiver;
- the winding-up judgment is published in a legal newspaper available in all the debtor's places of business.

This judgment is liable to stay of execution or appeal within eight days and 15 days respectively from the date of its publication.

Legal effects of winding-up procedure

The legal effects are as follows:

- setting up of various bodies in charge of carrying out the winding up procedure, such as an official receiver and creditors' meeting;
- a judge who is a member of the commercial court is appointed by the winding-up judgment as official receiver;
- the creditors meet regularly with the official receiver in order to approve the repayment proposals made by the debtor;
- the creditors' meeting is entitled to make all decisions relating to a fair running of the business;

- appointment of representatives of creditors to assist the receiver;
- appointment of a liquidator (generally a sworn-in chartered accountant at the Court of Appeal). The liquidator is in charge of assisting the debtor with running the business. He also acts as the creditors' legal representative;
- paying off creditors by the liquidation of the debtor's assets. This step implies the suspension of individual lawsuits against the debtor, the setting up of a composition to creditors, a body of creditors and temporary decisions.

The tax administration, secured creditors and the appointed liquidator remain fully entitled to take individual proceedings against the debtor.

KPMG contact partner

C.L. Andon
Audit 2000
01 BP 5682
Abidjan 01

Telephone: +225 21 10 91
Fax: +225 21 90 21

Jamaica

Legislation

The Jamaican Companies Act is based upon United Kingdom legislation. The provisions for insolvency procedures in Jamaica are, therefore, similar to those relevant in England and Wales prior to changes in the English legislation in 1986. The procedures set out in the section in this book dealing with England and Wales broadly apply for Jamaica with the exception of the administration procedures and the new law relating to directors.

The Jamaican Companies Act is currently under review and it is expected there will be amendments relating to administration procedures and directors' responsibilities.

Insolvency procedures

Receivership

There are different forms of receivership but usually it means the process whereby the holder of a registered charge against a company's assets appoints a receiver who assumes control of the company's assets and realises them in order to satisfy the claims of the secured creditor. The right to appoint a receiver is given in the security document, often referred to as a 'debenture', containing a floating charge and/or fixed charges over the debtor company's assets. Borrowings from banks are usually secured by a fixed and/or floating charge over the borrower's assets and are usually repayable on demand. Most receivers are appointed by banks. The powers of the receiver include the power to carry on the business and to receive income and realise assets; he is deemed to be the agent of the company unless and until the company enters into liquidation.

A body corporate is not qualified for appointment as a receiver of the property of a company.

There are provisions in the Companies Act for the giving of notice of appointment of a receiver and making returns to the Registrar of Companies.

Voluntary winding up

This is a solvent winding up under which the directors must have prepared a statutory declaration within the five weeks immediately preceding the resolution to wind up that, having made full inquiry, they are of the opinion that the company will be able to pay its debts in full with interest at the official rate within a period not exceeding 12 months from commencement of the winding up. Where a director makes such a declaration without reasonable grounds and the debts and interest are not paid within the specific period, the director is liable to a fine or imprisonment or both.

The assets and liabilities of the company are placed under the control of a liquidator who winds up the affairs of the company. A company may be wound up voluntarily:

- whenever the articles of association of the company provide for it to be dissolved, and the company in general meeting has passed a resolution requiring it to be wound up voluntarily;
- whenever the company has passed a special resolution requiring it to be wound up voluntarily;
- whenever members of the company have passed a resolution to the effect that it has been proved to their satisfaction that it cannot by reason of its liabilities continue its business, and that it is advisable to wind up the company.

A voluntary winding up is deemed to commence at the time of the passing of the resolution authorising the winding up. The effects of the commencement of winding up are that:

- the company shall cease to trade except as required for its beneficial winding up;
- the company's corporate powers and status continue until its affairs are wound up;
- upon the appointment of a liquidator all the powers of the directors cease.

Winding up subject to supervision of the court

When a resolution has been passed by a company to wind up voluntarily, the court may make an order directing that the voluntary winding up should continue but subject to such supervision of the court as the court thinks just. The company or any creditor of the company or any contributory may petition the court to order such supervision.

The most usual ground for a petition to the court is the inability of the company to pay its debts.

Winding up by the court

A company may be wound up by the court if:

- the company has by special resolution resolved that the company be wound up by the court;
- default is made in delivering the statutory report to the Registrar or in holding the statutory meeting;
- the company does not commence its business within a year from its incorporation, or suspends its business for a whole year;
- the number of members is reduced, in the case of a private company, below two, or, in the case of any other company, below seven;
- the company is unable to pay its debts;
- the court is of the opinion that it is just and equitable that the company should be wound up.

Section 204 of the Companies Act defines when a company is deemed to be unable to pay its debts. The date of commencement of winding up by the court is the date of presentation of the petition for the winding up.

The court shall appoint one or more persons to be called official liquidator or liquidators and all proceedings of the winding up of the company by the official liquidators are subject to the court's directions. The powers and duties of official liquidators are contained in the Companies Act.

As soon as the affairs of the company are fully wound up, the liquidator must make up an account showing the manner in which the winding up has been conducted and the property of the company disposed of.

Provisions are contained in the Companies Act relating to the giving of notice of appointment of liquidators, holding of meetings and making returns to the Registrar of Companies.

Striking off

Where the Registrar of Companies has reasonable cause to believe that a company is not carrying on business or in operation he may after enquiry and appropriate notice in the *Jamaica Gazette* determine that the company be struck off the register and dissolved.

Creditors

Secured creditors

A secured creditor is someone who holds a fixed or floating charge over property of the debtor. The holder of a charge has several courses of action available to him following default by the debtor, including the appointment of a receiver to the property which is the subject of the security, entering into possession as mortgagee or allowing the company or its liquidator to realise the security on behalf of the secured creditor.

Preferential creditors

In a winding up there shall be paid in priority to all other debts:

- all rates, charges, taxes, assessments or impositions, whether imposed or made by the government or by any public authority under the provisions of any law, and having become due and payable within 12 months next before the relevant date and not exceeding the whole of one year's assessment;
- all wages and salary (whether or not earned wholly or in part by way of commission) of any clerk or servant in respect of services rendered to the company during four months next before the relevant date, and all wages (whether payable for time or for piece work), of any workman or labourer in respect of services so rendered, provided that the sum to which priority is to be given under this paragraph shall not, in the case of any one claimant, exceed J$600;
- unless the company is being wound up voluntarily merely for the purposes of reconstruction or amalgamation with another company, or unless the company has at the commencement of the winding up under such a contract with insurers as is mentioned in s. 21 of the Workmen's Compensation Act, rights capable of being transferred to and vested in the workman, all amounts due in respect of any compensation or liability for compensation under the said Act accrued before the relevant date;
- all amounts by way of contributions for which the company is liable pursuant to ss. 4, 5 and 6 of the National Insurance Act and which have become due and payable before the relevant date;
- redundancy payments payable under the Employment (Termination and Redundancy Payments) Act;
- all amounts by way of contributions of which the company is liable pursuant to ss. 11 and 12 of the National Housing Trust Act and which have become due and payable before the relevant date.

Unsecured creditors

The term 'unsecured creditor' applies to a creditor having a claim which is neither covered by security nor has preferential status.

KPMG contact partner

Rolf Lanigan
KPMG Peat Marwick
The Victoria Mutual Building
6 Duke Street
PO Box 76
Kingston
Jamaica

Telephone: +1 (809) 922 6640
Fax: +1 (809) 922 7198

Japan

Legislation

The procedures which apply to corporate insolvency under Japanese law fall into two categories:

(a) Procedures for the liquidation and dissolution of companies:

- bankruptcy ('*hasan*') under the Bankruptcy Law;
- special liquidation ('*tokubetsu seisan*') under the Commercial Code.

(b) Procedures intended to promote the rehabilitation of companies:

- corporate reorganisation under the Corporate Reorganisation Law ('*kaisha kōsei*');
- company arrangement ('*seiri*') under the Commercial Code;
- composition ('*wagi*') under the Composition Law;
- compulsory composition under the Bankruptcy Law ('*kyōsei wagi*').

In addition to the above, a non-statutory voluntary arrangement ('*ninni seiri*') is commonly used for the liquidation/dissolution or rehabilitation of insolvent companies.

Insolvency procedures

Bankruptcy ('*hasan*')

If a company is unable to meet its payment obligations, or if it suspends payment of its debts (unless there is evidence that the company is able to meet its payment obligations), or if its total indebtedness is greater than the value of its assets, then a declaration of bankruptcy can be applied for by:

- any of the company's creditors;
- the company's directors; or
- the company itself.

Under Japanese law, bankruptcy applies to assets located in Japan. Recent international practices tend to allow extraterritorial authority of bankruptcy administrators, although there is at present no Japanese statute on this issue. A foreign company has the same status as a Japanese company under the Bankruptcy Law, provided that a foreign company's country of registration provides reciprocal treatment to Japanese companies. In addition, claims which may be enforced under the Civil Procedure Code are deemed to be located in Japan.

Following an application for declaration of bankruptcy, the court will examine the application documents and, after providing the debtor with the opportunity to state its opinion, may issue interim orders to preserve the company's assets. The application must be accompanied by a deposit to cover the costs of the procedure. When a declaration of bankruptcy is made, an administrator in bankruptcy is appointed by the court. The primary role of the administrator is to realise the assets of the company and to distribute the proceeds to the creditors. The administrator (commonly, a lawyer), once appointed, has the exclusive right to manage and control the assets of the bankrupt company and may allow the company to conduct limited trading activities in order to maximise the final distribution to creditors. In addition, the administrator can rescind executory bilateral contracts or request performance by the other party of its obligations in return for due performance by the bankrupt company.

Creditors' rights of set-off of debts created in good faith, which are provided under the Civil Code of Japan, may be restricted under the bankruptcy procedures, in particular where debts are created after the declaration of bankruptcy. In principle, secured rights, such as mortgages, can be exercised outside of the bankruptcy procedure.

Except in the case of secured creditors, creditors may only enforce their rights through the bankruptcy procedure. The administrator liquidates the assets constituting the bankruptcy estate and distributes the proceeds to the creditors according to their rights of priority and in proportion to the amount of their respective claims. The Bankruptcy Law invalidates:

- certain preferential acts in favour of particular creditors;
- compulsory execution proceedings and orders;
- provisional injunctions;
- provisional attachment orders.

Guarantees and collateral security agreements provided to the company remain valid under the bankruptcy procedure. Guarantors and security providers remain liable in respect of these.

Following completion of the distribution to creditors, the bankrupt company is dissolved.

Special liquidation ('*tokubetsu seisan*')

The special liquidation procedure is only available for joint-stock limited liability companies ('*kabushiki kaisha*' or '*KK*').

To institute the procedure, the shareholders must first have resolved, in general meeting, to dissolve the company voluntarily and to appoint a liquidator (usually a director). However, if it appears that:

- the company's debts will be greater than its assets; or
- if there will be material difficulty in liquidating the company

then the liquidator, the auditor, any creditor, or any shareholder of the company can apply to the court for a special liquidation order.

The purpose of the special liquidation procedure is to avoid the company being declared bankrupt and to distribute the company's remaining assets to its creditors and shareholders in an expeditious and equitable manner.

Under the procedure the following are suspended and no further proceedings can be commenced:

- compulsory execution proceedings and orders;
- provisional injunctions;
- provisional attachment orders.

In addition, the court may suspend any bankruptcy procedures or composition procedures which may be pending.

The liquidator prepares an agreement setting out the distribution of the company's assets to the creditors and the shareholders which, once approved by a certain majority in a creditors' meeting and by the court, becomes binding on all creditors. In principle, the agreement can treat certain creditors preferentially, but in practice this can make agreement difficult to achieve. If the court decides that agreement cannot be reached between the creditors then it may declare the company bankrupt. Bankruptcy procedures would then apply.

Creditors' rights of set-off of debts created in good faith, which are provided under the Civil Code of Japan, may be restricted under this procedure. Secured creditors can choose to join with the unsecured creditors or, in principle, to enforce their rights separately.

Corporate reorganisation ('*kaisha kōsei*')

The corporate reorganisation procedure is only available for joint-stock limited liability companies ('*kabushiki kaisha*' or '*KK*').

If a company appears to be unable, without material difficulty to its on-going business, to pay its debts as they fall due, or if it is considered that events may occur which could cause bankruptcy, then the following parties can make an application to the court for a corporate reorganisation:

- creditors with a certain minimum value of claims;
- shareholders with a certain minimum shareholding; or
- the company itself.

Following the application, the court considers the financial and business status of the company to determine if it is capable of rehabilitation. As part of this process, the court may appoint a provisional liquidator to manage the business and administer the assets. In addition, it may order certain measures to preserve those assets. The corporate reorganisation procedure applies to all company assets located in Japan. Again, international practice (not based on statutory grounds) is developing to allow extraterritorial expansion of the powers of liquidators and administrators. Claims which can be enforced under the Civil Procedure Code are regarded as being located in Japan.

This process of investigation can take in excess of a year for large companies. If the court finds probable grounds for the rehabilitation of the company then it may order commencement of the reorganisation. Typically, two administrators are appointed by the court, one a lawyer and one a businessman. All rights to manage the company and control its assets are vested in the administrators.

The administrators can rescind executory bilateral contracts or request performance by the other party of its obligations in return for due performance by the company. In addition, all litigation involving the company's assets, compulsory executions, provisional injunctions, provisional attachments, bankruptcy and other pending procedures are suspended.

Under the corporate reorganisation procedure, secured creditors are grouped together and may not exercise their rights outside of the procedure.

Rights of set-off can be exercised until the court deadline for submission of creditors' claims, after which time set-off is prohibited. Set-off may be restricted in the case of claims created in bad faith, or after the commencement of the procedure, or under circumstances involving fraudulent preference.

The administrators prepare a reorganisation plan, which may include:

- rescheduling the company's repayments;
- reduction or loss of shareholders' capital;
- secured and unsecured creditors waiving part of their claims.

The reorganisation plan takes effect once approved by a creditors' meeting and by the court, and is binding on all creditors. However, if agreement cannot be reached, the court may declare the company bankrupt. The bankruptcy procedures would then apply.

The corporate reorganisation procedure has proved to be effective in rehabilitating large companies. However, its disadvantages are that it takes a comparatively long time and that, from the perspective of shareholders and management, effective control of the company passes to the creditors.

Company arrangement ('*seiri*')

The company arrangement procedure is only available for joint stock limited liability companies ('*kabushiki kaisha*' or '*KK*').

Where there is a concern that a company may be unable to pay its debts, or that its debts may be greater than its assets, an application for a company arrangement can be made to the courts by:

- the directors and auditors of the company;
- creditors with a certain minimum value of claims; or
- shareholders with a certain minimum shareholding.

Once such an application has been made, provisional injunctions, all compulsory execution proceedings and orders, provisional attachments and other specified procedures are suspended. In addition, the court may take steps to preserve the company's assets.

In order to determine whether a company is capable of being rehabilitated under the company arrangement procedure, the court may appoint an inspector. However, the power to manage the company remains with the directors. Secured creditors can exercise their rights outside the company arrangement procedure, subject to the court's discretion to suspend enforcement procedures. Creditors' rights of set-off of debts created in good faith, which are provided under the Civil Code of Japan, may be restricted under this procedure.

The company's management prepare a plan of arrangement, covering such matters as deferral of payments and partial release from obligations, for acceptance and approval by the creditors and the court. If this plan is accepted and approved then it becomes effective. If not approved, or if it is considered by the courts that there is no hope of rehabilitation, then bankruptcy or composition proceedings may be commenced.

The company arrangement procedure has, in the past, proved effective in rehabilitating small companies. It provides management and shareholders with the opportunity to retain control of the company and its assets. The procedure is often used in preference to more formal approaches. In principle, the plan of arrangement requires the agreement of all of the creditors (secured and unsecured) and the court and, as such, it can be difficult to establish an acceptable plan. However, in practice, the court will generally approve the plan if it has the agreement of 90 per cent of the creditors.

Composition under the Composition Law ('*wagi*')

Any company can apply for composition if its circumstances are such that they may constitute grounds for bankruptcy.

Under this procedure, the potentially insolvent company proposes a plan of composition. The plan can only be put into effect after approval by a majority of creditors and the court. In the case where a plan of composition is not approved, the court may order bankruptcy proceedings.

The composition procedure is less formal than a corporate reorganisation and is favoured by smaller insolvent companies.

Compulsory composition under the Bankruptcy Law ('*kyōsei wagi*')

In order to continue its business, a company which has been declared bankrupt may offer a plan for partial release or rescheduling of indebtedness, or 'compulsory composition', to the courts.

If this plan is approved by the courts and the creditors, then the terms of the plan become effective. In practice, this procedure is only rarely used.

Voluntary arrangement ('*ninni seiri*')

In order to save costs and time, the creditors of an insolvent company may agree to arrange the affairs of the company without the supervision of the courts.

If successful, such voluntary arrangements can have a variety of outcomes, including:

- complete liquidation and dissolution of the company;
- rehabilitation of the company;
- the company being left dormant with its liabilities. A new company takes over the assets and business of the insolvent company and agrees to pay the debts of the insolvent company out of its future profits.

The voluntary arrangement procedure is commonly administered by a creditors' committee, elected by a meeting of the creditors.

KPMG contact partner

Colin Stuart
KPMG Peat Marwick
SKF Building, 8F
9–1, Shiba Daimon, 1-chome
Minato-ku
Tokyo 105
Japan

Telephone: +81 (3) 5400 7320
Fax: +81 (3) 5400 7330

Jordan

Legislation

Jordan insolvency legislation is included in Chapter 13 of the Companies Law No. 1 of 1989 and the Commercial Law No. 12 of 1996. Several changes are expected in the current legislation and a new Companies Law is expected to be out in early 1997.

Insolvency procedures

Liquidation

Liquidation is the statutory process for winding up the affairs of a company. A company can be liquidated either voluntarily, by a resolution adopted by its extraordinary general assembly, or mandatorily by a court order. The company shall not be dissolved until all procedures of its liquidation have been finalised.

After adoption of a resolution to liquidate the company, a liquidator is appointed whose duty is to supervise the operations of the company and safeguard its assets.

A company under liquidation must suspend its operations as of the date of commencing the liquidation procedures. The corporate status of the company continues to exist and it is represented by the liquidator until it is dissolved after finalising its liquidation procedures.

The party which decides to liquidate the company must provide the Controller of Companies and the public with a copy of its resolution.

The liquidation must settle the company's debts in accordance with the following order after deducting liquidation expenses:

- amounts due to employees of the company;
- amounts due to the Treasury or government;
- other amounts due in the order of priority established by the laws in force.

The liquidator must keep proper books and records and provide the court and the Controller with a statement of account duly audited by the liquidation auditor. After completing the liquidation process, the court will issue an order that the company be dissolved.

Bankruptcy

Bankruptcy applies to a merchant whose financial business is disrupted and ceases to meet its commercial debts as they fall due. A petition for bankruptcy may be made to the court by the individual or one of his creditors.

The court appoints an agent to manage the bankruptcy. The bankruptcy officer takes over the assets and books of the bankrupt person. The bankruptcy officer then prepares a balance sheet which is submitted to the court.

KPMG contact partner

Ghassan Tarazi
Khleif & Co.
PO Box 830 430
Amman 11183

Telephone: +962 (6) 681798
Fax: +962 (6) 681798

Kazakhstan

Legislation

Kazakh insolvency legislation is relatively new and undergoing continuous development. Under the Soviet system, all enterprises were deemed to be branches of the State, and therefore no bankruptcy was possible. Liquidation through reorganisation was possible, but it was an administrative and logistical exercise.

Although insolvency legislation has been passed in Kazakhstan and there is some evidence that insolvency proceedings have been instituted, the process is neither common nor even the automatic result of an irredeemable financial position. This is due partly to a lack of experience and partly to what seems to be a 'Soviet' belief that companies, once founded, cannot or should not die.

Current insolvency legislation is closely related to the legislation in Russia as both have evolved from the same system and Russian legislation is more readily accessible. Kazakh insolvency legislation is based on the Law on Insolvency (Bankruptcy), which was passed in April 1995.

Further development is certain and so these notes are merely indicative of the current situation.

Insolvency procedures

Types of insolvency procedure

- reorganisation — the business is placed in the hands of an external management, which may be charged with its rehabilitation;
- liquidation — this occurs (a) if a court has declared the enterprise insolvent, or (b) if the enterprise declares itself insolvent.

Insolvency courts

Insolvency cases are examined by 'arbitration' courts. Cases may be brought when claims have been outstanding for three months from the due date.

Parties to an insolvency action

The legislation recognises various parties in an insolvency action, including:

- proxy manager — the manager is authorised to carry on the business, recruit and dismiss employees, dispose of assets, call meetings of creditors, develop and execute a recovery plan;
- liquidator — the liquidator may dispose of assets, contest the validity of contracts completed up to six months prior to the initiation of arbitration proceedings, collect debts and receivables, form a liquidation committee and call a creditors' meeting;
- creditors;
- representatives of the workforce;
- debtor.

The proxy manager and/or liquidator must:

- have practical management experience;

- not have a criminal record;
- not be an officer of the debtor.

Petition

An insolvency action is initiated by a petition to the arbitration court from:

- the debtor, either the owner of the enterprise or its management — such a petition cannot be withdrawn;
- a creditor, after three months from the due date for payment for goods or services (the due date being defined as the date of delivery of a demand for payment by registered post);
- a procurator (public prosecutor), if the law of the Russian Federation requires the initiation of insolvency proceedings.

The court must rule within a month and either refuse the petition if it is established that the creditor's claim can be met or the defendant is solvent, or recognise the defendant as insolvent, in which case liquidation proceedings will be instituted.

If a petition is received from the debtor itself, the court may institute reorganisation or rehabilitation procedures rather than declaring the enterprise insolvent.

Reorganisation

Reorganisation of the enterprise may be considered if there is a real possibility that the solvency of the enterprise may be restored by selling off parts of the debtor organisation, reorganising it, or instituting some other economic measures. The arbitration court must review the plan and decide whether the enterprise should continue or the debtor should be declared insolvent and liquidation proceedings be instituted. The procedure may not last for more than 18 months although this may be extended for a further six months by the court.

Rehabilitation

If the enterprise can be restored to solvency as a result of financial aid by the owner or third parties, the arbitration court may institute rehabilitation proceedings. If an arbitration court rules in favour of rehabilitation, it must put the rehabilitation contract out to tender.

Within 12 months of the start of rehabilitation, the enterprise must have met at least 40 per cent of the combined creditor claims. Rehabilitation may not last for more than 18 months. Rehabilitation ceases when 18 months have elapsed or it is determined by the court that rehabilitation is ineffective, in which case liquidation proceedings must be instituted. Rehabilitation is deemed successful when all claims have been met.

Liquidation proceedings

Once a debtor has been declared insolvent, liquidation proceedings must continue. The arbitration court appoints a liquidation committee.

The committee has the duty to obtain the highest price by auction.

Claims secured by assets are satisfied outside the court.

The proceeds of the realisation of assets are distributed in order of precedence as follows:

- expenses related to the liquidation proceedings, expenses of the proxy manager and the liquidation committee;
- claims of individuals whom the debtor has injured or jeopardised;
- payment of the workforce, payments on contracts for author's rights and licensing;

- claims secured by assets;
- taxes and social security contributions;
- all other claims.

KPMG contact partner

Roger Munnings
KPMG
37 Ul. Novaya Basmannaya
3rd Floor
Moscow 107066
Russia

Telephone: +7 (502) 222 4030
Fax: +7 (502) 222 4024

Kenya

Legislation

Company law has not changed substantially since 1 January 1962 when the Companies Acts of 1959, 1960 and 1961 were amended and consolidated. The practitioners involved in liquidation, receivership and other corporate administrations work within a statutory framework comprising the Companies Act 1962 (ch. 486) supported by the Companies (Winding Up) Rules.

The insolvency law relating to individuals is in the Bankruptcy Act.

Insolvency procedures

Receivership

The terms of most charges or mortgages, which in all cases are limited in value because of stamp duty considerations, contain provisions for the appointment of a receiver and set out his powers. A floating charge debenture will normally confer upon the receiver the right of management and, in Kenya, there have been some examples of extended periods of management by receivers.

The receiver has a duty to deal with the claims of the preferential creditors and to settle them in priority to the amounts secured by means of a floating charge. The receiver has no more than a duty of care towards the unsecured creditors.

For the protection of the purchaser, a receiver, when disposing of the business, or substantial part thereof, is required to obtain a certificate from an independent practising accountant, under the provisions of the Transfer of Businesses Act, confirming that the sale price was the best one that could have been obtained on a timely basis.

Liquidation

An unpaid creditor may petition the court for the winding-up of a company. If a winding up order is made, the official receiver is appointed liquidator pending the holding of a meeting of members and creditors to vote on the appointment.

If the directors of a company find that the company cannot continue its business by reason of its insolvency, then they may call meetings of shareholders and creditors to resolve to wind up the company. This is termed a creditors' voluntary liquidation. If, for any other reason, it is desired to wind up a company and if the directors are of the opinion that it can meet its debts in full within a period not exceeding 12 months, the directors will swear a declaration of solvency and the members will pass a resolution to wind up. This is termed a members' voluntary winding up.

Scheme of arrangement

Where a compromise or arrangement is proposed between a company and its creditors, the court may order a meeting of creditors and the compromise or arrangement will be binding on all creditors of the same class, provided it is approved by a majority in number and a 75 per cent majority in value of those present in person or by proxy at the meeting.

Defunct companies

The Kenyan legislation gives power to the Registrar of Companies to strike defunct companies off his register. It is often possible for companies without any assets or liabilities to be dissolved in this way and thus avoid the cost of liquidation.

Who can be appointed?

- liquidators and receivers — no qualification is required to act as receiver or liquidator, though a body corporate may not be appointed. When an appointment is made out of court it is usual for a certified public accountant to act as liquidator or receiver;
- official receiver — the official receiver is an employee of the Department of the Registrar-General and is appointed as liquidator by the court upon the successful petition for the winding up of a company;
- special manager — an official receiver may, in certain circumstances, request the court's approval to appoint a special manager to assist in a liquidation. A special manager would usually be a certified public accountant;
- committee of inspection — creditors, at a meeting, may decide to appoint not more than five persons to this committee to look after their interests.

Creditors

Secured creditors

Holders of a charge or mortgage on property of a debtor as security for a debt are secured creditors, who can recover their debt wholly or in part from the assets of the debtor before the unsecured creditors.

Preferential creditors

The Companies Act provides for the payment of certain creditors in priority to creditors secured by a floating charge and unsecured creditors. These include:

- taxes and local rates due at the relevant date and due and payable within 12 months prior to that date;
- government rent not more than one year in arrears;
- wages and salaries subject to a maximum of Kshs4,000/- per employee and due within four months prior to the relevant date;
- National Social Security Fund contributions not more than one year in arrears.

Unsecured creditors

The claims of these creditors rank equally in a liquidation after the settlement of amounts due to secured and preferential creditors.

KPMG contact partner

Andrew Gregory
KPMG Marwick
PO Box 40612
Jubilee Insurance Exchange
Mama Ngina Street
Nairobi
Kenya

Telephone: +254 (2) 222 862
Fax: +254 (2) 215 695

Korea

Legislation

Where a company has ceased to pay its debts in the ordinary course of business or is unable to pay its debts as they fall due, protection of rights of the creditors is provided for in a number of laws. In cases where the liquidation procedure under the Commercial Code or the bankruptcy procedure under the Bankruptcy Act is taken with respect to a company, the company's business generally ceases to operate, whereas, if a company dishonours cheques, bills or notes drawn on itself, all of its transactions with the lending institutions become suspended.

In cases where a company discontinues paying its obligations as due under the Corporate Reorganisation Act, continuation of its business is not impeded; all obligations cease to be paid unless otherwise provided for in the reorganisation plan.

The Bankruptcy Act and the Corporate Reorganisation Act take precedence over the Commercial Code, the Civil Code or the Code of Civil Procedure.

Insolvency procedures

Relief under the Code of Civil Procedure

A creditor may recover a debt on compulsory execution under a court decision. (The related legal proceedings require a notarised document evidencing the debtor's refusal to pay its obligations.) In such a case, the court decision is valid solely with respect to the claims for which the legal proceedings were taken.

Where a company is in liquidation

All creditors are entitled to distribution of the company's residual assets in accordance with the order of priority as set by the liquidator of the company.

Relief under the Bankruptcy Act

When a company is no longer able to pay its obligations, the court, upon an application submitted by one of the directors of the company, may adjudicate it bankrupt.

The residual assets of the bankrupt company are to be distributed in accordance with the order of priority as determined under the Bankruptcy Act. Under the Bankruptcy Act, the status of an alien is the same as that of a Korean national, and the bankruptcy is effective solely with respect to the properties of the bankrupt company which exist in Korea. The bankrupt generally may be reinstated 10 years after adjudication of bankruptcy and may not depart from his dwelling place until reinstated. Because of such restrictions imposed on the bankrupt and the fact that only the directors of a company may apply for bankruptcy proceedings, in very few instances have companies applied for bankruptcy proceedings and been adjudicated bankrupt under the Bankruptcy Act.

Corporate reorganisation

Company reorganisation may be undertaken under the Corporate Reorganisation Act (CRA). The purpose of the CRA is to 'adjust the interests between creditors, shareholders and other interested persons with regard to a joint-stock company which is on the verge of insolvency due to financial difficulties but still regenerable, and to reorganise and rehabilitate the business of the company'. An alien is accorded the same status as a Korean national with regard to corporate reorganisation.

If a company is unable to pay its obligations as they fall due without impeding the continuation of its business, either creditors holding claims equal to one tenth or more of the company's capital, shareholders holding one tenth or more of the total shares issued by the company or the representative director of the company may file an application for commencement of reorganisation proceedings. Once the court has taken preservative measures with respect to the business and assets of the company, all debt payments, compulsory executions, auction sales of the assets, provisional attachments etc. cease unless otherwise specifically authorised by the court. The court appoints a receiver concurrently with the ruling for the commencement of reorganisation proceedings, and the receiver is required to prepare a reorganisation plan within two months from the date of his appointment after obtaining reports of the company's claims and obligations. A reorganisation plan requires the court's authorisation after its adoption by the creditors' committee. Unless otherwise specifically provided for in the reorganisation plan (which shows names of the creditors, amounts, repayment periods and other details of the obligations, and interest rates applicable during the corporate reorganisation period), no payments may be made to any of the creditors.

The order of priority with respect to the payment of obligations is as follows:

- reorganisation security rights (limited to the amount pledged in security);
- general reorganisation claims with priority rights;
- other general reorganisation claims;
- deferred reorganisation claims;
- preferred stockholders' shares;
- common stockholders' shares.

Claims for common benefits, such as the company's obligations which arise after the preservative measures have been taken, and salaries and retirement allowances of the company employees, shall be paid in preference to reorganisation claims.

If any modification is to be made (with respect to extension of the reorganisation period, the transfer of a part of the company's business or assumption of certain obligations of the company) to the reorganisation plan after reorganisation proceedings have commenced, either the modification should be authorised by the court after its adoption has been resolved by the creditors' committees or it may directly be made by the court's official powers.

If a person no longer remains in office who was a director or auditor of the company at the time when reorganisation proceedings commenced, he or she will not be eligible to be re-elected as a director or auditor after the reorganisation proceedings have been concluded.

KPMG contact partner

K. K. Suh
KPMG San Tong & Co.
15th Floor, Construction Center
71-2 Nonhyun-Dong
Kangnam-Ku
Seoul 135-701
Korea

Telephone: +82 (2) 3442 2345
Fax: +82 (2) 3442 3200

Kuwait

Legislation

The legislation regarding insolvency in Kuwait is very brief and covers only one page of Kuwaiti commercial law. The insolvency law is poorly developed and there is no efficient mechanism for dealing with personal or corporate bankruptcy or putting a business into receivership.

Insolvency procedures

The insolvency procedure commences when 75 per cent or more of the shareholders agree to liquidate the company, or the liquidation can commence with an order from the court upon request of major shareholders in the company.

Shareholders of the company can instigate the procedure and appoint the liquidator through an extraordinary meeting of shareholders or by court order. Once the liquidation procedure commences, the liquidator is in full control of running the company's business. However, the liquidator can continue the affairs of the company in order to meet the commitments and obligations made before liquidation but he should not make any new commitment regarding the company's business.

The liquidator controls the liquidation procedure and has the overall responsibility of realising the company's assets and paying its creditors in the context of insolvency legislation mentioned in Kuwaiti commercial law.

Creditors

Creditors holding security will continue to have the right to that security during the liquidation of the company. Creditors who receive preferential or special treatment are normally the employees of the company, the liquidator, the lawyer and government institutions who have the right to receive payment before commercial and other creditors.

Trading and other creditors (local and foreign) have the right to receive payment before any distribution to shareholders but after payment to preferential creditors.

Shareholders have the right to receive funds as a result of the liquidation of company assets after payment to all creditors has been made.

Other matters

Restriction and shortcomings of procedures

The legislation does not set a clear and detailed mechanism regarding liquidation procedure.

Timing and duration

Normally no time limit is set for liquidating the company.

KPMG contact partner

Masoud Sorkhou
KPMG Masoud & Co.
PO Box 3385
13034 Safat
Kuwait

Telephone: +965 2400121
Fax: +965 2400120

Latvia

Legislation

Insolvency legislation is regulated in the Act 'On Enterprises and Entrepreneurs Insolvency and Bankruptcy' which was implemented on 3 December 1991. Amendments to the Act have been made in January 1994 and in August 1995.

The Act regulates procedures on how an enterprise is declared insolvent or bankrupt and also the procedures on how creditors' claims are satisfied.

There are specific laws that regulate insolvency procedures for banks, other credit institutions and insurance companies.

Insolvency procedures

A company is presumed to be insolvent when it is not able to pay its debts within three months. A company is recognised as insolvent if:

- the debtor itself recognises its inability to pay off all debts;
- the court decides that the debtor cannot pay its debts;
- the debtor's actions convince creditors that they will not be able to recover their debts.

Insolvency may be initiated by the company's management or a creditor.

The court will consider approving one of the following insolvency procedures:

- voluntary arrangement;
- recovery;
- creditors' administration.

If none of the abovementioned procedures is feasible, the company is declared bankrupt.

Voluntary arrangement

It is possible to reach a voluntary arrangement if not less than two thirds of creditors who represent at least three quarters of total claims accept it. A voluntary arrangement is not allowed in cases of malicious bankruptcy. A voluntary arrangement is not allowed to settle claims relating to alimonies, liabilities of tax payments, other payments to the government and obligatory insurance payments.

Recovery of company

Where it is not possible to reach a voluntary agreement or establish a creditors' administration, the court will consult with the debtor for its views about possible recovery plans. The court decides which recovery plan is the best. The recovery period cannot be longer than 18 months. There is a requirement that within one year of starting the plan, the debtor should satisfy at least 40 per cent of creditors' claims.

Creditors' administration

Until a creditors' administration is approved, the business is run by a court-appointed administrator. The administrator's duties include:

- within two weeks organise a creditors' meeting;
- inform local government, State institutions and credit institutions about insolvency;
- evaluate the debtor's property and prepare a list of all liabilities.

The creditors in their meeting approve the administrator or ask the court to appoint a new one. At a creditors' meeting, decisions are approved by a majority of votes of creditors present.

The aim of a creditors' administration is to run the company in such a way as to avoid liquidation. It is possible to establish a creditors' administration only after the court's decision is accepted by creditors who represent at least three quarters of claims. As soon as a creditors' administration is approved, the company is run in accordance with the court's instructions.

A creditors' administration lasts for no longer than one year, but the court may extend this period by another year. A creditors' administration may be terminated in the following cases:

- the purpose of the creditors' administration is achieved;
- it is not possible to achieve the purpose of the creditors' administration;
- there is evidence of fraud.

Process of realising the assets of the company

Creditors in their meeting elect a body which the administrator manages to realise the company's assets in order to satisfy creditors. This body may invalidate any transaction entered into by the debtor within the previous 12 months if it unfairly prejudices creditors.

Creditors' claims must be notified to the administration within three months of the published notice of liquidation. Funds obtained during liquidation are distributed in the following order:

- debts to employees;
- taxes and other payments (debts) to State and local authorities;
- debts to suppliers (physical or legal persons) of unmanufactured agricultural goods;
- deposits to the social insurance institution for future monthly payments to employees relating to injuries incurred whilst at work;
- claims secured by a mortgage;
- expenses to compensate for damage to the environment, for land recultivation and for forest renewal;
- debts to creditors who have declared their demands within the prescribed term;
- debts to other creditors.

KPMG contact partner

Peter Graudums
KPMG
Kr. Valdemara lela 33–4
Riga LV-1010

Telephone: +371 733 3023
Fax: +371 733 3023

Lebanon

Legislation

Lebanon insolvency law is based upon the relevant legislation contained in the French Companies Law.

Changes in legislation are expected as the current law is outdated.

Insolvency procedures

Insolvency is declared by adjudication of the Court of Primary Jurisdiction in the principal place of business.

The management of the insolvent's estate is entrusted to a salaried proxy, the receiver. The number of receivers may, at any period, be raised to three who have to act collectively.

None of the family, relations or the relations by marriage of the insolvent up to the fourth degree inclusive may be appointed receiver.

Liquidation

Liquidation is the statutory process for winding up the affairs of a company. When the company has gone into liquidation, it is incumbent upon the receiver to make the declaration. The declaration must be lodged with the clerk of the court in the district where the company's head office is located.

Voluntary liquidation

This is initiated by management but after obtaining shareholders' approval. Creditors' confirmation is conveyed through a Commercial Court Ruling.

Compulsory liquidation

This is initiated by a creditor. The court normally makes a winding-up order and appoints the liquidator.

The liquidator prepares a statement showing the net assets of the company. A creditor should submit a signed proof of debt within eight days of the adjudication of insolvency. Afterwards, the liquidator deposits in the court clerk's office a statement of the debts which he has checked and the commissioner-judge's decision is taken in connection with each claim.

Bankruptcy

Bankruptcy applies to a trader or company whose financial business is disrupted and ceases to meet its commercial obligations. A petition of bankruptcy may be made to the court by the individual, one of his creditors or the public prosecutor. A receiver is appointed to manage the bankruptcy. The receiver carries out an inventory of the bankrupt's assets. A balance sheet is prepared and submitted to the court.

Scheme of arrangement

A scheme of arrangement is a court-approved arrangement between an individual or company and its creditors. This is usually entered into where the creditors are of the opinion that, if business activities continue as normal, they are more likely to recover their debts than if the company is wound up. A scheme of arrangement may be granted for total or partial relinquishment of the insolvent's assets.

Union

When no scheme of arrangement has been reached, the creditors shall be in a state of union. The commissioner-judge shall immediately consult them as much on the facts of management as on the utility of maintaining or replacing the receivers. The court shall appoint the receivers of the union.

Closure for insufficient assets

If at any time whatsoever, before the confirmation of the scheme of arrangement or the formation of the union, the course of the insolvency operations comes to a standstill due to lack of assets, the court, may, in the light of the commissioner-judge's report, pronounce the closure of the insolvency operations.

Creditors

The creditors are categorised as:

- pledges and preferential creditors over movable property;
- mortgagees and preferential creditors over immovable property;
- unsecured creditors.

KPMG contact partner

Riad A. Mansour
KPMG
Hamra Square Building
Beirut
Lebanon

Telephone: +961 (1) 348 710
Fax: +961 (1) 350 238

Lesotho

Legislation

- Insolvency Proclamation No. 51 of 1957;
- Companies Act 1967;
- regulations in terms of the Companies Act 1967 for winding up and judicial management of companies (ss. 166–276).

Insolvency procedures

- compulsory winding up by the court of an individual or partnership or company;
- members' or creditors' voluntary winding up of a company;
- voluntary surrender of estate by an individual;
- judicial management;
- schemes of arrangement or compromise.

Compulsory winding up

An insolvent's estate or company may be wound up by the court if:

- judgment has been obtained for a debt and cannot be satisfied or paid;
- any attempt is made to dispose of assets thereby prejudicing creditors or preferring one creditor above another;
- any attempt is made to compromise debts with creditors;
- written notice is given to any creditor that his debt cannot be paid;
- an executor of a deceased estate which is found to be insolvent petitions the court;
- a judicial manager makes application to the court;
- the debtor departs from his dwelling or otherwise absents himself with intent to delay the payment of his debts.

Voluntary winding up

The court may grant a voluntary winding up order if an individual petitions the court. No court order is required if a company has by special resolution resolved that it be wound up either by its members or creditors.

Judicial management

The court may grant a judicial management order when so petitioned by a director, member or creditor. Judicial management is a temporary moratorium to enable a company to surmount its financial problems under the management of a person specifically appointed for this purpose who acts in the place of the board of directors.

Scheme of arrangement or compromise

A scheme of arrangement or compromise may be proposed between the company in liquidation and its creditors or its members. Should the scheme or compromise be approved by creditors and sanctioned by the court the winding up order is set aside and the company is reinstated.

A private individual may also submit an offer of composition to his trustee for consideration by his creditors. However, any condition which makes the offer subject to the rehabilitation of the insolvent is of no effect.

Commencement and control of insolvency procedures

Insolvency procedures can generally be instituted by:

- anyone who is a creditor and has been unable to obtain settlement by legal means;
- directors, members, shareholders and an individual on his own recognisance;
- a judicial manager;
- an executor of an insolvent deceased estate;
- an *ex parte* application.

The effect once insolvency procedures have commenced is:

- to divest the company or individual of all assets which then vest in the master of the High Court until a liquidator or trustee is appointed by him;
- to stay civil proceedings;
- to cause trading to cease except in the case of judicial management, or where it is necessary to preserve an asset or by direction of the court on application by a liquidator;
- generally to curtail all activities except those of an individual who is entitled to earn an income but subject to certain restrictions and conditions;
- to make void every disposition of property (including rights of action) made after winding up has commenced, unless the court declares otherwise;
- to make void any attachment or execution order against the assets after the winding up has commenced;
- to make void, in the case of a company, every transfer of shares or alteration of the status of its members effected after winding up has commenced.

Controls, functions and duties are exercised by:

- the master of the High Court initially;
- a liquidator in the case of a company and a trustee in the case of an individual or a partnership who must account to the master of the High Court;
- the judicial manager in the case of judicial management.

The duties of the liquidator or trustee are:

- to investigate and report on the affairs of the company or insolvent, including contraventions by directors, members or individuals;
- to trace and realise all assets;
- to lodge a liquidation and distribution or contribution account with the master of the High Court.

The judicial manager continues the business of the company and reports to creditors on the viability of either continuing under judicial management or placing the company in liquidation.

Creditors

Secured creditors are entitled to value their security and prove their claims. On realisation of the security the creditor receives payment of the amount realised less administration costs. Any free residue resulting from assets realised, including any excess on secured assets realised, is awarded to preferential creditors such as the Receiver of Revenue, staff salaries and wages and audit fees within certain limits.

Thereafter:

- concurrent creditors are entitled to a pro rata share of whatever balance is available;
- foreign creditors enjoy the same considerations but payment in foreign currency is subject to government approval;
- shareholders are entitled to receive dividends only after all other creditors are settled in full;
- in the event of insufficient funds being available to cover liquidation costs, a contribution will be levied on the petitioning creditor and/or creditors who proved claims.

Other matters

Restrictions and shortcomings of the procedures

The Attorney General has asked interested parties for their comments on the 1957 Proclamation and relevant legislation with a view to producing a consolidation Act.

End result of the procedures

Being subject to the dictates and strict control of the master of the High Court, the present procedures ensure an equitable distribution of the proceeds of assets realised.

Duration and timing

Insolvency procedures may take from nine months to over two years to complete.

KPMG contact partner

Tjaart du Plessis
KPMG Administrators (Pty) Ltd
19th Floor
Carlton International Trade Center
Commissioner Street
2001 Johannesburg
South Africa

Telephone: +27 (11) 332 7111
Fax: +27 (11) 331 9517

Libya

Legislation

Procedures followed in cases of insolvency, dissolution, liquidation and bankruptcy in Libya are governed by legislation detailed by the relevant articles of the Libyan Commercial Code issued in 1953.

Insolvency procedures

Any merchant who is insolvent may, so long as his bankruptcy has not been declared, propose a composition to his creditors. Conditions of admission to the proceedings of composition are detailed by art. 707 of the Commercial Code.

An application for permission to compromise with creditors must be made by a request signed by the debtor, addressed to the tribunal of the town where the principal office of the firm is situated and stating the reasons which have caused his insolvency and the reason for the proposal for a compromise. He must present together with the request the accountancy records, a detailed balance sheet and an estimate of the assets as well as a list of his creditors.

The tribunal shall, if it considers the proposal to be admissible, declare the composition proceedings to be opened.

The procedure to be followed is detailed by art. 710 of the code which can be summarised as follows:

- a judge for the composition proceedings is delegated;
- a meeting of creditors is ordered to be convened;
- a judicial commissioner is appointed;
- the applicant shall deposit with the registry of the tribunal the amount presumed to be necessary for the entire proceedings.

During the composition proceedings a debtor shall retain the administration of his property and the management of his business under the supervision of the judicial commissioner and the guidance of the delegate judge.

A delegate judge shall, immediately after the order of admission to the composition proceedings, make a memorandum thereof under the last entry of the books submitted which are returned to the debtor, and shall be kept at the disposal of the delegate judge and the judicial commissioner.

The judicial commissioner shall proceed with the examination of the list of creditors and debtors which the debtor has presented together with the composition request.

The commissioner shall arrange for sending creditors the debtor's proposals and the date of the creditors' meeting.

The judicial commissioner shall prepare an inventory of the property of the debtor and an itemised report on the causes of his financial position, the conduct of the debtor, the proposals for a composition and the security offered to creditors. These documents are filed at the registry at least three days prior to the meeting of creditors.

If the judicial commissioner finds that a debtor has concealed or withheld any part of his assets; wilfully omitted to indicate one or more outstanding claims; declared any non-existent liabilities or committed any other act of fraud, the commissioner must immediately notify the delegate judge thereof, who shall, after making the appropriate investigation, obtain a bankruptcy declaration from the tribunal.

A meeting of creditors shall be controlled by the delegate judge.

At the meeting of creditors the judicial commissioner shall explain his report and the final proposal of the debtor. Any creditor may state the reasons for which he does not consider the approval for a composition admissible or acceptable or may declare any objections to the claims of creditors. A debtor shall have an opportunity of replying and of disputing, for his part, any claims — for which he must give the judge appropriate explanations.

A composition must be approved by a majority of the voting creditors representing two thirds of the total claims admitted to the vote.

In the minutes of a meeting of creditors the favourable and opposing votes of creditors shall be recorded with a statement of the names of the voters and the amounts of their relative claims. The minutes shall be signed by the delegate judge, the commissioner or registrar.

If the required majority of votes required is not attained, the delegate judge shall at once report to the tribunal which shall proceed in declaring the bankruptcy of the debtor.

If the required majority is attained, the delegate judge shall by an order published by posting on the noticeboard, call a hearing at which the parties shall appear before him not later than 30 days after the affixing of the order.

The tribunal shall, after verifying that the composition satisfies the conditions detailed by art. 728 of the Commercial Code, ratify the composition. If the conditions are not satisfied, it shall declare the debtor bankrupt.

Measures taken in ratification of the composition, appeals against ratification decisions, rejection and effects of a composition on creditors are explained in detail by arts 729, 730 and 731 of the Code.

After ratification of a composition the judicial commissioner shall supervise the implementation thereof in accordance with the procedure laid down. He shall report to the judge any actions which may have a detrimental effect on creditors.

Cancellation and annulment of a composition are governed by arts 868 and 869 of the Commercial Code. By cancelling a composition the tribunal shall declare the opening of bankruptcy proceedings.

KPMG contact partner

Ibrahim Baruni
PO Box 1054
Tripoli
Libya

Telephone: +218 (21) 3332225
Fax: +218 (21) 3332225

Lithuania

Legislation

Insolvency legislation is consolidated in the Law on Bankruptcy 1992, which includes some subsequent amendments. In addition, some relevant provisions can be found in the Law on Commercial Banks 1995. Lithuanian insolvency law basically follows the pattern of continental Europe. There are certain features which make it similar to German legislation, and there are some which make it similar to French (for example, insolvency set-off is not possible at present). It should be kept in mind that this body of legislation is still developing, especially due to the rapidly developing securities regulations. At present a new Bankruptcy Law is being drafted.

A certain body of case law already exists, but this does not have the same importance as in common law countries.

Insolvency procedures

Legal definition of insolvency

National law does not make a distinction between corporate insolvency and bankruptcy of an individual. As already mentioned, separate laws may contain special rules for different types of economic entities.

There is no special legal definition for insolvency. However, the law defines (a) the grounds for initiation of insolvency proceedings and (b) types of insolvency procedures.

Grounds

Grounds for the initiation of insolvency procedures are as follows:

- if an entity is insolvent, i.e., it cannot fulfil matured liabilities;
- if an entity's assets are less than its liabilities;
- if an entity disposes of its assets in such a way that its creditors have reason to believe that their claims will not be satisfied because of the disposition.

The petition for insolvency may be filed by creditors or the entity itself (owners or management).

Procedures

Extrajudicial

The insolvency proceedings may be initiated and carried on without judicial (i.e., court) review, if the following conditions are satisfied, namely, there are no claims pending in the courts against the entity, the entity's assets are sufficient to cover its liabilities, and the entity declares publicly that it is insolvent. The decision to apply extrajudicial procedure may be taken by a meeting of creditors.

Judicial

The insolvency is declared by the court upon submission of the petition accompanied with certain documents.

Voluntary arrangement ('*talkis sutartis*')

A creditor (or a group of them) may enter into a voluntary arrangement with the debtor. Such a multilateral agreement (or several bilateral agreements) should include the balance sheet of the debtor, a list of its debts, conditions upon which debts are rescheduled (restructured) and settled. The arrangement may be entered into if all the unsecured creditors consent to it. The voluntary arrangement shall be approved by the court, irrespective of which insolvency procedure is applied. Upon approval by the court of the arrangement, the state of insolvency of the entity is terminated.

Restructuring ('*reorganizavimas*')

This is a procedure carried out either by creditors, or a receiver, or owners of the entity by means of which its structure is changed and assets are transferred to other economic entities, also categories of activities are diversified in order to meet creditors' claims. (The restructuring procedure under insolvency law is to be distinguished from the one under company law.)

Restructuring may be started upon the court's decision if there is a possibility of restoring solvency of the entity, or selling part of the entity's assets to pay debts without discontinuing the business. The court will approve restructuring only if creditors with not less than two thirds of total claims consent to it.

The restructuring plan shall be approved by the court. Insolvency proceedings are suspended for the time the plan is in force, and are terminated as soon as the restructuring achieves its goals. In the case of failure, the court would renew the proceedings.

Rescue ('*sanavimas*')

Rescue is defined as measures of administrative, economic, financial character applied to the entity upon the financial guarantee of the State or other third persons in order to avoid insolvency. Recourse to rescue may be had if neither a voluntary arrangement is entered, nor restructuring is agreed.

Rescue may not last for more than 18 months. Within the first 12 months of the rescue, not less than one third of the total claims should be satisfied. The rescue is administered by persons having won the tender. Investments by those persons made during the rescue are treated as their participation in the entity (which can be equity and/or debt participation).

Liquidation ('*likvidavimas*')

An entity may be liquidated three months after the decision to liquidate is taken by the court (or its creditors under the extrajudicial procedure). Real estate of the entity shall be sold by a public auction. Liquidation of the entity shall be announced publicly and each of its creditors shall be informed separately. Upon liquidation of the insolvent entity, it is held that all of its obligations and all obligations towards the entity are matured.

Intentional insolvency

This is not a category of insolvency as such, but there are special legal provisions. It can be declared only by the court, upon having proof that an entity intentionally tried to avoid paying its creditors. If this is the case, the court shall examine all the contracts of the entity concluded within preceding the 12 months. Obligations of the intentionally insolvent entity crystallise when the court declares intentional insolvency.

Satisfaction of claims

When the court declares an entity insolvent, all payments are stopped.

The order of satisfaction of claims is as set out below:

- claims of the employees arising out of labour relations, and claims out of unsettled payments for purchased agricultural products;

- claims of Social Insurance Fund for unpaid mandatory contributions;
- secured creditors, expenses of administering the insolvent entity, claims to pay for goods supplied between declaring the entity insolvent and the decision to liquidate it, taxes;
- claims of unsecured creditors.

All the creditors are treated equally, irrespective of their nationality, origin of their capital, or ownership.

Mortgages and pledges on certain kinds of assets must be publicly registered in order to be valid and to qualify for the preferential treatment.

Insolvency practitioners

At present, there is no authorisation procedure for insolvency practitioners. Also, it is quite unusual to appoint a lawyer as a receiver. The law only sets out certain requirements to be a receiver (*'administratorius'*). Owners, directors or other heads of administration of the insolvent entity may not be appointed as receivers. It is quite normal that someone belonging to the former staff of an insolvent entity is appointed.

When appointed as a receiver, a person is liable for loss caused to the administered entity. Any action of the receiver leading to an increase in debts (liabilities) of the entity shall be approved by the court (with minor exceptions).

Validity of contracts

The receiver of an insolvent entity is entitled to contest before the court any contract entered by the entity within the 12 months preceding the insolvency, if 'a damage was done to the entity' because of the contract (art. 7 of the Law on Bankruptcy). It is quite difficult to outline a general trend in case law at present with regard to application of this provision by the courts. It is reasonable to say that there should be clear and unambiguous evidence presented that the contract was of an extraordinary character.

See also 'Intentional insolvency'.

Commercial banks and other financial institutions

National law sets out a more sophisticated legal regime with regard to the insolvency of commercial banks. The Bank of Lithuania as the supervising institution is given powers to involve itself and to regulate activities of a bank before legal proceedings can be started in the court. Depending on the circumstances of a case, a bank may have certain activities suspended. Such a situation is called 'temporary receivership', although it has little to do with the legal meaning of receivership as such. If the financial standing of a bank deteriorates, the Bank of Lithuania may appoint a receiver which would take over most of the powers of the board and of the supervisory council of the bank. The settlements of the bank under such a receivership are stopped, although the accrual of liabilities continues. The suspension of a bank's activities differs from insolvency, *inter alia*, with regard to set-off (it was quite often used during the latest banking crisis). As soon as the bank's financial position is restored, this receivership is lifted.

KPMG contact person

Leif René Hansen
KPMG Lietuva
Stulginskio 4, 4th floor
LT 2600 Vilnius

Telephone: +370 (2) 61 18 03
Fax: +370 (2) 62 08 51

Luxembourg

Insolvency procedures

Insolvency procedures under the framework of Luxembourg laws can be categorised into four broad areas. These include liquidations, both voluntary and court-ordered, controlled management (*gestion contrôlée*), suspension of payments and schemes of arrangements.

Liquidations

Liquidations in Luxembourg are initiated in a number of instances, some of which include the following:

- the company reaches the end of its term in accordance with its articles and memorandum of association. Companies are no longer required to state the duration of their existence and consequently, liquidations resulting from the end of their stated duration are rare;
- the company engages in illegal activities which can result in an order for the winding up of the company by local competent authorities;
- the shareholders of the company resolve to wind up the company (voluntary liquidation);
- an order to wind up the company is declared by the court of its own accord or upon petition by one or more creditors (court-ordered liquidation).

Of the reasons enumerated above, most liquidations are initiated either by the court or by shareholders.

Court liquidation

A court-ordered liquidation, usually arising from a petition lodged by one or more creditors against a company, results in the appointment of a 'sworn' liquidator ('*curateur*'). This liquidator is nominated by the court and is responsible for the liquidation of the company.

At the same time that a liquidator is nominated, the court also appoints a 'judge-commissioner' ('*juge-commissaire*') to the company. The judge-commissioner's role is to provide guidance and supervision to the liquidator in winding up the company.

Upon his appointment by the court, the liquidator becomes the sole legal representative of the company. The liquidator carries out his duties, which include realising assets and dealing with creditors' claims for the benefit of the company's creditors.

From the date of liquidation, all debts owed by the company crystallise and, as far as creditors' claims are concerned, interest on most debts ceases to accumulate.

The liquidator requires the approval of creditors in order to carry on the business of the company but otherwise has the ability to act and bind the company in all other undertakings.

Once a final list of creditors' claims has been established, and a dividend distributed where funds are available, the liquidator presents a report on his administration to the creditors. This report includes an account of the liquidator's receipts and payments.

The liquidator then reports to the court and requests the closure of his administration.

Voluntary liquidations

A voluntary liquidation is initiated by the shareholders of the company who resolve to wind up the company at a general meeting of shareholders in the presence of a notary public. At this same meeting the shareholders also appoint a liquidator, who can be any natural or legal person.

As soon as the company is in liquidation, the management is carried out by the liquidator instead of the directors. The liquidator's tasks include realising assets and dealing with the claims of creditors.

As with court liquidations, from the date of commencement of the liquidation, all debts owed by the company crystallise and, as far as creditors' claims are concerned, interest on most debts ceases to accumulate.

The liquidator requires the approval of shareholders at a general meeting in order to carry on the business of the company but otherwise has the ability to act for and bind the company in all other undertakings.

After the performance of his mandate, the liquidator reports on the conduct of his administration to the shareholders at a second general meeting. This meeting orders an audit of the liquidator's accounts.

A third and final general meeting puts an end to the liquidation and discharges the liquidator and the auditor of their respective liquidation mandates. This meeting must also be held before a notary public.

An alternative to the method described above is the liquidation of the entity involving an undertaking by the entity's parent company to pay all the liabilities of the entity. In this instance, a notary, once satisfied that the entity's shareholders are capable of underwriting the liabilities, carries out certain administrative formalities which effectively place the entity into liquidation.

Although this procedure is simple, quick and less costly, it should be used with care because of the far-reaching implications of the parent company's guarantee. It may be appropriate only for a company whose position is thoroughly known by the parent company.

Controlled management

This procedure is usually adopted where a company is in financial difficulties but is not yet insolvent. It allows a company to seek some relief through the reorganisation of its business or the proper realisation of its assets.

To that effect, an application for controlled management is made to the court setting out the grounds upon which relief is being sought. The application can be made at the instigation of the majority of directors or members of the company.

The application, with all its supporting documentation, must be able to show that the remedy being sought is capable of either ensuring the restoration of the business, or improving the conditions for realisation of assets, otherwise it will be rejected by the court.

If the court accepts the application, a judge is appointed to make a report within such period as the court decides. In practice, the appointed judge will arrange to be assisted by an expert to investigate the affairs of the company.

Once a judge has been appointed, the company may not, without his written consent, alienate, pledge or mortgage any of its assets or enter into any contracts, or receive any transferable capital, upon penalty of the transaction being declared void.

Once the investigating team submits a report of its findings to the court, the court either makes the order for controlled management and appoints a commissioner to supervise the company's assets, or the application is dismissed and a liquidation is ordered.

The commissioner must approve any disposal of the company's assets and also prepare a proposal for the reorganisation of the business or a systematic and orderly disposal of the company's assets. The proposed reorganisation must be approved by a majority of the creditors.

Suspension of payments

Suspension of payments is granted to a company which, as a consequence of extraordinary and unforeseen events, is temporarily obliged to cease making payments to its creditors. It effectively provides some relief to companies facing liquidity problems through no fault of their own.

An application for suspension of payments must be made to both the commercial court and the High Court of Justice. Experts are subsequently appointed to investigate the company's financial position.

The proposed suspension of payments must be approved by a majority of the creditors, representing more than 75 per cent of the claims, present at a meeting arranged by the Commercial Court.

The court also determines the duration of any suspension of payments and appoints one or more administrators who are responsible for supervising and controlling the company's business throughout the whole of the suspension period.

Judicial schemes of arrangement

This procedure is used when a company wishes to avoid being wound up either voluntarily or by the court by negotiating an acceptable arrangement with its unsecured creditors. It is a fairly complex procedure in that many formalities must be observed.

The scheme will only be passed if the majority of creditors, representing three quarters of all sums due, have accepted the company's proposal.

The company must apply to the court with its proposal for a scheme of arrangement. The application must include the grounds upon which the application is being made, a list of the assets available, a list specifying the names and amounts due to creditors and the proposal itself.

During these proceedings, the company may not dispose of, mortgage or otherwise deal with its assets, without the proper authority of the judge.

Before examining whether there are grounds to allow the petition, the court will appoint a judge to investigate the company's position. The judge is required to report to the court on his findings within eight days of his appointment. He may appoint experts to assist him in his investigation.

If the court determines there are grounds for commencement of proceedings to grant a scheme, it will convene a meeting of creditors for the purpose of voting on the scheme.

Secured creditors will only be able to vote in respect of their claims if they surrender their security. These creditors may, however, vote in the scheme without renouncing their security but only for an amount equivalent to one half of their claims.

If, in the course of considering an application for a scheme of arrangement, the court considers that the company is not acting in good faith, or if the processes outlined above fail, it may order the company bankrupt.

KPMG contact partner

Alan Boyn
KPMG Corporate Finance
31 Allée Scheffer
L-2520 Luxembourg

Telephone: +352 225 151
Fax: +352 225 171

Macau

Insolvency procedures in Macau are regulated by the laws of Portugal. Reference should be made, therefore, to the section in this book dealing with Portugal.

KPMG contact partner

Nick Etches
KPMG Peat Marwick
8th Floor, Prince's Building
GPO Box 50
Hong Kong

Telephone: +852 2522 6022
Fax: +852 2845 2588

Aloysius H. Y. Tse
KPMG Peat Marwick e Associados
23rd Floor D, Bank of China Building
Avenida Doutor Mario Soares
Caixa Postal 701
Macau

Telephone: +853 781 092
Fax: +853 781 096

Malawi

Legislation

The procedures for winding up a corporate body are dealt with in Part XII of the Companies Act 1984 which was promulgated on 1 April 1986. Consequently, the UK Companies Acts 1908 and 1913 which applied to Malawi before the enactment of the Companies Act 1984 no longer apply.

The winding up of a company may be either by the court or voluntary. Where it is decided that a company should be wound up, the liability of the members to the settlement of the company's debts and liabilities is restricted to the amount unpaid on the shares in respect of which that member is liable, or the amount undertaken by him to contribute to the assets of the company in the event of its being wound up. Dividends to members are only paid after all debts and other liabilities due by the company have been settled.

Insolvency procedures

Winding up by the court

Generally, a company may be wound up by court order on the petition of the company itself, or any creditor or person having an interest in the affairs of the company subject to the court being satisfied that the reasons given in the petition justify such a course of action.

Appointment of provisional liquidator

On acceptance of the winding up petition, the court may appoint the official receiver or any other person to be a provisional liquidator of the company. The provisional liquidator will exercise all the functions and powers of a liquidator in such manner as may be prescribed in the instrument of appointment prepared by the court.

In a situation where a provisional liquidator has not been appointed by the court, the official receiver will be the provisional liquidator until directed otherwise. The office of the liquidator may be filled or vacated by appointment or order of the court, the members or creditors of the company.

Duties of liquidator

Whilst in office, the liquidator of the company is empowered to take under his control all the property owned by the company being wound up or to which the company holds title. The liquidator may, with leave of the court and the committee of inspection, carry on the business of the company for its beneficial winding up for a period not exceeding four weeks after the date of the winding up order.

Additionally, the liquidator is required to establish the indebtedness and other claims against the company and arrange for an orderly settlement thereof within a given period. Similarly, he is required for the benefit of the company to dispose of the property held in trust by him at the best available offer and within the shortest period possible.

The functions of his office cease when the realisation of the property has been fully effected and the final dividend to the creditors has been distributed, following which an application to the court may be made to obtain approval of the dissolution of the company.

Rights of creditors

Claims by creditors are only endorsed by the court to the extent to which the company in liquidation is proved to be liable. Settlement of such claims is effected on priority bases starting with most secured creditors down to the unsecured creditors and by reference to the ability of the company to pay at any given moment. A final dividend (where part settlement is made in full satisfaction of the debt) to creditors, or settlement of the amounts owing, is made at the discretion of the liquidator or official receiver and liquidator of the company.

Voluntary winding up

A company may be wound up voluntarily if the life period of the company stipulated in its memorandum and articles expires or if it is resolved by a special resolution that the company be wound up.

Winding up commences when the special winding up resolution is passed and it becomes illegal for the company to continue carrying on the business except as is required for the beneficial winding up of that company. Before the resolution for winding up the company is passed, the degree of solvency of the company must be ascertained by the directors and a written declaration to the effect that the company, in their opinion, is in a position to pay all its debts and liabilities in full within a given period — normally not exceeding 12 months.

Insolvency

Where the liquidator (appointed by the company in a general meeting) is of the opinion that the company will not be able to pay its debts in full, he is required to call a meeting of the creditors, with minimum delay, with a view to presenting to them a statement of the assets and liabilities of the company.

Staying of members' voluntary winding up

After convening such a meeting, the winding up proceeds as if it was a creditors' voluntary winding up. At any time during the course of a voluntary winding up before the dissolution of the company, the company may, by a special resolution, resolve that the winding-up proceedings be stayed, subject to confirmation by the court. If confirmed, the liquidator can be discharged and the directors can henceforth resume the management of the company.

Other matters

Where a creditor has issued execution against the goods or land of a company or has attached any debt due to the company and the company is subsequently wound up, the creditor may not be entitled to retain the benefit of the execution or attachment against the liquidator unless he has completed it before the commencement of the winding up.

Any officer of the company being wound up who is found guilty of defrauding creditors of the company is liable to a fine of K5,000 and to imprisonment for a term of two years.

External companies

An external company in Malawi can be wound up by petition to the court and the provisions affecting the winding up of a locally incorporated company also apply to external companies.

KPMG contact partner

Farouk Sacranie
KPMG Peat Marwick
Able House
Hanover Avenue
PO Box 508
Blantyre
Malawi

Telephone: +265 620744
Fax: +265 620575

Malaysia

Legislation

Insolvency practitioners, i.e., liquidators and receivers and managers, are regulated within a statutory framework primarily comprising the Companies Act 1965, the Companies Regulations 1966 and the Companies (Winding up) Rules 1972.

Qualification for appointment

Appointments of receivers and liquidators are regulated by the Companies Act 1965 as follows:

Receivers

Only an approved liquidator or the official receiver may be appointed as the receiver of the property of a company. An approved liquidator is defined as a company auditor who has been approved by the Ministry of Finance as a liquidator. An official receiver means the official assignee or any other officer appointed under the Bankruptcy Act 1967. In addition, he must not be an undischarged bankrupt, a mortgagee of any property of the company, an auditor or an officer of the company.

Liquidators

Generally, only an approved liquidator or the official receiver may be appointed as liquidator or provisional liquidator of a company being wound up by the court. Provisional liquidators may be appointed after the presentation of a winding-up petition and before the making of a winding-up order. There are other provisions in the Companies Act that disqualify appointments as liquidators. For both types of voluntary winding up, a liquidator need not be an approved liquidator. However, in a creditors' voluntary winding up, his appointment must be approved by a majority of the creditors in number and value at a creditors' meeting.

Powers and duties

The powers and duties of a liquidator and a provisional liquidator are set out in the Companies Act 1965 and the Companies (Winding up) Rules 1972. Certain powers may only be exercised with the authority of either the court or of the committee of inspection. These powers relate to the continuation of business, payment of creditors, arrangements with creditors, compromising calls and debts and appointment of an advocate to assist the liquidator.

The powers of a receiver are set out in the debenture deed. These would normally include the power to take possession of and to sell the charged assets, power to carry on and manage the business of the company, power to borrow and the power to commence and continue legal actions against debtors and to defend actions against the company. The Companies Act also requires the receiver to perform certain duties and he may also apply to the court for directions in relation to any matter arising from the performance of his functions.

Other relevant legislation

Liquidators and receivers should also take note of other legislation in the performance of their duties, e.g. various tax legislation relating to the sale of the assets of the company and its trading profits (if any). The Employment Act 1955 is also important particularly in relation to retrenchment, termination benefits and notice period.

Insolvency procedures

Receivership

Appointment by the court

Application may be made to the High Court to appoint a receiver (or a receiver and manager) to assume custody of the assets of a company where its assets are deemed to be in jeopardy and it is necessary to protect them. The application can be made by unsecured and secured creditors of the company and a debenture is not necessary. A receiver appointed by the court is an officer of the court and is not an agent of the company. He must act in accordance with the terms of the order under which he is appointed.

Appointment by debenture holder

Upon appointment, a floating charge (if any) will crystallise into a fixed charge and the receiver will take control of the company's assets and realise them for the benefit of the debenture holder. A receiver and manager will only manage the business of a company if it will benefit the debenture holder, e.g., higher realisations from a going-concern sale or to run down stocks of raw material and/or work-in-progress. The powers of the receiver, which normally include the power of management, are contained in the debenture deed. Although a receiver is appointed by and responsible to the debenture holder, he operates as an agent of the company and has a responsibility to consider the interests of other creditors.

Liquidation

Members' voluntary winding up

A company may be wound up voluntarily under the following circumstances:

- where the memorandum or articles provide that the company be dissolved when the period fixed for its duration expires or a specific event occurs and the company in general meeting has passed an ordinary resolution to wind up voluntarily; or
- the company so resolves by special resolution.

Under this insolvency procedure the majority of the directors of the company must make a written declaration that they have made an inquiry into the affairs of the company and, at a meeting of directors, they have formed the opinion that the company will be able to pay its debts in full within a period not exceeding 12 months after the resolution to wind up. The company therefore has to be solvent before proceeding with a members' voluntary winding up.

The liquidator is appointed by the company in general meeting and upon his appointment all powers of the directors will cease and any transfer of shares or any alteration in the status of the members will be void. The company shall also cease to carry on its business except where the liquidator is of the opinion that it is for the beneficial winding up of the company. His powers and duties are set out in the Companies Act 1965.

Creditors' voluntary winding up

Creditors' voluntary winding up occurs when the directors of a company make a statutory declaration that the company cannot continue its business by reason of its liabilities and that separate meetings of shareholders and creditors have been summoned. This procedure therefore occurs when the company is insolvent. After the above declaration has been lodged with the Registrar of Companies and the official receiver, the directors shall appoint an approved liquidator to be the provisional liquidator.

A provisional liquidator has all the functions and powers of a liquidator in a creditors' winding up and his appointment shall continue until the appointment of a liquidator. The liquidator is nominated by the company in general meeting and approved by the creditors at their meeting. The creditors' nominee shall prevail if the company's nominee is not accepted by the creditors. The effect of a creditors' voluntary winding up and the powers and duties of the liquidator are similar to those in a members' voluntary winding up.

Compulsory winding up by the court

A company may be wound up under an order of the court on the petition of the company, any creditor, a contributory, the liquidator, the Minister and, in the case of a company carrying on a banking business, the central bank. The Companies Act provides for specific circumstances in which a company may be wound up by the court, which includes the inability of a company to pay its debts. Winding up shall be deemed to have commenced at the time of presentation of the petition to wind up.

The court may appoint the official receiver or an approved liquidator provisionally at any time after the presentation of a winding-up petition and before the making of a winding-up order. The provisional liquidator shall have all the powers of a liquidator subject to such limitations and restrictions as the court may specify in the order appointing him.

The liquidator is appointed by the court normally on the application of the petitioning solicitors. His powers and duties are set out in the Companies Act 1965.

After winding up has commenced, any disposition of the company's assets and any transfer of shares or alteration in the status of the members shall be void unless the court orders otherwise. In addition, any attachment, distress or execution put in force against the assets shall be void. When a winding-up order has been made, no action shall be taken against the company except with leave of the court. The liquidator would also require the approval of the court or the committee of inspection should he wish to continue the business of the company beyond four weeks after the date of the winding-up order.

Creditors

Secured creditors

A secured creditor is one who holds a mortgage, charge or lien on the assets of a debtor as security for a debt. He is in a position either at law or in equity to recoup partly or wholly from the assets of the debtor, with priority over unsecured creditors. If the security is in the form of a debenture, he may appoint a receiver or a receiver and manager over the charged assets of the debtor. In the case of a mortgage over land and/or property, he may commence foreclosure proceedings to sell the charged property by public auction.

Preferential creditors

The Companies Act 1965 classifies certain creditors in a company as preferential creditors who shall be paid in priority to all other unsecured debts. These preferential creditors are as follows:

- costs and expenses of winding up including petitioner's costs and liquidator's remuneration;
- wages and salaries not exceeding RM1,500 per employee in respect of services rendered within a period of four months before winding up commenced;
- amounts due in respect of workers' compensation under any written law;
- remuneration payable in respect of vacation leave;
- contributions due within a period of 12 months before the commencement of winding up relating to employees' provident funds or an approved retirement benefit scheme;
- amount of all federal tax assessed.

Unsecured creditors

Unsecured creditors include all creditors who are not secured or preferential creditors. They will only be paid after the claims of secured and preferential creditors have been fully settled during the course of a receivership or a liquidation. Unsecured creditors may petition to the court to wind up a company. Except in a members' voluntary winding up, they also have the right to determine whether a committee of inspection should be appointed to act with the liquidator, and to determine the members of the committee. In a creditors' voluntary winding up, they may appoint their nominee as liquidator if they so wish.

Priorities

The priority of payment in a liquidation is as follows:

- creditors secured by a fixed charge;
- preferential creditors except federal taxes;
- creditors secured by a floating charge;
- federal taxes;
- unsecured creditors.

In a receivership, the priority would be the same as above except that the receiver's costs would rank first and federal taxes and costs of winding up are not considered as preferential debts.

Costs incurred in realising the assets subject to a fixed charge would have to be paid before the secured creditor concerned. These costs would include the receiver's fees and expenses. Where the same assets are subject to more than one charge, the secured creditors would rank as specified, i.e., first charges, second charges etc.

Other matters

Liquidators must obtain tax clearance before making any distribution and this would normally take about 12 months to obtain. The liquidators would be personally liable if they made any distribution before tax clearance was obtained.

KPMG contact partner

Ooi, Woon Chee
KPMG Management Consulting
18th Floor Block B
Wisma Semantan
12 Jalan Gelenggang
Damansara Heights
50490 Kuala Lumpur
Malaysia

Telephone: +60 (3) 254 2233
Fax: +60 (3) 254 7005

Malta

Legislation

Maltese law on dissolution and winding up was the subject of a major overhaul with the enactment of the Companies Act 1995, in virtue of which local legislation has been carefully articulated to provide for important features which were absent from our law.

Other legislation regulating insolvency includes:

- the Commercial Code, in particular Part III on bankruptcy, applying only in the case of sole traders;
- the Civil Code, in particular those provisions on the ranking of creditors and on civil remedies which may be exercised by aggrieved parties;
- other specific statutes, including the Banking Act 1994 and the Insurance Business Act 1981 (the latter is due to be repealed and replaced by new legislation).

Insolvency procedures

Dissolution and winding up

A company shall be dissolved and wound up in two cases:

- where the company has by extraordinary resolution resolved that the company be dissolved and wound up by the court;
- where the company has by extraordinary resolution resolved that the company be dissolved and wound up voluntarily.

Voluntary dissolution and winding up

After filing of the extraordinary resolution the company is to cease to carry on business and any share transfers made without the sanction of the liquidator and any alteration in the status of the shareholders made, or to have effect, after the dissolution shall be void.

The directors of the company may decide to make a declaration of solvency confirming that they have made a full inquiry into the affairs of the company and are of the opinion that it will be able to pay its debts within 12 months from the date of dissolution. Where a declaration of solvency is drawn up, then the process is referred to as 'members' voluntary winding up' while if it is not drawn up then as 'creditors' voluntary winding up'.

Members' voluntary winding up

By extraordinary resolution, the company (or in default the court) is to appoint a liquidator and from that moment onwards, all the powers of the directors and of the company secretary shall cease. The liquidator is to call general meetings informing the shareholders of the financial situation of the company and to perform all acts conducive to the dissolution and consequent winding up, including the drawing up of a scheme of distribution according to the ranking of creditors. Following registration of the scheme of distribution and audited accounts and after the lapse of three months from the publication thereof the name of the company shall be struck off the register.

Creditors' voluntary winding up

The directors are to call a meeting of the creditors, following the general meeting at which the resolution to dissolve the company is passed, and at which the directors shall present a full statement of the position of the company's affairs together with a list of the creditors of the company and the estimated amount of their claims. The creditors and the company at their respective meetings are to appoint a liquidator by means of a resolution of the creditors and extraordinary resolution of the company. If different persons are so appointed, the person appointed by the creditors shall hold the post. If nobody is so appointed, the court shall intervene to do so. The creditors may also appoint not more than five representatives to form a liquidation committee and if such is formed, then the company may appoint up to five representatives of the contributories on the said committee. As in the case of a members' voluntary winding up, a scheme of distribution and audited accounts are to be prepared and filed with the Registrar of Companies so that the company will be eventually struck off the register.

Ranking of creditors and distribution of property

Subject to what is provided hereunder, the property of the company shall, on winding up, be applied in satisfaction of its liabilities *pari passu* and, unless otherwise provided, shall be distributed among the members according to their rights and interests in the company.

In drawing up the scheme of distribution the claims of all creditors would have to be satisfied in accordance with the legally established order of ranking, given below. It is to be noted that preferential treatment of specific debts arises not only out of the institutes of privileges and hypothecs regulated by the Civil Code, but also a considerable number of statutes dealing with widely varying subjects. In principle, privileges rank prior to hypothecs, and privileges and hypothecs may attach either to a particular asset of the debtor or to his general estate. Equally ranking privileges and equally ranking hypothecs are paid rateably.

The order of priority of creditors is as follows:

- winding up costs;
- wages due to employees in respect of an amount of Lm200 for each employee;
- income tax;
- debts due to pledgees;
- general privileges;
- debts due to a hotel keeper;
- wages of servants;
- supplier of provisions;
- value added tax;
- special privileges over movables;
- privileges over immovables;
- hypothecary debts according to the order of registration;
- unsecured claims.

Winding up by the court

A company may be dissolved and wound up by the court in the following cases:

- where the company has by extraordinary resolution resolved that the company be dissolved and wound up by the court;
- if the business of the company is suspended for an uninterrupted period of 12 months;

- where the company is unable to pay its debts.

A company is deemed to be unable to pay its debts either where a debt due by the company has remained unsatisfied, in whole or in part, after 24 weeks from the enforcement of an executive title against the company; or where it is proved to the satisfaction of the court that the company is unable to pay its debts, account being taken of the contingent and prospective liabilities of the company.

Furthermore, a company shall be dissolved by the court in the following cases:

- if the number of shareholders is reduced to below two and remains so for more than six months (unless it is a single-member company);
- where the number of directors is reduced below the statutory minimum and remains so for more than six months (the court may allow the company a period of 30 days within which to remedy the situation);
- where the court is of the opinion that there are grounds of sufficient gravity to warrant dissolution;
- where a definite period for the duration of the company has expired or an event occurs in terms of which the company is to be wound up (the court may allow the company a period of 30 days within which to remedy the situation).

Intervention of the court in any of the above cases shall be as a result of an application made either by the company in general meeting, by the board of directors, by a debenture holder, a creditor, by any contributory or by the Registrar. The court shall commence hearings during which the directors, secretary, contributories and creditors are entitled to make submissions. After the hearings the court may either dismiss or accede to the application or make provisional orders.

After a winding-up order is issued, the court may exercise various powers including the drawing up of a list of contributories and rectifying the register of members; causing the assets of the company to be collected and applied in the discharge of the company's liabilities in terms of law. Where the liabilities exceed the assets the court shall make an order for payment of the costs of the dissolution and winding up of the company in the order of priority it establishes having regard to the general order of priority established by law.

Liquidator

On the appointment of a liquidator, all the powers of the directors and of the company secretary shall cease. The liquidator may be vested with various powers which include:

- to bring any action or to defend any action or other legal proceeding in the name and on behalf of the company;
- to carry on the business of the company so far as may be necessary for its beneficial winding up;
- to pay creditors according to their ranking at law;
- to reach any compromise or arrangement with creditors or persons claiming to be creditors;
- to make calls on contributories or alleged contributories and to effect any compromise in relation to debts, liabilities and claims existing or alleged to be existing between the company and the contributories or other debtors;
- to represent the company in all matters and to do all such things as may be necessary for the winding up of the affairs of the company and distributing its assets.

Provisional administration, official receiver

A provisional administrator may be appointed by the court, after the filing of a winding-up application, to administer the estate or business of the company as the court may specify. The official receiver is to be appointed by the Minister responsible for the registration of partnerships who shall select such person from amongst public officers. The receiver is to carry out the investigations deemed necessary and to report thereon to the court and shall send to each creditor a statement of the company's affairs as prepared by the officers of the company. The receiver shall also investigate the affairs of the company and report thereon to the court. He is to remain in office until a liquidator is appointed. Once appointed, the liquidator is to start the process of liquidating the assets of the company in terms of law and once this process is completed the company is struck off the register.

Offences antecedent to dissolution or in the course of winding up

The Companies Act provides for what are commonly referred to as 'company law crimes', several of which may be committed either in the period preceding the dissolution of the company or further to the company being wound up, and include:

- where any past or present officer (director, shadow director, secretary and manager) of the company has within 12 months immediately preceding the date of dissolution or at any time after the dissolution, in any way concealed, removed, destroyed or otherwise disposed of any of the company's property or documents related thereto or acts fraudulently in acquiring property for the company or in acquiring the consent of the creditors;
- where an officer had the intention of defrauding the creditors in making a disposition;
- where officers do not cooperate fully with the liquidator in the winding-up procedure;
- where an officer misapplies, retains or becomes accountable for any money or other property of the company, or is guilty of any improper performance or breach of duty, he may be compelled to repay, restore or account for the property with interest or to contribute to the assets of the company in respect of the improper performance;
- other offences refer to situations where proper accounting records are not kept by the insolvent company and the company was at the time of dissolution unable to pay its debts;
- where fraudulent trading is engaged in: whereby business was carried out with the intent to defraud creditors — in such cases, the court may declare the parties to the said activities personally responsible, without any limitation of liability, for all or any of the liabilities of the company;
- where wrongful trading is said to be committed, when a company has been dissolved, by any person who was a director of the company and knew, or ought to have known prior to the dissolution of the company, that there was no reasonable prospect that the company would avoid being dissolved due to the insolvency.

Insurance Business Act 1981

This Act, which should soon be repealed, empowers the Minister of Finance to take the required action if an insurance company is 'conducting its business in a manner which is detrimental or hazardous to the public or to its policy holders', or has suspended or is about to suspend payment of its debts, or has been dissolved. In such cases, the Minister may, amongst other things:

- suspend or revoke the company's operating licence;
- appoint a person to assume full control over the company's assets and operations;
- order the company to wind up its business or its business in Malta;
- appoint a liquidator to wind up the affairs of the company.

Banking Act 1994

Where it appears to the Central Bank of Malta that a bank breaches any of the provisions of the Act; or no longer possesses sufficient own funds; or is likely to become unable to meet its obligations or can no longer be relied upon to fulfil its obligations towards its depositors or creditors; or has insufficient assets to cover its liabilities; or has suspended or is about to suspend payments; or by reason of the manner in which it is conducting or proposes to conduct its affairs, or for any other reason the interests of the depositors of the bank are threatened, it may take a series of actions which include:

- appoint a 'controller' to take control of the business of the bank;
- revoke or restrict its licence;
- order the bank to wind up its business or its business in Malta;
- appoint a person to act as liquidator to wind up the affairs of the bank.

A 'controller' appointed in terms of the Act assumes full control over the bank and its assets and his authority supersedes that of the directors, the liquidator, the curator in bankruptcy and the legal and judicial representatives of the company. He exercises all the powers, functions and duties of the bank, whether exercisable by the shareholders in general meeting or by the board of directors.

Where a bank considers that it is likely to become unable to meet its obligations or that it is about to suspend payment, it must inform the Central Bank of Malta in writing.

KPMG contact partner

Dr Louise Ellul Cachia Caruana
Joseph Tabone & Co.
3 V. Dimech Street
Floriana VLT.16
Malta

Telephone: +356 233 188
Fax: +356 234 647

Mauritius

Legislation

In Mauritius the main enactment governing winding up is embodied in the Companies Act 1984. Part XI of the Act relates specifically to winding up.

Winding up may be effected either by a court order or voluntarily. A voluntary winding up is in turn subdivided into members' and creditors' winding up.

Insolvency procedures

Winding up by the court

On hearing a petition, the court (i.e., the Bankruptcy Division of the Supreme Court of Mauritius) may dismiss it, adjourn the hearing or make any interim or other order that it thinks fit. The list of persons or corporate bodies who are entitled to present a petition is found in s. 216 of the Act along with the grounds upon which they can rely; security for costs has to be furnished prior to the hearing of the petition.

Within seven days of making the winding-up order, the petitioner has to lodge with the Registrar of Companies a copy of the order and the name and address of the liquidator appointed by the court. A copy of the order is delivered to the Official Receiver, the liquidator and the secretary of the company or such other person or in such manner as the court directs.

The liquidator so appointed takes control of all the property, movable and immovable, to which the company is or appears to be entitled. Within 14 days of the winding-up order a statement supported by an affidavit showing the assets and liabilities of the company, the creditors' names and addresses, the charges held by them and the dates on which they were created has to be delivered to the liquidator. Upon receipt of the statement of the company's affairs, the liquidator submits a preliminary report to the court as to the capital issued, subscribed and paid up and an estimate of the assets and liabilities together with the causes of the company's inability to honour its debts if such is the case.

When, in the opinion of the liquidator, any fraud or contravention of the Act has been committed, he may make further reports. By leave of the court any person may apply to have the winding up stayed.

The liquidator may summon a general meeting of the creditors or contributories for the purpose of ascertaining their wishes. The assets of the company will then be realised and all sums received are paid into a bank account. A notice is advertised in daily publications for creditors to file their proofs of claim, if any, and the court has its say. It may fix a date on or before which creditors have to prove their debts. Unless he has already completed the execution against any property of the company or attached any debts due to it, a creditor will not be entitled to retain the benefit of the execution or attachment. Any undue preference granted to a creditor is void or voidable.

In the event of the assets being insufficient to satisfy the liabilities, the court may make an order as to the priorities of any claims in such order as it thinks fit. A contributory may be ordered to pay any money due from him. When the liquidator has distributed a final dividend, if any, to the contributories, he may then apply to the court for an order that he be released and the company be dissolved. If such order is obtained, the company will then be considered as dissolved from the date mentioned therein.

Committee of inspection

If the need arises, and requests have been made by creditors or contributories, the liquidator may appoint a committee of inspection to act with him. Separate meetings of creditors and contributories are held for this purpose. Any difference as to the appointment or constitution of the committee is settled by the court.

Voluntary winding up

A company may be wound up voluntarily after the occurrence of an event, a lapse of time (as mentioned in the memorandum and articles) or by special resolution. The company has then to lodge with the Registrar of Companies a copy of such resolution and have it published in the *Government Gazette* and in two daily publications.

Members' winding up

Where the directors of a company have made an inquiry into the affairs of the company and at a meeting of directors they have formed the opinion that the company would be able to pay its debts within 12 months, they can make a declaration of solvency, and the voluntary winding up will be a members' voluntary winding up.

Where a liquidator is of the opinion that the company will not be able to pay its debts within 12 months he has to summon a meeting of the creditors forthwith and lay before them a statement of assets and liabilities of the company. In such a case the winding up will proceed as a creditors' winding up.

Creditors' winding up

If in the opinion of the directors a company is insolvent and it cannot continue business, then a creditors' winding up is carried out. The company must cease to carry on business unless, in the opinion of the liquidator, to do so would be beneficial. The corporate status and powers of the company will continue until its dissolution. Any transfer of shares or alteration in the status of the members will be void.

At a general meeting, the liquidator is appointed and his remuneration fixed. The liquidator can exercise certain powers of the court in such cases. Notices of a meeting of creditors are sent by registered post. The liquidator can be assisted in his task by a committee of inspection consisting of not more than five persons. The procedure for the realisation of assets, adjusting the rights of creditors and contributories is the same as in a winding up by the court.

General provisions for winding up

The property of a company will be applied *pari passu* in satisfaction of its liabilities and distributed among its members according to their rights and interests. The liquidator has to take into account that preferential claims have to be settled according to the laws of Mauritius and the relevant sections of the Civil Code relating to bankruptcy.

Where the affairs of the company have been fully wound up, the liquidator makes up an account showing how the winding up has been conducted and calls a general meeting of the company or, in the case of a creditors' voluntary winding up, a meeting of the company and the creditors, and he will lay the account before that meeting. Such a meeting is called by advertisement in two daily publications. Within seven days, a notice of the holding of the meeting is lodged with the Registrar of Companies and a copy thereof delivered to the Official Receiver.

The two legal officers controlling liquidators and the liquidation process are the Registrar of Companies and the Official Receiver (who is the administrative head of the Bankruptcy Division). Both are empowered to exercise control over the duties and conduct of liquidators. They monitor the actions of the liquidator and upon complaint they can cause prosecution to be instituted for any infringement of the Act.

In any form of winding up, the liquidator has to lodge a notice of his appointment within 14 days and deliver a copy to the Official Receiver. Within one month after the six months following his appointment and after every subsequent six months, the liquidator has to lodge an affidavit giving an account of his receipts and payments and the steps taken by him in the liquidation. Unclaimed dividends or money held for more than six months from the date it becomes payable, or any undistributed money, must be paid to the Official Receiver and be placed to the credit of the company's liquidation account. Any interest arising out of the investment of the money standing to the credit of the company's liquidation account is paid into the Consolidated Fund.

The court may, at any time within two years after a company has dissolved, make an order declaring the dissolution to have been void.

Rules may be made by the judges of the Supreme Court with respect to proceedings, practice and procedures of the court under this Act and generally in respect of winding up of companies. If no rules have been made then the rules of procedure used in England are followed except as to fees and costs where the tables of costs in bankruptcy rules are observed. The companies winding up rules made under the Bankruptcy Act are still in force.

Alternative simplified procedure for voluntary winding up

There is also an alternative simplified procedure for voluntary winding up of solvent companies. If the company has discharged all its debts and liabilities, any officer or member of the company may apply to the Registrar for a declaration of dissolution of the company. Prior to this the applicant has to publish a notice in the *Government Gazette* and in two daily publications and send by registered post to each director and to each member of the company, a notice to the effect that he proposes to apply for the dissolution of the company to the Registrar. If within 30 days no objection is lodged, the Registrar may dissolve the company.

KPMG contact partner

J. Jingree
KPMG
3rd Floor
12 Remy Ollier Street
Port Louis
Mauritius

Telephone: +230 280 8000
Fax: +230 208 3026

Mexico

Legislation

Insolvencies of corporations and businesses owned by individuals are regulated by the Bankruptcies and Suspension of Payments Law, which was enacted in April 1943. This law has never been amended and no changes are expected in the near future.

Insolvency procedures

The following insolvency procedures are available:

- bankruptcy;
- suspension of payments;
- '*concurso*'.

Even though on a very broad basis the term 'bankruptcy' is applicable to corporations and businesses owned by individuals, in dealing with the insolvency of a non-business activity the term '*concurso*' is applicable and it is regulated by the Civil Code; however, in practice it is not used very often (therefore it is not dealt with below).

Bankruptcy

Bankruptcies in Mexico may be regarded either as fortuitous (i.e., non-culpable), or due to bad management or fraudulent. The last two categories may be punished with prison for those responsible for the business administration.

A declaration of bankruptcy of an individual or a corporation is ordered by a judge at a creditor's request or at the request of the debtor.

The judge's resolution must include the appointment of a receiver (made by the judge) and of the creditors' committee (made by the creditors' board).

The judge must appoint the receiver from one of the following:

- a commercial bank;
- a chamber of commerce;
- an individual or corporation listed in the Commerce Register.

The judge must order the assurance and custody of all the debtor's goods in order that the receiver can sell them and distribute the proceeds among all the recognised creditors.

The receiver (known in Mexico as '*sindico*') who is also the liquidator, is in charge of the bankruptcy procedure. He manages the business administration while the bankruptcy is completed, is supervised during his appointment by the judge, and generally has full powers to carry on the business, to receive income and to realise assets.

The bankruptcy is completed if all debts are paid to creditors, or by creditors' agreement to receive a partial payment of their debts or because all assets owned by the debtor have been sold and the proceeds distributed among the creditors.

Suspension of payments

This is a procedure provided by Mexican legislation in order to prevent a bankruptcy. The suspension of payments is requested of a judge by any debtor. The judge authorises the debtor to suspend payments during a certain period of time, provided the board of creditors is in agreement. A receiver is also appointed by the judge to supervise the business administration, which is carried out by the debtor.

Creditors

Even though the principle of an equal division of assets amongst creditors of similar nature is fundamental to insolvency legal procedures, there are different categories of creditors:

- secured creditor — one who holds a mortgage on a debtor's property as security for the debt and who has the right to recoup partly or wholly from the disposition of that property in priority to an unsecured creditor;
- unsecured creditors — this term encompasses all creditors who are not secured creditors.

The legislation makes provision for the payment of certain creditors in priority to other unsecured creditors, such as debts for funeral and medical expenses incurred by the debtor's sickness or death, wages and salaries accrued during the 12-month period prior to the insolvency, unpaid federal and local taxes etc.

Other matters

Bankruptcy procedures are long and complex in Mexico. However, they are rarely used because insolvency conflicts are generally resolved by the suspension of payments procedure. This option is more common due to the fact that, in times of high inflation, creditors prefer to make an agreement with the debtor in order to recoup part of their debt in the short term than to wait until the bankruptcy is over.

KPMG contact partner

Gabriel Amante Dominguez
KPMG Cárdeñas Dosal SC
Bosque de Duraznos 55
Bosques de las Lomas
11700 Mexico City, DF
Mexico

Telephone: +52 (5) 7264343
Fax: +52 (5) 5968060

Moldova

Legislation

Moldovan insolvency legislation is relatively new and undergoing continuous development. Under the Soviet system, all enterprises were deemed to be branches of the State, and therefore no bankruptcy was possible. Liquidation through reorganisation was possible, but it was an administrative and logistical exercise.

Although insolvency legislation has been passed in Moldova and there is some evidence that insolvency proceedings have been instituted, the process is neither common nor even the automatic result of an irredeemable financial position. This is due partly to a lack of experience and partly to what seems to be a 'Soviet' belief that companies, once founded, cannot or should not die.

Current insolvency legislation is closely related to the legislation in Russia as both have evolved from the same system and Russian legislation is more readily accessible. Moldovan insolvency legislation is based on the Law on Insolvency (Bankruptcy), which was passed in March 1996. Since then the legislation has been considerably modified and developed by Presidential Decrees and other enabling legislation.

Further development is certain and so these notes are merely indicative of the current situation.

Insolvency procedures

Types of insolvency procedure

- reorganisation — the business is placed in the hands of an external management, which may be charged with its rehabilitation;
- liquidation — this occurs (a) if a court has declared the enterprise insolvent, or (b) if the enterprise declares itself insolvent;
- amicable settlement — the enterprise comes to an agreement with its creditors involving the deferral of payment of debts, payment by instalment, or debt forgiveness.

Insolvency courts

Insolvency cases are examined by 'arbitration' courts. Cases may be brought when outstanding claims have been outstanding for three months from the due date for repayment.

Parties to an insolvency action

The legislation recognises various parties in an insolvency action, including:

- receiver — the receiver may dispose of assets, act in an arbitration court to contest the validity of contracts completed up to six months prior to the initiation of arbitration proceedings, collect debts and receivables, form a liquidation committee and call a creditors' meeting;
- creditors;
- representatives of the workforce;
- debtor.

The receiver must:

- be an economist or lawyer;

- be a citizen of Moldova;
- have practical management experience;
- not have a criminal record;
- have a State licence to practise as a receiver.

Petition

An insolvency action is initiated by a petition to the arbitration court from:

- the debtor, either the owner of the enterprise or its management — such a petition cannot be withdrawn;
- a creditor, after the lapse of three months from the due date for payment for goods or services (the due date being defined as the date of delivery of a demand for payment by registered post);
- a procurator (public prosecutor), if it has been determined that a fictitious insolvency action has been initiated, or if the law of the Republic of Moldova requires the initiation of insolvency proceedings.

The court may either refuse the petition, if it is established that the creditor's claim can be met or the defendant is solvent, or it may recognise the defendant as insolvent, in which case liquidation proceedings will be instituted.

If a petition is received from the debtor itself, the court may decide to postpone the declaration of insolvency and instead institute rehabilitation or external management procedures.

Reorganisation

External management of the enterprise may be considered if there is a real possibility that the solvency of the enterprise may be restored by selling off parts of the debtor organisation, reorganising it, or instituting some other economic measures.

An arbitration manager is appointed by the court, and the remuneration of the manager is fixed by the creditors' committee and approved by the court.

The arbitration manager has three months in which to gain creditors' approval for a management plan involving the appointment of an external management.

External management may not last for more than 12 months if the enterprise has under 50 staff or 24 months otherwise.

The arbitration court must then review the results of the plan, and decide whether the management plan should continue or the debtor should be declared insolvent and liquidation proceedings be instituted.

Rehabilitation

In the event of a real possibility that solvency can be restored to the enterprise as a result of financial aid being given by the owner or third parties, the arbitration court may institute rehabilitation proceedings.

Within 12 months of the start of rehabilitation, the enterprise must have met at least 50 per cent of the combined creditor claims. Rehabilitation may not last for more than 12 months.

Rehabilitation ceases when 12 months have elapsed or it is determined by the court that rehabilitation is ineffective, in which case liquidation proceedings must be instituted.

Rehabilitation is deemed successful when all claims have been met and the insolvency action can be closed.

Liquidation proceedings

Once a debtor has been declared insolvent, liquidation proceedings must begin. The arbitration court appoints a receiver and the creditors' committee determines the receiver's remuneration.

The receiver has the duty, monitored by the creditors' committee, to obtain the highest price for the debtor's assets.

The proceeds of the realisation of assets are distributed in order of precedence as follows:

- expenses related to the liquidation proceedings;
- expenses of the arbitration manager and receiver;
- expenses related to the continuing operations of the enterprise;
- claims of individuals whom the debtor has injured or prejudiced;
- payment of the workforce;
- payments to the State Pension Fund;
- taxes and social security contributions;
- all other claims.

Amicable settlement

A settlement may be reached at any point in the insolvency proceedings if two thirds of all the creditors agree, and must be endorsed by the court. The settlement may be rendered void if (a) the terms are not satisfied, (b) the financial position of the debtor deteriorates, (c) the debtor infringes on the rights and interests of the creditors.

KPMG contact partner

Roger Munnings
KPMG
37 Ul. Novaya Basmannaya
3rd Floor
Moscow 107066
Russia

Telephone: +7 (502) 222 4030
Fax: +7 (502) 222 4024

Morocco

Legislation

Moroccan insolvency law is included in:

- Company Law 1996;
- Commercial Law 1913.

No changes in the current legislation are expected. A liquidator may be an experienced accountant in private practice or a shareholder.

Insolvency procedures

Liquidation

Liquidation is the statutory process for winding up the affairs of a company. There are three types of liquidation:

- legal liquidation: this is normally initiated when all the shares are the property of one shareholder, or when the duration fixed for the company expires, or when the purpose of the company is realised;
- voluntary liquidation: this is normally initiated by the board of directors who call an extraordinary general meeting of the shareholders. This meeting appoints a liquidator by majority;
- compulsory liquidation: any shareholder can present a winding-up petition to the court if he has good reasons.

As soon as the resolution or court order is received, the liquidator prepares a balance sheet for the company and an inventory.

The liquidator is charged with ending the business of the company, realising its assets and paying its creditors.

Bankruptcy

There is no specific procedure relating to bankruptcy in the law but it can be similar to compulsory liquidation.

Creditors

Creditors are categorised as:

- secured creditors: who hold a fixed or floating charge over the assets of the debtor;
- preferential creditors: who have priority in payment before unsecured creditors;
- unsecured creditors: all other creditors.

Government dues and salaries are normally paid before other creditors.

KPMG contact partner

Jamal Saâd el Idrissi
KPMG Audit-Maroc
30 rue Abou Faris al Marini
Rabat
Morocco

Telephone: +212 (7) 709 101
Fax: +212 (7) 709 122

Mozambique

Insolvency procedures

Insolvency (bankruptcy) procedures are regulated by the Civil Procedure Code.

The Code provides for three different insolvency procedures:

- preventive measures;
- confirmation or declaration of insolvency;
- liquidation of assets and payment of creditors.

Preventive measures

The law provides for alternatives to prevent a business from being liquidated and hence terminated as a going concern.

The business representatives, the creditors or the Attorney-General's Office can request the court to start the insolvency legal procedures.

Once this request has been received and accepted by the judge, the business is protected from any further execution, except for special creditors with preferential rights. Within 20 to 60 days from the initial decision of the judge a general meeting of all creditors should take place to ascertain the listing of the creditors.

The judge should also designate an administrator to control and support the debtor in the management of the assets of the business.

The debtor and the administrator should prepare a full listing of all creditors and the value of their debts. The list is made available to all interested parties and it can be challenged.

During this period it is also permissible for any creditor to present a proposal for a restructuring of the business.

The general meeting of creditors should then take place to ascertain the debts. The general meeting of creditors can decide on a restructuring of the business, which can include a moratorium, debt relief, or transformation of the business into a different legal entity.

Failing any agreement by the creditors the court immediately confirms and declares the business as insolvent.

The Civil Code provides some protection for creditors that do not agree with the restructuring of the business. To approve any business restructuring at least 75 per cent of creditors must vote in favour of it.

Confirmation or declaration of insolvency

Insolvency can be declared by the court upon the failure of any agreement by creditors and the debtor to rescue the business. Other situations in which the court can declare a business insolvent are:

- the business has stopped making payments;
- the whereabouts of the management and owners of the business are unknown, and any representatives are absent;
- misuse of the business assets such that the business is unable to fulfil its commitments.

The court can accept an application for the declaration of insolvency from any creditor or from the Attorney-General.

Upon the receipt of the application for the declaration of insolvency the court notifies the debtor and a hearing takes place where the court decides whether to issue the declaration of insolvency.

In cases where the insolvency is declared, the court appoints an administrator to manage the assets and the activities of the business.

The law provides for an appeal process against the court's decision that a business is insolvent.

Liquidation of assets and payment of creditors

The administrator of the business takes control of its assets.

The creditors then have the opportunity to present their claims. The administrator produces a listing of all the creditors, ranked in terms of priority, which is then filed in the court. The court should confirm this listing.

The administrator then proceeds with the actual liquidation of the assets. The assets of the business are sold in compliance with the rules for judicial executions. With the proceeds of the liquidation the creditors are paid in conformity with their seniority. Where the creditors rank equally and the proceeds of the liquidation are not enough to cover their debts, the liquidation proceeds are distributed pro rata.

The law distinguishes between a 'normal' insolvency and fraudulent insolvency. Fraudulent insolvency is a crime punishable by imprisonment for a period from two years up to eight years.

KPMG contact partner

Daniel Martins da Silva
KPMG
Prédio Progresso
Avenida 24 de Julho, 2096
3 Andar
Maputo
Mozambique

Telephone: +258 (1) 421892
Fax: +258 (1) 421899

Namibia

Legislation

- Insolvency Act No. 24 of 1936, as amended;
- Companies Act No. 61 of 1973, as amended;
- Regulations in terms of s. 15 of the Companies Act No. 61 of 1973, for winding up and judicial management of companies;
- Magistrates' Courts Act No. 32 of 1944, as amended, in terms of which provision is made for administration orders;
- Agricultural Bank of Namibia Act No. 13 of 1944, as amended.

Insolvency procedures

- compulsory winding up by the court of an individual or partnership or a company;
- members' or creditors' voluntary winding up of a company;
- voluntary surrender of estate by an individual;
- judicial management;
- schemes of arrangement or compromise.

Compulsory winding up

An individual insolvent's estate, or company may be wound up by the court if:

- judgment has been obtained for a debt and it cannot be satisfied or paid;
- any attempt is made to dispose of assets, thereby prejudicing creditors or preferring one creditor above another;
- any attempt is made to compromise debts with creditors;
- notice in writing is given to any creditor that his debt cannot be paid;
- an executor of a deceased's estate which is found to be insolvent petitions the court;
- a judicial manager makes an application to the court.

Voluntary winding up

The court may grant a voluntary winding-up order if an individual petitions the court. No court order is required if a company has by special resolution resolved that it be wound up either by its members or creditors.

Judicial management

The court may grant a judicial management order when so petitioned by a director, member or creditor. Judicial management is a temporary moratorium to enable a company to surmount its financial problems under the management of a person specifically appointed for this purpose who acts in the place of the board of directors.

Schemes of arrangement or compromise

A scheme of arrangement or compromise may be proposed between a company in liquidation and its creditors or its members. Should the scheme or compromise be approved by creditors and sanctioned by the court the winding-up order is set aside and the company is reinstated.

A private individual may also submit an offer of composition to his trustee for consideration by his creditors. However, any condition which makes the offer subject to the rehabilitation of the insolvent, is of no effect.

Commencement and control of insolvency procedures

Insolvency procedures can be instituted by:

- generally speaking, anyone who is a creditor and has been unable to obtain settlement by legal means;
- directors, members, shareholders and an individual on his own recognisance;
- a judicial manager;
- an executor of an insolvent deceased estate;
- an *ex parte* application.

The effect once insolvency procedures have commenced is:

- to divest the company or individual of all assets which then vest in the master of the High Court of Namibia until a liquidator or trustee is appointed by him;
- to stay civil proceedings;
- to cause trading to cease except in the case of judicial management or where it is necessary to preserve an asset;
- generally to curtail all activities except those of an individual who is entitled to earn an income but subject to certain restrictions and conditions;
- to make void every disposition of property (including rights of action) made after commencement of the winding up unless the court declares otherwise;
- to make void any attachment or execution order against the assets after the commencement of the winding up;
- to make void in the case of a company every transfer of shares or alteration of the status of its members effected after the commencement of the winding up.

Controls, functions and duties are exercised by:

- the master of the High Court of Namibia initially;
- a liquidator in the case of a company and a trustee in the case of an individual or a partnership who must account to the master of the High Court of Namibia;
- the judicial manager in the case of judicial management.

The duties of the liquidator or trustee are:

- to investigate and report on the affairs of the company or the insolvent including contraventions by directors, members or individuals;
- to trace and realise all assets;
- to lodge a liquidation and distribution or contribution account with the master of the High Court of Namibia.

The duty of a judicial manager is to continue the business of the company and to report to creditors on the viability of continuing under judicial management or placing the company in liquidation.

Creditors

Secured creditors are entitled to value their security and prove their claims. On realisation of the security the creditor receives payment of the amount realised less administration costs. Any free residue resulting from assets realised including the excess, if any, on secured assets realised is awarded to preferential creditors such as the Receiver of Revenue, staff salaries and wages within certain limits the auditor for up to N$2,000, etc.

Thereafter:

- concurrent creditors are entitled to a pro rata share of whatever balance is available;
- foreign creditors enjoy the same considerations but payment in foreign currency is subject to government approval;
- shareholders are entitled to receive dividends only after all other creditors are settled in full;
- in the event of insufficient funds being available to cover liquidation costs, a contribution will be levied on the petitioning creditor and/or creditors who proved claims.

Other matters

Restrictions and/or shortcomings of the procedures

The law of the Republic of South Africa is generally applied. However, since 1979 no amendments made by the Republic of South Africa to its laws are applicable in Namibia although certain amendments have been introduced by the transitional government while others are being considered.

End result of the procedures

Being subject to the dictates and strict control of the master of the High Court of Namibia, the present procedure ensures an equitable distribution of the proceeds of assets realised.

Duration and timing

Insolvency procedures may take nine months to two or more years to complete.

KPMG contact partner

Albie Basson
Second Floor, Bank Windhoek Building
262 Independence Avenue
Windhoek
Namibia

Telephone: +264 (61) 226511
Fax: +264 (61) 232309

Nepal

Legislation

Nepal does not have separate legislation covering insolvency. Corporate insolvency, which encompasses winding up and liquidation, is governed by the Company Act 1964.

The winding up of a company may be either:

- by the Registrar of Companies; or
- voluntary — creditors' or members'.

Insolvency procedures

Compulsory liquidation

There are specific grounds for compulsory winding up by the Registrar of Companies:

- the company passes a special resolution to that effect;
- the preliminary meeting is not convened or preliminary report not filed within the prescribed time;
- the company does not commence business within a year of registration or discontinues business for one year;
- the company is unable to pay its debts;
- the Registrar of Companies regards it as just and equitable that the company should be wound up;
- where the government stood surety for a loan and the company failed to pay off the debt.

The following may petition for the winding up:

- the company;
- any creditor;
- the Registrar of Companies.

The Registrar of Companies is required to appoint a person as a government liquidator for winding up the affairs of the company. He is also required to appoint an auditor to examine the accounts submitted by the liquidator.

Voluntary liquidation

A company may go into voluntary liquidation by passing a special resolution and notifying the Registrar of Companies. It is not permitted to continue business after the resolution is passed. The members are required to appoint a liquidator and an auditor to examine the accounts submitted by the liquidator. The liquidator exercises all such powers as are exercised by a government liquidator.

The decision to go into voluntary liquidation does not by itself prejudice the powers of the Registrar of Companies to initiate proceedings for compulsory winding up on receipt of an application from creditors or otherwise.

General

Upon a liquidator's appointment:

- the powers of the board and all of the company's officers ceases, unless the liquidator otherwise directs;
- the liquidator takes custody of all the books, records, documents and all assets owned by the company;
- the liquidator realises the property of the company for cash which is then distributed to creditors and members.

Distribution of sale proceeds

The liabilities of the company are paid out of the sale proceeds of assets in the following order:

- expenses incurred in liquidating the company;
- a secured creditor who holds a mortgage on the property of the debtor as a security for a debt;
- all wages and salaries of employees not exceeding Rs 500 each;
- rates and taxes having become due and payable to government or local authorities;
- loans obtained against assets of the company which had been attached within three months prior to the issue of liquidation order; and
- other debts.

No debts shall be paid nor other liabilities fulfilled which are lower in the order of priority unless the government liquidator is satisfied that those higher in the order of priority can be paid off.

Other matters

Compulsory liquidation is a laborious and lengthy process which could extend to several years.

Creditors seldom exercise their legal rights to take a company into liquidation to recover debts.

KPMG contact partner

T. R. Upadhyay
T. R. Upadhya & Co.
PO Box 4414
Kathmandu
Nepal

Telephone: +977 1 472 658
Fax: +977 1 474 178

Netherlands

Legislation

The Bankruptcy Act (*Faillissementswet*) contains the legislation relating to insolvency and bankruptcy. It was first enacted in 1893 and has been revised numerous times since then. Court decisions on the interpretation of the law are published regularly.

The Ministry of Justice is responsible for insolvency legislation. In every district court the registrar is bound to keep public records of those natural and legal persons who have fallen into bankruptcy within the court's territory. All bankruptcies are published in the *Official Gazette* (*Staatscourant*) and in at least one other newspaper. In addition, bankruptcies of all enterprises which are obliged to set forth and file their particulars with the Chamber of Commerce are to be registered in the Local Commercial Register.

Since 1987, legislation has been incorporated in company law whereby the members of the board of a Dutch company (or a branch of a foreign company operating in the Netherlands and its chargé d'affaires), may become liable on account of mismanagement. The burden of proof of such mismanagement is, in principle, with the receiver. However, mismanagement is assumed in the event that a company has failed to publish in time its financial statements in the manner required by law, and subject to contrary evidence, it is also assumed that if such publication has not taken place, mismanagement has been the cause of the bankruptcy.

Furthermore, legislation has been introduced to the effect that, outside bankruptcy, directors may become liable vis-à-vis fiscal and social security authorities in the event that a company remains in default in meeting its obligations under fiscal or social security legislation without having given due notice of it being unable to do so in the manner and at the time required by law.

Recent changes to legislation

Early in 1997 the Bankruptcy Act will probably be amended to include a regulation that provides for a reorganisation of the finances and debts of individuals who can no longer pay their debts. This regulation will enable the debtor to redeem his debts wholly or in part within five years at the most. After that period creditors lose their right to recover the remainder of their claims. Thus, the debtor will be protected from his creditors for years to come (as can be the case where a bankruptcy is terminated for lack of funds).

Application

All bankruptcy law applies nationwide to companies as well as individuals, independent of the place of residence in the Netherlands. There is no additional local legislation in this area.

Who can be appointed:

- receiver (*curator*): any person — generally an attorney;
- trustee (*bewindvoerder*): any person — generally an attorney.

Insolvency procedures

Moratorium (*surséance van betaling*)

Moratorium is a legal status introduced in bankruptcy law in 1925. In many cases it constitutes the prelude to a final bankruptcy. By judgment of the court the debtor is — at his own request — granted a suspension of payment. One or more trustees (*bewindvoerder*) are appointed who are to cooperate with the debtor. The debtor in a state of moratorium can dispose of his assets after having acquired permission from the trustees. First, a provisional moratorium is granted — usually for a period of three months, which can be extended with the court's permission; later a definite moratorium, for a period of 18 months, which can also be extended with the permission of the unsecured creditors.

Bankruptcy (*faillissement*)

Bankruptcy is a legal status which can be defined as an attachment on all assets and liabilities of a debtor who can no longer pay his debts. Bankruptcy relates to all assets and liabilities. The objective of the bankruptcy, in most cases following sale under execution, is to turn all the assets into money, so that proceeds can be distributed to the creditors in accordance with their specific (preferential) rights. The debtor completely loses the right to manage his own affairs; from the day of his adjudication onwards he can no longer legally dispose of his assets. A receiver and a supervising judge are appointed.

Method of appointment and nature of administration

A debtor is adjudicated bankrupt by the court if a petition is filed. This petition can be filed by:

- the debtor;
- one or more creditors;
- the public prosecutor for reasons of public interest.

In all cases it has to be proved that the debtor is in a situation where he has ceased paying his liabilities. If a creditor is filing a petition he has to prove that he has a claim and that there is more than one creditor. Consequently, a debtor can avoid bankruptcy if he can prove that:

- there is no valid claim;
- he is not in a situation where he has ceased paying his liabilities.

When the trustee, during the moratorium, asks for and is granted termination of the status of moratorium, the court can at the same time declare the debtor concerned bankrupt. In practice, termination of moratorium is always followed by adjudication of bankruptcy.

Persons involved in the administration of insolvent estates

There are no government officials directly involved in the management of bankruptcies. The court judgment contains the appointment of one or more supervising judges (*rechter-commissaris*), as well as the appointment of one or more receivers (*curator*).

The receiver is almost always an attorney. He manages the insolvent estate. In a number of cases the receiver needs the permission of the supervising judge when he wishes to commence legal proceedings on behalf of the estate. Further, the receiver normally asks permission when he has to make decisions with important implications. In general he keeps the supervising judge well informed of everything to do with the administration of the estate. Either together with the court's adjudication order or later, the court can appoint a committee of creditors, if the importance of the matter, or its specific character, show that this might be useful. Generally, the most important creditors are appointed. It is their task to assist and advise the receiver.

Nature of receivership

With the permission of the supervising judge and after having taken the advice of the creditors' committee, the receiver has to decide whether or not he will continue the business of the company and in what form.

Termination of bankruptcy

Bankruptcy can terminate in the following ways:

- the approval by the court of a composition, as proposed by a meeting of creditors. In this case creditors receive an agreed percentage of their claim. The debtor is discharged and he regains the right to manage his own property. Creditors waive the right to recover the remainder of their claims. The debtor is freed from his previous creditors;
- for lack of funds by order of the court if it appears that the balance to be recovered from the insolvent estate is insufficient to pay the expenses of the bankruptcy (receiver's salary, legal costs, costs incurred by an appraiser, etc.). The debtor regains the right to manage his own affairs; the creditors remain empowered to recover their claims later;
- when the plan of distribution of dividends, made up by the receiver, becomes irrevocable. This is a list of creditors, not being secured creditors, showing the sum due to each of them and the percentage of payment. Usually the receiver seeks a potential buyer for the enterprise or for part of its activities. If he does not succeed in finding one he has no choice but to liquidate the company.

In case of the termination of a bankruptcy, other than by a composition, a company (NV or BV) is automatically dissolved.

Liquidation

Liquidation is the process of winding up the affairs of a dissolved corporate body. The dissolved corporate body is obliged to add to its name the words '*in liquidatie*'.

In the case of dissolution as a result of bankruptcy the liquidation takes place in accordance with the Bankruptcy Act (*Faillissementswet*). The liquidation is proceeded to by the receiver (*curator*), appointed by the court.

If the company dissolves voluntarily and goes into liquidation, liquidators are appointed:

(a) by the articles of association or regulations of the company;

(b) by the body of the corporation that takes the decision to dissolve, i.e., the shareholders' meeting;

(c) by the court replacing liquidators as per (a) or (b) above, in case of their malfunction or if the company's debts apparently exceed its assets. Such appointment is made upon request by the public prosecutor or an interested party.

If the articles of association, the regulations or the corporate body taking the decision to dissolve do not appoint a liquidator, the managing directors will be liquidators. Corporate law continues to be applicable to companies in voluntary liquidation. Articles of association or regulations may, however, contain special rules concerning the position of the liquidator.

If a corporate body is dissolved by order of the court, the court appoints the liquidator. Liquidators, unlike receivers, are not required to follow special regulations governing their actions because law in this field has not yet been codified or enacted.

Creditors

The priority of creditors in the distribution of assets is mainly governed by the applicable provisions in the Civil Code. All property of the bankrupt at the date of the bankruptcy has to be distributed among the creditors, with the exception of the following assets:

- social security receipts;
- some strictly private property;
- alimony.

Other matters

Secured creditors

Secured creditors (e.g., holding mortgages or rights of pledge on the debtor's property, or having fiduciary property rights thereon) can simply enforce their security to the extent of its value. Such a secured creditor is called a separatist. However, when a secured creditor has realised his security and a balance remains due, he may file a proof of claim for the remainder of his claim. Finally, separatists do not share in the costs of administering the bankruptcy when they have exercised their rights.

Unsecured creditors

The receiver must distribute the proceeds realised from the property of the bankrupt in the following order:

- remuneration of the receiver and legal costs;
- debts of the estate (e.g., appraisement costs, lease of bankrupt's house);
- costs of the petition in bankruptcy;
- all tax claims;
- other creditors.

Based on an EC Directive, arts 1639aa ff. of the Civil Code were enacted, providing for automatic re-employment of employees on the same terms, on the transfer of an undertaking or a part thereof. It has now been accepted that these provisions are not applicable in the case of bankruptcy. They continue, however, to apply in the event of a moratorium and in the event of a voluntary liquidation.

KPMG contact partner

Jan D. van Muiswinkel
KPMG Restructuring Services BV
Burg. Rijnderslaan 10
Post Office Box 74500
1070 DB Amsterdam
The Netherlands

Telephone: +31 (20) 65 68 322
Fax: +31 (20) 65 68 325

Netherlands Antilles

Legislation

Procedures for initiating and conducting the dissolution of a company (or coming to an arrangement with creditors) are laid down in the Bankruptcy Decree of 1931.

Insolvency procedures

Procedures in general follow those of the Netherlands. A company may be wound up by the Attorney-General (if the company is deemed to be acting against the public interest) or by the court having been petitioned by creditors or debenture holders. There is a 'protection from creditors' provision, which is also instigated by the court having been petitioned by the company.

The court decides the effective date and appoints trustees. The trustees, usually a lawyer and an accountant, are empowered to demand and collect all outstanding debts and liabilities on shares. Notice of the arrangement must be placed in the *Official Gazette* and with the Commercial Register. The notice filed with the Commercial Register must set forth the scheme of distribution showing the basis for the division of the company's assets.

Rights of creditors and priorities of payment are the same as under Dutch law. Thus the trustees or liquidator, court and other government liabilities rank ahead of secured creditors.

After the notice of liquidation has been placed in the *Official Gazette*, at least three months must elapse before the liquidation can be finalised. In practice, compulsory liquidation takes much longer.

KPMG contact partner

Anthony Owers
KPMG Accountants
Kaya Flamboyan 5
PO Box 3082
Willemstad, Curaçao
Netherlands Antillies

Telephone: +599 (9) 325100
Fax: +599 (9) 375588

New Caledonia

Legislation

Insolvency procedures in New Caledonia are identical to the insolvency procedures in France. Reference should be made, therefore, to the section in this book dealing with France.

KPMG contact partner

Phillipe Ghillebaert
KPMG
85 avenue du Général de Gaulle
BP 2353
Nouméa
New Caledonia

Telephone: +687 275366
Fax: +687 276405

New Zealand

Legislation

There are two broad areas of New Zealand insolvency law and practice, namely:

- insolvencies applying to individuals, normally termed 'bankruptcies';
- insolvencies applying to companies, the terminology used varying according to the nature of the appointment.

The principal types are:

- receiverships, usually arising from the action of a secured creditor;
- liquidation, which may be by order of the court, or which may follow an initiative taken by the company;
- compromises without or with sanction of the court;
- statutory management, appointed by Order in Council.

Individual bankruptcies are governed by the Insolvency Act 1967 and its amendments.

Corporate insolvencies are governed by:

- the Receiverships Act 1993;
- the Companies Act 1955 and its amendments;
- the Companies Act 1993 and its amendments;
- the Companies Liquidation Regulations 1994;
- the Corporations (Investigation and Management) Act 1989.

From 1 July 1994 two Companies Acts have existed in New Zealand, the former Companies Act 1955 and the new Companies Act 1993. Due to extensive amendments to the 1955 Act, liquidation under the 1955 Act and the 1993 Act are virtually the same. The main difference is that the 1993 Act refers to working days and the 1955 Act to days. The actual times, however, are similar and will vary only slightly depending on when the appointment falls during the week, e.g., 21 days under the 1955 Act is 15 working days under the 1993 Act.

Transitional provisions

The former 1955 Act prior to amendment applies to all liquidations commencing prior to 1 July 1994 whereas the amended 1955 Act applies to companies registered under that Act in respect of liquidations commencing after 30 June 1994. All liquidations in respect of companies registered under the 1993 Act are governed by the Companies Act 1993.

Corporations (Investigations and Management) Act

This was designed to deal with complex corporate insolvencies which could not be dealt with satisfactorily under the existing legislation.

Role of commercial affairs division of the Ministry of Commerce

There are two broad business units concerned with company administration:

- the Companies Office which is principally concerned with company registration, prospectuses, general administration and special investigations;
- the New Zealand Insolvency and Trustee Service (Office of the Official Assignee) which is responsible for the administration of individual bankruptcies and court liquidations not handled by private liquidators.

Individual bankruptcies

In practice, the official assignee administers all adjudicated bankrupts.

Chartered accountants may act as trustees in a compromise which avoids bankruptcy.

Corporate insolvencies

The New Zealand insolvency and trustee service handles most of the court liquidations although some private liquidators are appointed. The appointment of a private liquidator often takes place at the time the company is first put into liquidation.

Appointments

New Zealand legislation is relatively silent on the issue of qualifications for appointment. Rather than spell these out it mentions those who cannot be appointed. In contrast to the situation in some other countries, New Zealand legislation has not to date made provision for the registration of liquidators or receivers. Nevertheless, the field is virtually dominated by chartered accountants in public practice.

Insolvency procedures

Remedies of secured creditor

A debenture holder has a number of courses of action open to him, including the appointment of a receiver and manager for the subject property. Where a lower-ranking creditor — for example, a second debenture holder — moves to appoint a receiver, or if the company is in liquidation, the secured creditor may rely on his security in the knowledge that the receiver or liquidator concerned is bound by law to pay out his claim first. A liquidator, however, may choose not to deal with property subject to a charge. Mortgagees can enter into possession of property and force its sale to recover the debt and other secured creditors can take steps to repossess the assets charged.

Remedies of unsecured creditors

The main courses open to unsecured creditors are:

- legal action resulting in an application to have the company put into liquidation by order of the court;
- arrange with the company to resolve to go into liquidation and have the liquidation conducted on behalf of the creditors by a liquidator appointed or approved by them;
- enter into a compromise as provided under the Companies Act.

Lenders to smaller companies have in recent years developed reservations about the effectiveness of a debenture security alone and therefore they usually ensure that advances are guaranteed by principal shareholders and often take security over assets outside the company structure.

Receivership

A receiver and manager sometimes trades on a business in order to ensure orderly realisation of the assets or sale as a going concern.

Although a receiver is appointed by and is responsible to the secured creditor, he is usually operating also as an agent of the company and has a common law and statutory responsibility (Receiverships Act 1993) to consider the interests of other creditors. The court, on the application of the debenture holder or other creditors, may appoint a receiver, who in practice is likely to be a chartered accountant.

Receivership action may be rapid and indeed is often the only method by which the assets of the company can be protected and the business brought under some form of control.

The powers of the receiver are set out in the Receiverships Act 1993 and the debenture deed. The practical and legal obligations of receivers and managers are onerous and complex. The receiver and manager has a statutory duty to obtain the best possible price for the sale of the company property. This forces receivers and managers to be seen to be taking all possible steps to achieve this in the course of selling separate assets and/or businesses.

It is clear that receivers and managers carrying on trading should obtain adequate indemnities from their principals to cover them against claims not recoverable out of realisations and not arising through their own negligence. Certain trading banks are showing some reluctance to provide such indemnities.

Liquidation

In New Zealand liquidations of companies unable to pay their creditors in full arise mainly in two ways:

- a creditor applies to the court for the company to be put into liquidation because of its inability to pay its debts (usually an unsatisfied statutory demand). The official assignee will be appointed liquidator unless the applicant has arranged for a private liquidator to accept appointment;
- the company resolves at a validly convened meeting or by entry in its minute book to appoint a liquidator.

The creditors have the right to have a meeting of creditors convened to appoint a liquidator of their choice.

Compromise

A compromise is an arrangement entered into between the company's creditors. There is no need for sanction by the court. It may be the only way of ensuring that the business of the company can continue in the long-term interests of its creditors and in order to preserve the company structure. This is sometimes desirable for taxation considerations.

Creditors

Preferential creditors

Given priority by the Companies Acts and the Receiverships Act 1993, preferential creditors rank ahead of debenture holders, but valid prior charges such as mortgages or chattels instruments will take precedence over the specific assets charged.

The ranking of preferential creditors among themselves is set out in a schedule to the Companies Act. As a general guide only, priorities in receiverships and liquidations are along these lines:

- receiver's and liquidator's expenses and remuneration;
- employees' wages including holiday pay entitlements and deductions subject to a limitation of NZ$6,000 for any one employee;
- goods and services tax and PAYE tax deductions due to the Inland Revenue Department.

Rent, although not preferential at law, is often treated as such in order to protect assets. Employees' claims for redundancy, whether pursuant to an agreement or not, may be acknowledged, but rank as unsecured.

Secured creditors

Secured creditors are those with claims supported by a mortgage, charge or lien on the property of the debtor as security for the debt and who are in a position either at law or in equity to recover amounts due wholly or partly from the assets secured, in priority to unsecured creditors.

The most common type of security is the debenture, which usually contains both a floating and fixed charge over the assets of the company, and is often supported by a mortgage over real property. Invariably there will be other secured creditors who will have valid claims over specific assets in priority to a floating charge debenture, including:

- prior mortgages;
- chattels instruments over fixed assets;
- hire-purchase agreements.

A partly secured creditor is able to prove in a liquidation for the portion of the debt not recovered under his security.

Unsecured creditors

These are all creditors not secured or ranking as preferential.

KPMG contact partner

Alan Isaac
KPMG
KPMG Centre
135 Victoria Street
Wellington
New Zealand

Telephone: +64 (4) 38 28 800
Fax: +64 (4) 80 21 224

Nicaragua

Legislation

Insolvencies of corporations and businesses owned by individuals are regulated by the Nicaraguan Trade Code, chapter No. 4 of Bankruptcies and Suspension of Payments Law, which was enacted in 1917.

The following insolvency procedures are available in Nicaragua:

- suspension of payments/insolvency;
- bankruptcy;
- out-of-court agreement.

Insolvency procedures

Suspension of payments/insolvency

This is when a merchant's assets exceed his liabilities, but he cannot pay his debts as they fall due. The debtor requests an extended term to pay obligations. The court gives approval provided that creditors agree.

The suspension of payments is only applicable to merchants. When a non-merchant entity's debts cannot be paid, it is considered insolvent.

The suspension of payments is a way to avoid bankruptcy among merchants. It is permitted when the following conditions are satisfied:

- the person must be a merchant;
- the merchant's assets must exceed its debts (if assets are insufficient, the merchant is automatically bankrupt);
- the merchant is unable to pay.

Bankruptcy

Bankruptcy is pronounced when a merchant ceases to pay his debts when his obligations exceed his assets. For bankruptcy to be effective the following circumstances must exist:

- the person (either natural or legal) must be a merchant;
- the person must have stopped making payments (provided that it does not have the benefit of suspension of payments).

There are three kinds of bankruptcy in Nicaragua:

- fortuitous (i.e., non-culpable);
- guilty; and
- fraudulent.

The last two categories may be punished with prison for those responsible for the business administration.

Bankruptcy procedures are the same for both local and foreign entities having branches or affiliated companies in Nicaragua.

Bankruptcy is declared:

- at the merchant's request (voluntary bankruptcy);
- when it is requested by legitimate creditors.

When the bankruptcy is requested by legitimate creditors it is ordered by a judge. The judge appoints a provisional procurator.

The judge must order the assurance and custody of all the debtor's goods in order that the provisional procurator can sell them and distribute the proceeds among all the recognised creditors.

The provisional procurator, who is also the liquidator, is in charge of the bankruptcy procedure. He manages the business administration while the bankruptcy is completed, and is supervised during his appointment by the judge, and generally has full powers to carry on the business, to receive income and to realise assets.

The bankruptcy is completed if all debts are paid to creditors, or by creditors' agreement to receive a partial payment of their debts or because all assets owned by the debtor are sold and the proceeds distributed among the creditors.

Out-of-court agreement

An agreement is the third solution for merchants affected by bankruptcy and it is tried before suspension of payments or bankruptcy declaration. It is an informal arrangement, agreed by a board of creditors, where they accept from the debtor what he offers and the difference is foregone.

KPMG contact partner

Humberto J. Hernández
KPMG Peat Marwick
Optica Visión 125 metros al Este
Reparto Bolonia
Managua, Nicaragua

Telephone: +505 (2) 66 6470
Fax: +505 (2) 66 4783

Nigeria

Insolvency procedures

Receivership

In a receivership the nature of the appointment made depends on the type of security held. A receiver or receiver and manager, who is usually a chartered accountant, may be appointed to take control of the specific assets charged, or even to take the management of the company away from its directors.

Where a company borrows money from a bank or some other lending institution, it normally gives the lender a debenture over its assets as security. The debenture usually provides for the appointment of a receiver or receiver and manager if requested to do so. It is not common, and no examples have been found, where a borrower has requested the lender to make the appointment.

Immediately upon appointment, the receiver or receiver and manager assumes control of the assets that are pledged as security to the lender; where all the company's assets have been pledged, the receiver and manager has control over the whole of the company, with power to manage given by the debenture. He acts as agent of the company.

The primary duty of the receiver and manager is to obtain sufficient funds from the assets of the company to repay the debenture holder. Usually, he does so by selling the business as a going concern or by selling the assets separately. In practice, in view of the general economic difficulties caused by the prevailing government economic recovery measures, a receiver and manager is expected to survey other available options which may assure full recovery in the longer term. Control by the receiver and manager in this case becomes prolonged.

The principal effect on the outside world is that the company's liabilities are effectively frozen at the date of the receiver's appointment, but, ironically, all lenders still continue to charge interest on the outstanding debts, thus increasing the balance intended to be recovered. The receiver collects money due to the company but is not directly responsible for paying liabilities owing by the company prior to his appointment. He is responsible for paying for any goods and services that are purchased or employed under his instruction.

He observes the following order of preference in the discharge of the company's debts:

- secured creditors (those to whom assets have been pledged);
- preferential creditors (employees, government departments and local government rates);
- unsecured creditors (suppliers of goods and services);
- shareholders.

Creditors' voluntary liquidation

In a creditors' voluntary liquidation the assets and liabilities of a company are placed under the control of a liquidator who terminates the affairs of the company in cooperation with its creditors.

The directors of the company decide that it is not possible for the company to continue to trade, and they call meetings of the shareholders and the company's creditors to explain the circumstances. The shareholders' meeting is held first and the company is formally placed in liquidation, and a liquidator is nominated.

Immediately afterwards, the meeting of creditors is held and the creditors are given the opportunity to inquire into the affairs of the company. The creditors either endorse the liquidator nominated by the shareholders, or appoint a liquidator of their own choice. Whoever is appointed by the creditors becomes the liquidator of the company and the control of the company passes entirely to him. A committee of inspection, usually composed of five of the creditors, is appointed at the meeting to represent the creditors' interests and sanction the actions of the liquidator.

The liquidator supervises the dissolution of the company and only allows the company to continue to trade in exceptional circumstances. His duty is to collect in all the assets of the company, and convert them into cash and to ascertain all the liabilities. When this task has been completed, he distributes the cash to the creditors and the company then ceases to exist.

The major effect of a liquidator being appointed to a company is that the company ceases to trade. A creditor who has security over an asset of the company is entitled to realise that security in order to satisfy the debt due to him, any funds surplus to that requirement being handed to the liquidator.

The following order of preference is observed in the discharge of the company's debts:

- secured creditors (those to whom assets have been pledged);
- preferential creditors (employees, government departments and local authority rates);
- unsecured creditors (suppliers of goods and services);
- shareholders.

Compulsory liquidation

As in a creditors' voluntary liquidation, the assets and liabilities of a company are placed under the control of a liquidator who terminates the affairs of the company. However, a compulsory liquidation is conducted in a more formal manner with regulations being enforced by the courts.

Any person who is a creditor of a company is entitled to make formal demand for payment of a debt due, failure to comply with that demand giving that person the right to petition to the court for the company to be wound up because it is unable to pay its debts.

The court hears the petition and, if it is satisfied that the company is insolvent, orders that the company be wound up. The official receiver, an officer of the Federal High Court of Nigeria, is appointed provisional liquidator and at that point control of the company passes entirely to him.

The provisional liquidator ensures that the assets of the company are secure and calls upon the directors of the company to prepare a detailed statement of affairs of the company. When this has been prepared the provisional liquidator calls a meeting of the creditors of the company and advises them of the company's history. The creditors either endorse the provisional liquidator as the liquidator or appoint another person as liquidator.

From that point onwards the liquidator does the same job as detailed under creditors' voluntary liquidation, but is required to file certain information with the court concerning the conduct of the liquidation. A committee of inspection may be appointed if the creditors so wish.

The effect of a company being placed into compulsory liquidation is the same as in a creditors' voluntary liquidation (see above) but creditors must make formal proof of their debts before the liquidator will admit their claims.

Members' voluntary liquidation

In a members' voluntary liquidation, a company which no longer wishes to exist, or which achieves the purpose for which it came into being, realises all its assets, discharges all its liabilities and distributes the surplus funds among the shareholders.

The directors of the company alone decide on the course of action because no outside parties will suffer any detrimental effect. It can only take place, however, if the company is able to discharge all its liabilities in full within a period of 12 months. The directors must swear an affidavit (statutory declaration of solvency) that the company will be able to do this and may appoint a liquidator of their own choosing.

The liquidator realises sufficient of the company's assets to discharge the company's liabilities. The remaining assets may be converted into cash or distributed in kind to the shareholders (for example, investments).

If the assets are insufficient to meet the liabilities of the company or if they cannot be realised within the 12-month period then the liquidation is converted to a creditors' voluntary liquidation (see above).

Striking off

Every company incorporated in Nigeria is registered with the Corporate Affairs Commission, Abuja. When a company ceases to exist it is struck off the register.

Many companies, either individually or as part of a group, become dormant. These companies frequently have no tangible assets, their balance sheets reflecting share capital and either a debit balance on reserve or an intercompany balance. The directors may write to the Registrar General, Corporate Affairs Commission advising him of the state of the company and request that it be struck off. The Registrar General issues public notices of his intention to strike off the company and, if no objections are received, the company ceases to exist.

KPMG contact partner

F O Akinbohun
KPMG Audit
Bolex House, Plot 33
Imam Dauda Street
Iganmu Industrial Estate
PO Box 549
Lagos
Nigeria

Telephone: +234 (1) 580 2110
Fax: +234 (1) 583 0579

Norway

Legislation

Norwegian insolvency and bankruptcy procedures are based on a system of codified law.

These rules are found in:

- the Bankruptcy Act (Act No. 58, 8 June 1984); and
- the Creditors Recovery Act (Act No. 59, 8 June 1984).

These apply both to corporate insolvency and personal bankruptcies.

In addition to the above statutes the Debt Arrangement Act (Act No. 99, 17 July 1992) contains rules relating to voluntary and compulsory debt arrangement for private persons.

In addition an important source of law is found in decisions of the court on the interpretation of the above statute law. Another source of law is contained in regulations issued by the Ministry of Justice and the preparatory works which preceded the Acts.

The Bankruptcy Act is divided into two main parts; the first part concerns court composition procedure (debt or debt arrangements) conducted through a court-appointed administrator. The second part concerns corporate insolvency and/or bankruptcy. Unlike, for example, English law, there are no distinctions under Norwegian legislation between corporate insolvency and personal bankruptcies. The expression 'bankruptcy' ('*konkurs*') under Norwegian law therefore applies to both corporations and individuals.

Insolvency procedure

Norwegian insolvency procedure is divided into three different levels or stages; the voluntary court composition procedure (debt arrangement), the compulsory court composition procedure and finally the bankruptcy procedure.

In addition to the above procedures, in recent years, several corporations and private persons have entered into private arrangements with creditors, solving financial difficulties in private instead of going through a formal insolvency procedure supervised by the courts.

Composition proceedings

It is only the debtor who can apply for composition proceedings under Norwegian law.

The purpose of the composition proceedings is normally to prevent liquidation of the debtor or corporation, and protect it from its creditors by applying to the bankruptcy court for assistance in reaching a permanent arrangement with the creditors.

To be able to apply, the debtor must be unable to pay its debts as they fall due, there must be an expectation that the debtor may obtain a debt rescheduling arrangement with its creditors, and the debtor must believe that its assets will be sufficient to cover its debts.

The application must contain a statement concerning the cause of the financial problems, a list of the debtor's assets and debts, including the names of all the creditors (for secured creditors, including the date when the debt was incurred and when it was secured) and a statement of the debtor's accounts.

The court can require the debtor to make an advance payment to the court to cover costs which are not covered by ordinary court fees, or to put up security to cover the costs.

If the bankruptcy court consents to open composition proceedings, it must appoint a creditors' committee to supervise the proceedings. The creditors' committee shall consist of a chairman (normally a lawyer) and between one and three members appointed from the creditors. On the recommendation of the creditors' committee, the bankruptcy court may appoint an auditor. The auditor is required to audit the debtor's accounts and finances and make a report to the creditors' committee.

The creditors' committee's main tasks are to assist the debtor to reach an agreement with the creditors and to represent and protect the creditors' interests. They have to inform the creditors involved of the court composition and ask them to submit their claims to the committee and must analyse and report to the court and the creditors on the debtor's financial position.

For the general public the debtor appears to continue to run its operations while the negotiations proceed. Initially the debtor is, however, controlled by the creditors' committee, which may instruct the debtor and its employees on what to do. The creditors' committee will also have power to decide that the debtor shall stop its operations during the composition proceedings, and for some transactions (for example the incurring of new debt) the debtor will need consent from the creditors' committee.

Voluntary composition proceedings

If the debtor and the creditors' committee believe that a scheme for settling the debt might be approved, they must propose the scheme.

The scheme may include:

- a postponement of debts;
- a reduction of debts;
- a disposal or liquidation of all or parts of the debtor's assets (without any reduction of liabilities);
- a disposal or liquidation of all or parts of the debtor's assets, but so that the debtor is released from any liability which is not settled by the liquidation;
- a combination of the above.

The voluntary composition has to include all creditors, but it is possible to keep outside the scheme secured and legally preferred claims, such as employees' claims for wages, ordinary tax and VAT claims, outstanding accounts which are secured by a right of set-off, and also outstanding debts less than a fixed sum agreed in the composition.

The proposal must be sent to the creditors who must be given at least two weeks within which to respond. To succeed with the arrangement to settle the debt, all creditors covered by the proposal must accept, or creditors representing at least three quarters of the aggregate value of the claims must accept and no creditors must object.

Compulsory composition proceedings

If the debtor fails to obtain consent from the creditors for a voluntary composition, it may try to obtain a compulsory settlement of debts. A request for a compulsory composition must be submitted to the bankruptcy court. The debtor must show that it has the support of at least 40 per cent of the aggregated amounts of the outstanding claims entitled to vote on a proposal for settling the debt.

These negotiations are also presided over by the creditors' committee.

If the bankruptcy court consents to the application, the creditors' committee must immediately publish the opening of such proceedings and ask the creditors to submit and specify their claims. The opening of such proceedings must be published in the Norwegian *Gazette* and must be formally registered in various registries.

To become binding, a proposal for compulsory composition must be approved by a majority in value and number of the creditors. The majority requirement varies depending on the amount of the debt which the proposal would offer to repay. This percentage must, however, not be less than 25 per cent payment to each creditor. If less than 50 per cent payment is proposed, two thirds of the voting creditors representing two thirds of the aggregated outstanding debts will have to accept the proposal if the compulsory composition is to succeed.

The result of the compulsory composition may be:

- a postponement on repayment of debts;
- a reduction to a certain percentage of the debtor's total debt (however, not less than 25 per cent payment to each creditor);
- a liquidation wholly or partly of the debtor's property, connected with reduction of his burden of debt; or
- a combination of the above.

The bankruptcy court must ratify the composition. There are circumstances in which the court may reject the proposal, despite acceptance by the creditors. If the creditors do not accept a proposal or if the court decides to reject the proposal, the court must terminate the composition proceedings and commence compulsory liquidation proceedings (i.e., the debtor is declared bankrupt).

Bankruptcy

The debtor itself, an unsecured creditor or the court of its own motion (for instance if compulsory composition proceedings have failed) may apply for an order to put the debtor into bankruptcy.

The debtor is declared bankrupt if it is 'insolvent'. Under Norwegian law a debtor is regarded as insolvent when it has a continuing (i.e., not merely temporary) inability to pay its debts as they fall due and/or its total liabilities exceed the value of its assets.

If the court decides that the debtor is insolvent and therefore opens bankruptcy proceedings, the court will appoint a temporary trustee (usually a lawyer) of the debtor's estate. The effect of such order is the confiscation or seizure of all assets of the debtor and the placing of these under the control of the trustee.

The order of the bankruptcy court is made public by registering it in the Company Registry (if the debtor is a company), the Movable Property Registry, the Land Registry, and in other relevant registries. It is also advertised in the newspapers and the Norwegian *Gazette* and in a newly established bankruptcy registry.

Once bankruptcy proceedings have been opened, the court and the temporary trustee will request all creditors to submit their claims to the trustee, and give them notice of the first creditors' meeting, which should be held within three weeks of the announcement of the court's order in the Norwegian *Gazette*.

At this creditors' meeting the trustee is appointed (usually the temporary trustee will be appointed as trustee). A creditors' committee is also appointed at this meeting, to advise the trustee on relevant matters.

The trustee must assess the assets of the debtor, secure and protect them against claimants, collect outstanding debts due to the debtor, pursue, enhance and dispose of the assets of the debtor in the best possible manner, compile and rank the claims, and propose dividend distributions to be approved by the court.

In conjunction with the creditors' committee, the trustee must prepare a report containing information on the debtor's business, accounting principles, the reasons for the insolvency situation, a statement of the assets and debts of the debtor, a statement as to whether any transactions prior to cut-off date are voidable and information on whether the debtor or its executives and/or officers should be prosecuted for any criminal offence due to its business methods.

This report must also recommend whether the debtor should be disqualified from establishing a new corporation or from acting as executive, non-executive or managing director in a new business for a period of two years.

This report is distributed to the creditors, the creditors' committee, the debtor, the court and the new bankruptcy registry.

If the trustee believes that the debtor may be guilty of a criminal offence prior to bankruptcy, the report must also be submitted to the public prosecutor's office.

When the liquidation is completed, final accounts are filed by the trustee. These accounts are sent to the court, the debtor and its directors. Once the accounts have been approved by the court, the trustee sends them to all the creditors.

The assets of the debtor are converted into money which is distributed amongst the creditors according to the following priorities:

- secured creditors (whose claims will be settled from the assets over which they have security);
- creditors whose claims arise during the bankruptcy proceedings and/or composition proceedings, provided priority for the claims was accepted by the creditors' committee during the proceedings;
- creditors with first-class priority claims (wages of the debtor's employees);
- creditors with second-class priority claims (ordinary taxes and VAT);
- ordinary unsecured claims;
- subordinated claims.

Bankruptcy proceedings are completed when the court has rendered its final decision on distribution of dividends to the creditors. The creditors may appeal such a decision.

On the recommendation of the trustee the court may, however, decide to suspend or discontinue bankruptcy proceedings before they are completed if there are insufficient assets in the estate to cover the costs of liquidation. If the debtor is a company, the trustee will notify the Company Registry when the bankruptcy proceedings are terminated, or suspended. The Company Registrar will then delete the debtor from the Registry.

Other matters

The Debt Recovery Act contains rules which enable the bankruptcy estate to set aside certain pre-liquidation transactions.

This Act also contains rules which enable the estate to enter into and continue the debtor's contracts with third parties, and rules on set-off of mutual claims against the debtor and its creditors.

Under Norwegian law both the Joint-Stock Company Act and the Companies Act have provisions on liability for officers of a corporation or a limited partnership. An officer may be liable for any damage intentionally or negligently caused by him as an officer of the company. During recent years such cases have become more and more frequent in Norway.

KPMG contact partner

Ole Kristian Aabø-Evensen
KPMG Law Advokatfirma DA
PO Box 150 Bryn
N-0611 Oslo
Norway

Telephone: +47 2207 2207
Fax: +47 2207 2201

Pakistan

Legislation

Insolvency proceedings for companies are regulated by the provisions of ss. 297 to 449 of the Companies Ordinance 1984.

Insolvency procedures

Winding up by the court

A company may be wound up by the court if:

- the company so resolves by special resolution;
- the company defaults in delivering the statutory report to the Registrar or in holding the statutory meeting or any two consecutive annual general meetings;
- the company does not commence its business within a year from its incorporation, or suspends its business for a whole year;
- the number of members of the company is reduced, in the case of a private company below two, or in the case of any other company below seven;
- the company is unable to pay its debts;
- the company is involved in unlawful or fraudulent activities, or is carrying on business not authorised by its memorandum;
- the company conducts its business in a manner oppressive to any of its members or persons concerned with the formation or promotion of the company or the majority shareholders;
- the company is run and managed by persons who fail to maintain proper and true accounts, or commit fraud, misfeasance or malfeasance in relation to the company;
- the company is managed by persons who refuse to act according to the requirements of the memorandum or articles or the provisions of the Companies Ordinance or fail to carry out the directions or decisions of the court or the Registrar or the authority given in the exercise of powers under the Companies Ordinance;
- being a listed company, it ceases to be such a company;
- in the opinion of the court it is just and equitable that the company should be wound up.

The winding up is deemed to commence at the time of presentation of the winding-up petition. The liquidator is appointed by the court and is known as the official liquidator.

Voluntary winding up

A company may be wound up voluntarily if the company so resolves by special resolution, or if the period fixed for the duration of the company by the articles expires or if an event specified in the articles occurs, by passing a resolution in general meeting.

A voluntary winding up is deemed to commence at the time of passing the winding-up resolution. The liquidator is appointed by the members in a members' voluntary winding up and by the creditors in a creditors' voluntary winding up. The company ceases to carry on its business, except so far as may be required for its beneficial winding up.

Winding up subject to supervision by the court

When a company has passed a resolution for voluntary winding up, the court may on its own motion or on the application of any person entitled to apply to the court for winding up a company, make an order that the voluntary winding up shall continue, but subject to such supervision of the court, and with such liberty for creditors, contributories or others to apply to the court, and generally on such terms and conditions, as the court thinks just.

Fraudulent preference

Any conveyance, mortgage, delivery of goods, payment, execution or other act relating to property made or done by or against a company within six months before commencement of its winding up is deemed fraudulent preference of its creditors and is invalid.

Effect of floating charge

Where a company is being wound up, a floating charge on the undertaking or property of the company created within 12 months of the commencement of the winding up shall, unless it is proved that the company immediately after the creation of the charge was solvent, be invalid except to the amount of any cash paid to the company at the time of, or subsequent to the creation of, and in consideration for, the charge, together with any surcharge on that amount at the rate of 1 per cent per month or part thereof or such other rate as may be notified by the Authority in the official *Gazette*.

Creditors

Where the company's assets are insufficient to meet its liabilities in full the following debts take precedence over debts due to holders of floating charges and before all other debts:

- all revenues, taxes, cesses and rates due from the company to the federal government or a provincial government or to a local authority at the relevant date and having become due and payable within the 12 months next before that date;
- all wages or salary for a period not exceeding four months and any compensation payable to any workmen under any law for the time being in force — up to Rs2,000 per employee;
- all accrued holiday remuneration;
- all amounts due in respect of insurance contributions payable by the company as employer;
- all sums due to any employee from a provident fund, pension fund, gratuity fund or any other fund for the welfare of the employees maintained by the company;
- the expenses of any investigation held in pursuance of ss. 263 or 265 in so far as they are payable by the company.

Where any payment has been made to an employee on account of wages, salary or accrued holiday remuneration out of money advanced by some person for that purpose, the person by whom the money was advanced shall, in winding up, have a right of priority in respect of the money so advanced and paid, up to the amount by which the sum in respect of which the employee or other person in his right would have been entitled to priority in the winding up has been diminished by reason of the payment having been made.

In the event of a landlord or other person distraining or having distrained on any goods or effects of the company within the three months next before the date of the winding-up order, the preferential debts shall be a first charge on goods or effects so distrained on, or the proceeds of the sale thereof, provided that, in respect of any money paid under any such charge, the landlord or other person shall have the same rights of priority as the person to whom the payment is made.

No distinction is made between local and overseas creditors.

KPMG contact partner

Masoud Neqvi
Taseer Hadi Khalid & Co.
1st Floor
Sheikh Sultan Trust Building No. 2
Beaumont Road
Karachi 75530
Pakistan

Telephone: +92 (21) 5671 761
Fax: +92 (21) 5685 095

Panama

Legislation

In the Republic of Panama there are basically two types of insolvency procedures:

- personal insolvency or bankruptcy, which relates to individuals;
- corporate insolvency, which relates to companies.

The Commercial Code of the Republic of Panama devotes a whole book, the third, to bankruptcy, from art. 1534 to art. 1648. The proceedings can be initiated by an insolvent individual or by a creditor seeking either to have the remaining assets of the bankrupt distributed among the creditors and thereby discharge the bankrupt from any further obligation or to restructure and reorganise the insolvent's debt structure.

On the other hand, the Panama Judicial Code provides, in Title XV (arts 1810 to 1936), that bankruptcy proceedings can either be voluntary or compulsory. Bankruptcy is voluntary when initiated by the bankrupt who conveys all his goods to his creditors. It is compulsory when it is presented by one or all of the creditors.

Corporate insolvency usually takes the form of a liquidation. The legislation governing liquidations is contained under Book III, Title III of the Commercial Code.

Insolvency procedures

Bankruptcy

A bankruptcy declaration is ordered by a judge in the district in which the bankrupt has its commercial domicile. It could be requested by:

- the bankrupt or the person who rightfully represents him;
- a legitimate creditor;
- the Public Ministry, if the bankrupt cannot be found or does not appoint a person to represent him in the fulfilment of commercial obligations.

Types of bankruptcy

- bankruptcy due to bad management;
- fraudulent bankruptcy.

Liquidation

A corporation can be liquidated either by order of the court or by the corporation voluntarily placing itself in liquidation. Whilst both administrations are similar there are significant differences in the methods of appointing the administrator and the duties bestowed upon him. In a court liquidation the court will order winding up of a corporation when the court considers that procedure is necessary. Alternatively, where the directors and shareholders of a corporation realise that the corporation is insolvent and cannot continue its operation, it is usual for the directors to convene a general meeting of the shareholders and creditors to place the corporation in voluntary liquidation.

A corporation in liquidation may not necessarily be bankrupt, but when a corporation is bankrupt, it always needs to be liquidated. The bankruptcy of a corporation also implies that of the general partners. Once the judge declares the bankruptcy of the corporation, he also declares, in a separate action, that of the bankrupt partners.

Bankruptcy of one or more of the partners does not imply bankruptcy of the corporation, but it will mean that the corporation is deemed to be dissolved.

The liquidation proceeding will be the one stated in the articles of incorporation. If they do not state any specific procedure, the liquidator must comply with the rules set forth in the Commercial Code.

Any person can be appointed as the liquidator by the corporation's shareholders. If an acceptable liquidator cannot be appointed, a creditor or shareholder may request the court to appoint a liquidator.

The function of the liquidator (usually a lawyer or an accountant) is to realise the corporation's assets, distribute the proceeds to the various classes of creditors and pay the expenses of the liquidation.

Voluntary winding up

Voluntary winding up means the winding up of a corporation when the shareholders do not seek the assistance of the court.

The assets and liabilities of the corporation are placed under the control of a liquidator who winds up the affairs of the corporation. Unless otherwise stated in the articles of incorporation a corporation may be wound up voluntarily:

- whenever the articles of incorporation of the corporation provide for it to be dissolved, and the corporation in general meeting has passed a resolution requiring it to be wound up voluntarily;
- whenever the corporation has passed a special resolution requiring it to be wound up voluntarily;
- whenever the shareholders have passed an extraordinary resolution to the effect that it has been proved to their satisfaction that the corporation cannot by reason of its liabilities continue its business, and that it is advisable to wind it up.

A voluntary winding up is deemed to commence at the time of the passing of the resolution authorising the winding up. The effects of the commencement of winding up are that:

- the corporation shall cease to trade;
- the corporation's corporate powers and status continue until its affairs are wound up;
- upon the appointment of a liquidator all the powers of the directors cease.

In practice the directors of a corporation decide that it is not possible or not necessary for the corporation to continue to trade and they call a meeting of the shareholders. The shareholders' meeting is held and the corporation is formally placed into liquidation by special resolution and a liquidator is nominated — unless, however, the appointment is delegated to the creditors. The winding up commences when articles of dissolution, containing the plan of dissolution and the name of the liquidators, are filed with the Public Registrar.

The liquidator has the duty to collect in all the assets of the corporation and convert them into cash, and to ascertain and pay all the liabilities of the corporation. When this task has been completed he distributes any surplus funds to the shareholders and, after filing the appropriate returns, the corporation is dissolved.

As soon as the affairs of the corporation are fully wound up the liquidator must make up an account showing the manner in which the winding up has been conducted and the property of the corporation disposed of.

Winding up under supervision of the court

When a resolution has been passed by a corporation to wind up voluntarily, the court may make an order directing such supervision of the court as the court thinks fair.

Any creditor of the corporation or any contributory may petition the court to order such supervision.

As in voluntary liquidation, the assets and liabilities of a corporation are placed under the control of a liquidator who terminates the affairs of the corporation. The liquidation is conducted in a more formal manner under the supervision of the court.

Any person who is a creditor of a corporation is entitled to make formal demand for payment of a debt due, and failure to comply with that demand will give that person the right to petition the court for the corporation to be wound up because it is unable to pay its debts.

The liquidator will take all necessary steps to secure the assets of the corporation and will call upon the directors of the corporation to prepare a detailed statement of the affairs of the corporation.

From that point onwards the liquidator will do the same job as has been detailed above under voluntary liquidation, but is required to file certain information with the court concerning the conduct of the liquidation. The effect of a corporation being wound up by the court is the same as in a voluntary liquidation (see above) but creditors must make formal proof of their debts before the liquidator will admit their claims.

Other matters

Creditors secured by chattel mortgage, mortgage or antichresis are preferred over any other and will not take part in the bankruptcy proceedings.

A creditor who has security over an asset of the corporation is entitled to realise that security in order to satisfy the debt to him, any funds surplus to that requirement being handed to the liquidator. In any case, the Panamanian legislation makes provision for the payment of certain creditors in priority of others. Priority is granted to the following, but not necessarily in the order presented:

- costs of liquidation including petitioning creditors' costs;
- debts in favour of the governmental entities in accordance with the date of registration;
- prescribed payments deductions;
- costs of any previous insolvency administrator;
- wages and salaries of employees.

KPMG contact partner

Francisco B. Vega
Avenida Nicanor de Obarrio
Calle 50, No. 54
PO Box 5307
Panama 5, Republic of Panama

Telephone: +507 263 5677
Fax No: +507 263 9852

Papua New Guinea

Legislation

Practitioners involved in liquidations, receiverships and other corporate administrations work within the statutory framework of the Companies Act, c. 146, which is based on Australian legislation.

There are provisions that disqualify the appointment of auditors, officers and mortgagees etc. of the debtor corporation to most of the above positions.

Insolvency procedures

Papua New Guinea insolvency law is divided into two distinct areas: the law relating to corporate insolvencies, which encompasses liquidations, receiverships, official managements and schemes of arrangement, and the law relating to individuals, which is contained in the Bankruptcy Act. In very broad terms the term 'liquidation' only applies to corporations whereas the term 'bankruptcy' only applies to individuals.

Receivership

A receiver and manager, appointed by a creditor holding security in the nature of an equitable mortgage, assumes control of the company's assets and realises them in order to satisfy the claims of the secured creditor. However, although the appointee is clearly acting for the secured creditor, the receiver and manager is the agent of the company and, further, has a common law responsibility to give due regard to the position of other creditors. A receiver appointed by the court must act in accordance with the terms of the order under which he is appointed.

Commonly, a company grants a mortgage charging the whole of its assets and undertaking. The instrument creating the charge confers on the holder of the mortgage or his trustee a right to appoint a receiver and manager where a condition precedent occurs, such as default in meeting a repayment obligation.

A secured creditor may elect not to exercise his rights to appoint a receiver and manager under the instrument and allow a liquidator to realise the assets which are subject to the charge provided there is acceptance by the liquidator of the validity of the security. The appointment of a receiver and manager can be implemented very quickly and with minimal dislocation to the company's business.

The receiver and manager may be appointed in terms of a floating charge, real property mortgage or other form of fixed or specific mortgage, or a Supreme Court order. The powers of the receiver and manager are usually contained within the security document or the instrument appointing him. The powers generally include full powers to carry on the business, to receive income and realise assets.

Agent for the mortgagee in possession

Following on from a mortgagee entering into possession of assets (and in some circumstances, an ongoing business) pursuant to powers contained in the mortgage or floating charge, the mortgagee may appoint an agent to do all things that the mortgagee is entitled to do in terms of the mortgage. This procedure may be implemented by a secured creditor more quickly than the appointment of either a receiver or receiver and manager and therefore provides a means to stabilise what may be a disorderly situation more promptly.

In addition, the law relating to priority payments does not require any payments in priority to the mortgagee's claim other than certain employee entitlements. The major disadvantages of this type of appointment are that if the mortgagee's agent carries on the business of the mortgagor, the mortgagee is assuming the risk for any losses that may be incurred. The agent for the mortgagee does not have the benefit of certain statutory rights and powers granted to other administrators to facilitate the objective of the administration.

This form of administration has only come to prominence in recent times and the law relating to it has not had the opportunity to develop. Accordingly, the law relating to this form of administration is likely to be subject to change as the administration is more widely used and aspects of it are brought to the attention of the courts and legislators.

Liquidation

A company can be liquidated either by order of the court or by the company voluntarily placing itself in liquidation. Whilst both administrations are similar there are significant differences in the method of appointing the administrator and the duties bestowed upon him. In a court liquidation the court will order the winding up of a company where it is of the opinion that it is just and equitable that the company be wound up. Alternatively where the directors and shareholders of a company realise that the company is insolvent and cannot continue its operations, the directors or creditors can convene a general meeting of the shareholders and creditors to place the company in liquidation.

Members' voluntary liquidation

Liquidation can be completed by solvent companies, which requires meetings of directors and shareholders including the making of a declaration of solvency. Usually an insolvency administrator is appointed to liquidate the assets, pay creditors and distribute the proceeds to shareholders.

Scheme of arrangement

A scheme of arrangement is a court-approved arrangement between a company and its creditors, providing either for a moratorium to pay the debt, or a barring arrangement whereby the company's creditors abandon the balance of their claims after receiving a specified distribution. This type of arrangement is usually entered into where the creditors are of the opinion that they are more likely to obtain a greater benefit from the company continuing its operations under the control of a scheme manager than if the company is wound up.

Official management

Official management is an arrangement, initiated by either the company or an unsecured creditor, that provides a moratorium period during which the company trades under the control of an official manager. The official manager must be of the opinion, and so must the creditors, that the company will be able to pay creditors' claims in full at some future point in time.

Who can be appointed?

- liquidator — with the exception of members' voluntary liquidations, only registered liquidators or registered official liquidators, being natural persons, can be appointed liquidators to corporations. Generally, only accountants in public practice with appropriate experience are registered as liquidators;
- receiver — only a registered liquidator may be appointed to act as a receiver of the property or part of the property of a company;
- official manager — any person who has consented in writing;
- scheme manager — only a registered liquidator can accept appointment to administer as scheme manager.

Creditors

The principle of an equal division of assets among creditors is fundamental to the whole statutory scheme, but there are some exceptions to the general rule, all of which are statutory in origin.

Secured creditors

A secured creditor is one who holds a mortgage, charge or lien on property of the debtor as a security for a debt, and is in a position either at law or in equity to recoup partly or wholly from that property in priority to unsecured creditors. A partly secured creditor is able to prove in a liquidation for the unsecured portion of the debt. A secured creditor has many courses of action available, and these include the appointment of a receiver to the property which is the subject of the security; entering into possession as mortgagee; or doing nothing, allowing the company or administrator to realise the security and then proving as an unsecured creditor (if the company is then in liquidation) for any remaining unpaid debt.

Priority claims

The Papua New Guinea legislation makes provision for the payment of certain unsecured creditors in priority to other unsecured creditors. The priority enjoyed by certain categories of creditors is an area that is the subject of much confusion due to the many authorities that give rise to priority laws. However, as a general guide to company liquidations and receiverships, priority is granted to the following but not necessarily in the order presented:

- costs of liquidation including petitioning creditors' costs;
- unremitted tax instalment deductions and withholding tax;
- costs of any previous insolvency administrator;
- wages and salaries not exceeding Kina 3,000 per employee;
- amounts due to employees in respect of holiday pay, long-service leave;
- injury compensation payments;
- municipal or local rates accrued within 12 months of the winding up.

Other matters

Insolvency administration and legislation in Papua New Guinea is highly sophisticated and provides a workable framework for creditors to exercise their legal rights to ensure that a company, unable to pay its debts, is placed in an appropriate form of insolvency administration. Similarly a debtor company is able to avail itself of the insolvency provisions to enable it to trade out of financial difficulties. Generally all forms of insolvency administrations are administered by accountants in public practice who have relevant qualifications.

KPMG contact partner

Rob Southwell
KPMG
2nd Floor, Mogoru Moto Bldg
Champion Parade
Port Moresby
Papua New Guinea

Telephone: +675 321–2022
Fax: +675 321–2780

Postal address

PO Box 507
Port Moresby
Papua New Guinea

All mail must be forwarded to the PO Box number.

Poland

Legislation

Insolvency procedures may be based on either:

- the Bankruptcy Decree of 24 October 1934 (with amendments), which regulates the bankruptcy procedure; or
- the Settlement Proceedings Decree of 24 October 1934 (with amendments), which regulates the general settlement procedure.

Insolvency procedures

Bankruptcy

The Bankruptcy Decree applies to all business entities except governmental and municipal units, major public service companies (e.g., Polish State Railways, Polish Post, etc.) and entities which do not need to have their economic activity registered.

Grounds for bankruptcy declaration

Companies are declared bankrupt if they are insolvent. Generally, a company is deemed to be insolvent if it fails to pay its debts or its property is not sufficient to cover its debts.

Motions for bankruptcy declarations can be filed in court by the debtor or any of its creditors. Debtors who cease payment of their debts must file a motion for a bankruptcy declaration. Where the debtor is a legal entity, this duty rests on the normal representatives or liquidators of the legal entity. However, if an application for the initiation of settlement proceedings has been filed (see below), the duty to apply for a bankruptcy declaration is waived.

Bankruptcy procedure

Bankruptcy proceedings are usually commenced in the district court which has jurisdiction over the area where the debtor's main plant or business is located. The court may require advance payment of the costs of the proceedings from the creditor who files the motion. At the creditor's request, and before deciding on the motion, the court may issue interim orders securing the debtor's property.

The court decision declaring bankruptcy includes, *inter alia*, a summons to creditors to produce claims within a designated time, and the appointment of a judge-commissioner and a bankruptcy receiver. The date of the court decision is automatically the date of the bankruptcy declaration. Bankruptcy declarations are published in the official court journal (*Monitor Sądowy i Gospodarczy*), as well as in the local press.

After the declaration, bankruptcy proceedings are conducted by the judge-commissioner except those parts which are reserved for the court. The judge-commissioner, *inter alia*, directs the proceedings and supervises the receiver.

The receiver takes over and administers the bankrupt's property, and carries out the liquidation. In particular, the receiver informs the tax authorities and creditors about the bankruptcy of the debtor. The receiver is entitled to demand information on the bankrupt's property from offices, institutions and other persons who have this information.

After the time designated in the summons to creditors to produce their claims expires, the receiver requests the bankrupt to make a statement on the claims submitted, in particular, acknowledging them or not. The receiver then submits a draft list of creditors to the judge-commissioner, who determines the list of claims.

At this stage, the bankrupt may come to a settlement with the creditors. Creditors participating in the settlement act together as an assembly (the 'assembly of creditors'). The settlement is adopted by creditors if creditors with two thirds of the total number of claims vote in favour of it. The settlement will become effective if it is approved by the court.

The judge-commissioner may appoint a creditors' council if this is necessary, or if creditors holding at least 20 per cent of the total amount of the claims so require. The council, *inter alia*, assists and supervises the receiver and gives opinions at the receiver's request. It may demand explanations from the receiver and examine books and documents concerning the bankruptcy. Certain actions may only be taken by the receiver with the consent of the creditors' council.

Results of bankruptcy declaration

The bankrupt is required to declare and relinquish all property, commercial books, correspondence and other documents. The bankrupt cannot use or dispose of his or her property, or property acquired in the course of the proceedings, from the date of the bankruptcy declaration. Legal actions of the bankrupt concerning the bankruptcy estate are ineffective. The court may apply special measures if the debtor attempts to conceal his or her property, or prevent the calculation of its value.

Distribution of estate funds

Claims are paid in the following order:

- costs of bankruptcy proceedings;
- receiver's costs and costs of executing contracts approved by the receiver;
- taxes incurred during the last two years before bankruptcy plus interest and the costs of execution;
- social insurance (ZUS) incurred during the last year before bankruptcy;
- funeral costs of the bankrupt and medical costs of last illness before bankruptcy (if a natural person);
- other liabilities, including claims, plus interest accrued during the last year before bankruptcy;
- interest on claims not satisfied in the above categories;
- fines and penalties;
- claims stemming out of gifts or donations.

If the amount to be distributed is not sufficient to cover all dues of the same category, they are covered on a pro rata basis. If all claims have been fully satisfied, the residue of the property of incorporated bankrupts is distributed among shareholders in proportion to the amount of shares held by them.

Guarantees

The following debts are guaranteed by special guarantee funds:

- bank deposits — by the Polish Bank Guarantee Fund;
- insurance payoffs — by the Insurance Guarantee Fund;
- salaries — by the Social Claims Guarantee Fund.

The amount of the sums guaranteed are limited under the applicable statutes.

Settlement proceedings

An economic entity may apply to the court for the commencement of settlement proceedings with creditors, if it has ceased to pay debts, or foresees this happening, due to exceptional circumstances beyond its control. The purpose of these settlement proceedings is to protect the debtor from bankruptcy. They are initiated and conducted under the Settlement Proceedings Decree.

Settlement proceedings are usually commenced in the district court which has jurisdiction over the area where the debtor's main plant or business is located. They are opened upon the court's decision, and are conducted by a judge-commissioner, except for those actions which are reserved for the court. The judge-commissioner is appointed by the court.

The court also appoints an executive supervisor, who supervises the debtor's enterprise, closes its books and examines the balance sheet submitted by the debtor and the condition of the debtor's enterprise. The supervisor's consent is required before the debtor can dispose of any part of its estate, or assume obligations which exceed the scope of ordinary administration.

Creditors participating in the settlement act together as an assembly. The settlement is adopted by creditors if creditors with two thirds of the total number of claims vote in favour of it. The settlement will become effective if it is approved by the court.

In principle, the settlement can only cover the deferment of debts, spreading payment of debts into instalments, reduction of the amount of debts and securing debts. Certain types of debts may not be covered by the settlement proceedings, for example, taxes, social insurance premiums, debts resulting from labour contracts and debts secured by pledges or mortgages.

KPMG contact person

Artur Zurek
KPMG Polska Sp. z o.o.
LIM Center — Marriott Hotel, IX floor
Al. Jerozolimskie 65/79
00–697 Warsaw, Poland

Telephone: +48 (39) 120 381
Fax: +48 (39) 120 384

Portugal

Legislation

The legal regime for bankruptcy in Portugal is governed by arts 1, 27 and 122 to 249 of Decree Law No. 132/93 of 23 April 1993 which approved the 'Code for Special Processes of Companies' Recovery and Bankruptcy' as amended by Decree Law no. 127/96 of 8 August 1996.

Insolvency procedures

In legal terms a company is considered to be in a situation of bankruptcy if it cannot, due to a lack of own means or credit, comply on time with its obligations.

The situation of insolvency, which leads to the bankruptcy of companies, can be caused directly by market conditions in which the company operates. In this case the bankruptcy is regarded as non-intentional and non-negligent. Bankruptcy can however, arise from serious negligence or imprudence on the part of the management board of the company, or by actions carried out with the intent to prejudice creditors. In the first case, the bankruptcy is considered to be non-intentional but negligent and in the second case it is called fraudulent bankruptcy. In both cases there is criminal responsibility on the part of the members of the management board.

Situations that the law determines as insolvency on the part of the debtor are the following:

- failure to fulfil one or more obligations which by their amount or circumstances demonstrate the impossibility of the company being able to satisfy its obligations on time;
- departure of the company's shareholders or members of its management board, which is related to a lack of liquidity in the company, without designation of a responsible substitute, or the abandonment of the establishment in which the company has its head office or carries out its main activity;
- destruction or misappropriation of goods, fictitious establishment of credit or any other abnormal procedure which reveals the intention of the company to put itself in a situation that would make it impossible to comply with its obligations.

Initiation of the process

The company, through its management board, has a duty to present itself in a court and request its declaration of bankruptcy within 60 days after the first situation mentioned above (failure to fulfil one or more obligations) has taken place. It may if it sees fit make a request for the application of a process of recovery.

The Public Attorneys, as well as any other creditor, can, under any circumstances and regardless of the amount or nature of its debt, request the declaration of bankruptcy of a company whenever any of the three abovementioned situations occur.

The process of bankruptcy, as well as all the procedural incidents that occur in it, are considered special processes and are of an urgent nature. Therefore they have precedence over normal court business. The procedural steps taken are sequential, and are only suspended during judicial holidays.

The competent court for the initiation of the bankruptcy process is the court for the district where the company has its main establishment or where the company has its head office.

Request for bankruptcy

The request for bankruptcy is carried out by a written petition which must set out the following:

- identification of the company;
- indication of the members of the management board of the company;
- description of the facts that form the reasons for the bankruptcy declaration.

Where the bankruptcy request is presented by the company it should furthermore be accompanied by the following documents:

- description of all creditors and their respective addresses, with an indication of the amounts of their debts, due dates and guarantees of which they have the benefit;
- description and identification of all actions and executions pending against the company;
- copies of the last accounting records, of the balance sheet, inventory, profit and loss accounts and the books of the last three years;
- copy of the minute which documents the discussions leading to the request;
- indication of other means of evidence (testimonial or documented).

When the bankruptcy request is presented by a creditor or by the Public Ministry, the request has to indicate the origin, nature and amount of debts due and the basis for the bankruptcy request. Documents should be presented by the creditor or Public Ministry to prove the existence of a debt together with any other document that they may have regarding the company in bankruptcy and also other means of obtaining additional evidence.

With the presentation of the petition of bankruptcy, the debts of the company with regard to third parties cease to earn interest.

The judge, after receiving the petition, will order that a number of bodies be directly informed. These are the State, the workers' commission of the company, the company (where it did not itself make the request for the process) and the 10 largest creditors. These can then, within 14 days, petition the court on their intention to adopt one of the following three actions:

- no actions (accepting what will be proposed);
- claiming amounts due; or
- opposing the bankruptcy request.

The other creditors will be informed through a publication in the official gazette (*Diário da República*), and have 28 days to provide their views in the same terms.

If at this stage there are creditors who hold debts which represent 75 per cent of the global amount of debts and oppose the bankruptcy request, the judge shall immediately order that the process be converted into a company recovery process.

If this does not occur within 21 days, the judge has to analyse the information presented by the creditors and decide on the continuation of the action. This court decision is very important since following this stage the process will be concluded. Therefore:

- in this order, the judge should analyse the petitions presented and should there be opposition to the bankruptcy on the part of creditors that represent 30 per cent of the total creditors, the judge shall order the continuation of a recovery process;
- on the other hand, if there is no opposition to the bankruptcy request the judge shall declare immediate bankruptcy;
- if on the part of any creditor, or the part of the company (if it did not make the request for the process) there is any opposition to the bankruptcy request, the judge, in this court order will call for a court hearing. This hearing is to be carried out within seven days, all parties being notified and having to present on the day and time set, new documents and witnesses.

In the court hearing, the judge, after hearing initial legal evidence, will make a summary of the relevant facts and advise if he intends to hear further evidence, in order to call witnesses.

Within seven days of the court hearing the judge shall pronounce sentence. It is, however, important to stress that the petitioner of a bankruptcy process can, up until the time of sentence, renounce the process, independently of the wishes of other creditors, who in this case would have to present a new bankruptcy request.

Declaration

The formal declaration which orders the bankruptcy of the company shall:

- nominate the liquidator for the bankruptcy and the members that make up the creditors' commission;
- order the seizure of all the company's goods and all accounting records;
- order the delivery of information to the Public Attorneys, where evidence of crime exists;
- if a single person is bankrupt, establish his residence;
- establish a timetable of between 20 and 60 days for creditors to claim their debts.

The sentence is registered at the Commercial Companies Registrar and published in the State and local journal.

The consequences of the bankruptcy declaration are the following:

- vesting of the liquidator as the only representative of the bankrupt;
- prohibition of the disposal of present or future assets except as expressly decided by the liquidator;
- immediate closure of accounting books;
- prevention of the members of the management board of directors of the bankrupt company, or individual bankrupts from being nominated for identical positions in commercial companies, State companies, cooperative societies and associations which carry out any economic activity.

The bankruptcy has several consequences with regard to the business of the company:

- all of the company's obligations are due and enforceable;
- cessation of interest on all liabilities;
- cessation of any credit privileges of the State, local authorities and social security institutions, these now being payable as common debts;
- possibility of annulment, for the benefit of the bankrupt estate, of the following acts:
  - acts that involve a decrease of the net worth of the bankrupt which were agreed without payment in the two years before the beginning of the bankruptcy process;
  - acts carried out on an onerous basis by the bankrupt company in the six months before the date of the beginning of bankruptcy with companies controlled by it or controlled by the same shareholders or members of the management board;
- contracts for payment made by the company with third parties, such as supply contracts, agency contracts, work contracts, etc. may be terminated.

Liquidation management

The liquidator can effect all normal business transactions. He must ensure that the bankrupt's rights are protected, investigate the extent of the bankruptcy, the business conditions relating to the trade and the reasons for the occurrence of the insolvency.

Receivables must be collected with due diligence and the liquidator may file suits against debtors as necessary. He may obtain authorisation from the trustee to obtain assistance from the bankrupt for the management of the liquidation.

The activity of the liquidator is audited by a commission made up of three to five creditors, denominated as a creditors' commission and chosen between the various classes of creditors and those interested in the liquidation of the company.

Verification of liabilities

All claims for money owed by the bankrupt may be presented to the court by any creditor on declaration of bankruptcy. Within five working days of the termination of the period of time given by the court to the creditors to make their claims, the liquidator must present a list of all known creditors to the court for which no claims have been made. Amounts claimed by creditors or listed as unclaimed may be contested by the bankrupt within the period established by the judge.

For amounts neither contested nor requiring additional documentary evidence, the court recognises the debts and determines the effective date of the bankruptcy. Where evidence of proof of the debts is required, the judge proceeds to obtain such proof, investigations to be concluded within a period of 60 days. When the period of investigation is completed, the process is reviewed by a representative of the Public Attorneys and, within 14 days, the court determines the date of the bankruptcy trial.

The judgment determines the order of preference for the payment of creditors and the effective date of the bankruptcy is declared. The following may appeal against the court's decisions:

- the petitioners;
- the bankrupt;
- the administrator;
- the Public Attorneys.

Liquidation of the assets

After the declaration of the effective date of the bankruptcy, the liquidator, under the supervision of the creditors' commission, may sell all the assets of the bankrupt if it is considered necessary.

Both the creditors and the bankrupt can make written objections to the court against irregular or prejudicial acts carried out by the liquidator during the course of the liquidation. When the liquidation is completed, the liquidator calls together the creditors for an examination of the books of account and other related documents, after which they have 14 days to make any claims.

Preferential creditors

Creditors with charges on the assets of the company are paid first out of the proceeds arising from the sale of such assets.

Ordinary creditors

If the amount on deposit with the bank, arising from the liquidation of the assets, exceeds 5 per cent of the total amount due to ordinary creditors, a distribution is made to them on a pro rata basis, as authorised by the court after receiving the opinion of the representative of the Public Attorneys.

Incidental procedures

There are two types of appeals which can take place in a bankruptcy process:

- an opposition to the declaration of bankruptcy, which can be made by any of the interested parties in the process within seven days of sentence on the ground of any matter of fact or right in law;
- an appeal against a decision of the judge in opposition to the declaration.

The effect of the presentation of these incidental provisions is to suspend the liquidation of the assets and the subsequent liquidation process until the decision is made final.

Other matters

There are some special provisions relating to the bankruptcy of companies as follows:

- the declaration of bankruptcy of one or more stockholders of a company does not necessarily mean that the company will be declared bankrupt;
- the declaration of bankruptcy of a company will result in the declaration of bankruptcy of any unlimited liability stockholders of that company;
- a company may initiate bankruptcy proceedings through the medium of any one of its stockholders or its management — a decision of a stockholders' general meeting is required and evidence of the minutes of such decisions must be shown;
- creditors of the company will be paid in preference to the company's stockholders with unlimited liability;
- any stockholders with capital that is not fully paid up will be required by the administrator to pay up such capital in full at the date of the declaration of bankruptcy;
- debenture holders can only claim an amount up to the issue price of the debentures if known, otherwise the nominal value and after taking into account all repayments already made relating to such debentures.

KPMG contact partner

Mark Gibbins
KPMG Peat Marwick
Edificio Avis
Av. da Boavista, 3477–3521
1, Salas 102–104
4100 Pôrto
Portugal

Telephone: +351 (2) 619 9010
Fax: +351 (2) 617 7821

Puerto Rico

Legislation

Puerto Rico falls within the jurisdiction of the United States Federal Bankruptcy Code and insolvency procedures in Puerto Rico are similar to the insolvency procedures in the United States. Reference should be made, therefore, to the section in this book dealing with the United States of America.

KPMG contact partner

Jose J. Gil de Lamadrid
KPMG Peat Marwick
American International Plaza
250 Munoz Rivera Avenue
11th Floor
Hato Rey 00918
San Juan
Puerto Rico

Telephone: +1 (787) 7566020
Fax: +1 (787) 7546175

Qatar

Legislation

Liquidation of companies is covered by the Qatar Company Law 1981, under the title 'Companies Winding up and Liquidation'.

Insolvency procedures

A company may be wound up in the following circumstances:

- expiry of the period set for the company;
- bankruptcy;
- amalgamation;
- court order.

In addition to the above, if the company sustains losses exceeding half of its capital, the board of directors should convene an extraordinary general meeting to consider the winding up of the company or any other necessary measures. If the board fails to do so, each shareholder is entitled to request the winding up.

Winding up is undertaken by a liquidator appointed by a general meeting or by the court.

KPMG contact partner

Munzer Dajani
KPMG Peat Marwick
Suite 7, 5th Floor
Commercial Bank of Qatar Building
Doha
Qatar

Telephone: +974 329698
Fax: +974 425626

Romania

Legislation

Insolvency legislation was consolidated in a recent Act, Law No. 64/1995, regarding the procedure of judicial reorganisation and liquidation, replacing the provisions of the Commercial Code of 1887. The legal provisions covering directors' duties and penalties in relation to insolvent companies are contained in this law and in the Company Law No. 31/1990. Other legal provisions in this matter are contained in:

- Commercial Code;
- Law No. 76/1992 establishing a specific procedure for commercial debt recovery;
- Governmental Ordinance No. 11/1996 regarding the forced execution of debts due to the State budget;
- Civil Code;
- Civil Proceedings Code.

Insolvency legislation provides the following insolvency procedures:

- debt recovery procedure according to the provisions of the Commercial Code and of Law No. 76/1992;
- voluntary liquidation according to the provisions of Company Law No. 31/1990;
- judicial reorganisation and liquidation according to the provisions of Law No. 64/1995.

Insolvency procedure

Debt recovery and realisation of securities

Common procedure

A creditor who is owed money which is not paid when due can issue proceedings against the debtor, including proceedings for attachment of the debtor's movable goods, including money. The creditor is required to make a deposit with the court equal to half of the claim, in the case of attachment of money, and one third of the claim in the case of attachment of land or goods. A court fee, depending on the amount claimed, is to be paid. The court can order attachment of movable goods even when payment of a debt is not due where it can be shown that there is a risk that the debtor may conceal its assets or diminish the value of any security given for the debt. The court gives notice of the attachment to the debtor and a court official seals the goods by taking an inventory and placing the court's official stamp on the goods. In the case of attachment of money the court gives notice to the third-party debtor.

A creditor who has obtained a judgment can enforce that judgment against movable goods. In order to do so he must get the judgment stamped by the court as an 'enforceable title'. In the case of debts representing an obligation to repay money under a loan agreement with a bank and in the case of mortgages it is not necessary to obtain a judgment because such loan agreements and mortgages represent enforceable titles.

The holder of an 'enforceable title' must get the relevant court officials or bailiffs to 'seal' the goods before proceeding further with realisation.

The procedure for the realisation of assets which have been attached or 'sealed' following the obtaining of an 'enforceable title' or which are the subject of a pledge or mortgage is as follows:

Realisation of movable goods:

- the court fixes a date for sale by public auction;
- the goods are auctioned until sufficient funds have been realised to discharge the judgment debt;

Realisation of monetary assets, i.e., debts:

- the court gives notice to the third-party debtor;
- third-party debtor is then bound to pay the creditor rather than the original debtor;

Realisation of immovable property:

- the court gives notice to the debtor that if the amount of the judgment debt is not paid the property subject to the mortgage will be sold;
- thirty days after such notice, a court official draws up a report including a description of the property. A date for the sale is fixed by the court;
- where there are several creditors with claims against the debtor the court draws up a list showing the order of priority of creditors including mortgagees. Notice of the sale is posted at the court at the place where the property is situated;
- the sale is by public auction.

Special procedure

Law No. 76 sets out certain procedures to be followed where companies have defaulted in payment of sums due for more than 30 days. The law provides for payment of certain minimum penalties for late payment. The parties can specify higher penalties.

The law provides that a company which has unpaid debts outstanding for more than 30 days from the due date is in a state of 'payment incapacity'. Any creditor can give notice to the debtor of such payment incapacity after the expiry of the period of 30 days.

The creditor may commence proceedings claiming the amount due plus penalties. The court fee is 10,000 Lei (currently about £2), irrespective of the amount of money claimed. The application has priority over other court proceedings.

Once a creditor has obtained a judgment he is entitled to attach assets of the debtor company as described above. Law 76 also contains provisions imposing obligations on debtors including in particular:

- ceasing payment to suppliers in advance;
- ceasing distribution of profits;
- ceasing payments of bonuses and other compensation to managers.

One of the grounds giving shareholders the right to seek liquidation is bankruptcy of the company. Accordingly, an insolvent company can be voluntarily liquidated using the following procedure.

The liquidators are appointed at a general meeting of shareholders at which the decision to liquidate is taken by the majority specified in the by-laws. If the by-laws make no provision, the resolution must be unanimous. If the requisite majorities are not met any shareholder can apply to the court for appointment of liquidators.

The appointment of liquidators must be notified to the Registry of Commerce.

In addition to powers conferred on them by the shareholders (by the same majority as is required for their appointment), the liquidators can:

- sue or be sued for the purposes of the liquidation;

- carry out any transactions necessary for the liquidation;
- sell by public auction the real estate and chattels of the company — the assets cannot be sold as a single lot;
- settle disputes;
- liquidate and realise debts owed to the company;
- issue commercial paper, take unsecured loans and do any other necessary acts.

The liquidators cannot mortgage the assets of the company unless authorised by the court.

From the amounts realised the liquidators must discharge the liabilities to creditors before paying any sums to shareholders.

Where the amounts realised are insufficient to discharge the liabilities to unsecured creditors, the payments to such creditors will be made pro rata to their indebtedness.

Judicial reorganisation and liquidation

Concerned persons and jurisdiction

Law No. 64/1995 concerning the procedure of judicial reorganisation and liquidation applies both to individual merchants and companies. All the procedures stipulated by the law are of exclusive competence of the court in whose jurisdiction the headquarters of the debtor are located.

Commencing procedure

The procedure of judicial reorganisation and liquidation is commenced when the debtor, or one or more creditors having an unpaid debt against the debtor who ceased payments for a period of more than 30 days, or Chamber of Commerce and Industry, if the cessation of payments is public knowledge, presents a winding up petition to the court. By Government Ordinance No. 11/1996, the bodies under the Ministry of Finance's authority are permitted to present a petition, in their capacity as creditors of unpaid taxes due to the State budget. The debtor will be informed in two days about the registration of the creditors' petition and can oppose the declaration of cessation of payments in the court within five days after receiving the notice. A judgment will be issued admitting or rejecting the debtor's opposition.

After the registration of the winding up petition, the court orders a notice to be sent to to the debtor, to the creditors and to the Registry of Commerce where the debtor is registered. The notice will state the commencment of the procedure and the convening of the creditors' meeting within 30 days after registration of the petition or within 20 days after the rejection of the debtors' opposition, as the case may be. A syndic judge will be appointed to carry out all the legal actions related to the reorganisation and liquidation procedure, including measures to deal with assets and all categories of creditors etc. In the meantime, the debtor loses all power in relation to the administration of its business and all claims are handled by the syndic judge.

Persons and bodies involved in judicial reorganisation and liquidation procedures

- the court;
- the syndic judge — a judge named by the president of the court in charge of the supervision of all reorganisation and/or liquidation acts;
- the administrator — appointed by the court if the creditors' meeting decided to appoint an administrator to take charge of the management of the debtor's business;
- the liquidator — appointed by the court following the proposal of the syndic judge, the liquidator assists the syndic judge in all operations relating to the liquidation;

- the creditors' meeting — formed by the debtor's creditors to approve the reorganisation or liquidation plan as well as proposals for the sale of assets made by the syndic judge;
- the creditors' committee — three to five creditors appointed in the first creditors' meeting to assist the syndic judge in all the operations related to the reorganisation and/or liquidation.

The administrator or liquidator must be a chartered accountant, authorised accountant registered with the professional body or a person having a university degree in economics or law with at least five years of economics or law practice.

Proposals

The debtor or the creditors may make proposals for a detailed plan which provides one of the following:

- reorganisation — a process to enable the debtor to continue and reorganise its business under the control of a syndic judge and with the sanction of the court;
- sale of debtor's assets — an organised process of realisation of assets by selling all or part of the debtor's assets under the control of a syndic judge and with the sanction of the court;
- liquidation — a formal process of realising a debtor's assets and distributing the proceeds to creditors in accordance with their rights under the control of a syndic judge and with the sanction of the court.

The proposed plans must be approved by the syndic judge and submitted for approval at the creditors' meeting. Subsequently the plan, when approved by the creditors, will be confirmed by the court.

Reorganisation

The debtor will be required to complete the structural changes stipulated by the reorganisation plan, under the supervision of the syndic judge, within one year. The court can order the extension of the reorganisation period if it was registered as an improvement of the activity and will increase the sums which are to be distributed to the creditors, under the supervision of a competent person. If the court approves the continuation of the debtor's activity this extension would be for no more than one year. The creditors may oppose an extension of the reorganisation period.

Liquidation

Where a liquidation plan is approved, or when a reorganisation plan is not successful, the court will order liquidation. The syndic judge, assisted by the liquidator, will proceed to realise the debtor's assets, distribute the proceeds to the creditors and pay the expenses of the liquidation. The syndic judge is permitted to sell perishable goods or other goods which will diminish in value or where the cost of preserving goods is excessive. The assets must be sold item by item at public auction, following a valuation. The assets cannot be sold in one lot except in the case of items which remain unsold at the auction.

Every six months, from the date of liquidation, the syndic judge will report to the court on the progress of the liquidation. The report will include details of asset realisations and a plan for distribution of the proceeds to the creditors.

The order of distribution is as follows:

- liquidation expenses;
- payment of the credits granted by banks during the reorganisation period;
- secured creditors;
- judicial expenses and remuneration of administrator, liquidator and other experts;
- preferential creditors;

- debts resulting from trade operations conducted by the syndic judge or by the administrator during the reorganisation and/or liquidation period;
- administrative expenses;
- unsecured non-preferential creditors;
- shareholders or partners in accordance with their respective rights;
- others.

Creditors

Secured creditors

A secured creditor is someone who holds a fixed or floating charge over the debtor's property. Mortgages over immovables are to be registered in the Register of Real Estate and pledges in the Register of Pledges.

Preferential creditors

In liquidations, creditors for certain types of claims have priority in payment before unsecured creditors. Preferential claims are:

- six months' duties due by the debtor to third parties;
- living expenses of the debtor and his family at an amount established by the court;
- in the case of an individual merchant, six months' arrears of wages due;
- taxes and other duties due to the State;
- social security duties.

Unsecured creditors

An unsecured creditor is a creditor having a claim which is neither secured nor has preferential status.

Other matters

The court can decide at the syndic judge's request to end the procedure if it concludes that there are insufficient assets to cover the liquidation expenses and no creditors offer funding.

By closing the procedure the debtor will be discharged of its obligations unless it is found guilty of fraud.

Directors and statutory auditors of insolvent companies can be held personally liable for debts incurred as a result of wrongful trading, if their actions are deemed to be criminal. If a criminal judgment is issued against the directors or statutory auditors they will be disqualified from holding other directorships.

KPMG contact partner

François Gontard
KPMG
Str. Ion Campinean Nr. 11 Et. 4
Sector 1
Bucharest
Romania

Telephone: +40 (1) 312 2554
Fax: +40 (1) 312 2809

Russia

Legislation

Russian insolvency legislation is relatively new and undergoing continuous development. Under the Soviet system, all enterprises were deemed to be branches of the State, and therefore no bankruptcy was possible. Liquidation through reorganisation was possible, but it was an administrative and logistical exercise.

Current insolvency legislation is based on the Civil Code of the Russian Federation and the Law on Insolvency (Bankruptcy), which was passed in 1992. Since then the legislation has been considerably modified and developed by Presidential Decrees, Government Resolutions, Orders of the State Property Committee and other enabling legislation. An important innovation was the establishment of a Federal Department of Insolvency under the State Property Committee to handle State-owned enterprises that are insolvent. Further development is certain and so the notes in this chapter are only indicative of the situation.

The economic restructuring of society means that many enterprises fall within the definitions of the insolvency law, and yet it would be socially unacceptable to prevent them from continuing to trade. In Moscow alone, it has been reliably reported that two-thirds of Moscow's manufacturing enterprises are insolvent and technically bankrupt. In 1995 the Federal Insolvency Department was responsible for 20,000 enterprises in Russia. Bankruptcy proceedings against enterprises that have not paid wages for extended periods are being accelerated.

Insolvency procedures

Types of insolvency procedure

- reorganisation — the business is placed in the hands of an external management, which may be charged with its rehabilitation;
- liquidation — this occurs (a) if a court has declared the enterprise insolvent, or (b) if the enterprise declares itself insolvent;
- amicable settlement — the enterprise comes to an agreement with its creditors involving the deferral of payment of debts, payment by instalment, or debt forgiveness;
- bankruptcy — an individual registered as an entrepreneur can be declared bankrupt by a court when he/she is unable to meet creditor demands. The business registration is made null and void.

Insolvency courts

Insolvency cases are examined by 'arbitration' courts. Cases may be brought when outstanding claims are greater than 500 times the monthly minimum wage (as of 1 January 1996, the monthly minimum wage is 63,250 roubles — equivalent to US$14 — and hence the insolvency threshold is about US$7,000) and the claims have been outstanding for three months from the due date for repayment.

Insolvency courts exist in all the main administrative regions of Russia, Moscow and St Petersburg being the only cities with this status.

Parties to an insolvency action

The legislation recognises various parties in an insolvency action, including:

- arbitration manager — the arbitration manager is authorised, *inter alia*, to carry on the business, recruit and dismiss employees, dispose of assets, call meetings of the creditors, and draw up a plan for an external management and execute the plan;
- receiver — the receiver may dispose of assets, act in an arbitration court to contest the validity of contracts completed up to six months prior to the initiation of arbitration proceedings, collect debts and receivables, form a liquidation committee and call creditors' meetings;
- creditors;
- representatives of the workforce;
- debtor.

The arbitration manager and/or receiver must:

- be an economist or lawyer;
- have practical management experience;
- not have a criminal record;
- not be an officer of the debtor.

Petition

An insolvency action is initiated by a petition to the arbitration court from:

- the debtor, either the owner of the enterprise or its management — such a petition cannot be withdrawn;
- a creditor, after the lapse of three months from the due date for payment for goods or services, the due date being defined as the date of delivery of a demand for payment by registered post;
- a procurator (public prosecutor), if it has been determined that a fictitious insolvency action has been initiated, or if the law of the Russian Federation requires the initiation of insolvency proceedings;
- tax authorities.

The court may either refuse the petition if it is established the creditor's claim can be met or the defendant is solvent, or it may recognise the defendant as insolvent, in which case liquidation proceedings will be instituted.

If a petition is received for the debtor enterprise to be reorganised, the court may decide to postpone the declaration of insolvency and instead institute rehabilitation or external management procedures.

Reorganisation

External management of the enterprise may be considered if there is a real possibility that the solvency of the enterprise may be restored by selling off parts of it, reorganising it, or instituting some other economic measures. An arbitration manager is appointed by the court, and the remuneration of the manager is fixed by the creditors' committee and approved by the court. The arbitration manager has three months in which to gain creditors' approval for a management plan involving the appointment of an external manager.

External management may not last for more than 18 months. The arbitration court must then review the results of the plan, and decide whether the management plan should continue or the debtor should be declared insolvent and liquidation proceedings be instituted.

Rehabilitation

If an enterprise can be restored to solvency through the injection of financial aid from the owner or third parties, the arbitration court may institute rehabilitation proceedings. Rehabilitation is not possible if insolvency proceedings are reopened within 36 months. If an arbitration court rules in favour of rehabilitation, it must put the rehabilitation contract out to tender.

Within 12 months of the start of rehabilitation, the enterprise must have met at least 40 per cent of the combined creditor claims. Rehabilitation may not last for more than 18 months. Rehabilitation ceases when 18 months have elapsed or it is determined by the court that rehabilitation is ineffective, in which case liquidation proceedings must be instituted. Rehabilitation is deemed successful when all claims have been met and the insolvency action can be closed.

Liquidation proceedings

Once a debtor has been declared insolvent, liquidation proceedings must continue. The arbitration court appoints a receiver and the creditors' committee determines the receiver's remuneration. The receiver has the duty, monitored by the creditors' committee, to obtain the highest price for the debtor's assets.

The liquidation proceedings must also include representatives of the workforce and other interested parties.

The proceeds of the realisation of assets are distributed in order of precedence as follows:

- expenses related to the liquidation proceedings;
- expenses of the arbitration manager and receiver;
- expenses related to the continuing operations of the enterprise;
- claims of individuals whom the debtor has injured or jeopardised;
- payment of the workforce;
- payments to the State Pension Fund;
- taxes and social security contributions;
- creditor claims;
- claims of shareholders who are members of the workforce;
- claims of other shareholders;
- all other claims.

Injured individuals, the workforce claiming payment, and taxes and social security contributions are considered privileged creditors.

Voluntary liquidation

An enterprise may declare voluntary liquidation in the event of its managers determining that it can no longer meet its obligations or restore solvency. The receiver is appointed by the enterprise's creditors.

Amicable settlement

A settlement among the non-privileged creditors may be reached at any point in the insolvency proceedings; it may not infringe on the settlement of the privileged claims and must be endorsed by the court. Creditors must receive at least 35 per cent of their settlement within two weeks of the settlement date. The settlement may be rendered void if (a) the terms are not satisfied, (b) the financial position of the debtor deteriorates, (c) the debtor infringes on the rights and interests of the creditors.

KPMG contact partner

Roger Munnings
KPMG
37 Ul. Novaya Basmannaya
3rd Floor
Moscow 107066
Russia

Telephone: +7 (502) 222 4030
Fax: +7 (502) 222 4024

Saint Lucia

Legislation

Insolvency procedures are governed by the provisions of Chapter 244, Title IV of the Commercial Code of St Lucia with respect to liquidations and receiverships and the provisions of Title IX with respect to bankruptcies. The legislation is based largely on the UK Companies Act of the early 1900s. This is likely to change in the near future as Parliament has passed the Companies Act No. 19 of 1996. In the Act, when it becomes effective, receiverships will be dealt with under ss. 288 to 301. Part IV of the Act (ss. 370–491)) deals with liquidations and bankruptcies. This new legislation is part of the program of harmonisation of legislation in the CARICOM region.

Insolvency procedures

Bankruptcy

Bankruptcies are not common. Bankruptcy procedures are conducted by order of the court which may make a 'receiving order' on a petition presented either by a creditor or the debtor.

Liquidation

Liquidations of companies may be commenced:

- by the court;
- by creditors (through the court);
- voluntarily, i.e., by members of a company;
- subject to the supervision of the court (on application by either creditors or members).

A liquidator, more often than not a practising public accountant, is appointed either by the court or named in the winding-up resolution made by the members of the company. He must be an individual.

Upon appointment, a liquidator takes possession of all of the property of the company and is vested with power to sell such property or to carry on the business of the company so far as may be necessary for its beneficial winding up. He may appoint a special manager for that purpose.

When the property of the company is realised, the liquidator is to apply it in payment of:

- costs, charges, etc. necessarily incurred, including the liquidator's remuneration;
- pre-preferential debts;
- secured creditors (first out of the proceeds of their security);
- unsecured creditors, *pari passu*;
- members' distribution according to their rights and interests in the company.

Receivership

A receiver is usually appointed in accordance with provisions contained in a debenture or mortgage deed instrument. Only an individual may be appointed receiver.

A receiver is required to take possession of the assets secured either by a fixed or floating charge and, if the company is not being wound up, must pay the debts of the company (or borrower) which in every winding up are required to be paid in priority to all other debts.

A receiver or receiver and manager may carry on the business of the borrower if such course will enhance or prevent the deterioration of the assets coming into his possession.

A receiver is usually indemnified by the secured creditor against any claims against him other than those caused by his negligence.

KPMG contact partner

Frank V. Myers
KPMG Peat Marwick
PO Box 1101
Morgan Building
L'Anse Road
Castries
St Lucia

Telephone: +1 (758) 45 31471
Fax: +1 (758) 45 36507

Seychelles

Legislation

Insolvency procedures in the Republic of Seychelles are governed by the Companies Act 1972, ss. 202 to 308.

Insolvency procedures

There are two types of insolvency procedures:

- by the court;
- voluntary (members' or creditors').

Winding up by the court

Application for winding up may be made to the court by:

- the company (following a special resolution);
- any creditor, shareholder, contributory or debenture holder or any combination thereof;
- the Registrar under s. 190(3).

The official receiver or a liquidator appointed by the court controls the winding up and no action or proceeding can be commenced or proceeded with against the company except with the leave of the court.

The functions and duties of the liquidator are:

- to bring or defend any action or other legal proceeding in the name and on behalf of the company;
- to carry on the business of the company so far as necessary for winding up purposes;
- to appoint a legal adviser;
- to discharge all the remaining assets and liabilities in a manner acceptable by law;
- to summon meetings of creditors and shareholders;
- to exercise the power of the court of settling a list of contributories.

At the completion of the winding up the court will order the dissolution of the company.

Voluntary winding up

Voluntary winding up is instigated by the company. A members' voluntary winding up requires a special resolution by the members that the company be wound up or, where the company cannot pay its debts, a general resolution. A creditors' voluntary winding up requires a resolution by the creditors at a meeting called by the company.

The liquidator is appointed either by the members or by the creditors and the company ceases to carry on business except so far as may be required for the benefit of the winding up.

The functions and duties of the liquidator are the same as for a winding up by the court (see above).

The company is dissolved three months after the liquidator has lodged his final accounts and a return of the holding of a general meeting (members' voluntary) or a creditors' meeting (creditors' voluntary).

Creditors

The following factors apply to meetings:

- creditors are entitled to vote in proportion to the amount of their debt;
- a resolution is binding on all creditors where more votes are cast in favour than against;
- creditors can form a quorum where aggregate debts form 10 per cent of total debts or claims against the company.

Creditors must prove their debts within a time fixed by the court.

The priorities among creditors are as follows:

- secured creditors:
  - secured by a fixed charge;
  - secured by a floating charge (subject to preferential creditors).
- preferential creditors:
  - taxes assessed on the company up to 31 December preceding the date on which the winding-up order was made;
  - wages and salaries in respect of the four month period before the date of the winding-up order or resolution;
  - loans;

  (The above three categories rank equally among themselves and are to be paid in full, unless the assets of the company are insufficient, when they will abate proportionately; and so far as the assets available to pay all its liabilities are insufficient, have priority over claims of creditors and debenture holders secured by general floating charges and are to be paid accordingly out of such property.)
- ordinary creditors.
- shareholders.

Other matters

The Companies Act was passed in 1972 and is currently being amended. A revised Act is expected to be in force in 1997.

KPMG contact partner

C. Smith
KPMG Peat Marwick
Kingsgate House
PO Box 396
Victoria
Mahé
Seychelles

Telephone: +248 224955
Fax: +248 224692

Sierra Leone

Legislation

The legislation relating to insolvency procedures in Sierra Leone is embodied in the Sierra Leone Companies Act, c. 249 of the Laws of Sierra Leone.

Insolvency procedures

There are three forms of insolvency procedure:

- receivership;
- creditors' compulsory winding up; and
- creditors' or members' voluntary winding up.

Receivership

A receiver and manager is usually appointed under powers contained in an instrument such as a debenture trust deed or by the court in other circumstances where the security is in jeopardy, and the property is to be realised for the benefit of the secured creditor. Usually, an accountant or solicitor is appointed, although joint appointments are quite common. The appointment of a receiver means the powers of directors are suspended. The receiver's rights and duties would normally be set out in the debenture trust deed. The receiver's task is completed when payment has been made to the debenture holders.

Compulsory winding up

A court order for compulsory winding up is made on the petition of a creditor when the company cannot pay its debts. The court will appoint the official receiver as liquidator and no one can proceed against the company without the permission of the court.

Due notice must be given of the appointment to the Registrar of Companies within 21 days. The duties of a liquidator are stipulated in legislation as is the priority in which the company's debts are to be paid. Notice with regard to the final dissolution of the company must be published in the official *Gazette*.

Voluntary winding up

This may be either a creditors' or a members' voluntary winding up. In the case of the former the creditors' choice of liquidator will take precedence over that of shareholders if there is disagreement. A committee of inspection comprised of creditors and shareholders may be appointed to assist the liquidator.

For a members' voluntary winding up there must be a declaration of solvency by the directors that the company will pay all its debts within a period not exceeding 12 months and the statement must be delivered to the Registrar of Companies for registration.

KPMG contact partner

Raymond Davies
KPMG Peat Marwick
Ludgate House
Wallace-Johnson Street
Freetown
Sierra Leone

Telephone: +232 (22) 222061
Fax: +232 (22) 228149

Singapore

Legislation

The principal legislation governing corporate insolvency in Singapore is the Companies Act, c. 50.

Insolvency procedures

The insolvency procedures available are as follows:

- receivership;
- judicial management;
- scheme of arrangement;
- liquidation.

Receivership

Generally, the appointment of a receiver or receiver and manager is made by a debenture holder pursuant to the powers provided in the debenture. The appointee must act in accordance with the powers set out in the debenture and, provided he has the power to do so, he may carry on the business, i.e., to act as receiver and manager. The receiver operates as an agent of the company and is primarily responsible to his appointee who is the secured creditor. All assets charged to the debenture holder come under the control of the receiver who is to dispose of such assets and repay the secured debts owing to the debenture holder except that, where there are insufficient funds available, the proceeds of assets under a floating charge are utilised to settle preferential creditors in priority to claims of the debenture holder. There is no fixed duration in which the receivership must be completed. However, the continuation of the business operations may be disrupted by the appointment of a liquidator, repossession of assets held under hire-purchase, leasing or retention of title, etc.

Where there is no debenture, the court may appoint a receiver if it is satisfied that the assets of the company are in jeopardy and the appointment of a receiver is in the interest of all parties concerned. A receiver appointed by the court must act in accordance with the terms of the court order.

Judicial management

This procedure was introduced to afford financially troubled but viable companies a chance to rehabilitate themselves. Under the legislation, the court, on application of any interested parties, including the company or its directors, may make an order to place the company under judicial management so as to achieve one or more of the following:

- the survival of the company or its undertaking as a going concern;
- the approval of a compromise or a scheme of arrangement with the creditors under s. 210 of the Companies Act;
- a more advantageous realisation of the company's assets than in a winding up.

A judicial management order, when given, is effective for a period of 180 days from the date of the making of the order.

Unless it is in the public interest to do so, the court may not grant an order unless it is satisfied that the holder of a debenture secured by a floating charge over the whole (or substantially the whole) of the company's assets will not oppose the making of the order and has not or will not exercise its right to appoint a receiver and manager. Once an order is made, all proceedings and actions against the company are stayed. No steps can be taken to enforce any charge or security over the company's property or to repossess goods under hire-purchase and leasing agreements or goods under retention of title.

The judicial manager has very wide powers. With the approval of the court, he has the power to dispose of properties under fixed charge, hire-purchase and leasing agreements or retention of title, provided the proceeds thereof are accounted to holders of the fixed charge or the owners of such property.

The judicial manager acts as agent of the company. He is personally liable on any contract entered into by him but is entitled to be indemnified out of the property under his control or custody. He is required, within 60 days of his appointment, to make a proposal for the approval of the creditors for achieving the underlying objectives of his appointment.

Scheme of arrangement

Section 210 of the Companies Act provides that the court may order a meeting of creditors to consider a compromise or arrangement between a company and its creditors or a class of creditors. The court may approve the compromise or arrangement, subject to such alternatives or conditions as it thinks just, if at the meeting held pursuant to the court order a majority of creditors holding three-fourths in value agree to the compromise or arrangement. Upon approval by the court the terms of the compromise or arrangement will bind all creditors or class of creditors, as the case may be.

In practice, it is generally acknowledged that the legal procedures are cumbersome and time-consuming. Consequently, new legislation relating to judicial management was introduced to facilitate, among other things, compromises with creditors.

Liquidation

An insolvent company can be liquidated either voluntarily by convening a general meeting of the shareholders and creditors or compulsorily by an order of the court. Once a company is placed in liquidation, no legal proceedings or actions against the company can be commenced without the leave of the court. General creditors must file proofs of debt with the liquidator and amounts admitted will rank equally for distribution from the balance available after payment of preferential creditors.

Preferential creditors

In a winding up, preferential payments to be made in priority to all other unsecured creditors are:

- costs and expenses of the winding up including the remuneration of the liquidator;
- wages and salary of any employee not exceeding five months' salary or $7,500, whichever is the lesser — wages and salary are defined to include amounts payable to a subcontractor of labour, payment in lieu of notice of termination and retrenchment benefits;
- amounts due on workmen's compensation accrued before the commencement of winding up;
- outstanding contributions to any approved superannuation or provident funds for the preceding 12 months;
- amounts payable in respect of vacation leave;
- taxes.

Where there are insufficient sale proceeds, wages and salary, contributions to provident funds and vacation pay rank in priority to holders of a floating charge.

With the exception of taxes, the above list of priority payments applies to receiverships and, where the sale proceeds are insufficient, payment to preferential creditors is to be made out of the proceeds of assets under the floating charge.

KPMG contact partner

Michael W. T. Ng
KPMG Peat Marwick
16 Raffles Quay #22-00
Hong Leong Building
Singapore 048581

Telephone: +65 321 0606
Fax: +65 225 0984

Slovakia

Legislation

Owing to the enforcement of centrally planned economic principles, bankruptcy and settlement procedures were not applied for more than 40 years in the former Czechoslovakia, from 1948 up to 1989. Thus, it was more than obvious, that both bankruptcy and settlement needed to be quickly incorporated into the legal system after the 1989 political change. This was done by Act No. 328/1991 Coll. on Bankruptcy and Settlement which came into effect on 1 October 1991 and substantially affected the enforcement of the bankruptcy law. However, there was a 'temporary regime' under which no insolvency-related bankruptcy could be declared or filed until 1 October 1992.

After the separation of the Czech and Slovak Republics the bankruptcy law has been incorporated into the Slovak legal system. The Slovak Parliament approved the same Act (No. 93/1993 Coll.) but deferred the effective date until 31 May 1994.

Furthermore, the bankruptcy law has been amended as follows:

- prior to declaration of bankruptcy, mandatory proceedings to revitalise the debtor were introduced in 1994: the so-called arrangement (reorganisation) or negotiation proceedings. For agricultural debtors and debtors operating in the transport and telecommunications industry a special bankruptcy procedure was introduced together with the mandatory ecological evaluation of their debts;
- the Act on Bankruptcy and Settlements is not to be applied if the National Property Fund is a debtor;
- exception from the Bankruptcy Act has been extended to the State budgetary and contributory organisations, municipalities and other legal entities established by special laws;
- in 1996 the so-called 'strategically important enterprises' were fully exempted from the bankruptcy law.

Insolvency procedures

Creditors

In bankruptcy proceedings the creditors have different rights. The secured creditors who hold mortgages or other collateral on the debtor's assets are entitled to separate satisfaction of their claims (by disposal of the assets in question).

Other creditors' claims are to be satisfied in the following sequence:

- claims ensuing after the declaration of the bankruptcy proceeding — so-called administration claims, (taxes, fees, remuneration of the administrator, employees' claims etc.);
- claims of the bankrupt's employees payable for the three preceding years (first-class claims);
- taxes, fees, social security contributions arisen within the last three years (second-class claims);
- other claims (third-class claims).

Debtors

Any legal entity can become a debtor except for the following:

- entities established by a special law (e.g., National Property Fund, National Bank of Slovakia etc.);
- municipalities;

- budgetary and contributory organisation;
- strategically important enterprises as defined in a special law.

Courts

In dealing with bankruptcies, settlements and negotiations regional first-degree commercial courts are authorised to act. The Supreme Court deals with appeals and complaints.

Other institutions and bodies involved

- the Slovak government is authorised to declare bankruptcy if such a proposal was submitted against the debtor operating in the area of telecommunications and transportation;
- a government body as a founder of a particular enterprise takes part at the creditors' meetings if a bankruptcy proposal was submitted against the debtor operating in telecommunications or transport;
- the National Property Fund performs tasks similar to those of a founder provided it has more than 34 per cent of shares of the company concerned;
- during arrangement (reorganisation) proceedings, the creditors' meeting (or general assembly of domestic creditors) decides upon a revitalisation project for the debtor and elects the board of creditors as an executive body for the debtor;
- in bankruptcy proceedings a meeting of creditors can be convened. A creditors' committee may be established as an advisory body to the administrator and the court;
- the bankruptcy administrator is appointed by the court from a list of administrators. The court may appoint an administrator-assistant in order to administer specific assets;
- the settlement administrator is a person appointed by court in order to conduct a settlement proceeding.

Bankruptcy proceedings

According to the Bankruptcy and Settlement Act, a debtor is bankrupt if:

- at least two creditors are unpaid during a period longer than three months and the debtor is not able to meet his outstanding financial obligations); or
- the debtor has more liabilities than assets — this applies only to business entities.

After filing for bankruptcy, a mandatory arrangement (reorganisation) proceeding must commence. The petitioner has to submit a list of creditors with the amount of their claims and to convene a meeting of domestic creditors (Slovak residents). A board of creditors should be elected, which controls the company's business activities, appoints and recalls managers of the company, and approves a reorganisation plan. The election of the board must be registered in the Commercial Register and in the Real Estate Register.

The Act No. 122/1993 Coll. which amended the Act on Bankruptcy and Settlement, introduced arrangement proceedings as an 'early mandatory stage' to be commenced prior to actual bankruptcy and settlement proceedings. This concept represents the most serious problem since it slows the entire bankruptcy proceedings considerably. In addition, foreign creditors are excluded from participation in the arrangement proceeding. On the other hand, all domestic creditors are equal to each other, regardless of the extent of their claims.

If the arrangement fails to revitalise the debtor, the court declares bankruptcy proceedings and appoints an administrator of the assets. The court invites creditors to file their claims within 30 days.

During the bankruptcy proceedings, only the administrator is authorised to manage the debtor's assets. The bankrupt company is wound up and all claims crystallise. The administrator compiles a list of the bankrupt's assets based on the results of an extraordinary inventory, balance sheet, and financial statements on the day of the declaration of the bankruptcy. The administrator makes up a list of claims for the purpose of distributing the assets.

Creditors must file two copies of their claims with the court, with the reason for the claim and the relevant documents. Foreign creditors must appoint a representative for service of documents otherwise the court appoints such a person. The court reviews the submitted applications. The process of realisation of the assets is carried out by the court at an auction, or by the administrator, with the court's consent.

Prior to issuing a court resolution on the distribution of the assets, the bankrupt may propose a compulsory settlement. He must offer the full satisfaction of the priority claims (first- and second-class claims) and satisfaction of at least one third of other claims within one year. A prerequisite for the court's confirmation of such a settlement is the approval by a three-quarters majority of the third-class creditors present at the hearings. If the court confirms the compulsory settlement, the bankruptcy proceeding is terminated and liquidation is not carried out, since the company's reorganisation has been successful.

There is also an extra-judicial settlement in bankruptcy proceedings; the negotiation or bargaining procedure. The debtor may negotiate with every creditor the amount of the claim and the manner in which the claim will be satisfied. A creditor's approval must be in a deed with a verified signature. Upon agreement with the administrator the court cancels the bankruptcy proceeding.

After the resolution approving the final record and remuneration for the administrator is passed, the court decides on the distribution of the assets. Eventually, the court issues a resolution terminating the bankruptcy proceeding, if:

- the distribution schedule has been implemented;
- the necessary conditions for holding bankruptcy proceedings are not met (no assets available);
- the compulsory settlement was approved;
- all creditors have agreed with the bankrupt's proposal of extra-judicial settlement.

Settlement (composition) proceedings

Voluntary settlement (composition) with creditors may take place before bankruptcy. Only the debtor can file a settlement proposal with the court. The settlement offered must be more favourable to the creditors than bankruptcy proceedings. The law sets out several strict conditions to eliminate fraudulent settlement proposals. If the court permits the settlement, it notifies the Commercial Register and the Real Estate Register. The debtor continues to operate his business activities with some restrictions that protect the creditors' claims.

The settlement administrator appointed by the court usually supervises the debtor's activity. The court approves the proposed settlement if a majority of the creditors agree to it. If the debtor meets all his obligations as set out in the settlement proposal, the balance of creditors' claims not satisfied are ignored.

Judicial practice and new legislation

There are general considerations such as totally overloaded commercial courts, and a general lack of practical experience in dealing with bankruptcy laws that affect the overall efficiency of bankruptcy implementation. In addition, there is almost no awareness of the importance of bankruptcy regulations amongst managers.

Courts take up to several months to declare bankruptcy proceedings. If the proceedings are commenced after this time, the whole process of the bankruptcy can take several years. There have been only approximately 70 bankruptcies officially declared, so far, whilst commercial courts have processed over one thousand petitions. Every third petition has had formal flaws, and every fifth other flaws.

There is a strong demand from businesses to abolish the mandatory arrangement proceeding prior to the bankruptcy declaration or at least to simplify it. However, such an amendment to the bankruptcy law has not been drafted yet.

KPMG contact partner

Bert Damstra
KPMG Slovensko
Francisciho 4
811 08 Bratislava
Slovak Republic

Telephone: +42 (7) 536 1436
Fax: +42 (7) 536 1462

Slovenia

Legislation

The Compulsory Settlement, Bankruptcy and Liquidation Act provides the conditions for the commencement of proceedings for compulsory settlement and bankruptcy as well as the financial reorganisation of companies subject to bankruptcy proceedings.

Insolvency procedures

Bankruptcy proceedings

Bankruptcy proceedings are initiated against debtors with a long history of insolvency or over-indebtedness.

Debtors are independent entrepreneurs, commercial companies, cooperatives, State-owned companies and other legal and natural persons determined by special Acts.

Bankruptcy proceedings cannot be initiated against debtors:

- whose property value is not sufficient to cover the costs of the proceedings;
- with only one creditor.

The proposal for the commencement of bankruptcy proceedings may be filed by creditors, the debtor himself, or a personally liable shareholder.

Bankruptcy proceedings are executed by the competent court in the town where the company in question is located, and are conducted by a bankruptcy senate (composed of three judges, of which one is the senate president), bankruptcy administrator and a creditors' board. A creditors' board must be established upon the request of creditors representing at least 50 per cent of all claims.

The application for bankruptcy proceedings is reviewed by the senate. Once bankruptcy proceedings have been initiated:

- an insolvent estate is formed (comprising the whole of the debtor's property);
- all employment contracts are terminated;
- a bankruptcy administrator (receiver) is appointed by the bankruptcy senate. All management powers are passed to the bankruptcy administrator.

Creditors' claims must be filed with the senate within two months of the bankruptcy proceeding being proclaimed in the *Official Gazette* of the Republic of Slovenia. If the creditor does not report the claim within this term, he loses his right to be paid from the distribution of the bankruptcy estate.

During the bankruptcy procedure the debtor may finish any business already underway that will enhance or preserve the insolvent's estate. Approval for this is given by the bankruptcy senate.

After obtaining approval of the creditors' board and the administrator and on the basis of expert opinion, the senate may proceed with the sale of the debtor's assets or business by public auction or call for bids.

A receiver represents the debtor and has the following powers and duties:

- preparation of a bankruptcy balance sheet;
- recovery of debts owed to the debtor;
- realisation of the debtor's bankruptcy estate;
- preparation of draft final bankruptcy statement.

If the bankruptcy estate does not exceed 10 million Slovenian tolars, abridged bankruptcy proceedings apply.

Compulsory settlement

Before or during bankruptcy proceedings, a debtor can propose a compulsory settlement. The debtor may carry on business (with some limitations), in spite of being in compulsory settlement proceedings.

Compulsory settlement proceedings are conducted by a senate of three judges, a creditors' board and the compulsory settlement administrator (who is appointed by a court).

Creditors' claims must be filed with the senate within 30 days of the compulsory settlement being proclaimed in the *Official Gazette* of the Republic of Slovenia. When the senate approves a compulsory settlement, it may appoint a compulsory settlement administrator. The debtor may classify the claims and offer different conditions of repayment to each class.

The debtor must prepare a financial reorganisation programme within two months of proposing compulsory settlement. In this plan he indicates how he anticipates repaying his creditors. If the plan includes offering reduced payments, the percentage offered should not be less than:

- 50 per cent if payment is within one year;
- 60 per cent if payment is within two years;
- 100 per cent if repayment is within three years.

Creditors vote on the proposed settlement. Those in favour must represent at least 60 per cent of the total amount of claims and the decision must be confirmed by the senate. If the 60 per cent vote is not obtained, the senate rejects compulsory settlement and initiates bankruptcy proceedings.

Confirmed compulsory settlements bind all creditors, including those who voted against compulsory settlement and any unknown creditors.

Review of past transactions

The creditors and bankruptcy administrator (receiver) have the right to appeal against any legal action taken by the debtor during the year prior to the beginning of the bankruptcy procedure, if such action led to:

- one of the creditors being preferred;
- disposal of the debtor's assets at an undervalue;
- loss of certain material rights;
- commitment to certain material obligations.

An appeal against the above may be filed within six months from the commencement of bankruptcy proceedings. The action is brought against persons who benefited unlawfully.

However, it is open to anyone who benefited from such actions to prove that he was not aware of the poor economic or financial situation of the debtor.

Creditors

Creditors have different rights according to their legal status. In bankruptcy, creditors are divided into three groups:

- secured creditors — the bankruptcy procedure does not affect the right to special payment from certain assets of the debtor;
- unsecured creditors — there are two types of unsecured creditors. Certain creditors for costs, expenses and business debts incurred during the liquidation period have preferred status. All other unsecured creditors are paid pro rata from the remaining proceeds. But, even among such creditors there are statutory priorities for payment of employees;
- creditors claiming retention of title — before the sale of assets takes place, any owners of assets not belonging to the insolvent may claim their return.

KPMG contact person

Marjan Kristan
KPMG Slovenija d.o.o.
Dunajska 21
61000 Ljubljana
Slovenia

Telephone: +386 (61) 1321 042
Fax: +386 (61) 1321 261

Solomon Islands

Legislation

Corporate insolvency and reconstruction is governed by the Companies Act (c. 66) which is essentially the UK Companies Act 1948.

Insolvency procedures

The winding up of a company may be either:

- by the court;
- voluntary; or
- subject to the supervision of the court.

Winding up by the court usually occurs when a company is unable to pay its debts.

Voluntary winding up may be by the members or creditors, but requires a company's directors to declare solvency before it can proceed.

Where a company has passed a resolution for voluntary winding up, the court may make an order that it shall continue but subject to such supervision as the court thinks fit.

The Companies Act further provides for the appointment of receivers and managers either:

- by the court upon an application on behalf of the debenture holders or other creditors; or
- out of court under the powers contained in any instrument.

Other matters

The liquidation and dissolution of cooperative societies can only follow an order of the Registrar of Cooperative Societies in terms of the Cooperative Societies Act (c. 73).

The Bankruptcy Act 1994 has been enacted to replace the Bankruptcy Act 1914 of UK (being one of the statutes of general application adopted by Solomon Islands upon independence in 1978). However, the Solomon Islands legislation has still not been signed into force.

KPMG contact partner

Andrew Dickinson
KPMG
The KPMG Centre
45 Clarence Street
Sydney
NSW 2000
Australia

Telephone: +61 (2) 9335 7000
Fax: +61 (2) 9299 7077

South Africa

Legislation

- Insolvency Act No. 24 of 1936, as amended;
- Companies Act No. 61 of 1973, as amended;
- regulations in terms of s. 15 of the Companies Act No. 61 of 1973, for winding up and judicial management of companies;
- Magistrates' Courts Act No. 32 of 1944, as amended, in which provision is made for administration orders;
- Close Corporations Act No. 69 of 1984 as amended;
- Land Bank Act No. 13 of 1944 as amended;
- Agricultural Credit Act No. 28 of 1966 as amended;
- Administration of Estates Act No. 66 of 1965 as amended.

Insolvency procedures

- compulsory winding up by the court of an individual or partnership, company or close corporation;
- members' or creditors' voluntary winding up of company or close corporation;
- voluntary surrender of estate by an individual;
- judicial management;
- schemes of arrangement or compromise.

Compulsory winding up

An insolvent's estate, company or close corporation may be wound up by a court if:

- judgment has been obtained for a debt and cannot be satisfied or paid;
- any attempt is made to dispose of assets, thereby prejudicing creditors or preferring one creditor above another;
- any attempt is made to compromise any debts;
- notice in writing is given to any creditor that his debt cannot be paid;
- a court applies s. 34 of the Administration of Estates Act;
- a judicial manager makes an application to court;
- a creditor, by motion to the court, applies for a winding-up order.

Voluntary winding up

No court order is required if a company or close corporation has by special resolution resolved that it be wound up either by its members or creditors.

Judicial management

The court may grant a judicial management order upon application by a director, member or creditor.

Judicial management is a temporary moratorium to enable a company to surmount its financial problems under the management of a person specifically appointed for this purpose who acts in the place of the board of directors.

Scheme of arrangement or compromise

A scheme of arrangement or compromise may be proposed between a company, its creditors or its members, whether it is in liquidation or not. Should the scheme or compromise be approved by creditors and sanctioned by the court the winding-up order is set aside and the company is reinstated.

A private individual may submit an offer of compromise to his trustee for consideration by his creditors. However, any condition which makes the offer subject to the rehabilitation of the insolvent, is of no effect.

50 per cent of the members of a close corporation may submit an offer of composition to the liquidator for consideration by its creditors.

Commencement and control of insolvency procedures

Insolvency procedures can be instituted by:

- generally speaking anyone who is a creditor and has been unable to obtain settlement by legal means;
- directors, members, shareholders and an individual;
- a judicial manager;
- an executor of an insolvent deceased;
- an *ex parte* application.

The effect once insolvency procedures have commenced is:

- to divest an individual of all assets which then vest in the Master of the Supreme Court until a trustee is appointed by him;
- to place the property of a company or close corporation in the custody and under the control of the Master of the Supreme Court until the appointment of a liquidator;
- to stay civil proceedings;
- to cause trading to cease except in the case of judicial management or where it is necessary to preserve an asset;
- generally to curtail all activities except those of an individual who is entitled to earn an income but subject to certain restrictions and conditions;
- to make void every disposition of property (including rights of action) made after commencement of the winding up unless the court declares otherwise;
- to make void any attachment or execution order against the assets after the commencement of the winding up;
- to make void in the case of a company or close corporation every transfer of shares or alteration of the status of its members effected after the commencement of the winding up.

Controls, functions and duties are exercised by:

- the Master of the Supreme Court initially;
- a liquidator in the case of a company or close corporation and a trustee in the case of an individual, trust or a partnership, who is accountable to the Master of the Supreme Court and creditors;

- a judicial manager in the case of judicial management.

The duties of the liquidator or trustee are:

- to investigate and report on the affairs of the company, close corporation or insolvent including contraventions by directors, members or individuals;
- to trace and realise all assets;
- to lodge a liquidation and distribution of contribution account with the Master of the Supreme Court.

The duty of a judicial manager is to continue the business of the company and to report to creditors on the viability of continuing under judicial management or placing the company in liquidation.

Creditors

Secured creditors

Secured creditors are entitled to value their security and prove their claims. On realisation of the security the creditor receives payment of the amount realised less administration costs. The excess, if any, on secured assets realised is awarded to preferential creditors such as the Receiver of Revenue, staff salaries and wages within certain limits, auditors for fees up to R5,000 etc.

Concurrent creditors

Concurrent creditors are entitled to a pro rata share of whatever balance is available for distribution from the free residue.

Foreign creditors enjoy the same considerations but payment in foreign currency is subject to SA Reserve Bank approval.

Shareholders are entitled to receive dividends only after all other creditors are settled in full, including interest.

In the event of insufficient funds being available to cover liquidation costs, a contribution will be levied on the applicant creditor and creditors who proved claims.

Other matters

Restrictions and/or shortcomings of the procedures

The South African Law Commission is reviewing and modernising the Insolvency Act and the statutory provisions regarding the liquidation of companies and close corporations. The statutory provisions applicable to the liquidation of other institutions such as pension funds, banks, insurance companies and cooperatives will also receive attention and the Law Commission will consider to what extent, if at all, the provisions regarding compromises with creditors in terms of the Agricultural Credit Act 1966, should be included in the investigation. In short, it is intended to consolidate all the overlapping provisions regarding insolvency in a single Act.

End result of the procedures

Being subject to the dictates and strict control of the Master of the Supreme Court, the present procedures ensure an equitable distribution of the proceeds of assets realised.

Duration and timing

Insolvency procedures may take from nine months to two or more years to complete.

KPMG contact partner

Tjaart de Plessis
KPMG Administrators (Pty) Ltd
19th Floor
Carlton International Trade Centre
Commissioner Street
2001 Johannesburg
South Africa

Telephone: +27 (11) 332-7111
Fax: +27 (11) 331-9517

Spain

Legislation

The legislation that supports the Spanish bankruptcy and suspension of payments system is the following:

- 1989 Companies Act (*Real Decreto-Ley 1564/1989 de 22 de diciembre, por el que se aprueba el Texto Refundido de la Ley de Sociedades Anónimas*);
- 1995 Limited Liability Companies Act (*Ley 2/1995 de 23 de marzo, de Sociedades de Responsabilidad Limitada*);
- 1885 Commercial Code (*Código de Comercio del 22 de agosto de 1885*);
- Suspension of Payments Act (*Ley de Suspensión de Pagos de 26 de julio de 1922*).

Insolvency procedures

Suspension of payments (transitional insolvency)

This procedure is carried out when the debtor is insolvent, but an agreement between the debtor and his creditors can be achieved in order to defer payment of debts and thereby avoid bankruptcy. This agreement generally provides full payment to creditors over an extended period of time or a reduced payment within a short time period.

The procedure may only be applied for by the debtor. The application must include a balance sheet, a list of creditors with their respective balances and due dates, a report explaining the reasons for the insolvency, the means by which the creditors will be repaid, and the approval of the composition proposal by the board of directors. The applicant's account books must be submitted with the application.

The judge appoints three trustees ('*interventores*') to oversee the composition proceedings. One of the trustees is selected from among the creditors. All of the debtor's transactions must be approved by the trustees, who must report regularly to the judge. The documents submitted to the court are examined and, once an opinion thereon is received from the trustees, the judge either declares the debtor temporarily insolvent or bankruptcy proceedings are begun. A creditors' meeting is convened by the judge to discuss the suspension of payments proposal. At least 60 per cent of unsecured outstanding debts must be represented at the meeting. A simple majority vote representing at least 75 per cent of the debts present results in the composition being accepted.

Bankruptcy (definitive insolvency)

Bankruptcy leads to the liquidation of the debtor's assets. It can be applied for by the debtor, one of his creditors, or the court of its own motion. As soon as bankruptcy proceedings are opened, all debts become due and payable and the debtor may no longer run his business. The debtor may contest the opening of bankruptcy proceedings if he can prove that he has paid all overdue amounts. The bankruptcy must be recorded in all legal registers.

A commissioner and a depositary administrator are appointed by the court to convene a creditors' meeting to appoint three trustees ('*síndicos*') to administer, prepare an inventory of and sell the company's assets, collect the debts and prepare a statement of affairs. The commissioner acts as an intermediary between the trustees and the judge. All available funds are distributed to the creditors in accordance with their category. They can be especially privileged (like creditors for salaries owed six months before bankruptcy, or those specifically contemplated in the Civil and Commercial Code), privileged by mortgage, or unsecured. If the bankruptcy is considered fraudulent, the debtor will be civilly as well as criminally responsible. The responsibility of the shareholders is limited to the value of their shares.

There is no difference between national or foreign creditors in the insolvency procedures, the duration of which, whether definite or transitional, depends on the circumstances involved.

KPMG contact partner

Vicente Muñoz
KPMG Peat Marwick
Edificio Torre Europa
Paseo de la Castellana, 95
28046 Madrid
Spain

Telephone: +34 (1) 555 5363
Fax: +34 (1) 555 0132

Sudan

Legislation

In Sudan, insolvency is based on the Sudanese Companies Act 1925. The Act defines the company as one formed and registered under it and having the liability of its members limited to the amount if any, unpaid on the shares respectively held by them. According to s. 148 of the 1925 Act, the methods of winding up may be either by the court, voluntary or subject to the supervision of the court.

Despite the fact that the Act has been revised, the definitions and insolvency procedures described below remain unchanged.

Insolvency procedures

Winding up of a company by the court

This is done in any of the following circumstances:

- if a special resolution has been passed by the company that it should be wound up by the court;
- non-deposit of the statutory report or if the first ordinary general meeting is not held;
- if the company has not started operations since the date of its incorporation or if it ceases to operate for a period of one year;
- if the number of members becomes less than two in the case of a private company or less than seven in the case of other companies;
- failure to pay its debts;
- if the court decides that it is fair and just to liquidate the company.

The court may appoint official liquidators to perform winding-up duties instead of the company's board of directors.

Voluntary liquidation

A company may be liquidated voluntarily upon the passage of a certain period of time or occurrence of a certain event if this is prescribed in its articles of association. A company may also be liquidated voluntarily if a special or extraordinary resolution is passed that it should be liquidated. In this latter case, the liquidation date is the date on which the decision has been taken and the company should place a notice in the newspapers within 10 days.

Winding up subject to supervision of the court

This happens when a company has by special or extraordinary resolution resolved to wind up voluntarily. The court may make an order that the voluntary winding up shall continue but subject to such terms and conditions as the court thinks just.

A liquidator is appointed and may be removed by the court. However, the court will consider the wishes of creditors and contributories in relation to the appointment of liquidators.

KPMG contact partner

KPMG
A.L. Hassan
Khartoum Insurance Co. Building
PO Box 731
Khartoum

Telephone: +249 (11) 773749
Fax: +249 (11) 771481

Suriname

Legislation

The Bankruptcy Act which forms part of the Commercial Code contains legislation relating to insolvency and bankruptcy. It was first enacted in 1935 and has been revised several times since then. Suriname insolvency and bankruptcy procedures in general follow those of the Netherlands. Therefore, reference should be made to the section of this book dealing with the Netherlands.

Insolvency procedures

Moratorium

Moratorium is a legal status introduced in the Bankruptcy Act in 1935. At his own request, a debtor may be granted a suspension of payment by the court when he is unable to pay his debts. The court appoints one or more trustees who, together with the debtor, manage and control the debtor's affairs. This means, for instance, that the debtor cannot dispose of the assets without the cooperation, permission or assistance of the trustee(s). If the debtor acts against this, his estate cannot be held liable.

First, a provisional moratorium is granted, usually for a period of three months. This period can be extended with the court's permission. Subsequently, a definite moratorium is granted by the court for a period of at most 18 months. The court is entitled to extend this period for at most another 18 months. No definite moratorium is granted if in the court's opinion there is a risk that the debtor will try to prejudice his creditors or there is no prospect that the debtor will be able to pay his creditors. In practice, if this occurs, the court will declare the debtor bankrupt.

Bankruptcy

Bankruptcy is a legal status which can be defined as an attachment on all assets and liabilities of a debtor who can no longer pay his debts. The objective of the bankruptcy is to sell all the assets of the debtor so that proceeds can be distributed to the creditors in accordance with their rights. The debtor in a state of bankruptcy loses the right to manage his own affairs.

Adjudication

A debtor is adjudicated bankrupt by the court if a petition is filed by:

- the debtor;
- one or more creditors;
- the public prosecutor for reasons of public interest.

In all cases it has to be proved that the debtor is in a situation where he has ceased paying his liabilities. A creditor filing a petition should prove that he has a claim and that there is more than one creditor. Consequently, a debtor can avoid bankruptcy if he can prove that there is no valid claim and he can pay his debts.

Administration of the insolvent estate

The court adjudication order contains the appointment of a supervising judge as well as the appointment of one or more receivers. The receiver, who is normally an attorney, actually manages the insolvent's estate. The receiver should keep the supervising judge well informed of all matters relating to the administration of the estate. For certain decisions, such as the termination of employment, the termination of a rental contract and the commencing of legal proceedings on behalf of the insolvent estate, the receiver needs the permission of the supervising judge.

The court can appoint a committee of creditors. Generally, the most important creditors are appointed. The purpose of the committee of creditors is to assist and advise the receiver.

Nature of receivership

With the permission of the supervising judge and after having taken the advice of the creditors' committee, the receiver has to decide whether or not he will continue the business of the company and in what form. In many cases the receiver seeks a potential buyer for the enterprise or for part of its activities. If he does not succeed in finding one he has no choice but to liquidate the company.

Termination of the bankruptcy

Bankruptcy can be terminated in the following ways:

- by the approval by the court of a composition, as proposed by a meeting of creditors. The creditors receive an agreed percentage of their claim. The debtor is discharged and he regains the right to manage his own property. The creditors waive the right to recover the remainder of their claims. The debtor is freed from his previous creditors;
- by order of the court, if it appears that the balance to be recovered from the insolvent estate is insufficient to pay for the expenses of the bankruptcy (receiver's salary, legal costs, costs incurred by an appraiser, etc.). The debtor regains the right to manage his own affairs. The creditors remain empowered to recover their claims later.

In case of the termination of a bankruptcy, other than by a composition, a company is automatically dissolved.

Liquidation

The Commercial Code contains legislation applicable to liquidation. Liquidation is the process of winding up the affairs of an insolvent corporate body. Such a corporate body is obliged to add to its name the words 'in liquidation'. The liquidation of a company can take place voluntarily or as a result of bankruptcy. If it takes place as a result of bankruptcy, the liquidation is handled by a receiver appointed by the court.

All property of the bankrupt at the date of the bankruptcy has to be distributed among the creditors, with the exception of the following assets:

- social security receipts;
- certain strictly private property;
- alimony.

Creditors

Secured creditors

Secured creditors (e.g., holding mortgages or rights of pledge on the debtor's property, or having fiduciary property rights thereon) can simply enforce their security to the extent of its value. Such a secured creditor is called a separatist. However, when a secured creditor has realised his security and a balance remains due, he may file a proof of claim for the remainder of this claim. Separatists do not share in the costs of administering the bankruptcy when they have exercised their rights.

Unsecured creditors

The receiver must distribute the proceeds realised from the property of the bankrupt in the following order:

- remuneration of the receiver and legal costs;
- debts of the estate (e.g., appraisement costs, lease of bankrupt's house);
- all tax claims;
- other creditors.

KPMG contact partner

Michael Lutchman
KPMG Suriname
Van 't Hogerhuysstraat 9–11
Paramaribo
Suriname

Telephone: +597 476764
Fax: +597 474585

Swaziland

Legislation

- Insolvency Act No. 81 of 1955, as amended;
- Companies Act No. 7 of 1912, as amended;
- Financial Institutions Order No. 23 of 1975, as amended;
- Swaziland Development and Savings Bank Order No. 49 of 1973.

Insolvency procedures

- compulsory winding up by the court of an individual or partnership or company;
- members' or creditors' voluntary winding up of a company;
- voluntary surrender of estate by an individual;
- schemes of arrangement or compromise.

Compulsory winding up

An insolvent's estate or company may be wound up by the court if:

- judgment has been obtained for a debt and cannot be satisfied or paid;
- any attempt is made to dispose of assets thereby prejudicing creditors or preferring one creditor above another;
- any attempt is made to compromise debts with creditors;
- notice in writing is given to any creditor that his debt cannot be paid;
- an executor of a deceased estate which is found to be insolvent petitions the court;
- any other just case.

Voluntary winding up

The court may grant a voluntary winding-up order if an individual petitions the court. No court order is required if a company has by special resolution resolved that it can be wound up either by its members or creditors.

Scheme of arrangement or compromise

A scheme of arrangement or compromise may be proposed between the company in liquidation and its creditors or its members. Should the scheme or compromise be approved by creditors and sanctioned by the court the winding-up order is set aside and the company reinstated.

A private individual may also submit an offer of composition to his trustee for consideration by his creditors. However, any condition which makes the offer subject to the rehabilitation of the insolvent is of no effect.

Commencement and control of insolvency procedures

Insolvency procedures can be instituted by:

- generally, anyone who is a creditor and has been unable to obtain settlement by legal means;

- directors, members, shareholders and an individual on his own recognisance;
- an executor of an insolvent deceased estate;
- an *ex parte* application.

The effect once insolvency has commenced is:

- to divest the company, or individual, of all assets which will then vest in the master of the High Court until a liquidator or trustee is appointed by him;
- to stay civil proceedings;
- to cause trading to cease except in the case where it is necessary to preserve an asset;
- generally to curtail all activities except those of an individual who is entitled to earn an income but subject to certain restrictions and conditions;
- to make void every disposition of property (including rights of action) made after commencement of the winding up unless the court declares otherwise;
- to make void any attachment or execution order against the assets after the commencement of the winding up;
- to make void in the case of a company every transfer of shares or alteration of the status of its members effected after the commencement of the winding up.

Controls, functions and duties are exercised by:

- the master of the High Court initially;
- a liquidator in the case of a company and a trustee in the case of an individual or a partnership who must account to the master of the High Court.

The duties of the liquidator or trustee are:

- to investigate and report on the affairs of the company or insolvent, including contraventions by directors, members or individuals;
- to trace and realise all assets;
- to lodge a liquidation and distribution or contribution account with the master of the High Court.

Creditors

Secured creditors are entitled to value their security and prove their claims. On realisation of the security the creditor receives payment of the amount realised less administration costs up to the amount of the claim.

Any surplus resulting from assets realised is awarded to preferential creditors such as the Commissioner of Taxes, staff salaries and wages within certain limits and statutory contributions to the provident fund.

If there is no surplus, the Commissioner of Taxes and certain staff salaries and wages take precedence over secured creditors.

Thereafter:

- concurrent creditors are entitled to a pro rata share of whatever balance is available;
- foreign creditors enjoy the same considerations but payment in foreign currency is subject to approval by the Central Bank;
- shareholders are entitled to receive dividends only after all other creditors are settled in full;

- in the event of insufficient funds being available to cover liquidation costs, a contribution will be levied on the petitioning creditor and/or creditors who proved claims excluding preferential creditors.

Other matters

End result of the procedures

Being subject to the dictates and strict control of the master of the High Court, the present procedures ensure an equitable distribution of the proceeds of assets realised.

Duration and timing

Insolvency procedures may take nine months to two or more years to complete.

KPMG contact partner

John Hayter
KPMG
Imfumbe Building
Warner Street
Mbabane
Swaziland

Telephone: +268 42 891
Fax: +268 41 929

Sweden

Legislation

Rules are to be found in the new Bankruptcy Act 1988 and the Reorganisation of Business Act 1996 but there are several additional laws applying in tandem with those main Acts. The main statutory framework is as follows:

- Bankruptcy Act (1987: 672);
- Priority Rights Act (1970: 979);
- Reorganisation of Business Act (1996: 764).

Insolvency Procedures

In Sweden the following insolvency procedures are available:

- private (informal) reorganisation;
- public business reorganisation;
- bankruptcy.

Apart from lawyers there are special credit organisations (*Ackordscentraler*) in some major cities to assist creditors and debtors to negotiate and establish a business reorganisation.

Private (informal) reorganisation

This procedure is neither subject to court proceedings nor specific legislation. It is a reorganisation suggested by the debtor to which all creditors, if it includes a composition, must agree. It generally provides more funds distributable to the creditors but as it requires acceptance from all creditors it is often not successful.

Public business reorganisation

In 1996 the Swedish parliament enacted a new Reorganisation of Business Act which replaced the old Composition Act. The new law is influenced by the US Chapter 11 rules. This new procedure may be used to obtain a business reorganisation, subject to court proceedings. The procedure is started by a petition to court for reorganisation of the business, made by either the debtor or a creditor (if accepted by the debtor) followed by a suspension of all payments. All creditors must be notified of this suspension. Together with the petition for reorganisation of business the debtor also must apply to have an administrator (‘*rekonstruktör*’) appointed to examine the debtor’s financial situation and to safeguard the interests of the creditors. The application will include a recent balance sheet, an explanation of the reason for the insolvency and a brief description of the reorganisation proposal. In most cases the application is accepted by the court, which appoints an administrator, who must have certain qualifications, normally a lawyer with good knowledge of the insolvency laws or an official of an *Ackordscentral*.

A court order for business reorganisation involves a general prohibition on enforced collection and execution of debts arising prior to that date. It also prohibits creditors from terminating an ongoing contract provided that the debtor honours his obligations or security is furnished to the creditor in question. If needed, a creditors’ committee may be appointed, which the administrator is to consult on important matters.

The administrator’s duties include supervising the debtor’s business in order to ensure that the best interests of the creditors are considered, although the debtor is still in full possession of the business. The administrator must notify the creditors of the proceedings, advise them of the proposed reorganisation details and request their acceptance thereof. A very important task for the administrator is to consult the creditors on the reorganisation proposal.

If the reorganisation includes a proposal which is not accepted by all creditors, the debtor may apply to the court, requesting that public composition proceedings begin. This application must contain details of the proposed composition, such as timing of proposed payments, a recent inventory (no older than three months), the latest financial statements of the company and a report from the administrator. This report must comment on whether the debtor has acted fraudulently, whether the proposed composition is in the creditors' interests and a statement that 40 per cent of the creditors (in number and amount) are willing to support the composition. The debtor must, if requested by a creditor, testify under oath before the court that the deed of inventory is correct. The court then decides whether the application should be accepted.

Under a public composition secured creditors are to be paid in full unless they have agreed otherwise. Debts due to the tax authorities have priority and employees must be fully paid. The tax authorities sometimes, but not often, agree on a reduction of their claims. All ordinary creditors must be treated alike. If the proceedings are commenced, a creditors' meeting is convened to vote on the proposed composition. A majority of 60 per cent (both in number and amount) is needed when it is proposed that unsecured creditors are to receive at least 50 per cent. A majority of 75 per cent is needed when the proposal gives less than 50 per cent. During a business reorganisation procedure it is possible to overturn certain transactions entered into prior to the suspension of payments, as in bankruptcy (see below). The proceedings before the court normally take three to four months but can be extended. A public composition is binding on all creditors, even unknown ones. The proceedings end when the debtor fulfils the terms of the composition or is adjudicated bankrupt.

Bankruptcy

The debtor or a creditor may apply to the court to start bankruptcy proceedings. The court has to decide whether or not the debtor is insolvent (cannot pay his debts now or in the foreseeable future). If the debtor is insolvent, a receiver will be appointed by the court. The receiver must be a lawyer with relevant experience. The receiver decides how to deal with the property in question and will consult the creditors and the authority supervising the bankruptcy.

One of the primary tasks for the receiver is to sell the debtor's assets and distribute the proceeds among the creditors. The receiver can, if it is considered beneficial, continue to run the business of the company for a short time in order to ensure that it can be sold at the best possible price. One of the receiver's duties is to negotiate with the debtor's employees concerning termination of their employment.

Transactions made before the bankruptcy petition can, under certain circumstances, be reversed and the goods or money in question recovered for the bankrupt estate. This is the case, for example, where a transaction is deemed to be particularly unfair to the other creditors, when goods or money have been given away or when large sums of money have been paid only a short time before the bankruptcy petition.

The receiver has to make up an inventory of the bankrupt's estate including the creditors' names and addresses. This inventory is then submitted to the bankruptcy court. The court calls a meeting to be held one to two months after the bankruptcy decision. At this meeting representatives of the company, i.e. board members and managing director, have to testify under oath that the deed of inventory is correct. The creditors are normally notified of this meeting by a receiving order published in the daily papers.

If the receiver considers it necessary, a special procedure will be initiated whereby the creditors lodge proof of their claims. If such a procedure is initiated, the creditors known to the receiver will be notified by the court. This procedure is normally used only when unsecured creditors are likely to receive only partial payment.

Even during a bankruptcy it is possible for the creditors to agree on a composition. The rules are similar to the public composition, but seldom used, since this procedure does not enable the company to continue its business after the composition.

The receiver makes a report concerning the circumstances surrounding the insolvency. This report contains the reasons for the bankruptcy, whether there is a reason to believe that representatives of the company can be suspected of any fraud and whether there might be pre-insolvency transactions which could be challenged.

When closing the bankruptcy, the receiver proposes a dividend to be paid to the different creditors. The creditors are paid according to their priorities of payment, where secured creditors, taxes and salaries are paid before creditors without specific priority. Creditors can appeal to the court against the proposed payments.

Liquidation

A liquidator can be appointed to a corporation, a trading partnership or an incorporated society in order to terminate the business of the company. The liquidator is often a lawyer but can also be a director of the company. The decision to liquidate a company is normally taken at a shareholders' meeting. Under certain circumstances a board member, a managing director or a shareholder can apply to the court for the liquidation of the company.

When the company has entered into liquidation, the liquidator is the only person authorised to sign on behalf of the company. The liquidator will discontinue the company's business and advertise for creditors to lodge proof of their claims within six months. When all known liabilities have been paid, the liquidator gives a final statement to the shareholders, who formally agree that the liquidation is closed and the company dissolved.

KPMG contact partner

Sven Andrén
KPMG Bohlins AB
Tegelbacken 4
PO Box 16106
S-103 23 Stockholm
Sweden

Telephone: +46 (8) 723 91 00
Fax: +46 (8) 10 52 58

Switzerland

Legislation

Legislation on debt collection and bankruptcy is enacted by the Federal State. The new Federal Law on Debt Collection and Bankruptcy was enacted in 1997. In addition, a great number of decrees and other enactments exist to supplement the statutory provisions.

Insolvency Procedures

Swiss law distinguishes between three types of enforcement of debts by writ:

- distraint;
- enforcement of a lien;
- bankruptcy.

The first two are special executions, i.e., only certain parts of the debtor's property are seized, whereas the last is a general execution, i.e., all the debtor's property is seized.

Bankruptcy mainly applies to corporate bodies and individuals who are recorded in the commercial register as, for example, a sole trader, a member of a general partnership or in a similar capacity. Individuals are otherwise only subject to distraint. This is a procedure which involves items of the debtor's property being seized and subsequently realised in favour of the prosecuting creditor, in so far as this is necessary to meet the debt. In most cases, therefore, individuals cannot be made bankrupt by their creditors. On the other hand, every debtor is free to ask for his own bankruptcy by filing a declaration of insolvency in court. If the debt is secured, collection will also be by enforcement of a lien against the debtor who is subject to bankruptcy. This involves the pledged property being realised in favour of the secured creditor.

Bankruptcy proceedings

The purpose of bankruptcy is the compulsory liquidation of the whole of a debtor's property and the distribution of the proceeds to the creditors, according to their ranking. To achieve this, all property in the possession of the debtor at adjudication of bankruptcy constitutes the bankrupt's estate. Property subject to a lien or mortgage is included in the bankrupt's estate subject to the preferential right vested in the secured creditors.

Various bodies are involved in a bankruptcy. First of all, a bankruptcy court investigates whether the requirements for adjudication have been fulfilled. This includes a creditor having carried out the debt collection procedure successfully and then having demanded adjudication of bankruptcy. Bankruptcy can be adjudicated without debt collection proceedings if the debtor himself declares his insolvency to the bankruptcy court or in cases of fraud or if the debtor stopped all payments. The management (board of directors) of a limited company is bound to make this declaration as soon as its debts are no longer covered by its assets. Analogous provisions apply to exempt private limited companies and cooperative associations.

The receivers are in charge of the bankruptcy. They have to attend to all the affairs necessary for conserving and realising the bankrupt's estate. Their rights and duties are primarily laid down by law and pertinent enactments. The receivers are appointed by the creditors' meeting, which decides whether it wants this function to be assumed by the bankruptcy office or one or more persons whom it elects. In either case, the creditors' meeting may appoint a committee of inspection from among its members to supervise the administration of the receivership and to decide on matters of far-reaching importance.

Compositions and schemes of arrangement

The composition agreement or deed of arrangement is more lenient than bankruptcy. Its purpose is to enable the debtor, with the approval of a majority of creditors to the terms of the composition or arrangement, to discharge his debts according to a draft he has drawn up, and which is in keeping with his financial resources. A composition or scheme of arrangement is generally in the best interest of the creditors as it avoids involuntary liquidation and, therefore, the debtor's assets can generally be realised more favourably. This increases the dividend which can be paid to the creditors.

A debtor wishing to have the benefit of a composition or scheme of arrangement has to submit the scheme or draft composition agreement to the competent court. A creditor having carried out the debt collection procedure successfully may also ask for a composition or scheme of arrangement for his debtor. If, on the basis of examination, the court deems the debtor worthy of composition or arrangement, it grants him a moratorium of up to six months and appoints a trustee. Prolongation of the moratorium is possible up to 24 months. During this time, no debt collection proceedings can be instituted or continued. The debtor is allowed to continue running his business under the supervision of the trustee. The power granted by the court to the trustee may vary from simple supervision of the debtor's business up to full decision making power by the trustee.

The trustee summons a creditors' meeting to debate the petition for composition or arrangement. The creditors decide whether the proposed agreement should be accepted or rejected. If the necessary majority of creditors accept the agreement, it must then be approved by the competent court, to which the trustee makes his recommendation. One of the conditions for approval is that full payment of the proved claims of preferential creditors is ensured. Upon court approval of the deed of composition or arrangement, it becomes binding upon all creditors.

Composition

Composition is where the debtor agrees to pay a fixed proportion of each creditor's debt. The debts are satisfied in the form of a fixed dividend which is paid out within a certain period of time or is divided into instalments payable at fixed intervals. The debtor's business can be carried on.

Letter of respite

If the debtor only temporarily finds himself in financial difficulties, he will strive for a letter of respite, i.e., a limited extension of time which should enable him to recover financially. The creditors do not abandon their claims. They merely grant the debtor new terms of payment for settling his non-recurring or successive debts.

Liquidation arrangement (deed of assignment)

By means of a liquidation arrangement, the debtor assigns all or part of his property to the creditors. They divide up the proceeds among themselves and abandon the amount of the debt which is not repaid. Like bankruptcy, this arrangement generally leads to the liquidation of the debtor's business. Assignment is a possibility where the proceeds are expected to be better than in bankruptcy proceedings.

Who can be appointed?

Most functions in connection with debt collection and bankruptcy are exercised by government offices or officials, but there are three functions which can also be taken on by non-governmental persons or organisations:

- receivership — either the State bankruptcy office or one or more persons can take on receiverships. No special professional requirements are laid down by law but in practice trust or auditing companies or lawyers are generally appointed unless the bankruptcy office assumes this function;
- trustee — anyone, in principle, can be appointed to act as trustee in composition proceedings, but generally only experts, such as trust or auditing companies or lawyers, take on this function;
- liquidator — the comments relating to trustees above also apply to liquidators.

Creditors

Basically, the principle of equal treatment of creditors prevails, but absolute uniformity would not be altogether fair. Consequently, the law lays down a specific ranking according to which the creditors are to be paid. Only debts of the same rank are treated equally.

Secured and unsecured creditors

Secured creditors are those who hold a mortgage, charge or lien on property of the debtor as a security for their debt. The pledged property, i.e., the returns of its realisation, is used for the preferential payment of the relevant secured creditor. Normally, a secured creditor only has the option of enforcing a lien against the debtor, i.e., realising the pledged property, in order to bring about payment of this debt. In a few cases debt collection by bankruptcy is also possible provided that the debtor is subject to this type of debt collection proceeding.

The term 'unsecured creditor' includes all creditors whose debts are not secured. According to the principles mentioned earlier, unsecured creditors can collect their debts from the debtor by distraint or bankruptcy. Each creditor whose debt is not paid can make the debtor bankrupt, provided he is subject to bankruptcy.

Priority claims

For the payment of those creditors without security, Swiss bankruptcy law makes provision for a ranking, placing the debts in three categories. The first two categories stand in priority to one another, whilst the third category includes ordinary debts. In practice, this system of priority means that the creditors of one category are only entitled to the proceeds when the creditors of the category ranking above them have been paid in full. Creditors of the same category rank equally among themselves.

Of the two preferential categories, there are 10 types of debt which enjoy a privilege in bankruptcy, for example, wage claims going back six months prior to adjudication.

Attachment

Attachment enables a debtor's property located in Switzerland and subject to distraint to be seized temporarily if satisfaction of the creditor's claims seems to be threatened on account of the debtor's circumstances or conduct.

The attachment will be granted by the attachment authority (generally a judge) at the place where the property to be attached is located if there are grounds of attachment and the creditor substantiates his claim. The debt must be due and may not be secured by pledge. Grounds of attachment can be:

- the debtor has no fixed abode;
- the debtor makes funds or property disappear or flees from justice;
- the debtor is in transit;
- the creditor possesses a provisional or final certificate of loss;
- the debtor is not a Swiss resident.

The last can only be put forward as a ground of attachment if the debtor does not have a business establishment in Switzerland and has not elected a special domicile in Switzerland. Attachment used to entitle a creditor to institute debt collection proceedings and bring legal action at the place of attachment in Switzerland until the Lugano Convention came into force on 1 January 1992. Since then considerable restrictions have been imposed in this respect for debtors residing in signatory States.

If these requirements are satisfied, the attachment authority will issue a writ of attachment. The creditor can be obliged to provide security because he is liable for any damages arising out of unwarranted attachment. The debt collection officer brings the property under the custody of the law by issuing an attachment order.

The request for attachment must describe the property to be attached and state where it is located. If it is not possible to give an exact description, a general description of the goods according to their category may be sufficient provided that the location and ownership are known. However, a description like 'all the debtor's assets with bank X' is insufficient.

The creditor is obliged to follow up the attachment by bringing legal action or instituting debt collection proceedings within 10 days of the attachment order being served, otherwise the attachment becomes void.

KPMG contact partner

Dr Peter Herzog
Esther Nägeli
KPMG Fides Peat
Badenerstrasse 172
CH 8004 Zürich
Switzerland

Telephone: +41 (1) 249 3131
Fax: +41 (1) 249 2319

Taiwan

Legislation

The main statutes governing liquidation, composition and bankruptcy procedures are: the Company Law, last amended in December 1983, and the Bankruptcy Law, last amended in December 1980:

- the board of directors shall apply to the court for adjudication of bankruptcy when the company's assets are deemed as insufficient to cover its debts (Company Law 211);
- a debtor unable to honour its debts shall have them liquidated through legal proceedings as prescribed in the Bankruptcy Law (Bankruptcy Law 1).

Insolvency procedures

Two types of insolvency procedure are provided in the Bankruptcy Law, 'composition' and 'adjudication of bankruptcy':

- composition — a debtor unable to honour its debts may apply to the court or the local chamber of commerce for composition, prior to filing an application for adjudication of bankruptcy by the court;
- adjudication of bankruptcy — a debtor unable to honour its debts may apply to the court for adjudication of bankruptcy.

Composition

The debtor may apply to the court or the local chamber of commerce for composition and submit to such authority a status report of assets, a list of creditors and debtors, a composition proposal, and the guarantee to be provided. A meeting of all related creditors shall be held if the application for composition is successful. Where composition is processed through the local chamber of commerce, it is deemed to be effective when the proposal is passed at the creditors' meeting and a composition contract, executed by both the creditors and the debtor, is sealed by the local chamber of commerce and signed by its chairman.

Alternatively, where composition is processed through the court, it is deemed to be effective when the proposal is passed at the creditors' meeting and then approved by the court.

The debtor is then legally eligible to instigate composition procedures before the court and the related application must be filed before applying for adjudication of bankruptcy. Currently, only merchants who are also members of the local chamber of commerce are eligible to apply for composition before that chamber of commerce. However, these procedures must be undertaken before applying for adjudication of bankruptcy.

Once composition procedures are commenced, the following conditions are effective:

- the debtor may continue to operate its business;
- any gratuitous transaction entered into by the debtor subsequent to the application for composition is void;
- all onerous acts done by the debtor subsequent to the application for composition beyond the scope of normal managerial acts or of the ordinary business shall take no effect upon the creditors;
- after the application for composition has been approved, civil execution procedures may not be commenced or continued against the debtor, except in the case of secured and preferential obligatory claims;
- the composition shall take no effect upon creditors with security or preference rights, unless they agree to waive their rights;

- the rights of the creditors toward the guarantor of the debtor and other joint debtors shall not be affected by a composition;
- a promise by the debtor to give creditors any extra benefits not prescribed in the composition plan shall take no effect.

Supervisor

After the application for composition through the court has been approved, the court shall designate a judge to serve as the supervisor and select a certified public accountant or a person elected by the local chamber of commerce or one or two other appropriate persons to serve as assistant supervisor(s). The supervisor shall act as the chairman of the creditors' meeting and report to the court the final decision resolved at such meeting. Where a composition is processed through the chamber of commerce, the chamber may appoint members of the chamber, certified public accountants or other specialists to inspect the creditor's properties and books, supervise the management of the debtor's business, and stop any act of the debtor prejudicial to the interests of the creditors. In the course of conducting a composition, the debtor may continue its business but shall be subject to the supervision of the supervisor and the assistant supervisor. The supervisor and the assistant supervisor may inspect all the books, documents and properties related to the business of the debtor.

Assistant supervisor

For a composition processed through the court, certified public accountants, persons recommended by the local chamber of commerce or other appropriate persons can be appointed as assistant supervisors. The assistant supervisor shall supervise the management of business by the debtor and stop any action of the debtor prejudicial to the interests of creditors; preserve current assets and business receipts of the debtor, while allowing expenses necessary to the management of the business and maintenance of the debtor's family; complete the preparation of the list of creditors; and investigate the business of the debtor, his properties and the values thereof. In exercising these functions the assistant supervisor is subject to the direction of the supervisor. The creditors' meeting is presided over by the supervisor. The assistant supervisor shall be present at the meeting of creditors.

Classification and legal rights of creditors in a composition are as follows:

- secured creditors — a creditor holding a pledge, mortgage or lien on property of the debtor prior to adjudication of bankruptcy shall claim the right of exclusion in respect of such property even while composition is in process;
- preferential creditors — remuneration for the assistant supervisors, unpaid business taxes and interest accrued thereon, unpaid customs duties etc. must be paid in full before creditors without security;
- ordinary creditors — a creditor without priority or preference rights can claim only those assets which remain after creditors with security or preference rights have been paid, in accordance with the provisions in the composition proposal;
- shareholders — shareholders who are also the creditors may exercise their rights as creditors with security or preference rights, or as ordinary creditors as stated above.

There are restrictions/drawbacks of composition procedures and an application for composition shall be dismissed in any of the following circumstances:

- where the application is not in line with the aforementioned provisions and the applicant fails to make amendments thereto after being ordered to do so within a fixed period;
- where the applicant has, as a result of composition or bankruptcy, been sentenced to imprisonment in accordance with the provisions of this law;
- where the applicant fails to fulfil the agreed conditions after a composition or reconciliation was approved by the court;

- where the applicant, upon being summoned by the court, fails to appear without any justifiable reason, or appears before the court but fails to make a genuine statement, or refuses to produce relevant documents.

The debtor shall be present at the creditors' meeting and answer the inquiries raised by the supervisor, the assistant supervisor or the creditors. If the debtor, after being duly notified, fails to be present at the creditors' meeting without any justifiable reason, or the application for composition is rejected by the court or the chamber of commerce, or the composition is not approved by the court, the chairman shall call off the meeting and make a report thereof to the court. The court shall then declare the debtor bankrupt.

The court shall cancel the composition upon the creditors' application, in the event that the creditors at the creditors' meeting expressed disagreement to the conditions of the composition, did not attend, in person or by proxy, the creditors' meeting at the time when the resolution for a composition was adopted, and can prove that the composition shows bias in favour of the interests of other creditors and is therefore prejudicial to their own rights, or the creditors prove that the debtor has made a false report on his debts, concealed his properties or promised to give extra benefits to one or some of the creditors, or that the debtor fails to comply with the conditions required by the composition. When the composition is cancelled, the court shall declare the debtor bankrupt.

The composition procedure provides that:

- a creditor with security can claim his right of exclusion in respect of the property for which he holds a pledge, mortgage or lien irrespective of the composition procedures, unless he agrees to waive his secured right;
- a creditor with preference is entitled to be paid in full prior to the ordinary creditors, unless he agrees to waive his preference right;
- an ordinary creditor can only be paid in accordance with the composition conditions.

Adjudication of bankruptcy

A creditor who petitions for adjudication of bankruptcy must state in the petition the nature and the amount of the debt and details of the debtor's inability to pay. With the petition the debtor must submit a statement on the status of its assets and a list of creditors and debtors. The court shall declare bankruptcy or dismiss the petition by a ruling within seven days from receipt of the petition. A trustee shall be appointed when the court makes an adjudication of bankruptcy. All the creditors must report their debts to the trustee within a certain period, after which the trustee will produce a list of assets. The creditors' meeting is called by the court and a court judge shall be appointed as the chairman. After the first meeting of creditors is held, the trustee distributes the assets to the creditors in accordance with a distribution list previously approved by the court. The court will announce the end of the bankruptcy procedure as soon as the report of final distribution prepared by the trustee is submitted.

Unless otherwise stipulated, bankruptcy may be declared upon the petition of the creditors or the debtor. In the event that the debtor's property is insufficient to cover the debts and there is no heir to assume the remaining debts, the heir or the property manager, or the executor can apply for adjudication of bankruptcy. In addition, if the court finds out in the course of a civil suit procedure or a civil execution procedure that the debtor is unable to pay off its debts, it may declare the debtor bankrupt.

Once bankruptcy is declared, the following conditions shall prevail:

- the court may, if it deems necessary, request the post office or the telegraph office to forward to the trustee in bankruptcy letters and telegrams addressed to the bankrupt;
- the bankrupt shall not depart from the place of his domicile or residence without the permission of the court;
- when it deems necessary, the court may summon or arrest the bankrupt;

- if it is believed that the bankrupt may escape, conceal himself, destroy or abandon his properties, the court may issue a warrant to detain the bankrupt;
- the bankrupt shall, as a result of the adjudication of bankruptcy, lose the right to manage and dispose of the properties which should belong to the bankrupt's estate;
- the bankrupt's debtors are not permitted to make direct payments to the bankrupt for debts owing to him;
- when bankruptcy is adjudicated against a lessee, the trustee in bankruptcy may terminate the lease even if the lease has a fixed term;
- the trustee in bankruptcy will apply to the court to avoid any gratuitous or onerous acts done by the debtor prior to the adjudication of bankruptcy, if such acts are prejudicial to the creditors' rights and are avoidable in accordance with the provisions of the Civil Code.

Trustee

The trustee in bankruptcy shall be a certified public accountants or a person similarly qualified for the administration of the estate in bankruptcy. The trustee will maintain the books, documents and assets handed over by the bankrupt and will take action to safeguard the assets and rights as stipulated in the bankruptcy procedures. Immediately upon the completion of final distribution, the trustee in bankruptcy will submit a report on the distribution to the court.

Supervisor

Persons appointed at the creditors' meeting will supervise the bankruptcy proceedings on behalf of the creditors.

Classification of creditors involved in bankruptcy procedures are as follows:

- secured creditors — a person who has a pledge, a mortgage or a lien on the properties of the debtor prior to the adjudication of bankruptcy will have the right of exclusion in respect of such properties. Creditors who have the right of exclusion exercise their right without complying with the bankruptcy procedure;
- preferential creditors — obligatory claims entitled to priority in the properties of the bankrupt's estate shall be repaid in advance of other obligatory claims;
- ordinary creditors — an ordinary creditor can claim only that property which remains after obligatory claims entitled to priority in the property of the bankrupt's estate are paid, according to the distribution list approved by the court.

The bankrupt's estate consists of:

- all properties belonging to the bankrupt at the time of adjudication of bankruptcy and the claim on properties to be made in future;
- properties acquired by the bankrupt after adjudication of bankruptcy and before the close of the bankruptcy.

The rights solely belonging to the bankrupt himself and the properties against which an attachment is prohibited are exempted from being included in the bankrupt's estate.

If the resolution passed at the creditors' meeting is contrary to the interests of the creditors in bankruptcy, the court may, upon the application of the trustee in bankruptcy, the inspector or the creditors in bankruptcy who expressed disagreement, prohibit the execution of the resolution.

Bankruptcy procedures provide that:

- a creditor with security can claim his right of exclusion in respect of the property for which he holds a pledge, mortgage or lien, irrespective of the bankruptcy procedures;
- a creditor with preference is entitled to priority in the properties of the bankrupt's estate above creditors with subsequent priority or ordinary creditors, according to the distribution list approved by the court;
- an ordinary creditor can claim only that property which remains after obligatory claims entitled to priority in the property of the bankrupt's estate are paid, according to the distribution list approved by the court;
- the creditors are not allowed to claim for outstanding debts after the bankruptcy procedures are concluded.

KPMG contact partner

Wu-Yee Chang
KPMG Peat Marwick
6th Floor
18 Chang An East Road, Sec 1
Taipei 104
Taiwan

Telephone: +886 (2) 567 6996
Fax: +886 (2) 523 8797

Tajikistan

Legislation

Tajik insolvency legislation is relatively new and undergoing continuous development. Under the Soviet system, all enterprises were deemed to be branches of the State, and therefore no bankruptcy was possible. Liquidation through reorganisation was possible, but it was an administrative and logistical exercise.

Although insolvency legislation has been passed in Tajikistan and there is some evidence that insolvency proceedings have been instituted, the process is neither common nor even the automatic result of an irredeemable financial position. This is due partly to a lack of experience and partly to what seems to be a 'Soviet' belief that companies, once founded, cannot or should not die.

Current insolvency legislation is closely related to the legislation in Russia as both have evolved from the same system and Russian legislation is more readily accessible. Tajik insolvency legislation is based on the Law on Insolvency (Bankruptcy), which was passed in 1992. Since then the legislation has been considerably modified and developed by Presidential Decrees and other enabling legislation.

Further development is certain and so these notes are merely indicative of the current situation.

Insolvency procedures

Types of insolvency procedure

- reorganisation — the business is placed in the hands of an external management, which may be charged with its rehabilitation;
- liquidation — this occurs (a) if a court has declared the enterprise insolvent, or (b) if the enterprise declares itself insolvent;
- amicable settlement — the enterprise comes to an agreement with its creditors involving the deferral of payment of debts, payment by instalment, or debt forgiveness.

Parties to an insolvency action

The legislation recognises various parties in an insolvency action, including:

- receiver — the receiver may dispose of assets, act in an arbitration court to contest the validity of contracts completed up to six months prior to the initiation of arbitration proceedings, collect debts and receivables, form a liquidation committee and call a creditors' meeting;
- creditors;
- representatives of the workforce;
- debtor.

Petition

An insolvency action is initiated by a petition to the arbitration court from:

- the debtor, either the owner of the enterprise or its management — such a petition should be made before three months have elapsed after the due date for payments that cannot be met and cannot be withdrawn;

- a creditor, after the lapse of three months from the due date for payment for goods or services.

The court may either refuse the petition if it is established that the creditor's claim can be met or the defendant is solvent, or it may recognise the defendant as insolvent, in which case liquidation proceedings will be instituted.

If a petition is received from the debtor itself, the court may decide to postpone the declaration of insolvency and instead institute rehabilitation or external management procedures.

Reorganisation

The arbitration court may institute rehabilitation proceedings if there is a real possibility of financial aid being given by the owner or third parties. If an arbitration court rules in favour of rehabilitation, it must put the rehabilitation contract out to tender.

Liquidation proceedings

Once a debtor has been declared insolvent, liquidation proceedings commence with the arbitration court appointing a receiver. The liquidation proceedings must also include representatives of the workforce and other interested parties.

The receiver has a duty to obtain the highest price for the debtor's assets. The proceeds of the realisation of assets are distributed in the following order:

- expenses related to the liquidation proceedings;
- expenses of the receiver;
- expenses related to the continuing operations of the enterprise;
- payment of the workforce;
- payments to the State Pension Fund;
- taxes and social security contributions;
- creditor claims;
- claims of shareholders who are members of the workforce;
- claims of other shareholders;
- all other claims.

Payments to the workforce and taxes and social security contributions are considered privileged creditors. Claims secured by assets are settled outside the liquidation proceedings.

Voluntary liquidation

An enterprise may declare voluntary liquidation in the event of its managers determining that it can no longer meet its obligations or restore solvency. The receiver is appointed by the enterprise's creditors.

Amicable settlement

A settlement among the non-privileged creditors may be reached at any point in the insolvency proceedings; it may not infringe on the settlement of the privileged claims and must be endorsed by the court. Creditors must receive at least 35 per cent of their settlement within a year of the settlement date, 40 per cent within 18 months, and 50 per cent after two years. The settlement may be rendered void if (a) the terms are not satisfied, (b) the financial position of the debtor deteriorates, (c) the debtor infringes on the rights and interests of the creditors.

KPMG contact partner

Roger Munnings
KPMG
37 Ul. Novaya Basmannaya
3rd Floor
Moscow 107066
Russia

Telephone: +7 (502) 222 4030
Fax: +7 (502) 222 4024

Tanzania

Legislation

The provisions relating to liquidation, receivership and other corporate administrations are embodied in the Companies Ordinance 1932 (c. 212), as amended in 1987, which is supported by the Companies (Winding-up) Rules.

The insolvency law relating to individuals is in the Bankruptcy Act.

Insolvency procedures

Receivership

The terms of most charges or mortgages, which in all cases are limited in value because of stamp duty considerations, contain provisions for the appointment of a receiver and set out his powers. A floating charge debenture will normally confer upon the receiver the right of management.

The receiver has a duty to deal with the claims of the preferential creditors and to settle them in priority to the amount secured by means of a floating charge. The receiver has no more than a duty of care towards the unsecured creditors.

Liquidation

An unpaid creditor may petition the court for the winding up of a company. If a winding-up order is made, the official receiver is appointed interim liquidator pending the holding of a meeting of members and creditors to vote on the appointment of a liquidator.

If the directors of a company find that the company cannot continue its business by reason of its insolvency, then they may call meetings of shareholders and creditors to resolve to wind up the company. This is termed a creditors' voluntary liquidation. If, for any other reason, it is desired to wind up a company and if the directors are of the opinion that it can meet its debts in full within a period not exceeding 12 months, the directors will swear a declaration of solvency and the members will pass a resolution to wind up. This is termed a members' voluntary winding up.

Scheme of arrangement

Where a compromise or arrangement is proposed between a company and its creditors the court may order a meeting of the creditors and the compromise and arrangement will be binding on all creditors of the same class, provided it is approved by a majority in number and a 75 per cent majority in value of those present in person or by proxy at the meeting.

Defunct companies

The Tanzania legislation gives power to the Registrar of Companies to strike defunct companies off his register. It is often possible for companies without any assets or liabilities to be dissolved in this way and thus avoid the cost of liquidation.

Who can be appointed?

- liquidators and receivers — no qualifications are required to act as receiver or liquidator, though a body corporate may not be appointed. When an appointment is made out of court it is usual for a certified public accountant to act as liquidator or receiver;

- official receiver — the official receiver is usually appointed as liquidator by the court upon the successful petition for the winding up of a company;
- special manager — an official receiver may, in certain circumstances, request the court's approval to appoint a special manager to assist in liquidation. A special manager would usually be a certified public accountant;
- committee of inspection — in the case of liquidations, creditors, at a meeting, may decide to appoint not more than five persons to this committee to look after their interests.

Creditors

Secured creditors

Holders of a charge or mortgage on property of a debtor as security for a debt are secured creditors, who can recover their debt wholly or in part from the assets of the debtor before the unsecured creditors.

Preferential creditors

The Companies Act provides for the payment of certain creditors in priority to creditors secured by a floating charge and unsecured creditors. These include the following:

- taxes and local rates due at the relevant date and due and payable within 12 months prior to that date;
- wages and salaries subject to a maximum of TShs 4,000/- per employee and due within four months prior to the relevant date.

Unsecured creditors

The claims of these creditors rank equally in liquidation after the settlement of amounts due to secured and preferential creditors.

KPMG contact partner

Andrew Gregory
KPMG Peat Marwick
PO Box 40612
Jubilee Insurance Exchange
1st Floor
Mama Ngina Street
Nairobi
Kenya

Telephone: +254 (2) 222 862
Fax: +254 (2) 215 695

Thailand

Legislation

The present Bankruptcy Act was enacted in 1940 and came into force on 1 January 1941. It has subsequently been amended in 1968 and 1983.

Insolvency procedures

Only officials of the court can be appointed as official receiver by the Minister of Justice to administer the affairs of the bankrupt.

Bankruptcy

A creditor may institute a bankruptcy case in the following circumstances:

- the debtor is insolvent;
- the debt is not less than Bt 50,000 if the debtor is an individual, or Bt 500,000 if the debtor is a legal entity;
- the debt is a liquidated sum, payable immediately or in the future.

In a bankruptcy case, an official receiver can only be appointed by the Minister of Justice. When the court issues a receiving order, the official receiver will automatically be empowered to act on behalf of the debtor to perform duties such as calling for creditors to submit claims, issuing a public announcement about control of the debtor's assets, seizing of property, managing of the business and property, acting on behalf of the debtor in a civil case, calling a creditors' meeting, or offering a compromise settlement of debts. The receiver may borrow money required for the management of the debtor's property with the court's approval, and can require a debtor to obtain a life insurance policy.

Participation for repayment of debt

A resident creditor is required to file an application to participate in the payment of his outstanding debt to the official receiver within two months from the date of advertisement of the receiving order. But, in the case of a non-resident creditor, the official receiver may grant an extension of a further two months.

Prior to filing the application, a non-resident creditor must prove to the official receiver that the Thai creditors may enjoy the same right to participate in repayment for the debts in his country, and agree to relinquish the property of the debtor he has acquired, if any, outside Thailand for the common benefit of all the creditors.

Adjudication order

After the making of a receiving order, the official receiver will hold a meeting of creditors to decide whether or not the debtor should be adjudicated bankrupt. If the meeting so decides, the court will issue the adjudication order declaring the debtor legally bankrupt.

Priorities in distribution

Upon the making of an adjudication order, the receiver shall seize all properties of the debtor for the benefit of the creditors. In general, distributions of the proceeds are made in order of priority as follows:

- cost of bankruptcy, including court fees;
- expenses of the official receiver in managing the debtor's estate;
- court fees for collecting the debtor's property and court and counselling fees of the petitioning creditor;

- taxation due within six months preceding the order for control of the property;
- wages of the debtor's employees;
- other debts.

Discharge of bankrupt

The bankrupt may apply to the court for his discharge after adjudication on the ground that he has co-operated with the official receiver in managing his properties for the common benefit of the creditors. The official receiver, however, may oppose this. The court has a wide discretion to decide according to the individual circumstances.

Liquidation

A company can either be liquidated by order of the court, by the company voluntarily placing itself in liquidation, or because of bankruptcy. A company in liquidation may not necessarily be bankrupt, but when a company is bankrupt it always needs to be liquidated. However, if the liquidator of a company determines, in the process of liquidation, that the company has insufficient assets to cover its liabilities, the liquidator is responsible for requesting the court to order the company bankrupt in order that the official receiver can take over the responsibilities of receivership under the Bankruptcy Act.

Any person can be appointed as the liquidator by the company's shareholders. If an acceptable liquidator cannot be appointed, the public prosecutor, a creditor or a shareholder may request the court to appoint a liquidator.

Creditors

Secured creditors

A secured creditor is one of the following:

- a holder of a mortgage;
- a holder of a pledge;
- a holder of a right of retention; or
- a holder of a preferential right in the same manner as a pledge.

Secured creditors normally have priority in recouping their claims from the properties of the debtor even if they do not enforce their rights under a bankruptcy case. A secured creditor may institute bankruptcy proceedings:

- if the debt cannot be fully recovered through such property;
- he relinquishes the secured property for the common benefit of all the creditors.

Unsecured creditors

Any creditor other than a secured creditor, described above, is considered an unsecured creditor.

KPMG contact partner

Saridphol Chompaisal
KPMG Peat Marwick Suthee Ltd
9th Floor, Sathorn Thani Tower II
92 North Sathorn Road
Bangkok 10500
Thailand

Telephone: +66 (2) 236 6161
Fax: +66 (2) 236 6165

Trinidad and Tobago

Legislation

The laws of Trinidad and Tobago are based on pre-1939 English law. Accordingly, insolvency procedures bear certain similarities to those in England. There is at present in draft a new Companies Act which is patterned more on a Canadian model which, if and when enacted, will affect existing insolvency procedures.

Insolvency procedures

Receivership

Receivers are most commonly appointed by lenders under the terms of mortgage debentures where there has been a failure by the borrower to repay the debt to the lender on request. No body corporate can be appointed receiver. Receivers must file accounts of receipts and disbursements with the Registrar every six months. There is a specific order of discharge of liabilities by which receivers are guided. Upon discharge of the liability to the debenture holder, or disposal of all assets, whichever comes first, the receiver must file a notice of ceasing to act which effectively terminates his appointment.

Winding up

The winding up of a company may be either:

- by the court;
- voluntary;
- subject to the supervision of the court.

Winding up by the court

A company may be wound up by the court if:

- the company has passed a special resolution requiring that it be wound up by the court;
- default is made in delivering the statutory report to the Registrar or in holding the statutory meeting;
- the company does not commence its business within a year from its incorporation, or suspends its business for a whole year;
- the number of members is reduced in the case of a private company below two, or, in the case of any other company, below seven;
- the company is unable to pay its debts;
- the court is of the opinion that it is just and equitable that the company should be wound up.

The Companies Ordinance, s. 162, defines when a company is unable to pay its debts. The date of commencement of winding up by the court is the date of presentation of the petition for the winding up.

The court may appoint one or more persons as liquidator(s) and all proceedings are subject to the court's directions. The powers and duties of the liquidator are set out in the Companies Ordinance.

Voluntary winding up

A company may be wound up voluntarily:

- whenever the articles of association of the company provide for it to be dissolved and the company in general meeting has passed a resolution requiring it to be wound up voluntarily;
- if the company resolves by extraordinary resolution that the company be wound up voluntarily;
- if the company resolves by extraordinary resolution to the effect that it cannot, by reason of its liabilities, continue its business and that it is advisable to wind up.

A voluntary winding up is deemed to commence at the time of passing the resolution for voluntary winding up.

The effects of the commencement of winding up are that:

- the company shall cease to trade;
- the company's corporate powers and status continue until its affairs are wound up;
- upon the appointment of a liquidator all the powers of the directors cease.

As soon as the affairs of the company are fully wound up, the liquidator must make up an account showing the manner in which the winding up has been conducted and the property of the company disposed of.

Where the winding up continues for more than one year, the liquidator must make up an account for each 12-month period and present it to a general meeting of the company each year.

Winding up under supervision of the court

When a company has passed a resolution for voluntary winding up, the court may make an order that the voluntary winding up shall continue but subject to such supervision of the court as the court thinks just. The company or any creditor of the company or any contributory may petition the court to order such supervision.

A body corporate may not be appointed as liquidator of a company.

KPMG contact partner

Herman C. Rodriguez
KPMG Peat Marwick
PO Box 1328
Scotia Centre
56–58 Richmond Street
Port of Spain
Trinidad

Telephone: +1 (809) 623 1081
Fax: +1 (809) 623 1084

Tunisia

Insolvency procedures

There are two procedures for dealing with corporate insolvency in Tunisia:

- the rehabilitation scheme for firms in difficulty (as set out in Law No. 95–34 of 17 April 1995, which replaced the previous system of preventive scheme of composition);
- the bankruptcy procedure.

Rehabilitation scheme for firms in difficulty

The rehabilitation scheme for firms in difficulty is a special legal procedure which helps firms (whether incorporated or not) which are experiencing difficulties in paying their debts and maintaining employment. This procedure is granted only to firms which have not reached a point of no return. The scheme may be either:

- preventative, which is applicable before the default of payments: an amicable settlement; or
- curative, which is applicable when default of payment has occurred: a judicial settlement.

Preliminary phase

The public accounting services, the work inspection function, the National Social Security Fund, and the auditor of the company in difficulty are responsible for notifying the 'Follow-up Commission for Economic Companies' if they become aware of any issue which threatens the viability of a firm. The information gathered by the Follow-up Commission for Economic Companies is available to the courts.

Amicable settlement

The procedure is started by the firm's general manager applying to the relevant court for an amicable settlement with creditors. The court nominates a mediator who is responsible for helping to arrange an agreement between debtor and creditors.

A settlement is approved if creditors whose claims amount to more than two thirds of the total debts agree. The settlement consists of the following measures:

- a discount or a rescheduling of the debts;
- postponement of interest;
- any other measure to assist in the repayment of the debt.

Effect of the agreement

- actions which try to recover previous claims are postponed until the end of the agreement term. However, if, during the course of the agreement, a statement of default is pronounced, the agreement is terminated;
- the court may decide to reschedule all debts which are not contained in the agreement.

Judicial settlement

The procedure is started at the request of the firm's general manager, of any creditor, or by the president of the relevant court.

The court nominates a judge, and a certified public accountant, who is responsible for reviewing the company's economic situation and the ways of assisting it.

The judge submits a settlement plan to the Follow-up Commission for Economic Companies and draws up a report for the court about the possibility of settlement.

Results of a judicial settlement

- there is a moratorium during which time:
  - the court nominates a judicial administrator whose function is to develop a settlement plan (to allow for the continuation of the company's activity or its sale). This judicial administrator has the power to manage the company's business;
  - there is a postponement of all legal actions in respect of previous debts, postponement of deferred interest and of all time limits on legal actions;
  - all the proved debts are listed according to their order and priority (for payment);
- the continuation of the company's activity in conformity with the plan;
- the partial or total sale of the company.

However, if the court refuses the request for a judicial settlement or if the proposed plan is not considered viable, the debtor is declared bankrupt.

Bankruptcy

The court declares bankruptcy:

- by a written declaration of the debtor or his legal representative, board of directors for a limited company and manager for a private limited company;
- by the application of one or more creditors;
- automatically.

The judgment declaring bankruptcy provides for the appointment of:

- a judge superintendent (member of the court) entrusted with supervising the management of the bankruptcy;
- one to three syndics acting as court attorneys who will be entrusted with the management and the settlement of the bankrupt's estate.

The superintendent judge may appoint one or more supervisors to deal with creditors and assist him in supervisory duties.

Results of the bankruptcy

For the bankrupt party there is:

- the loss of all his civic rights;
- the loss of the right to manage the business and all his property as long as he is in bankruptcy.

For existing creditors and privileged creditors there is:

- the postponement of individual actions;
- debts are payable immediately;
- interest on debts stops accruing;
- the postponement of some actions started by the bankrupt.

The simple scheme of composition is a contract between the bankrupt party and his creditors which usually provides for payments to be rescheduled or a partial reduction of debts. It can also provide for the bankrupt party passing some or all of his assets to his creditors.

The creditors' union is the solution in which the bankrupt's assets are sold and the proceeds divided between the creditors. Creditors are paid according to the following order of priority:

- privileged creditors;
- normal creditors;
- shareholders.

KPMG contact partner

Rached Fourati
Cabinet Rached Fourati
KPMG Tunisie
7 rue de Mauritanie
1002 Tunis Belvedere
Tunisia

Telephone: +216 (1) 793 544
Fax: +216 (1) 783 568

Turkey

Legislation

In Turkey insolvency matters are regulated by the Code of Execution and Bankruptcy. The Code has undergone many extensive changes since 1929, the latest comprehensive amendment being in 1985.

Bankruptcy is the only type of insolvency procedure available in Turkey. Outside bankruptcy, there are only execution procedures for the collection of individual debts. Only merchants and business associations are subject to bankruptcy proceedings.

Although it cannot be considered as an alternative to bankruptcy, concordat is also possible under Turkish law (see below).

Insolvency procedures

Bankruptcy

A person (natural or legal) can only be declared bankrupt through a judgment given by the Commercial Court of First Instance. The procedure is started by an official request to the court, and the court declares a person bankrupt after investigating and determining that (a) the debtor is a merchant or a business association and (b) the debtor is insolvent.

The application to the court can be made by the debtor or by the creditors of the debtor seeking the collection of a particular debt.

If the debtor is a natural person or an unlimited liability company the application by the debtor to the court is not compulsory. However the directors of a limited liability company or a corporation are obliged to commence bankruptcy proceedings if the company is found to be insolvent.

The official declaration by the court of bankruptcy is very important. Not only the date but the exact hour is cited as well.

At the moment of declaration all effects of bankruptcy come into force. Any transactions made by the bankrupt on his estate after the moment of declaration are null and void.

The bankruptcy officer, a government employee working under the control of the Court of Execution, sends notices and invites all the bankrupt's creditors to attend a meeting.

The meeting of creditors elects the bankruptcy management. Those elected, upon approval by the court, constitute the bankruptcy management board. This board has direct power to manage and liquidate the bankrupt estate.

The bankruptcy management board identifies the goods and properties contained in the estate. The board determines and lists all the debts, sells everything in the estate and distributes the money among the creditors on a pro rata basis.

At the moment when bankruptcy is declared by the court, all debts of the bankrupt become due and payable. Interest on debts (other than debts secured by pledge or mortgage) ceases to accrue.

All creditors are required to attend the meeting of creditors and are required to have their claims registered by the bankruptcy management, which prepares the final list of claims. The creditors may object to this list on the grounds that their own debt is not properly listed or that any other debt listed should be taken out. It is up to the court to decide on such objections and eventually declare the list final.

Of the creditors with security only those who have pledges on movable property and those who have mortgages on immovable property receive priority in payment. When the collateral is sold, the money is used to pay the secured debt plus interest. Only after secured creditors are fully paid can the remaining portion, if any, be added to the general creditors' pool.

Among other creditors, employees of the bankrupt, his family members for alimony claims and the State (taxes, dues and fines, etc.) have priority in that order.

The remaining portion of the estate is distributed among ordinary creditors on a pro rata basis. There is no difference between foreign and domestic creditors.

Shareholders of bankrupt companies are not considered as creditors. Therefore they are paid only after all the creditors are fully satisfied.

The main shortcoming of the bankruptcy procedure is the time factor. Although the law states that the liquidation should be finalised in six months, it normally takes from three to five years.

In a country like Turkey with high inflation this time factor, plus the rule that stops the running of interest, make bankruptcy proceedings extremely detrimental to the creditors.

Concordat

Either before or after a declaration of bankruptcy the debtor has the right to offer concordat to his creditors. The offer might be to pay a certain percentage of the debts or to pay 100 per cent after a certain period.

The creditors meet and vote on the offer. If it is accepted by two thirds of the total amount of debts and two thirds of the number of creditors, the concordat goes into effect binding also the creditors who voted against it.

As long as the debtor conforms with the provisions of the concordat, he retains full powers to deal with the estate.

KPMG contact partner

Turhan Yetkin
Yetkin Yeminli Mali Musavirlik AS
Barbaros Bulvari
Gurel Apt, A Blok No:41 D:13
Besiktas
Istanbul
Turkey

Telephone: +90 (212) 259 72 85
Fax: +90 (212) 258 35 48

Turkmenistan

Legislation

Turkmen insolvency legislation is relatively new and undergoing continuous development. Under the Soviet system, all enterprises were deemed to be branches of the State, and therefore no bankruptcy was possible. Liquidation through reorganisation was possible, but it was an administrative and logistical exercise.

Although insolvency legislation has been passed in Turkmenistan and there is some evidence that insolvency proceedings have been instituted, the process is neither common nor even the automatic result of an irredeemable financial position. This is due partly to lack of experience and partly to what seems to be a 'Soviet' belief that companies, once founded, cannot or should not die.

Current insolvency legislation is closely related to the legislation in Russia as both have evolved from the same system and Russian legislation is more readily accessible. Turkmen insolvency legislation is based on the Law on Insolvency (Bankruptcy), which was passed in October 1994. Since then the legislation has been considerably modified and developed by Presidential Decrees and other enabling legislation.

Further development is certain and so the notes in this chapter are merely indicative of the current situation.

Insolvency procedures

Types of insolvency procedure

- reorganisation — the business is placed in the hands of an external management, which may be charged with its rehabilitation;
- liquidation — this occurs (a) if a court has declared the enterprise insolvent, or (b) if the enterprise declares itself insolvent;
- amicable settlement — the enterprise comes to an agreement with its creditors involving the deferral of payment of debts, payment by instalment, or debt forgiveness.

Parties to an insolvency action

The legislation recognises various parties in an insolvency action, including:

- administrative manager — the manager is authorised to carry on the business, recruit and dismiss employees, dispose of assets, call meetings of the creditors, and draw up a plan for an external management and execute the plan;
- receiver — the receiver may dispose of assets, act in an arbitration court to contest the validity of contracts completed up to six months prior to the initiation of arbitration proceedings, collect debts and receivables, form a liquidation committee and call creditors' meetings;
- creditors;
- representatives of the workforce;
- debtor.

Petition

An insolvency action is initiated by a petition to the arbitration court from:

- the debtor, either the owner of the enterprise or its management — such a petition cannot be withdrawn;

- a creditor, after the lapse of two months from the due date for payment for goods or services, the due date being defined as the date of delivery of a demand for payment by registered post.

The court may either refuse the petition if it is established that the creditor's claim can be met or the defendant is solvent, or it may recognise the defendant as insolvent, in which case liquidation proceedings will be instituted.

If a petition is received for the debtor enterprise to be reorganised, the court may decide to postpone the declaration of insolvency and instead institute rehabilitation or external management procedures.

Reorganisation

External management of the enterprise may be considered if there is a real possibility that the solvency of the enterprise may be restored by selling off parts of the debtor organisation, reorganising it, or instituting some other economic measures. An administrative manager is appointed by the court. Adminstrative management may not last for more than 18 months.

The arbitration court must then review the results of the management, and decide whether it should continue or the debtor should be declared insolvent and liquidation proceedings be instituted.

Rehabilitation

In the event of a real possibility for solvency being restored to the enterprise as a result of financial aid being given by the owner or third parties to the enterprise, the arbitration court may institute rehabilitation proceedings. Rehabilitation may not last for more than 18 months, which can be prolonged by the court for a further six months. Rehabilitation ceases when 18 months have elapsed or it is determined by the court that rehabilitation is ineffective, in which case liquidation proceedings must be instituted. Rehabilitation is deemed successful when all claims have been met and the insolvency action can be closed.

Liquidation proceedings

Once a debtor has been declared insolvent, liquidation proceedings commence with the arbitration court appointing a receiver.

The receiver has a duty to obtain the highest price for the debtor's assets. The proceeds of the realisation of assets are distributed in the following order:

- expenses related to the liquidation proceedings;
- expenses of the administrative manager and receiver;
- expenses related to the continuing operations of the enterprise;
- claims of individuals whom the debtor has injured or prejudiced;
- payment of the workforce;
- payments to the State Pension Fund, allowances for the year prior to the institution of the insolvency action, payments on contracts for authors' rights and licensing;
- taxes and social security contributions;
- creditor claims;
- claims of shareholders who are members of the workforce;
- claims of other shareholders;
- all other claims.

Injured individuals, the workforce claiming payment, and taxes and social security contributions are considered privileged creditors.

Claims secured by assets are settled outside the liquidation proceedings.

Voluntary liquidation

An enterprise may declare voluntary liquidation in the event of its managers determining that it can no longer meet its obligations or restore solvency. The receiver is appointed by the enterprise's creditors.

Amicable settlement

A settlement among the non-privileged creditors may be reached at any point in the insolvency proceedings if two thirds of the creditors consent; it may not infringe on the settlement of the privileged claims and must be endorsed by the court. The settlement may be rendered void if (a) the terms are not satisfied, (b) the financial position of the debtor deteriorates, (c) the debtor infringes on the rights and interests of the creditors.

KPMG contact partner

Roger Munnings
KPMG
37 Ul. Novaya Basmannaya
3rd Floor
Moscow 107066
Russia

Telephone: +7 (502) 222 4030
Fax: +7 (502) 222 4024

Turks and Caicos Islands

Legislation

The laws of the Turks and Caicos Islands are based on English law and thus insolvency procedures are similar to those in England and Wales. Such laws include Part V of the Companies Ordinance 1981.

Insolvency procedures

Receivership

Receivers are most commonly appointed by lenders under the terms of mortgage debentures where there has been a failure by the borrower to repay the debt to the lender when requested to do so.

The receivership procedures are similar to those set out in the section on England and Wales except that the term 'administrative receiver' is not used in the Turks and Caicos Islands and no meeting of creditors has to be called by the receiver. The procedures provide a speedy remedy and allow the company to continue to trade.

Voluntary winding up

Voluntary winding up means the winding up of a company by the shareholders without the involvement of the court. The assets and liabilities of the company are placed under the control of a liquidator who winds up the affairs of the company.

A company may be wound up voluntarily:

- whenever the articles of association of the company provide for it to be dissolved, and the company in general meeting has passed a resolution requiring it to be wound up voluntarily;
- whenever the company has passed a special resolution requiring it to be wound up voluntarily;
- whenever the company has passed an extraordinary resolution to the effect that it cannot by reason of its liabilities continue its business, and that it is advisable to wind up the company.

A voluntary winding up is deemed to commence at the time of passing the resolution authorising the winding up. The effects of the commencement of winding up are that:

- the company shall cease to trade;
- the company's corporate powers and status continue until its affairs are wound up;
- upon the appointment of a liquidator all the powers of the directors cease.

As soon as the affairs of the company are fully wound up, the liquidator must prepare an account showing the manner in which the winding up has been conducted and the property of the company disposed of.

Winding up under supervision of the court

When a resolution has been passed by a company to wind up voluntarily, the court may make an order directing that the voluntary winding up should continue but subject to such supervision of the court as the court thinks just. The company or any creditor of the company or any contributory may petition the court to order such supervision.

Compulsory winding up

A company may be wound up by the court whenever:

- the company has passed a special resolution requiring the company to be wound up by the court;
- the company does not commence its business within a year from its incorporation, or suspends its business for the space of a whole year;
- the members are reduced in number to less than five;
- the company is unable to pay its debts;
- the court is of the opinion that it is just and equitable that the company should be wound up.

The Companies Ordinance, s. 93, defines when a company is deemed to be unable to pay its debts. The date of commencement of winding up by the court is the date of presentation of the petition for the winding up.

The court shall appoint one or more persons to be called official liquidator. All proceedings in the winding up of the company by the official liquidator are subject to the court's directions. The powers and duties of the official liquidator are contained in the Companies Ordinance 1981.

Striking off

A company may be dissolved under the provisions of Part VI of the Companies Ordinance 1981 where:

- the Registrar of Companies has reasonable cause to believe that it is not carrying on business or is not in operation;
- it is being wound up and the Registrar of Companies has reasonable cause to believe that either no liquidator is acting, or the affairs of the company are fully wound up.

The striking off of any company under this Ordinance shall not affect the liability, if any, of any director, officer and member of the company, and such liability shall continue and may be enforced as if the company has not been struck off. Any property vested in or belonging to any company struck off the register under this Ordinance shall thereupon vest in the Financial Secretary of the Turks and Caicos Islands.

Using this procedure, a company may be dissolved at minimum cost and there is no need for a liquidator.

KPMG contact partner

Gary Brough
KPMG
Mayfair House, The Centre Mews
PO Box 357
Providenciales
Turks and Caicos Islands
British West Indies

Telephone: +1 (809) 946 4613
Fax: +1 (809) 946 4619

Uganda

Legislation

Company law has not changed since 1 January 1961 when the current Companies Act was enacted. The provisions relating to liquidation, receivership and other corporate administrations are embodied in the Companies Ordinance 1961 (c. 85), which is supported by the General (Winding up) Rules.

The insolvency law relating to individuals is in the Bankruptcy Act.

Insolvency procedures

Receivership

The terms of most charges or mortgages which in all cases are limited in value because of stamp duty considerations, contain provisions for the appointment of a receiver and set out his powers. A floating charge debenture will normally confer upon the receiver the right of management.

The receiver has a duty to deal with the claims of the preferential creditors and to settle them in priority to the amounts secured by means of a floating charge. The receiver has no more than a duty of care towards the unsecured creditors.

Liquidation

An unpaid creditor may petition the court for the winding up of a company. If a winding-up order is made, the official receiver is appointed interim liquidator pending the holding of a meeting of members and creditors to vote on the appointment of a liquidator.

If the directors of a company find that the company cannot continue its business by reason of its insolvency, then they may call meetings of shareholders and creditors to resolve to wind up the company. This is termed a creditors' voluntary liquidation. If, for any other reason, it is desired to wind up a company and if the directors are of the opinion that it can meet its debts in full within a period not exceeding 12 months, the directors will swear a declaration of solvency and the members will pass a resolution to wind up. This is termed a members' voluntary winding up.

Scheme of arrangement

Where a compromise or arrangement is proposed between a company and its creditors, the court may order a meeting of creditors and the compromise or arrangement will be binding on all creditors of the same class, provided it is approved by a majority in number and a 75 per cent majority in value of those present in person or by proxy at the meeting.

Defunct companies

The Ugandan legislation gives power to the Registrar of Companies to strike defunct companies off his register. It is often possible for companies without any assets or liabilities to be dissolved in this way and thus avoid the cost of liquidation.

Who can be appointed?

- liquidators and receivers — no qualification is required to act as receiver or liquidator, though a body corporate may not be appointed. When an appointment is made out of court it is usual for a certified public accountant to act as a liquidator or receiver;

- official receiver — the official receiver is usually appointed as liquidator by the court upon the successful petition for the winding up of a company;
- special manager — an official receiver may, in certain circumstances, request the court's approval to appoint a special manager to assist in the liquidation. A special manager would usually be a certified public accountant;
- committee of inspection — in the case of liquidations, creditors, at a meeting, may decide to appoint not more than five persons to this committee to look after their interests.

Creditors

Secured creditors

Holders of charges or mortgages on property of a debtor as security for a debt are secured creditors, who can recover their debt wholly or in part from the assets of the debtor before the unsecured creditors.

Preferential creditors

The Companies Act provides for the payment of certain creditors in priority to creditors secured by a floating charge and unsecured creditors. These include:

- taxes and local rates due at the relevant date and due and payable within 12 months prior to that date;
- wages and salaries subject to a maximum of Ush 4,000/- per employee and due within four months prior to the relevant date.

Unsecured creditors

The claims of these creditors rank equally in a liquidation after the settlement of amounts due to secured and preferential creditors.

KPMG contact partner

Andrew Gregory
KPMG Peat Marwick
PO Box 40612
Jubilee Insurance Exchange
1st Floor
Mama Ngina Street
Nairobi
Kenya

Telephone: +254 (2) 222 862
Fax: +254 (2) 215 695

Ukraine

Legislation

Regulations for insolvency procedures in Ukraine are contained in the Law of Ukraine 'On bankruptcy' adopted by the Supreme Council of Ukraine on 14 May 1992, with updates on 17 June 1993, 25 February 1994 and 14 May 1995. The Ukrainian Rada are reviewing proposals for extensive changes to bankruptcy law.

Numerous other legal Acts also incorporate rules of law and procedures relating to bankruptcy. Among these are:

- the Law 'On business associations';
- the Law 'On enterprises';
- the Law 'On foreign investments'.

A considerable number of rules relating to bankruptcy are contained in the Arbitration Procedure Code (APC), and implementation of letters of the National Bank of Ukraine (NBU). Bankruptcy cases are adjudged solely by arbitration courts designated under the APC.

Insolvency procedures

Under current insolvency legislation bankruptcy means 'the failure of any legal entity subject to business activity to meet in a set time period its budgetary liabilities and the claims of creditors due to the lack of liquidity of its assets'. 'Debtors' are defined as legal entities registered as a subject of business activity who are able to meet creditors' claims and to repay debt.

Bankruptcy cases are initiated exclusively against legal entities and not against separate structural units such as representative offices, departments or branches. An individual is not entitled to be a debtor under Ukrainian insolvency law. By definition, an individual cannot be bankrupt and subject to administration. In contrast to other countries, Ukrainian legislation uses the terms bankruptcy and insolvency interchangeably.

An individual may participate in the litigation as a creditor irrespective of whether the case was commenced by the individual's own claim or following a creditors' report issued by the official press body of the Supreme Rada of Ukraine.

The Law of Ukraine 'On bankruptcy' does not apply to foreign legal entities and international companies with permanent residence outside Ukraine.

Stages of bankruptcy

- sanation — a process in which an individual or legal entity applies to the arbitration court to assume the debt;
- trusteeship — a process similar to sanation in which a trustee over the debtor's property is authorised by the arbitration court;
- liquidation — an arbitration court instituted procedure when there are no means of sanation or trusteeship for the debtor.

Sanation and trusteeship are not strictly processes of bankruptcy. When sanation or trusteeship is instituted, any bankruptcy proceedings are terminated because the debt is assumed by another party. Liquidation is the legal consequence of bankruptcy.

The debtor can reserve the right to choose the procedure of reorganisation or bankruptcy if the application to institute bankruptcy was the debtor's own initiative.

Insolvency practitioners

The ability to act as a liquidator, sanator or trustee in bankruptcy proceedings is provided by order of the arbitration court. Individuals or legal entities wishing to participate in the sanation of the debtor must submit a written claim to the court specifying the conditions on which the debt will be assumed.

Petition

Bankruptcy procedures are, in all cases, initiated by a written claim filed by either the debtor or a creditor to the arbitration court.

The arbitration court must follow certain procedures before instituting proceedings against the debtor. In particular, the court must decide whether 'preliminary claims' have been declared to the debtor and whether the claims were met by the debtor within a month. Preliminary claims are not required if the case is initiated by the public prosecutor. Cases are initiated by the public prosecutor when the question of insolvency is raised by the Ukrainian tax inspectorate or by other local authorities.

The requirement to file preliminary claims was introduced under the Arbitration Procedure Code to ensure protection against unjust and fraudulent claims.

Sanation

A process in which an individual or legal entity applies to the arbitration court to assume the debt. The sanator specifies conditions in the application under which the debt will be assumed. The individual or legal entity that wishes to participate in the sanation process has one month from the date of publication of bankruptcy proceedings to file an application with the arbitration court.

The arbitration court will issue a resolution upon the sanation process at the end of the one-month period.

The conditions of sanation are subject to agreement with creditors before the arbitration court will issue a final resolution on the sanation. If adopted, such a resolution must contain:

- an agreement between the debtor and sanator on transferring the debt;
- the reorganisation of the debtor as a legal entity;
- the description of the sanator's payments to the creditors including the terms and conditions of repayment.

When the sanation process is agreed the arbitration court will discontinue the bankruptcy procedure.

Trusteeship

A process similar to sanation, in which a trustee is authorised by the arbitration court to take control over the debtor's property.

In general, the bank providing cash payment and services to a debtor will act as trustee. If the debtor is a State-owned enterprise the duties of trustee will be performed by the State Property Fund.

Liquidation

If sanators are not available to assume the debt or the creditors do not agree to proceed with conditions laid down by sanation, the arbitration court will decide the commencement of bankruptcy proceedings against a debtor. The court is authorised to announce the debtor as bankrupt.

The arbitration court appoints liquidators from a number of creditors' representatives or other financial bodies. If the debtor is a State-owned enterprise then the State Property Fund will be established as the liquidator.

The liquidators are required to set up a commission to investigate the financial position of the debtor and to realise assets. If there is property left after satisfying creditors' claims, the debtor may return to normal trading or other business activity.

From the moment the debtor is declared bankrupt the following consequences will ensue:

- business activity of the debtor is terminated immediately;
- a liquidation commission takes charge over a debtor's property;
- the debtor's liabilities are deemed to have expired;
- all fines and interest incurred by the debtor are cleared.

There are no punitive measures taken against a bankrupt company. The present insolvency legislation does not include any restrictions on company personnel (managing directors, chief accountant, etc.) to engage in future commercial activity. However, if a bankrupt company was engaged in fraudulent activity, including tax evasion, leading to bankruptcy, criminal punishments are established under the Criminal Code.

Creditors

Secured creditors

Secured creditors, being creditors secured by mortgage bonds, are preferential to other distributions, but rank after payment of the costs of the arbitration court and the liquidation proceedings.

Preferential creditors

Creditors for other types of claims have priority in payment after secured creditors. Preferential claims, in order of priority, include:

- obligations to the enterprise's employees, if the bankrupt is a State-owned enterprise, except for the contributions of employees to the authorised fund of the enterprise or stocks held by employees;
- local State taxes and non-tax payments due to the State budget.

Unsecured creditors

The term 'unsecured creditor' applies to creditors not secured by mortgage bonds or not having preferential claims.

Claims of creditors not guaranteed by mortgage bonds rank in priority to contributions of employees to the authorised fund of State enterprises and payments on stocks of the enterprise in the possession of employees.

KPMG contact partner

Graeme Edwards
KPMG
Luteranska 25
Kiev 252024
Ukraine

Telephone: +380 (44) 2934095
Fax: +380 (44) 2293175

United Arab Emirates

Legislation and insolvency procedures

At present there is no federal or emirate law or regulation which comprehensively governs insolvency in UAE although some statutes provide guidance on the subject. The courts in UAE have not developed a standard approach to deal with cases of insolvency, and a few specific cases have been governed by individual emiri decrees. Thus the rights and obligations under insolvency, for both companies and individuals, and the procedures relating to liquidation and receivership, are largely dealt with case by case.

However, the federal laws and emiri decrees provide a framework and guidance for courts to deal with these cases. The federal laws which contain provisions regarding bankruptcy, liquidation, receivership and priority are the Federal Commercial Companies Law, No. 8 of 1984 (FCL), the Federal Civil Transactions Code, No. 5 of 1985 (CTC) and the Federal Labour Law, No. 8 of 1980.

Commercial Companies Law

The FCL provides for dissolution and liquidation of companies by a liquidator appointed by the shareholders of the company or a court of law. The liquidator is empowered to collect assets, to provide public notice of the liquidation and to settle debts.

If there are insufficient assets to pay all the debts then the liquidator may effect payment to the creditors on a pro rata basis. The FCL does not define preferred creditors, but other federal statutes discussed below provide some guidance on priority creditors.

The FCL came into effect on 1 January 1985 but the regulations implementing the law have not yet been issued and so it is impossible to evaluate, at this stage, how the law will be implemented.

Civil Transactions Code

The CTC contains provisions governing liquidation of partnerships. However, while the courts have generally applied the provisions of CTC to commercial as well as civil or non-commercial matters, a federal court has in one instance held that CTC provisions do not apply in a commercial context.

The CTC provisions are broadly similar to the FCL provisions discussed above but also set out the substantive rights of preference among creditors, according secured creditors priority over unsecured creditors.

Emiri decrees

In certain specific cases, appointment of receivers, liquidation and priority among creditors have been dealt with by emiri decree. In one instance the distribution of the assets was carried out in the following order of priority:

- liabilities and expenses of the receivership;
- fees and taxes of the emirate and the federal governments;
- employee salaries and other labour entitlements;
- secured debts up to the amount secured;
- unsecured debts;
- proprietors' share of assets.

Conclusion

Insolvency law in the UAE continues to be dealt with ad hoc. However, some statutory guidance is now available and it is expected that over a period of time the uncertainties inherent in an ad hoc approach will give way to a comprehensive statutory scheme.

KPMG contact partner

Andrew Neden
KPMG Peat Marwick
PO Box 3800
City Tower 1
KPMG Level
Sheikh Zayed Road
Dubai
United Arab Emirates

Telephone: +971 (4) 310222
Fax: +971 (4) 310202

United Kingdom

England, Wales and Northern Ireland

Legislation

Insolvency legislation is consolidated in the Insolvency Act 1986 in England and Wales and the Insolvency (Northern Ireland) Order 1989 in Northern Ireland. The law relating to directors' duties and penalties in relation to insolvent companies is contained in the Company Directors Disqualification Act 1986 and the Companies (Northern Ireland) Order 1989. There is also a considerable amount of case law.

Insolvency law is divided into two areas: the law relating to corporate insolvencies, which encompasses liquidations, administrative receiverships and administrations, and the law relating to individuals (known as 'bankruptcy').

Insolvency procedures

Insolvency procedures in England, Wales and Northern Ireland include:

- receivership — a limited process where a person is appointed to administer specific property owned by a debtor company, on behalf of the person holding a fixed charge or mortgage over the property;
- administrative receivership — a process similar to receivership but usually extending to all the assets owned by a debtor company and covered by a floating charge. A floating charge is said to hover over a debtor company's assets until some default is made in the terms, at which time it becomes fixed on the assets then in existence;
- administration — a process to enable a company to reorganise its business under the control of an administrator and with the sanction of the court;
- liquidation — a formal process of realising a company's assets and distributing the proceeds to creditors in accordance with their rights;
- voluntary arrangement — a procedure to enable a company or an individual to enter into a scheme of arrangement with creditors with the minimum of court involvement;
- bankruptcy — a formal method of realising an individual's assets and distributing the proceeds among the creditors.

Receivership

There are different forms of receivership but usually it means the process whereby the holder of a floating charge appoints an 'administrative receiver', who assumes control of the company's assets and realises them in order to satisfy the claims of the secured creditors. The right to appoint an administrative receiver is given in the security document, often referred to as a 'debenture', containing a floating charge and probably also fixed charges over the debtor company's assets. Borrowings from banks are usually secured by a fixed and/or floating charge over the borrower's assets. The borrowings so secured are usually repayable on demand and in consequence most administrative receivers are appointed by banks. The powers of the administrative receiver include the power to carry on the business and to receive income and realise assets; he is deemed to be the agent of the company unless and until the company enters into liquidation.

An administrative receiver has a duty to seek the highest price possible on the date that he realises assets and in so doing he has an oblique responsibility to all creditors. However, he has a legal responsibility to his appointor and also to the preferential creditors who are entitled to be paid before the floating charge holder. Any surplus remaining on completion of the receivership must be passed to the directors or to the liquidator because an administrative receiver has no power to pay unsecured claims.

The administrative receiver reports to his appointor as they may agree. He must also send a report to and hold a meeting of unsecured creditors within three months of his appointment (unless the court directs otherwise). A committee of creditors may be established. He files an annual summary of his cash transactions with the Registrar of Companies but is not subject to audit.

The executive powers of the directors effectively cease on the appointment of an administrative receiver, who then assumes full powers to direct all functions of the company to which he has been appointed.

The order of application of funds by an administrative receiver is as follows:

- creditors secured by way of a fixed charge, out of the proceeds of their security after costs of realisation;
- administrative receivership costs, including trading expenses;
- the administrative receiver's remuneration;
- preferential creditors;
- creditors secured by way of a floating charge.

Any surplus is then passed to the company or, if the company is in liquidation, its liquidator.

Administration orders

When a company is in financial difficulties and is unable, or likely to become unable, to pay its debts, the directors, shareholders or a creditor can apply to the court for the appointment of an administrator. The court will make the appointment if it is likely to lead to the survival of the company, or part of its business, as a going concern or if it will lead to a more advantageous realisation of the assets than would be the case in a liquidation.

Before the court makes an administration order, it first gives the holder of a floating charge the opportunity to appoint an administrative receiver. If the opportunity is taken, the application for an administrator will fail unless there are reasons to consider the floating charge invalid.

The administrator has three months (or longer if the court allows) to produce a 'statement of proposals' or scheme by which he intends to achieve his objectives. If the scheme is approved by creditors, the administrator puts it into effect and reports to a committee of creditors.

If the scheme is not approved, or fails in its objectives, the company is likely to go into liquidation. If the scheme proves successful, the administration order may eventually be lifted and the company return to normal trading.

During an administration the creditors at the date of the appointment will not be able to press their claims or obtain repayment unless the scheme allows. No steps may be taken to enforce any security over the company's property or to repossess goods in the company's possession, except with the consent of the administrator or the leave of the court. If an administrator wants to dispose of company assets over which there is a fixed charge, such as mortgaged property or assets subject to hire-purchase or retention of title, he first has to get court permission, and the proceeds of realisation will be repayable to the particular secured creditor up to the limit of his security.

The administrator's remuneration and expenses, and debts and liabilities incurred by him, are payable out of the company's assets ahead of any other claims except those of creditors with a fixed charge.

Liquidation

Liquidation is the statutory process for winding up the affairs of a company. The two most common forms are creditors' voluntary liquidation and compulsory liquidation. The first is initiated by the directors who call a meeting first of shareholders and then of the creditors. The meeting of shareholders may nominate a liquidator. The creditors' meeting may confirm the shareholders' nominee as liquidator or replace him with their own choice.

Compulsory liquidation is usually commenced when a creditor presents a winding-up petition to the court, which then normally makes a winding-up order in respect of the debtor company. The official receiver, an official of the Department of Trade (or Department of Economic Development, in Northern Ireland) becomes liquidator; in due course he may call a meeting of the creditors at which they choose whether or not to appoint a liquidator in place of the official receiver.

The function of the liquidator is to realise the company's assets and distribute the proceeds to the various classes of creditors and pay the expenses of the liquidation. The order of distribution is as set out below:

- those holding a fixed charge over property are to be paid out of the realisations, less costs of realisation;
- expenses of liquidation;
- liquidator's remuneration;
- preferential creditors;
- creditors holding a valid floating charge security;
- unsecured, non-preferential creditors;
- interest on unsecured creditors' claims;
- shareholders in accordance with their respective rights.

A company may be wound up voluntarily by means of a members' voluntary liquidation if all its liabilities including interest, can be paid in full within a period of 12 months.

Insolvency practitioners

An authorisation is required before a person may act in any of the following capacities: liquidator, provisional liquidator, administrator, administrative receiver, supervisor of a company's voluntary arrangement, trustee in bankruptcy or individual's deed of arrangement and supervisor of an individual's voluntary arrangement.

Creditors

Secured creditors

A secured creditor is someone who holds a fixed or floating charge over property of the debtor. The holder of a fixed charge has several courses of action available to him following default by the debtor, including the appointment of a receiver to the property which is the subject of the security, entering into possession as mortgagee or allowing the company or its liquidator to realise the security on behalf of the secured creditor. The holder of a floating charge can appoint an administrative receiver (see under Receivership above).

Preferential creditors

In liquidation, creditors for certain types of claims have priority in payment before unsecured creditors. Preferential claims include one year's unremitted employee tax deductions and social security contributions, wages and salaries not exceeding £800 per employee, accrued holiday pay and six months' unremitted value added tax. In administrative receivership, preferential creditors rank ahead of repayments to the holder of a floating charge, but not a fixed charge.

Unsecured creditors

The term 'unsecured creditor' applies to a creditor having a claim which is neither covered by security nor has preferential status.

Other matters

Directors

Legislation provides sanctions against directors of insolvent companies, including 'shadow directors' (i.e., those who in practice have the influence of a director although not formally appointed). Apart from being criminally liable in extreme circumstances, directors can be held personally liable for debts incurred as a result of wrongful trading, i.e., trading beyond the point at which creditors are likely to be paid. They may also be disqualified from holding other directorships. (Directors who are disqualified in England and Wales under the Company Directors Disqualification Act 1986 may not hold office as a company director in Northern Ireland. However, a Northern Ireland director disqualified under the Companies (Northern Ireland) Order 1989 is not similarly barred from holding a directorship in a company registered in England and Wales.)

Scotland

Legislation

Commercial legislation in Scotland is derived from Roman law and it differs from commercial legislation in England. While some legislation is common to both countries, many statutes or parts of statutes apply only to one or the other. The insolvency legislation is in the latter category.

The legislation applicable to insolvency in Scotland underwent considerable change in 1985 and 1986 when the following statutes came into force:

- the Insolvency Act 1986 (together with the Insolvency Practitioners Regulations 1986, the Insolvency (Scotland) Rules 1986 and the Receivers (Scotland) Regulations 1986);
- Company Directors Disqualification Act 1986 (together with the Insolvent Companies (Reports on Conduct of Directors) (No 2) (Scotland) Rules 1986);
- the Bankruptcy (Scotland) Act 1985 (together with the Bankruptcy (Scotland) Regulations 1985) subsequently revised and amended by the Bankruptcy (Scotland) Act 1993.

Further rules are provided in the Rules of Court of the Court of Session and in the Rules of the Sheriff Courts.

In addition to the statutes there is a considerable volume of case law applicable to insolvency.

Insolvency procedures

Insolvency procedures in Scotland include:

- receivership of companies;
- administration of companies;
- liquidation of companies;
- sequestration of individuals and partnerships;
- voluntary trust deeds for creditors of individuals.

Receivership of companies

In accordance with the Insolvency Act 1986 a receiver may be appointed by a creditor holding a floating charge over all or part of the assets of the debtor company, or by the court. He is agent of the company and not of the holder of the floating charge.

In addition to the powers contained in the Act, the receiver has such additional powers as may be granted to him by the instrument creating the floating charge. In distinction from the law of England where the receiver may or may not be a manager, a receiver in Scotland is always a manager and he has statutory powers to carry on the business. On appointment he assumes control of the company's assets and he may realise them either on a going-concern basis or piecemeal. The proceeds are applied first in payment of the claims of the preferential creditors and next in payment of the claim of the floating charge creditor. He has no statutory responsibility towards the unsecured creditors but nevertheless he has a duty to look to their interests. If there is any surplus remaining after payment of the floating charge creditor it will be necessary to put the company into liquidation (if a liquidator has not already been appointed) and the receiver, after meeting his costs, will pay the balance to the liquidator who is responsible for paying any dividends to the ordinary creditors.

The circumstances in which a receiver may be appointed are specified in the instrument creating the floating charge or alternatively the provisions of the Act apply.

Where a company goes into liquidation and certain of the assets are subject to a floating charge the liquidator is obliged to meet the claim of the holder of the floating charge to the extent of the relevant assets after meeting the claims of the preferential creditors but in priority to the claims of the unsecured creditors.

The appointment of a receiver can in appropriate circumstances be implemented very quickly and usually more quickly than the appointment of a liquidator.

Administration of companies

An administrator can act virtually as a receiver in cases where there is no floating charge under which a receiver could be appointed. The administrator is effectively the manager of the company and he is appointed by the court under an administration order. The court will make such an order if it considers that it is likely to achieve the survival of the company as a going concern or a more advantageous realisation of the company's assets than would be effected on a winding up.

The petition to the court for the administration order is made by the company, the directors or a creditor or by all or any of those parties. The administrator is nominated in the order and the term of his appointment is specified.

The administrator may do all such things as may be necessary for the management of the affairs, business and property of the company and he is specifically granted the same powers as those of a receiver. The administrator is required to submit his proposals for the salvation of the company to a meeting of creditors. The creditors may approve the proposals with or without modification but in the event of modification the administrator's consent is required.

Liquidation of companies

There are two principal methods of winding up (or liquidating) insolvent companies:

- winding up by the court;
- creditors' voluntary liquidation.

The legislation for both methods is contained in the parts of the Insolvency Act 1986 which apply to Scotland and in the relevant rules and regulations.

In a winding up by the court the petition may be presented either to the Court of Session or to the appropriate sheriff court. It may be presented either by the company, the directors, any creditor or a contributory (a shareholder) or by all or any of those parties. When the court makes the winding-up order it appoints at the same time an interim liquidator. Within 28 days the interim liquidator is required to summon separate meetings of creditors and contributories for the purpose of electing a liquidator in place of the interim liquidator (and he may in fact be the interim liquidator). In the event that the contributories and the creditors elect different persons as liquidator the nominee of the creditors is appointed.

If on presentation of the winding-up petition the court decides not to appoint an interim liquidator it may appoint a provisional liquidator to carry out whatever functions the court may confer on him. A provisional liquidator's powers are usually limited.

In a creditors' voluntary liquidation the members of the company resolve that by reason of its liabilities the company cannot continue its business and accordingly it should be wound up voluntarily. The members nominate a liquidator. The members' meeting is followed within 14 days by a meeting of the creditors and if the creditors choose to nominate a different person as liquidator, as in the case of winding up by the court, the creditors' nominee is appointed.

In both types of liquidation the principal duty of the liquidator is to gather in and realise the assets of the company and to apply the proceeds in satisfaction of the claims of the creditors according to the creditors' rights. He may carry on the business of a company only to the extent that it is beneficial for the winding up.

Sequestration of individuals and partnerships

The judicial form of bankruptcy of individuals and partnerships is sequestration under the Bankruptcy (Scotland) Act 1985. The petition for sequestration is presented to the Court of Session or to the appropriate sheriff court. It may be presented:

- by the debtor himself provided he has the concurrence of a qualified creditor or creditors (i.e., creditors with debts amounting in total to £1,500); or
- by a qualified creditor or creditors provided the debtor is 'apparently insolvent' and the apparent insolvency was constituted within four months before the petition was presented; or
- by a trustee acting under a voluntary trust deed.

On making the award of sequestration the court appoints an interim trustee. Subsequent to changes in legislation in 1993, the Accountant in Bankruptcy, an official of the Court of Session, will be appointed interim trustee unless the sequestration petition specifically states that an insolvency practitioner has agreed to act as an interim trustee. The interim trustee's primary functions are to safeguard the debtor's estate and to administer the sequestration until a permanent trustee is appointed, to ascertain the reason for the debtor's insolvency and to ascertain the state of his liabilities and assets. If the Accountant in Bankruptcy is interim trustee, he may appoint an insolvency practitioner as his agent to administer the case on his behalf.

In cases where an insolvency practitioner is interim trustee, he must convene a meeting of creditors within 28 days of the date of award of sequestration. If the Accountant in Bankruptcy is interim trustee, he must advise creditors within 60 days of the award of sequestration whether he intends to call a meeting of creditors. Unless a meeting of creditors elects someone other than the interim trustee as permanent trustee, the interim trustee will automatically be appointed as permanent trustee.

The permanent trustee's functions are broadly in line with those of the liquidator in a company winding up. The conduct of the sequestration is supervised by the accountant in bankruptcy. The Act imposes significant procedural and administrative duties on the permanent trustee, particularly in relation to the timing of events and providing the Accountant in Bankruptcy with information.

Voluntary trust deeds for creditors

The judicial process of sequestration may be avoided if the debtor is prepared voluntarily to grant a deed whereby his estate is conveyed to a trustee for the benefit of his creditors generally. The deed is referred to as a 'trust deed'. A trust deed is considerably less formal than a sequestration, and it can usually be completed more quickly, but it is not suitable in all cases. For practical purposes the functions of a trustee under a trust deed are the same as those of a trustee in sequestration without the procedural and administrative chores, and the involvement of the Accountant in Bankruptcy is minimal.

Insolvency practitioners

No person may act as a liquidator, receiver, administrator or trustee unless he is qualified as an insolvency practitioner in accordance with the Insolvency Act 1986. Broadly this means that the person concerned is the holder of an insolvency permit issued by a recognised professional body, for example, the Institute of Chartered Accountants of Scotland, which has rules for securing that its members who wish to act as insolvency practitioners are fit and proper persons so to act and that they meet acceptable requirements as to education, practical training and experience.

Creditors

The principle of an equality of division of assets among creditors is fundamental to the whole statutory scheme and to the voluntary schemes. However, there are some exceptions to this general rule, all of which have a statutory basis.

Secured creditors

A secured creditor is one who holds a heritable security, a charge or lien on property of the debtor as security for a debt (e.g., a floating charge or a hire-purchase agreement) and who is in a position to recoup partly or wholly from the assets which are the subjects of the charge or lien in priority to unsecured creditors. A partly secured creditor is entitled to claim in an insolvency as an ordinary creditor for the unsecured portion of the debt.

A creditor secured by a charge on heritable property is entitled to sell the property in satisfaction of his debt irrespective of whether the debtor has gone through a formal or informal process of insolvency.

A creditor secured by a floating charge has the statutory right to appoint a receiver.

A hire-purchase creditor has a right embodied in the hire-purchase agreement with the debtor to repossess and sell the goods subject to the hire-purchase agreement.

Preferential creditors

The Insolvency Act 1986 and the Bankruptcy (Scotland) Act 1985 both provide for the payment of certain creditors in preference to other unsecured creditors.

The principal preferential creditors are the expenses of the insolvency procedure; wages and salaries including holiday pay currently due for payment (subject to statutory limitations); income tax deducted from emoluments for one year; national insurance contributions for one year; value added tax for six months; and certain legal expenses.

Where a bank (or other person) has advanced money for the payment of salaries and wages to a company, partnership or individual which becomes insolvent, the bank is entitled to the preference that the employees otherwise would have had.

Unsecured creditors

The term 'unsecured creditor' includes all creditors who are neither secured nor preferential.

Other matters

Disqualification of directors

The Company Directors Disqualification Act 1986 requires the liquidator, receiver or administrator to make a report to the Secretary of State on the conduct of the directors of the company. If the report is adverse, the

Secretary of State is empowered to apply to the court for a disqualification order whereby the person concerned will be disqualified from acting as a director for the period specified in the order.

KPMG contact partner

Mike Wheeler
KPMG
20 Farringdon Street
London
EC4A 4PP
United Kingdom

Telephone: +44 (171) 311 1000
Fax: +44 (171) 311 3606

United States of America

Legislation

United States law governing formal business and personal financial reorganisations or liquidations is divided between federal and state law. Most significant formal reorganisations or liquidations are administered under the jurisdiction of the federal bankruptcy court pursuant to the Bankruptcy Reform Act of 1978, Pub L No. 95–598 (which, with subsequent amendments, the latest being the Bankruptcy Reform Act of 1994, are collectively referred to as the Bankruptcy Code). The Bankruptcy Code was intended to establish processes to achieve two sometimes contradictory objectives: (a) collection and equitable distribution of the debtor's assets, and (b) relief from debt for the benefit of the debtor.

The new Bankruptcy Code grants original and exclusive jurisdiction to the United States federal district courts.

Insolvency procedures

The Bankruptcy Code of the United States is divided into two separate areas. The first area, including Chapters 1, 3 and 5 of the Code, applies generally to all kinds of bankruptcies, regardless of what type of relief a debtor or its creditors opt for. This area contains general provisions such as definitions, rules of construction, administration procedures, rights and obligations of debtors, and claims by the creditors. The second area, including Chapters 7, 9, 11 and 13 offer a debtor or creditor specific kinds of relief. Chapter 12 offers a family farmer relief, Chapter 7 provides for liquidations, Chapter 9 applies to the adjustment of debts of an insolvent municipality or other governmental unit, Chapter 11 governs reorganisations and Chapter 13 provides for the adjustment of debt of small businesses and individuals with regular income.

Liquidation

A Chapter 7 case is a liquidation of all of the debtor's assets and a consequent discontinuance of its business. It can be brought about voluntarily by the debtor or involuntarily by the filing of a petition by the creditors. The objective of a Chapter 7 case is to marshal the assets of a debtor as expeditiously as possible, and then liquidate and distribute the proceeds of those assets to creditors in accordance with the statutory scheme.

Reorganisation

A Chapter 11 case is generally commenced with the intention of reorganising the business of the debtor. The objective is to continue the business as a going concern under the protection of the bankruptcy court. The debtor attempts to identify the causes of its financial distress, and scale down or close inefficient operations, reject leases and other agreements, effect changes in management, obtain new financing and engage in mergers, sales of assets or other dispositions. The major goal of a Chapter 11 case is to negotiate and confirm a Chapter 11 plan which repays to creditors designated amounts of money (or percentages of debt) and/or an equity interest and creates an ongoing, viable business entity.

Plan of reorganisation

The debtor has the exclusive right to file a plan for 120 days (plus additional time at the discretion of the bankruptcy court) after filing the bankruptcy petition.

Thereafter, any party in interest, including the trustee, a creditors' committee, or a creditor, may file a plan if (a) a trustee has been appointed; (b) the debtor does not file within the 120-day period; or (c) the debtor files a plan within the 120 days but fails to obtain the required consent within 180 days. The Bankruptcy Code specifies the contents of a plan of reorganisation. A plan must: designate classes of claims and classes of interest; specify the classes of claims or interests that are impaired and unimpaired; provide the same treatment for each claim or interest of a particular class; provide adequate means for the plan's execution; prohibit the issuance of non-voting equity securities and provide for an appropriate distribution of voting power among the various classes of equity securities. A plan must contain only provisions consistent with the interest of creditors and equity security holders, and with public policy.

The court holds a hearing on confirmation of the plan at which any party in interest may interpose objections. A condition of confirmation is acceptance by each class of creditors and by the shareholders. Two thirds in amount and more than half in number of each class of creditors must accept the plan. Two thirds in amount, regardless of number, is required for shareholders. At least one class of claimants must accept the plan. If a class does not accept the plan, it may, nevertheless, be confirmed if the court finds that the class remains unimpaired by the plan.

Who can be appointed?

US trustees

The US trustee is to be an employee of the Executive Branch, and is under the direct supervision of the US Attorney-General. The US trustee, and his assistants, manage, appoint, and supervise panels of private trustees in the administrative aspects of the bankruptcy case in all districts.

Private trustees

In a Chapter 7 liquidation case, an independent, disinterested trustee represents the estate and has the duty of marshalling the assets and administering the distribution of proceeds. The trustee is generally appointed by the US trustee from a standing panel of trustees, but may be elected by creditors.

Trustees are empowered to retain attorneys, accountants, appraisers and other necessary professionals; to sue and be sued, to sell or lease property of the estate; and to avoid certain pre-petition transfers of the debtor for the benefit of unsecured creditors.

A trustee must account for property received, investigate the financial affairs of the debtor, examine claims and make appropriate objections to improper claims, oppose the discharge of the debtor if warranted and fulfil a reporting obligation to the court, government agencies and other parties.

Debtor-in-possession

In a Chapter 11 reorganisation case, the management of the debtor continues to operate the business as a debtor-in-possession unless a trustee is appointed. A debtor-in-possession has the same duties and powers as a trustee, including the power to retain attorneys and accountants. A trustee is only appointed upon a showing of fraud, dishonesty or mismanagement. The duties and powers of a Chapter 11 trustee are similar to those of a Chapter 7 trustee.

Examiners

In reorganisation cases under Chapter 11, the court may appoint an examiner rather than a trustee, upon a showing that such appointment is in the best interests of creditors or that the fixed liabilities of the debtor exceed a certain level. The duties of the examiner are the same as those of a trustee to the extent that the examiner shall investigate the affairs of the debtor, its financial condition, its operation and the desirability of its continuance. The examiner shall file a report of the results of his investigation, and distribute it as directed by the court.

Creditors' committees

Creditors' committees are appointed in Chapter 11 cases from among the persons who hold the largest claims of a particular kind against the debtor. Unsecured creditors' committees are regularly appointed and other committees of creditors or equity security holders may be appointed upon request. A creditors' committee performs an oversight function and may consult with the trustee or debtor concerning case administration, investigate the assets and liabilities and financial affairs of the debtor, participate in the negotiation and formulation of a plan, and request appointment of a trustee or examiner if warranted. Each of these committees also has the power to retain accountants and attorneys.

Creditors

The reform of the Bankruptcy Law through the enactment of the Bankruptcy Code is intended to balance more equitably the interests of different classes of creditors, and give greater recognition to the interests of general unsecured creditors who enjoy no priority in the distribution of the assets of the debtor's estate.

Secured creditors

For purposes of the Code 'creditor' means an entity that has a claim against the debtor that arose at the time of or before the filing of a petition in bankruptcy. A 'security agreement' is the agreement that creates or provides for a security interest. A 'security interest' is the lien created by such an agreement and includes a mortgage obtained on real property.

The Bankruptcy Code focuses on concepts which affect the collateral of a secured creditor, the relationship between the secured party and the debtor's estate, and methods by which a secured party's interest in collateral may be protected.

The filing of a petition in bankruptcy effects an 'automatic stay' of creditor activity aimed at enforcement of rights against the debtor or against the property of the estate obtained prior to commencement of bankruptcy proceedings. However, the Bankruptcy Code authorises the courts to grant relief from the automatic stay at the request of a 'party in interest' which would include a secured creditor. The trustee or debtor-in-possession is required to provide a method of protection such as '(1) requiring the trustee to make periodic cash payments to the secured creditor, to the extent that the stay . . . or grant of a lien . . . results in a decrease in the value of the secured creditor's interest in such property or by providing to the secured creditor an additional or replacement lien to the extent that such stay, use, sale, lease, or grant results in a decrease in the value of the secured party's interest in such property' (11 USC §361(1), (2)). These two methods are based on the idea that a secured creditor should receive the value of his bargain. Additionally, the court is authorised to condition or prohibit the use, sale or lease of property when it is necessary to provide adequate protection to a secured creditor's interest in the property (11 USC §363(e)). Where a creditor is under-secured the claim will be treated as secured to the extent of the value of the collateral, and unsecured as to any balance.

Unsecured creditors

Unsecured creditors include anyone who holds a pre-petition claim against the debtor with no security interest. A claim includes a right to payment whether or not such right is reduced to judgment, liquidated, unliquidated, fixed, contingent, matured, unmatured, disputed, undisputed, legal, equitable, secured or unsecured; or a right to an equitable remedy for a breach of performance if such breach gives right to a payment, whether or not such right is reduced to judgment, fixed, contingent, matured, unmatured, disputed, undisputed, secured or unsecured (11 USC 101 (5)(A) and (B)). The effect of this broad definition is to ensure that all legal obligations of the debtor will be dealt with in the bankruptcy proceeding, irrespective of the nature of the debt.

Unsecured creditors may petition the bankruptcy court to commence a Chapter 7 or 11 bankruptcy case against a debtor involuntarily. With certain exceptions, an involuntary petition must be filed by at least three creditors each of which holds a claim that is not contingent and is not subject to a bona fide dispute, and only if the unsecured portions of the petitioners' claims aggregate at least $10,000. The petitioning creditors must show that the debtor is generally not paying its debts as they become due or that within 120 days prior to the filing of the petition a custodian was appointed or took possession of substantially all of the debtor's property.

In a Chapter 7 liquidation case, the holders of allowable, unsecured claims may elect a committee of not less than three or more than 11 creditors. In a Chapter 11 case, the committee is not elected by the creditors but is appointed by the US trustee and will ordinarily be composed of representatives of the seven largest unsecured claims against the debtor. The committee may consult with the trustee in connection with the administration of the estate and make recommendations to the trustee as well as submit questions to the court regarding the administration of the estate.

Priority claims

Precedence is given to certain kinds of unsecured debts in the order they will receive distribution from the estate. Generally, secured debts are the first to be satisfied out of the estate's assets. After the secured debts are satisfied, the unsecured debts are paid. Certain types of unsecured debts have been given a priority over general claims as well as an order among themselves. Creditors' claims not entitled to priority are general claims and are satisfied pro rata from the remaining assets of the estate after secured and priority claims are paid.

First priority in the distribution of unsecured claims is given to administration expenses, This is intended to include most taxes incurred during the administration of the estate. Second priority goes to creditors who dealt with a debtor subject to an involuntary petition after commencement but prior to either appointment of trustee or order for relief. Third priority is held by wage claimants up to a maximum of $2,000. Fourth priority is given to contributions to employee benefits plans such as pension, health or life insurance plans. Fifth priority is given to consumer creditors arising from deposits for purchase or lease of property or services for consumer purposes. The sixth and last general priority lies in favour of governmental units for unsecured claims for taxes of various kinds.

Other matters

The United States Bankruptcy Code provides a workable method by which creditors are equitably treated, and the debtor is given a realistic 'fresh start' after bankruptcy. The role of the accountants in bankruptcy proceedings is essential. No trustee, debtor-in-possession or creditor committee can effectively do its job without the professional assistance, knowledge and cooperation of qualified accountants and attorneys. Bankruptcy proceedings require a close working relationship between the accountants and attorneys so that the ultimate results for the clients can be maximised.

KPMG contact partner

Dale R. Metz
KPMG Peat Marwick LLP
99 High Street
Boston, MA 02110-2371
USA

Telephone: + 1(617) 988-1038
Fax: + 1(617) 988-0800

Uruguay

Legislation

Uruguayan legislation for bankruptcy and liquidation is mainly contained in:

- Book IV, Commercial Code, for insolvency in a commercial activity (except corporations);
- Act No. 2.230 of 2 June 1893, regarding the liquidation of corporations.

Insolvency procedures

Insolvency regulations provide different types of procedures:

- bankruptcy, in a narrow sense (*quiebra*);
- pre-bankruptcy scheme of arrangement (*concordato preventivo, concordato en la quiebra*).

Bankruptcy

Anyone conducting a business who ceases to pay his debts is liable to be adjudicated bankrupt by decision of the competent court following his own admission of insolvency, the petition of one or more creditors or by the court of its own motion. The bankruptcy adjudication removes control of administration of the debtor's present and future property from the debtor.

The competent court appoints a receiver who assumes wide administration powers over the bankrupt company's assets in order to dispose of them and satisfy the creditors on an equal basis, after satisfying priority creditor's debts.

Although one of the leading principles of the Uruguayan bankruptcy procedure is the equality of division of assets among creditors, legislation provides for the payment of certain creditors before others.

Secured creditors do not have to wait for the result of the bankruptcy procedure to take action against the debtor's property. They are in a position (stated by law) to recoup, wholly or partly, their debts in priority to unsecured creditors.

The first step of the bankruptcy procedure consists of an examination of the company's accounts and the preparation of a detailed inventory of all its assets by the receiver. Within the time limit fixed by the court, creditors must present to the receiver a statement of claims. Subsequently, he submits for the court's approval a report on the bankrupt business. A creditors' meeting is called in order to verify the debts and to enable the receiver to prepare a list of the bankrupt's liabilities. If within a term of 10 days after this list is prepared, the debtor does not present a scheme of arrangement, the receiver begins the liquidation of the assets. They are sold in the best possible way and the proceeds divided among all creditors. Finally, the receiver draws up a definitive statement of accounts and the court decrees the end of the bankruptcy procedure.

A bankruptcy procedure may involve criminal consequences and prevents the bankrupt, for a certain period, from carrying out any business activity.

Scheme of arrangement

A scheme of arrangement is a court-approved arrangement between a company and its creditors, mainly providing for a moratorium, relief from part of the debt, or both.

The company does not lose administration powers over its assets, but a scheme manager is appointed by the court and has a general power of control over the business. This type of arrangement is usually entered into when the creditors are of the opinion that they are more likely to obtain a greater benefit if the company continues operating under the control of a scheme manager than from winding up.

Other matters

The Uruguayan parliament is considering introducing an important reform to insolvency legislation in order to make it more efficient in preserving both debtors' and creditors' rights.

KPMG contact partner

Jorge Barsantini
KPMG Uruguay Ltda
Plaza de Cagancha 1335 of. 702
11100 Montevideo
Uruguay

Telephone: +598 (2) 924 546
Fax: +598 (2) 921 337

Uzbekistan

Legislation

Uzbek insolvency legislation is relatively new and undergoing continuous development. Under the Soviet system, all enterprises were deemed to be branches of the State, and therefore no bankruptcy was possible. Liquidation through reorganisation was possible, but it was an administrative and logistical exercise.

Although insolvency legislation has been passed in Uzbekistan and there is some evidence that insolvency proceedings have been instituted, the process is neither common nor even the automatic result of an irredeemable financial position. This is due partly to lack of experience and partly to what seems to be a 'Soviet' belief that companies, once founded, cannot or should not die.

Current insolvency legislation is closely related to the legislation in Russia as both have evolved from the same system and Russian legislation is more readily accessible. Uzbek insolvency legislation is based on the Law on Insolvency (Bankruptcy), which was passed in May 1994. Since then the legislation has been considerably modified and developed by Presidential Decrees and other enabling legislation.

Further development is certain and so these notes are merely indicative of the current situation.

Insolvency procedures

Types of insolvency procedure

- reorganisation — the business is placed in the hands of an external management, which may be charged with its rehabilitation;
- liquidation — this occurs (a) if a court has declared the enterprise insolvent, or (b) if the enterprise declares itself insolvent;
- amicable settlement — the enterprise comes to an agreement with its creditors involving the deferral of payment of debts, payment by instalment, or debt forgiveness.

Parties to an insolvency action

The legislation recognises various parties in an insolvency action, including:

- proxy manager — the proxy manager is authorised to carry on the business, recruit and dismiss employees, dispose of assets, call meetings of the creditors, and draw up a plan for an external management and execute the plan;
- receiver -- the receiver may dispose of assets, act in an arbitration court to contest the validity of contracts completed up to six months prior to the initiation of arbitration proceedings, collect debts and receivables, form a liquidation committee and call a creditors' meeting;
- liquidation committee — the committee is required to draw up a liquidation plan;
- creditors;
- representatives of the workforce;
- the debtor.

Petition

An insolvency action is initiated by a petition to the arbitration court from:

- the debtor, either the owner of the enterprise or its management — such a petition cannot be withdrawn;
- a creditor, after the lapse of three months from the due date for payment for goods or services, the due date being defined as the date of delivery of a demand for payment by registered post; or
- a procurator (public prosecutor), if it has been determined that a fictitious insolvency action has been initiated, or if the law of the Russian Federation requires the initiation of insolvency proceedings.

The court may either refuse the petition if it is established that the creditor's claim can be met or the defendant is solvent, or it may recognise the defendant as insolvent, in which case liquidation proceedings will be instituted.

If a petition is received for the debtor enterprise to be reorganised, the court may decide to postpone the declaration of insolvency and instead institute rehabilitation or external management procedures.

Reorganisation

In the event of there being a real possibility of solvency being restored to the enterprise as a result of financial aid being given by the owner or third parties to the enterprise, the arbitration court may institute rehabilitation proceedings. Rehabilitation is not possible if insolvency proceedings are reopened within 36 months.

Within 12 months of the start of rehabilitation, the enterprise must have met at least 40 per cent of the combined creditor claims. Rehabilitation may not last for more than 18 months, which can be prolonged a further six months. Rehabilitation ceases when 18 months have elapsed or it is determined by the court that rehabilitation is ineffective, in which case liquidation proceedings must be instituted.

Rehabilitation is deemed successful when all claims have been met and the insolvency action can be closed.

Liquidation proceedings

Once a debtor has been declared insolvent, liquidation proceedings commence with the arbitration court appointing a receiver. The liquidation proceedings must also include representatives of the workforce and other interested parties.

The receiver has a duty to obtain the highest price for the debtor's assets. The proceeds of the realisation of assets are distributed in the following order:

- expenses related to the liquidation proceedings;
- expenses of the proxy manager and receiver;
- expenses related to the continuing operations of the enterprise;
- claims of individuals whom the debtor has injured or prejudiced;
- payment of the workforce;
- payments to the State Pension Fund;
- taxes and social security contributions;
- claims secured by assets;
- creditor claims;
- claims of shareholders who are members of the workforce;
- all other claims.

Injured individuals, the workforce, and taxes and social security contributiions are considered privileged creditors.

The liquidator will be monitored by a creditors' committee, which will also determine the receiver's remuneration.

Amicable settlement

A settlement among the non-privileged creditors may be reached at any point in the insolvency proceedings with the consent of two thirds of the creditors; it may not infringe on the settlement of the privileged claims and must be endorsed by the court. Creditors must receive at least 35 per cent of their settlement within two weeks of the settlement date. The settlement may be rendered void if (a) the terms are not satisfied, (b) the financial position of the debtor deteriorates, (c) the debtor infringes on the rights and interests of the creditors.

KPMG contact partner

Roger Munnings
KPMG
37 Ul. Novaya Basmannaya
3rd Floor
Moscow 107066
Russia

Telephone: +7 (502) 222 4030
Fax: +7 (502) 222 4024

Vanuatu

Legislation

At the time that the New Hebrides gained independence in 1980 from joint rule by France and England, the laws applicable to companies were, to a large extent, those which had been developed from the English legal system. The majority of companies were registered under the former British laws which were applicable in the New Hebrides. Running parallel with this system there was also the French legal system under which companies could be registered. These two systems continued after the New Hebrides gained independence and changed its name to Vanuatu. In 1986 a new act entitled the Companies Act (c. 191) was introduced which brought together the two previous systems and required the re-registration of all French companies and conversion to English-style companies. Insolvency law in Vanuatu is based principally upon the English system.

Insolvency procedures

The winding up of a company in Vanuatu may be either by the court or voluntary.

Court winding up

A company may be wound up by the court for the following reasons:

- the passing of a special resolution that the company be wound up by the court;
- default in delivery of the annual return;
- non-commencement or suspension of business for a whole year;
- reduction in the number of members below the prescribed minimum;
- inability of the company to pay its debts;
- the court considers that the company should be wound up;
- the company is in persistent breach of its duties or obligations under law;
- non-appointment of a secretary or directors;
- non-payment of annual fees;
- non-determination of registered office or absence of statutory records;
- the company is being carried on for an unlawful purpose.

The procedure for a court winding-up can be commenced either by the company or its creditors. On the making of a winding-up order, the court would normally appoint the official receiver ('receiver') of companies. The court retains control of the winding-up procedure throughout the period of winding up, until a final report is prepared by the receiver.

A statement of the company's affairs is required to be submitted to the receiver within 14 days from the date of the court order. Following the receipt of the statement of affairs the receiver is required to make a report to the court in respect of the amount of capital issued, the reason why the company has failed and whether, in his opinion, fraud has been committed.

For the purpose of conducting the winding up the court may appoint a liquidator. In the case where a liquidator is not appointed by the court, the receiver carries out the duties of the liquidator of the company. A liquidator appointed by the court may resign or may be removed by the court. The liquidator's powers conferred by the court shall be subject to the control of the court, as are his fees.

The liquidator in a winding up by the court shall have the power, with the sanction either of the court or of a committee of inspection, to bring or defend actions in the name of and on behalf of the company. He may also carry on the company's business so far as may be necessary for the beneficial winding up of the company and he may appoint a legal practitioner to assist him in the performance of his duty. The liquidator may pay any classes of creditors in full or compromise or make arrangements with creditors with the sanction of the court or the committee of inspection. The liquidator has the power to sell the company's assets, to carry out acts on the company's behalf and to use the company's seal where necessary, and to do all such things as may be necessary for winding up the affairs of the company and distributing its assets.

The liquidator is required to keep proper books of the transactions during the liquidation period and is required at least twice a year to prepare an account of his receipts and payments which are required to be audited. The court may make an order for inspection of the books of the company by the creditors.

Following the final distribution of all available funds, a statement of receipts and payments is prepared by the liquidator and submitted to the court for approval. On receipt of the court's approval the liquidator obtains a discharge from his duties, and an announcement is made through the *Government Gazette* that the company has been struck off.

Voluntary winding up

A company may be wound up voluntarily by a members' resolution if it is able to pay all its debtors. However, if a declaration of solvency cannot be made then a voluntary winding up must be made by a resolution of the creditors. A creditors' voluntary winding up is governed by the same procedures as those set out above in respect of a court liquidation, except that the creditors have similar powers to those of the court in respect of the appointment, receipt of reports and final discharge of the liquidator.

Receivership

Receivers and/or managers are able to be appointed to a company to manage the property of the company secured by floating and fixed charges or under the powers contained in any other instrument on behalf of the charge holders. Where land in Vanuatu forms part of security a court appointment is also required.

The powers of the receiver are conferred by the instrument under which he was appointed and regulated by the Companies Act and English law.

Upon appointment the receiver is required to notify the company and the Financial Services Commission ('FSC') and request a statement of affairs be provided by the directors within 14 days. The receiver is required to lodge the statement within two months with the FSC and debenture holders together with any comments thereon.

The receiver is also required to forward an abstract of receipts and payments to the FSC on a semi-annual or annual basis and at the conclusion of the appointment.

Scheme of arrangement

If the creditors of a company so agree, a scheme of arrangement can be put in place with the sanction of the court.

A 'manager' is appointed to administer a scheme of arrangement. The primary objectives of the scheme manager are to save the company from liquidation or receivership, and to trade out of the difficulties such that the creditors are paid in accordance with the compromise that is reached when the scheme is put in place.

This type of arrangement is sometimes referred to as a voluntary administration, and it affords a greater level of control by the company over the company's affairs than a full liquidation or receivership.

Creditors

Preferential treatment is given to wages and salaries, accrued holiday pay, and certain payments to the government for rates and taxes. Such liabilities are paid in priority to all other creditors. The treatment of foreign creditors is no different to that of local creditors. Any remaining funds after all creditors have been paid would be returned to the shareholders.

KPMG contact partner

Bill Hawkes
KPMG
PO Box 212
Port Vila
Vanuatu

Telephone: +678 22 091
Fax: +678 23 665

Venezuela

Legislation

Practitioners involved in liquidations, corporate administrations and who act as syndics operate within the statutory framework of the Venezuelan Commercial Code.

Insolvency procedures

Insolvency procedures in the Venezuelan Commercial Code are applied in relation to all persons who are unable to fulfil their financial obligations. Insolvency procedures include:

- liquidation;
- administration by syndic;
- scheme of arrangement.

Two further categories of insolvency exist:

- insolvency of a deceased trader (limited to the year following death);
- insolvency of a retired trader (for a period of five years following retirement and only if payment of liabilities ceased before retirement).

Liquidation

Liquidation procedures may be described as follows:

- 'in arrears' and 'amicable liquidation'. A trader whose assets exceed his liabilities but who, through unforeseen lack of cash, finds himself compelled to postpone payment to his creditors will be considered as being 'in arrears' and may apply to the appropriate commercial court for authorisation to deal with his affairs by way of 'amicable liquidation';
- serious insolvency. The court may order the winding up of a company which, not being 'in arrears', ceases to pay its liabilities.

Every insolvent trader must give written notice of insolvency to the proper commercial court within three days of ceasing to pay creditors, giving reasons for the insolvency. The court will then decide the appropriate course.

An undischarged bankrupt cannot continue or resume trading. Payment of liabilities in full entitles the bankrupt to be discharged even after his death.

A liquidator must be a person with business experience. A syndic must be a lawyer. A syndic must be:

- over 21 years of age;
- not an undischarged bankrupt;
- not a spouse or relative of the bankrupt;
- not a creditor whose claim is disputed.

The creditors may resolve that they themselves should conduct the liquidation. Provided the resolution is passed by a majority of the creditors shown in the debtor's records, the court, without prejudice to any criminal proceeding which may be brought, will authorise liquidation by the creditors.

Three types of insolvency are recognised by the Venezuelan Commercial Code:

- fortuitous (i.e., non-culpable);
- culpable;
- fraudulent.

The last two types are dealt with under the Criminal Code, which also covers the actions of antecedents and issue of the bankrupt who had knowledge of the situation or who received or hid the insolvent's assets.

Administration by syndic

Under the Commercial Code a syndic represents all the creditors and has power to manage, protect and realise the company's assets. A syndic is appointed by the court. He may be dismissed at any time on application to the commercial court by the insolvent company, by its creditors or by former officers of the company on the grounds of inexperience, negligence, fraud or conspiracy.

Scheme of arrangement

At any stage of insolvency proceedings an agreement may be reached between the debtor and his creditors, provided all the creditors agree. For example, they can agree to terminate or suspend the insolvency process. In order for the agreement to be effective it must be sanctioned by the commercial court, which will have received a report from the syndic on the nature of the insolvency and the propriety of the agreement.

The agreement with the debtor does not deprive creditors of their right to pursue third-party guarantors for the full amount of their claims.

Creditors may reach such an agreement with a 'culpable' debtor but not with a 'fraudulent' debtor.

Creditors

A preferential or secured creditor is generally one who has a charge or mortgage on the debtor's assets.

Where there is to be an agreement between a debtor and his creditors, preferential and secured creditors may attend the first meeting of creditors, but may not vote in the proceedings unless they give up their rights of priority. If they vote they will be taken to have renounced their entitlement to priority.

Other creditors are all those not in the above category. Such creditors may resolve that they themselves should conduct the insolvency proceedings. They may nominate three candidates for appointment as a syndic from whom the court will appoint one together with a creditors' committee to supervise the liquidation.

Preferential claims

The Venezuelan Commercial Code provides for the payment of preferential and secured creditors. Creditors without such priority will receive dividends from the proceeds of realisation of the debtor's assets in proportion to their agreed claims. The syndic makes such distributions only after deducting the costs and disbursements of the liquidation and any allowance made to the debtor including statutory legal costs.

Other matters

The Capital Market Law contains certain provisions, which protect the stockholders of companies regulated by the National Securities Commission in case of their bankruptcy or liquidation. In this situation the National

Securities Commission personnel may act as liquidator or syndic, according to the Venezuelan Commercial Code.

The Venezuelan Income Tax Law provides special privileges over other creditors in favour of the National Treasury to collect income taxes, fines and interest on delayed payments. Only salaries and other rights derived from the labour law or collective labour contracts, and creditors secured by mortgages or pledges have prior rights over the National Treasury.

KPMG contact partner

Jorge L. Rodriguez
Alcaraz Cabrera Vazquez
Edifico Selemar, Piso 12
Apartado No. 5972
Calle Los Mangos Con Av.
Francisco Solano
Sabana Grande
Caracas 1050-A
Venezuela

Telephone: +58 (2) 706 7711
Fax: +58 (2) 762–0448

Virgin Islands (British)

Insolvency procedures

Receivership

As there is no local statutory law regarding receiverships, reference is made to English common law which applies in the British Virgin Islands.

Where a company borrows money from a bank or some other lending institution it will usually give the lender a mortgage debenture over its assets as security. That mortgage debenture will normally state that the lender may appoint a receiver, or receiver and manager, if certain events occur. The most common events are the failure of the borrower to repay the debt to the lender when requested to do so, or the occurrence of one or more specified events which may put the security in jeopardy.

Immediately following his appointment, the receiver, or receiver and manager, assumes control of assets that were charged as security to the lender. In nearly all cases, all of a company's assets have been pledged and the receiver therefore has control of the whole of the company's assets with the power to manage it given to him by the debenture.

The primary duty of the receiver and manager, who acts as agent of the company, is to realise sufficient assets of the company to repay the lender who has security over the assets. In so doing he must act with reasonable regard to the rights of the company and other creditors. He will attempt to do this either by selling the business as a going concern or by selling the assets separately.

The principal effect on the outside world is that the company's liabilities are effectively frozen at the date of the receiver's appointment. The receiver will collect moneys due to the company but is not directly responsible for paying liabilities owing by the company prior to his appointment. He is responsible for paying for any goods and services that are purchased or employed under his instruction and he will make payments to the statutory preferred creditors (if any) and then to the debenture holder. Arguably, redundancy payments under the BVI Labour Code Act have the status of preferential debts but no other BVI statute gives creditors preference in receivership.

Voluntary liquidation

The Companies Act does not differentiate between a creditors' winding up and a voluntary winding up. However, the shareholders may delegate the power of appointing a liquidator to the creditors or a committee of creditors.

The International Business Companies Act ('IBC Act') does distinguish between the winding up of a solvent or insolvent company. The voluntary winding up of an international business company ('IBC') occurs under the provisions of the IBC Act but if the directors or members, at the time of passing the winding-up resolution, or the liquidator after his appointment, have reason to believe that the company is insolvent they must give notice of the fact to the Registrar of Companies and then all winding-up and dissolution proceedings take place under the provisions of the Companies Act.

In a voluntary liquidation, the assets and liabilities of a company are placed under the control of a liquidator who terminates the affairs of the company. Unless otherwise resolved, the powers of the directors cease upon the appointment of a liquidator.

In practice the directors of a company incorporated under the Companies Act decide that it is not possible or not necessary for the company to continue to trade and they call a meeting of the shareholders. The shareholders' meeting is held and the company is formally placed into liquidation by special resolution and a liquidator is nominated, unless the appointment is delegated to the creditors. For an IBC the directors must approve a plan of liquidation, which must be approved by a resolution of members. The winding up of an IBC commences when articles of dissolution, containing the plan of dissolution, are filed with the Registrar or on such subsequent date, not exceeding 30 days, as may be specified in the articles of dissolution.

The liquidator supervises the winding up of the company and is only permitted to continue to trade in exceptional circumstances. His duty is to collect in all the assets of the company and convert them into cash, and to ascertain and pay all the liabilities of the company. When this task has been completed he distributes any surplus funds to the shareholders and, after filing the appropriate returns, the company is dissolved. The assets of an IBC, and also of a company incorporated under the Companies Act, where the company's articles of association permit, may be distributed *in specie*.

A creditor who has security over an asset of the company is entitled to realise that security in order to satisfy the debt due to him, any funds surplus to that requirement being handed to the liquidator. Certain creditors have priority over others, as defined by legislation. In broad terms the priorities are:

- employees (for small amounts prescribed in the Companies Act);
- secured creditors (those to whom assets have been charged including land and house taxes under the Registered Land Act);
- unsecured creditors (proportionately if the assets are insufficient for them to be paid in full);
- shareholders.

Winding up by the court

As in a voluntary liquidation, the assets and liabilities of a company are placed under the control of a liquidator who terminates the affairs of the company. The liquidation is conducted in a more formal manner under the supervision of the court.

Any person who is a creditor of a company for US$240 or more is entitled to make formal demand for payment, and failure to comply with that demand will give that person the right to petition the court for the company to be wound up because it is unable to pay its debts.

The liquidator will take all necessary steps to secure the assets of the company and will call upon the directors of the company to prepare a detailed statement of affairs of the company.

From that point onwards the liquidator will do the same job as has been detailed above (under voluntary liquidation) but is required to file certain information with the court concerning the conduct of the liquidation. The effect of a company being wound up by the court is the same as in a voluntary liquidation (see above) but creditors must make formal proof of their debts before the liquidator will admit their claims.

Striking off

Every company incorporated in the British Virgin Islands is registered with the government's Registrar of Companies. When a company ceases to exist it is struck off the register.

Many companies, either individually or as part of a group, become dormant. If such a company is incorporated under the Companies Act the directors may write to the Registrar of Companies and suggest that the Registrar may wish to strike it off the register. At any time after the striking off, the company or a member thereof (but not a creditor) may apply to the court to have the name of the company restored. In the case of an IBC that has been struck off for failing to comply with certain statutory requirements, the IBC or any member, creditor or liquidator thereof may apply to the court to have the name of the company restored.

A company licence fee is payable annually except in the year of incorporation and if the fee is not paid by the due date in any year, the name of the company will, within time limits, be struck off the register automatically.

A company incorporated under the Companies Act may, within two months of being struck off under the terms of the above, and an IBC within three years of being struck off, apply to the Registrar to restore the name to the register.

Other matters

Under existing legislation there are very few restrictions on who may act as receiver or liquidator but, in general, an accountant or solicitor is appointed.

KPMG contact partner

John J. Greenwood
KPMG
Tropic Isle Building
PO Box 650
Road Town, Tortola
British Virgin Islands

Telephone: +1 (809) 494 5800
Fax: +1 (809) 494 6565

Yemen

Legislation

Yemeni insolvency law is based upon the relevant legislation in the Middle East, mainly in the Arab countries and Egypt in particular. The legislation is included in the following:

- Commercial Law — Law No. (32) of 1991;
- Company Law — Law No. (34) of 1991;
- Banks Law — Law No. (36) of 1991.

No major changes in these laws are expected.

A competent commercial court may appoint the following:

- liquidator;
- insolvency manager.

Auditors and officers of the debtor company or firm are normally disqualified from acting as either a liquidator or insolvency manager unless the court decides otherwise.

Insolvency procedures

Liquidation

Liquidation is the statutory process for winding up the affairs of a company. This process may be:

- voluntary liquidation — this is normally initiated by the directors who call a meeting of the shareholders/partners who, by majority, appoint a liquidator. The creditors normally meet shortly afterwards and confirm the nomination or replace him with their own choice;
- compulsory liquidation — this is normally initiated when a creditor presents a winding up petition to the court. The court then normally makes a winding-up order and appoints the liquidator. The winding up of commercial or specialised banks can be requested by the Central Bank of Yemen which supervises and controls their activity.

As soon as the resolution or court order is received the liquidator prepares the financial statements of the company as at either the date of the court order or the date of the company's resolution. After receiving the various claims from the creditors, the liquidator prepares a final report and submits it to the court for approval.

Bankruptcy

Bankruptcy applies to a trader or company whose financial business is disrupted and ceases to meet its commercial debts as they fall due. A petition of bankruptcy may be made to the court by the individual, one of his creditors or the public prosecutor.

The court appoints a person to manage the bankruptcy, known as the bankruptcy manager. The bankruptcy manager carries out an inventory of the bankrupt's assets and takes over the assets, books of account and documents of the bankrupt company. The bankruptcy manager then prepares a balance sheet and a detailed report which is to be submitted to the court.

Other forms of insolvency administration are set out in the Yemeni Bank's law and the Central Bank of Yemen Law.

Scheme of arrangement

A scheme of arrangement is a court-approved arrangement between an individual or company and its creditors, mainly providing either for a moratorium of time to pay the debt or relief from part of the debt, or both. This type of arrangement is usually entered into where the creditors are of the opinion that, if the business activities continue as normal, they are more likely to recover their debt than if the company is wound up. This arrangement is more popular than a composition since the scheme is discussed and decided in court.

Composition

A composition is a compromise whereby the debtor agrees to pay a certain amount to each unsecured creditor whilst continuing the company's business. The composition may stipulate time limits to pay and may also discharge the debtor or part of the debt. If agreement from a majority of the creditors is reached the composition is submitted to court for approval.

Creditors' union

Creditors may believe that the only means of recovering their debts is by providing financial assistance to the debtor. A union of creditors is formed where the debtor fails to apply for a composition or the debtor applies for a composition, which is later annulled or rescinded. The court must approve the union of creditors and agree the level of financial assistance required.

In practice, creditors prefer to arbitrate rather than go to the courts for settling disputes with their debtors. In general, Yemeni commercial courts have little experience of insolvency proceedings since formal insolvency is very rare.

Creditors

The creditors are categorised as:

- secured creditors — someone who holds a fixed or floating charge over the assets of the debtor;
- preferential creditors — someone who has priority in payment before unsecured creditors;
- unsecured creditors — all other creditors.

Preferential creditors normally include all government dues, social insurance and amounts due to employees. However, the courts have in certain recent cases awarded payments to employees before secured creditors.

KPMG contact partner

Mohamed Zohdi Mejanni
Mejanni, Hazem Hassan & Co.
PO Box 10556
Sana'a
Republic of Yemen

Telephone: +967 (1) 265 141
Fax: +967 (1) 267 094

Zambia

Legislation

Zambia was formerly the British Colonial Protectorate of Northern Rhodesia, gaining independence in 1964. After indepenence, many chapters of the former British based legislation were retained. In 1994, the Companies Act was introduced which closely follows the UK Companies Act in all material respects with specific provisions for financial and banking institutions. Reference should be made, therefore, to the section in this book dealing with England and Wales.

KPMG contact partner

Graham J Barnhurst
Kambendekela House
Dedan Kimathi Road
Lusaka
Zambia

Telephone: +260 (1) 228874
Fax: +260 (1) 225903

Zimbabwe

Legislation

- Insolvency Act (c. 6:04);
- Companies Act (c. 24:03);
- Companies (Winding Up) Rules 1972.

Insolvency procedures

- compulsory winding up by the court of an individual, partnership or company;
- members' or creditors' voluntary winding up of a company;
- voluntary surrender of estate by an individual;
- judicial management;
- schemes of arrangement or compromise.

Compulsory winding up by the court

By far the most common insolvency procedure, compulsory winding up by the court, commences with a petition to the High Court by the company, a creditor who has been unable to obtain settlement by other legal means, a judicial manager or an executor of a deceased estate; if granted, a provisional liquidation order is issued and the person nominated in the petition becomes the provisional liquidator (or trustee in the case of an individual or partnership).

The effect of the provisional winding-up order is to stay any legal actions for or against the company or estate and to render void any attachments or executions made against the assets after the commencement of the winding-up order, or any transfer of shares or change in status of the shareholders.

In the case of a company, the provisional liquidator immediately assumes control and proceeds to recover all the assets and property of the company both movable and immovable. He has numerous powers in terms of the Companies Act, but may not dispose of the assets prior to the first statutory meeting without the authority of the court.

If no notice of opposition is lodged, the court will confirm the provisional liquidation order after a period of 21 days. Thereafter, the master convenes the first statutory meeting within one month for the purpose of allowing creditors to prove their claims and to elect a liquidator.

Once appointed, the liquidator is granted the additional power to sell, by public auction or otherwise, the movable and immovable property of the company. Within the next few months, the liquidator must convene the second statutory meeting to be held before the master for the purpose of allowing the proof of further claims and for the consideration of his report, which should be circulated to all known creditors prior to the date of the meeting.

This report should deal with such matters as the capital structure of the company, the estimated amount of its assets and liabilities, the causes of its failure, whether proper books and records have been maintained as required by the Companies Act, the progress and prospects of the liquidation and whether, in his opinion, there is need for further inquiry into the conduct of the company's business and the reasons for its failure.

Six months from the date of his appointment as liquidator and every six months thereafter, the liquidator must lay before the master a set of accounts consisting of a receipts and payments account and a plan of distribution. The accounts must lie open for inspection by creditors and any other interested persons, for a period of 14 days. Upon confirmation of the account by the master, the liquidator proceeds to pay out the dividends to the proved creditors and lodges the receipts with the master. Any requirement may be varied with the approval of the master.

If there are insufficient funds available to cover liquidation costs a contribution is levied on the petitioning creditor and those who prove claims.

Members' and creditors' voluntary winding up

A voluntary winding up may take one of two forms, either a members' voluntary or creditors' voluntary, and in both cases all that is required is for the company to pass a special resolution to the effect that it be wound up voluntarily. This is the major difference from a compulsory winding up. Other significant differences relate to:

- the appointment, powers and remuneration of the liquidator, which are determined by the members or creditors as the case may be;
- the proof of creditor claims, which are lodged directly with the liquidator for his acceptance or amendment;
- the meetings of creditors, which are convened by and held before the liquidator.

However, the end result in both modes of winding up is to divest the directors of their powers, so that the liquidator may sell the assets of the company and distribute the proceeds to the creditors according to their claims.

Judicial management

The court may grant a judicial management order when so petitioned by a director, member or creditor.

Judicial management is a temporary moratorium to enable a company to surmount its financial problems under the management of a person specifically appointed for this purpose who acts in place of the board of directors and reports to creditors on the viability of continuing under judicial management and the possible need to place the company in liquidation.

Scheme of arrangement or compromise

A scheme of arrangement or compromise may be proposed between a company in liquidation and its creditors or its members. Should the scheme or compromise be approved by creditors and sanctioned by the court the winding-up order is set aside and the company is reinstated.

A private individual may also submit an offer of compromise to his trustee for consideration by his creditors. However, any condition which makes the offer subject to the rehabilitation of the insolvent, is of no effect.

Creditors

There are three main categories who may prove claims with the provisional liquidator:

- those holding some form of security (e.g., a mortgage bond, hire-purchase agreement, landlords, hypothec or lien);
- those who receive preferential treatment (e.g., pension, medical and insurance funds, portion of wages claims, income tax and sales tax claims and farmers' stop orders);
- those with ordinary (concurrent) claims.

Secured creditors are paid from the proceeds of the assets which form the subject of their security, and the liquidator prepares a separate receipts and payments account (designated an encumbered assets account) for each creditor. The proceeds from the sale of the unsecured assets are shown in the general receipts and payments account (designated the free residue account) and the preferential creditors' claims are paid from the account in their order of preference. Upon satisfaction of the preferential claims, the residue is divided amongst the ordinary creditors pro rata to the value of their claims. In the unlikely event of a surplus remaining after payment of all claims, the funds are distributed to the shareholders.

Foreign creditors enjoy the same considerations as local creditors but payments in foreign currency are subject to the approval of the Reserve Bank. However, claims in foreign currency are not admissible. Such claims must be converted into Zimbabwe dollars as at the date of liquidation and must be accompanied by a certificate from a commercial bank attesting to the rate used.

Other matters

Duration of procedures

Insolvency procedures may take from nine months to two or more years to complete.

KPMG contact partner

Peter Bailey
KPMG
Club Chambers
Corner Baker Avenue/3rd Street
Harare
Zimbabwe

Telephone: +263 (4) 707 661
Fax: +263 (4) 707 669